D1594386

GRASSROOTS FASCISM

WEATHERHEAD BOOKS ON ASIA

WEATHERHEAD EAST ASIAN INSTITUTE, COLUMBIA UNIVERSITY

WEATHERHEAD BOOKS ON ASIA

WEATHERHEAD EAST ASIAN INSTITUTE, COLUMBIA UNIVERSITY

LITERATURE   DAVID DER-WEI WANG, EDITOR

Ye Zhaoyan*Nanjing 1937: A Love Story*, translated by Michael Berry (2003)

Oda Makato, *The Breaking Jewel*, translated by Donald Keene (2003)

Han Shaogong, *A Dictionary of Maqiao*, translated by Julia Lovell (2003)

Takahashi Takako, *Lonely Woman*, translated by Maryellen Toman Mori (2004)

Chen Ran, *A Private Life*, translated by John Howard-Gibbon (2004)

Eileen Chang, *Written on Water*, translated by Andrew F. Jones (2004)

Writing Women in Modern China: The Revolutionary Years, 1936–1976, edited by
    Amy D. Dooling (2005)

Han Bangqing, *The Sing-song Girls of Shanghai*, first translated by Eileen Chang, revised and
    edited by Eva Hung (2005)

Loud Sparrows: Contemporary Chinese Short-Shorts, translated and edited by Aili Mu, Julie Chiu, and
    Howard Goldblatt (2006)

Hiratsuka Raichō, *In the Beginning, Woman Was the Sun*, translated by Teruko Craig (2006)

Zhu Wen, *I Love Dollars and Other Stories of China*, translated by Julia Lovell (2007)

Kim Sowŏl, *Azaleas: A Book of Poems*, translated by David McCann (2007)

Wang Anyi, *The Song of Everlasting Sorrow: A Novel of Shanghai*, translated by Michael Berry with
    Susan Chan Egan (2008)

Ch'oe Yun, *There a Petal Silently Falls: Three Stories by Ch'oe Yun*, translated by Bruce and
    Ju-Chan Fulton (2008)

Inoue Yasushi, *The Blue Wolf: A Novel of the Life of Chinggis Khan*, translated by
    Joshua A. Fogel (2009)

Anonymous, *Courtesans and Opium: Romantic Illusions of the Fool of Yangzhou*, translated by
    Patrick Hanan (2009)

Cao Naiqian, *There's Nothing I Can Do When I Think of You Late at Night*, translated by
    John Balcom (2009)

Park Wan-suh, *Who Ate Up All the Shinga? An Autobiographical Novel*, translated by Yu Young-nan and
    Stephen J. Epstein (2009)

Yi T'aejun, *Eastern Sentiments*, translated by Janet Poole (2009)

Hwang Sunwŏn, *Lost Souls: Stories*, translated by Bruce and Ju-Chan Fulton (2009)

Kim Sŏk-pŏm, *The Curious Tale of Mandogi's Ghost*, translated by Cindy Textor (2010)

The Columbia Anthology of Modern Chinese Drama, edited by Xiaomei Chen (2011)

Qian Zhongshu, *Humans, Beasts, and Ghosts: Stories and Essays*, edited by Christopher G. Rea,
    translated by Dennis T. Hu, Nathan K. Mao, Yiran Mao, Christopher G. Rea, and
    Philip F. Williams (2011)

Dung Kai-cheung, *Atlas: The Archaeology of an Imaginary City*, translated by Dung Kai-cheung,
    Anders Hansson, and Bonnie S. McDougall (2012)

O Chŏnghŭi, *River of Fire and Other Stories*, translated by Bruce Fulton and Ju-Chan Fulton (2012)

LIST CONTINUES ON PAGE 348

Grassroots

FASCISM

THE WAR EXPERIENCE OF THE JAPANESE PEOPLE

YOSHIMI YOSHIAKI

TRANSLATED AND ANNOTED BY ETHAN MARK

COLUMBIA UNIVERSITY PRESS   NEW YORK

COLUMBIA UNIVERSITY PRESS
Publishers Since 1893
New York   Chichester, West Sussex

First published in Japanese by University of Tokyo Press in 1987.
Copyright © 1987 Yoshiaki Yoshimi
Translation copyright © 2015 Columbia University Press
All rights reserved

Library of Congress Cataloging-in-Publication Data

Yoshimi, Yoshiaki, 1946–
   [Kusa no ne no fashizumu. English]
   Grassroots fascism : the war experience of the Japanese people = Kusa no ne no fashizumu : Nihon minshu no senso taiken / Yoshiaki Yoshimi ; Ethan Mark, translator.
       pages cm — (Weatherhead books on Asia)
   Summary: "A profile of the Asia Pacific War, the most important and still the least understood experience of Japan and Asia's modern history—as seen and lived by ordinary Japanese"—Provided by publisher.
   Includes bibliographical references and index.
   ISBN 978-0-231-16568-6 (cloth : alkaline paper) — ISBN 978-0-231-53859-6 (ebook)
   1. World War, 1939–1945—Personal narratives, Japanese. 2. Japan—History—1926–1945—Biography.
3. World War, 1939–1945—Campaigns—Pacific Area. 4. Fascism—Japan—History—20th century. 5. Japan—Politics and government—1926–1945. I. Title.

D811.A2Y5913 2015
940.53'52—DC23

2014017123

Columbia University Press books are printed on permanent and durable acid-free paper.
This book is printed on paper with recycled content.
Printed in the United States of America

C 10 9 8 7 6 5 4 3 2 1

References to Internet Web sites (URLs) were accurate at the time of writing.
Neither the author nor Columbia University Press is responsible for URLs
that may have expired or changed since the manuscript was prepared.

JACKET + BOOK DESIGN BY VIN DANG

CONTENTS

GRASSROOTS FASCISM

Translator's Introduction
THE PEOPLE IN THE WAR

ETHAN MARK

From 1939 to 1940, Japan not only expended more than ten billion yen and suffered more than one hundred thousand deaths in battle. It also absorbed several hundred thousand repatriated soldiers who had accumulated raw experiences of China and its battlefields, who had developed a deep fear of China's resistance that involved the country's entire people, and who had hardened in their determination to fight on. The Japan of this period was thus a Japan different from before. One by one, people returning from the battlefield—along with people at home who had been supporting the war—were becoming earnest and beginning to give it their all.

YOSHIMI YOSHIAKI, *Grassroots Fascism*

The study of wartime Japan and its empire is a study of extremes.[1] Staggering was the scale of the misery and destruction visited upon Japan's neighbors and ultimately upon Japanese as well. Staggering was the brutality and barbarity associated with Japan's military aggression, immortalized in such infamous signifiers as the "Rape of Nanjing," "Unit 731," the "comfort women," the "Bataan Death March," the Thai-Burma Railway, and the *rômusha*; staggering too the violence of the Allied response, culminating in a hail of fire- and atom bombs dropped on largely defenseless Japanese cities. As the merciless killing fields of China expanded into a "War Without Mercy" with the Western allies, the conflict ensnared not only millions of soldiers but also the lives and livelihoods of much larger numbers of Asian and Pacific civilians, finally imploding upon Japan's domestic population in a gruesome manmade holocaust.[2]

Nearly seventy years after Japan's defeat, the legacies of this brutal conflict continue to haunt the present. What drove Japan on this bloody course? What exactly happened, and who or what was responsible? In recent times, ongoing criticism from Japan's neighbors over silence on the subject, or worse, historical whitewashing, seems to meet only with noisy and aggressive responses from unapologetic Japanese nationalists, including some within government ranks. With so many questions seemingly remaining unanswered, the image persists of a postwar Japan unable to account for—or to own up to—the sins of its past. For many observers, comparison with the historical reckoning of postwar Germany reveals a Japanese society somehow still not mature enough to come to terms with its wartime behavior.

There is an ironic continuity here, for ever since the Second World War, a purported social immaturity has also been the most common explanation offered not only for postwar Japan's failure to reckon properly with its wartime past but indeed for Japan's wartime behavior itself. Allying itself with Nazi Germany and fascist Italy, Japan was of course not the only nation at the time that pursued aggression abroad and repression at home, committing shocking atrocities in the process. But if few might still agree with General Douglas MacArthur's racist occupation-era characterization of Japan as "a nation of twelve-year-olds," the image persists of a wartime Japanese imperialism and a Japanese social system that were somehow less evolved or advanced than those of its European counterparts, retaining uniquely "premodern" or "semifeudal" cultural characteristics.[3] European fascism might have deployed Teutonic or Roman myths to "sanction aggression, but the myths were never presented as literal truth," reads one still-influential East Asian history textbook. In wartime Japan, in contrast, "it was not necessary to disinter archaic myths, [for] these were still alive . . . Japan was not fully modern."[4] Where the broader study of the Second World War and its place in global history is concerned, such characterizations would seem to dismiss Japan's experience as exceptional and peripheral in its relevance to the "main story," offering little in the way of contributing to our understanding of the Second World War or of fascism as modern global phenomena. If the Second World War in Europe was a clash of the forces of modernity—mass society and mass politics, democracy and totalitarianism, capitalism and communism—Japan's war appears here as an anachronism, the brutal, blind rampage of a society stuck at an earlier stage of development.[5]

Emphasized in such accounts is the distinctive staying power of the inter-war Japanese regime, anchored by the unwavering, "irrational" devotion of the Japanese people to their emperor. In German and Italian fascism, mass fascist movements "from below" battled with rival mass socialist movements and seized control over the state, toppling the old regime; in wartime Japan, what-ever political unrest there was appeared to play out only at the top, among fac-tions of its military and civilian ruling elites. Violent acts of political extremism against the existing order came from a handful of young officers from within the ranks of the military itself. Among them and in the wider society, the emperor's authority was never questioned, and his representatives remained firmly in the saddle. If there was something akin to Western fascism in Japan—an assertion many scholars dispute in the first place[6]—this evidence suggests that it could not have been more than a primitive version of the European original, a unilat-eral "fascism from above" foisted by an all-powerful state upon a society con-ditioned by tradition and indoctrination not to think or to act autonomously.[7]

In searching for the origins, driving forces, and culprits of Japan's disastrous wartime adventure, Western and Japanese scholars alike have therefore typ-ically started at the top, in the structures, institutions, and cultural traditions that presumably dictated and manipulated national behavior in the absence of a "fascism from below." Japanese scholars of the first postwar decades generally saw the war as an inevitable consequence of fundamental social deficiencies dating back to the nature of the 1868 Meiji Restoration and indeed continuing into the postwar present. Reflecting the critical Marxian orientation dominant among them through at least the 1970s, most of these did not stop at the villainy of the state or the military as such but attempted to explain Japan's disastrous imperial course by focusing on the specific needs of an expanding but imma-ture Japanese capitalism and its interdependent relationship with "semifeudal" landed and military elites from the time of the Meiji settlement onward. They viewed the intensified militarization of society and the military showdown with China and the Western powers in the Pacific as a reactionary attempt to shore up this "Emperor System" (*tennôsei*) in crisis, in the context of a global crisis of capitalism.

In contrast, mainstream Western scholars of the early postwar decades such as Edwin O. Reischauer, ideologically at odds with Marxist critiques of capitalism and imperialism and more positive about Japan's modernization, were more sanguine. They argued that under enlightened civilian leadership, Japan's prewar development had shown signs of promise in a healthy, democratic, liberal capitalist direction—a direction happily resumed, with American encouragement, after World War II. In this characterization, the war itself appeared as a dramatic misstep on the way to modernity, in which Japan's normally pragmatic and reasonable civilian leaders had been temporarily overwhelmed by an aggressive, irrational, "militarist" clique. The leadership of this troublesome group was roughly represented by those whom the United States and their allies singled out for high-profile war crimes trials held in Tokyo in the late 1940s. It was they who were seen to have taken advantage of the sense of crisis generated by the Great Depression, a subservient public, and insufficiently autonomous public institutions to engineer repression at home and a disastrous expansionary adventure abroad. Notably, the membership of this group did *not* include the emperor himself, whose wartime role was essentially characterized—both by the Allies and most subsequent mainstream Western scholarship—as little changed from what it had been for centuries: a passive, tragic figure in the eye of someone else's political storm.

A third line of analysis, unique in enjoying wide influence both in Japan and outside of it, was formulated very soon after the war by the brilliant political theorist Maruyama Masao. Maruyama hewed closer to the mainstream Japanese scholarly interpretation in seeing the disaster as an inevitable consequence of "feudal" social and political structures willfully exploited and manipulated by the Meiji regime and in highlighting prewar Japan's economic "backwardness." But he shared with Western analysts a focus on fundamental shortcomings in Japan's modern cultural development. Specifically, he argued that the location and identity of the emperor within the prewar regime, combining both religious and political supremacy in one and the same person, had thwarted the development of a mature, Western-style civil society, with its clear and rational divisions between the spheres of church and state, the public and the private, the moral and the political. The result was a prewar society whose values were determined not within the independent, rational mind and conscience of each individual, as Maruyama contended was the case in the modern West, but externally and "situationally," in reference to the national body and to the "absolute value" at its center—the emperor. Within this scheme, it was one's relative proximity to the emperor that determined not only one's social status but also one's behavior, values, and attitude toward others, even as the emperor himself remained a passive player. Orders and oppression emanating from those closer to the center were passed along to those further outside, accompanied by little or no sense of individual responsibility for one's actions. Members of Japan's armed forces, positioned in the Meiji Constitution under the direct command of the emperor, had viewed themselves as practically a race apart from their fellow civilian Japanese, let alone vis-à-vis "foreigners" under Japanese imperial subjugation. In these notions of externalized values and a "system of irresponsibility," Maruyama sought to explain both the savagery of Japan's war crimes on the one hand and an apparent inability to acknowledge or take responsibility for them on the other. For progressive intellectuals such as Maruyama, postwar Japan needed to seek a way forward to a more responsible and autonomous popular life by nurturing what had been thus been fatally lacking until Japan's surrender: a sense of what he called individual subjectivity.

> August 15, 1945, the day that put a period to Japanese imperialism, was also the day when the "national polity," which had been the foundation of the entire ultranationalist structure, lost its absolute quality. Now for the first time the Japanese people, who until then had been mere objects, became free subjects and the destiny of this "national polity" was committed to their own hands.[8]

Despite the great differences between these conventional storylines, there was an ironic correspondence between them. Whether narrated by Japanese or non-Japanese, from the political left or right, the agents of Japan's wartime history were Japan's political, military, and economic elites, the impersonal structures and forces of socioeconomics, and/or "the Japanese" conceived as a single ethnocultural whole. Up to the present day, these conceptual and political frameworks have inhibited a deeper, more nuanced understanding and assessment of the subjective war experience and role of the mass of the Japanese people themselves. Furthermore, by placing the onus of the war on Japan's "feudalistic" ruling groups (variously defined) in combination with a certain general social and cultural underdevelopment, these conventional narratives cast ordinary people as victims of a sinister state, effectively absolving them from direct responsibility for the war. Like the bombs that rained upon them from the sky, the war remained not so much something that ordinary Japanese had actively shaped and participated in as something that overtook them from above. The unspeakable horror of the atomic bombs in particular, and the fact that Japan's citizenry remain the only people ever subjected to them, only added ammunition to a general sense of victimhood. Throughout the period since the war's end, this problem of what Carol Gluck has called "history in the passive voice" has helped undergird a pervasive Japanese reticence regarding questions of war responsibility.[9]

Despite their vocal criticism of Japan's insufficient reckoning with its wartime crimes, more often than not, overseas commentators too have furthered this basic understanding of Japan's war as primarily a "top-down" affair. The extent of the dominance of such perspectives up to the present day is reflected in statements from officials of the People's Republic of China, the wartime society that suffered most at Japanese hands, with a political leadership ideologically committed to the eradication of all traces of "Japanese fascism" then and now. The last three decades have seen increased PRC criticism of Japanese war "amnesia" and encouragement of domestic awareness of Japanese aggression, including the construction of memorial museums at Nanjing and Mukden and extensive coverage in the educational curriculum, whipping up anti-Japanese sentiments in the younger generation for nation building and international ends. Yet ever since the early postwar era, even PRC spokesmen have made a consistent policy of distinguishing between the Japanese state, which they hold primarily responsible for Japanese militarism, and the Japanese people, whom they do not. Whether American or Chinese, such postwar positions have been shaped not only by a shared conception of a distinctive Japanese wartime social "backwardness" but also by a pragmatic geopolitical interest in producing a narrative of the war that makes sense of a painful past while allowing for the fostering of alliances with strategic partners in the Japan of the present. With few exceptions, the end result outside of Japan has in any case been the same as that within: a tenacious inattention to the active role of ordinary Japanese as wartime participants and perpetrators.

As a young historian researching prewar popular political movements in the early 1970s, Yoshimi Yoshiaki (b. 1946) became increasingly struck—and troubled—by this systematic inattention to popular experiences of the war period, along with the virtually universal silence on questions of popular war responsibility. Imbued with the progressive convictions of a scholarly generation that came of age amid the political struggles of the late 1960s, he was dissatisfied with the near-universal academic focus on elites and abstract social structures that rendered the story of the Japanese experience of the war "a history without people in it." After many years of research, stops and starts, the end result was *Grassroots Fascism*: a radically different vantage on the wartime experience from the "bottom-up" and a unique, bold attempt to break out of the constricted confines of "history in the passive voice."

Taking us on a narrative journey that begins with the war's troubled early 1930s beginnings and culminates in the disaster of defeat and the promise of a new beginning in 1945, moving adeptly and systematically between the home front and the diverse variety of "fronts" that distinguished Japan's far-flung Asian imperium, *Grassroots Fascism* exposes us to a remarkable array of popular voices deftly assembled from sources such as diaries, government archives, and memoirs. Along the way Yoshimi presents a carefully nuanced and historicized portrait of everyday, nonelite Japanese in all their real-life complexity and ambiguity not only as victims of, but also as *active participants* in, the wartime struggle for hegemony in Asia and social renovation at home. *Grassroots Fascism* is also at special pains to include equally penetrating accounts of the experience of Japanese ethnic minorities and imperial subjects, including Okinawans, Koreans, and Taiwanese, engaged in their own complex personal and group negotiations of the wartime enterprise.

In taking Japan's "common people" as protagonists and letting them in effect tell their own story of the war as it evolved, *Grassroots Fascism* reveals to us a 1930s and 1940s Japan that defies historiographical convention. Viewed from the bottom up, there unfolds before us a complex modern mass society, with a corresponding variety of popular roles and agendas. The comfortable, transparent "black and white" of conventional narratives of victims and villains is boldly exchanged for the translucent "grey" of a Japanese people cast as both victim and victimizer. In this and in its ingenious deployment of source material to evoke the wartime experience in three dimensions of vividness and diversity, Yoshimi's study elevates scholarly discussion of the nature and dynamics of Japan's wartime experience—and of "Japanese fascism"—to a bold new level.

The scholarly relevance of *Grassroots Fascism* extends in fact far beyond the study of modern Japan alone. In providing a balanced and comprehensive vantage on the mental world of the "common people" not only unknown in the Japanese wartime context but indeed extremely rare in the study of *any* historical social context, *Grassroots Fascism* represents a model of social and cultural history writing.[10] It is also groundbreaking in its social and geographical inclusiveness, providing an account of how the war was experienced "on the ground" by the full sweep of "Japanese subjects" in the length and breadth of the wartime empire. Most remarkably, as vividly reflected in the citation that heads this essay, this empirewide perspective is deployed not only for the sake of inclusion itself but also as analytical method: experiences of home front and battlefront, of imperial metropole and periphery, are seen not simply in isolation from one another but in interaction, as intimate and interrelated determinants in the evolving shape and evolution of fascism both at home and abroad. In its relation of the Second World War to the evolution—and destruction—of empire, *Grassroots Fascism* thus represents a significant contribution to the study of the Second World War as global history.

In recent years and with increasing effectiveness, scholarship informed by a postcolonial problematic has sought to reveal the hidden yet essential interrelationship and interdependence of the history of modern Europe with that of its colonies.[11] Yet the history of the Second World War remains among the strongest of Eurocentric bastions, its imperial aspects relegated to the periphery of conventional narrative and knowledge. European fascism is conceived of as a fundamentally domestic enterprise, with the war envisioned essentially in terms of a conflict between European nation-states. A pervasive scholarly blind spot regarding the imperialist identity of "the democracies" against which Italy and Germany went to war, alongside the fact that Italy and Germany essentially set about building new empires in earnest only after their fascist regimes were already developed, has made it easy for scholars erroneously to conceive of their imperialism as a *byproduct* of fascism, rather than exploring the degree to which their fascism was itself determined within a broader, longer-term global context of competing imperialisms. The project of revealing the central role of empire in the Second World War and in fascism necessitates an overcoming of the Eurocentric assumptions built into the study of the war and of fascism itself. It is only recently and belatedly that scholarship on the European experience of the Second World War is taking its first, tentative steps toward incorporating empire and imperialism into the story of fascism, not simply as an external "symptom" of the inherent aggression of fascist regimes but as an integral and dynamic determinant of the shape and evolution of fascist movements and ideas in Europe and across the globe.[12]

In contrast, students of wartime Japan, particularly those of Yoshimi Yoshiaki's caliber, have not had to wait for advanced postcolonial theory to perceive the centrality of the imperial dimension, and the historical interaction between metropole and colony, in the making of the Second World War and of fascism. In Japan as in Europe, the rise of the modern nation-state, capitalism, political institutions, even democratic movements, came in tandem with—and were dependent on—the building and maintenance of an empire. In a dialectical development, the war in Asia, and the particular shape of Japanese fascism, assumed the form that it did in large part because the peoples of Asia refused to be merely the passive objects of these sorts of nation-building projects and imperial rivalries any longer. While Eurocentrism and inter-European tensions distracted Europeans (and have distracted conventional scholars ever since) from the global crisis in the imperial order that lay at the heart of the Second World War, Japan had no choice but to confront it from the beginning. In a properly global historical perspective that includes Asia and the centrality of empire, the Second World War itself can indeed be said to have started in July 1937—four-and-a-half years before Japan attacked Pearl Harbor and more than two years before Germany attacked Poland—when Chinese nationalist forces returned fire at Marco Polo Bridge. In the face of an increasingly aggressive and exploitative Japanese interventionism in China, against a Japan that was, like its European counterparts, so heavily invested in its empire that it could hardly contemplate a future without it, the empire struck back. Unable to overcome this challenge but also unable to imagine an alternative to empire, Japan responded in China with the inhuman ruthlessness and brutality characteristic to modern colonial war against an "obstinate" opponent perceived as racially and culturally inferior; in deepening desperation, Japan then raised the regional and global stakes by challenging Western imperial hegemony across the breadth of Asia. With exceptional vividness, *Grassroots Fascism* reveals that in going to war Japanese of all walks of life envisioned, engendered, and sought to overcome an imperial crisis and that this in turn defined the evolving nature— and radicalization—of "Japanese fascism" itself.

In its revelation of a center-periphery dynamic in the evolution of fascism that positions it even now at global history's conceptual and narrative cutting edge, *Grassroots Fascism* is testimony to a striking phenomenon in scholarship on modern Japan that remains mostly hidden from global view behind a triple barrier of language, unfamiliarity, and Eurocentrism: Its powerful potential as a globalizer of Eurocentric conceptual models. Wittingly or not, attempts to find nuance and "make room" for Japan's modern experience within Western-derived paradigms such as capitalism, imperialism, and fascism have at times propelled scholars of modern Japan to innovations and broader perspectives that anticipated subsequent developments in, and even transcended, the narrower field of vision of their Western counterparts.[13]

Yet if its global relevance has in some ways only become clearer with the years, *Grassroots Fascism* also remains an intensely engaged reflection of its particular postwar place and time. Originally aimed primarily at a contemporary Japanese audience, it is animated as much by the presentist questions of the legacy of the war for the postwar and the moral issue of war responsibility as it is by the empirical question of how the war was experienced and engendered. As such it remains a passionate story with a progressive message that is at once place specific and universal: If we are to learn from our parents' mistakes rather then repeat them, we must first understand them for what they were.

Over the last two decades, Yoshimi's boldness and steadfastness in investigating such difficult questions has gained wide attention. Outside of Japan, he is best known for his research into the wartime "comfort women" system.[14] In the early 1990s, Yoshimi's uncovering of indisputable evidence of the wartime state's systematic involvement in the "comfort women" system compelled a historic apology from an uneasy Japanese government, bringing him a hero's status on the political left and an equally infamous standing among Japan's increasingly vocal right. The language barrier has heretofore prevented *Grassroots Fascism* from garnering equal attention outside of Japan. Originally published more than twenty-five years ago, its revelations remain no less profound, no less politically charged, and no less relevant today.[15]

A brief look at Yoshimi's personal origins does not suggest the most likely candidate for such bold endeavors. Born shortly after the war ended in a mountain village in Yamaguchi Prefecture in the very west of Japan's main island of Honshū—a postwar bedrock of the ruling conservative LDP party—he was the fifth son of an impoverished elementary school teacher "on the conservative side."[16] Hiroshima was nearby, and stories circulated of survivors returning to the village in rags, but Yoshimi's immediate family had been lucky enough to suffer no direct losses in the war. As such neither the war nor politics were discussed at home, but patriotism—a now discredited commodity among many Japanese—was in fact strongly encouraged.[17] Yoshimi's father insisted on raising the flag on national holidays, even if his was the only house on the block doing so. As the child of such a household, Yoshimi was expected to show similar dedication. Assuming him to be the fourth-grader most likely to know the national anthem by heart, his elementary school principal once spontaneously called on him to sing it at a school assembly (with a hearty laugh, Yoshimi recently recalled his embarrassment when he forgot the words halfway through)![18]

Both physically and spiritually, Yoshimi's adolescence was thus spent at a far remove from the political center of Tokyo, rocked at the time by movements for democratization that peaked in mass demonstrations against the renewal of the U.S.-Japan Security Treaty (AMPO) in 1960. Participants in these movements had experienced the hardships of the wartime and immediate postwar eras firsthand, out of which emerged a powerful idealism and a concrete resentment against the hypocrisy of a conservative older generation that had led Japan to war and now continued to rule, in a Cold War alliance with the United States, in the name of "peace and democracy." Although "the waves of AMPO didn't reach as far as farming villages," the young Yoshimi Yoshiaki too was moved by the progressive ideals and promises of his postwar times. As a middle-school student, he was deeply impressed by the postwar constitution's protections of individual rights as explained to him by his civics teacher, a recent graduate of Hiroshima University, particularly in that they "extended even to people out in little villages like mine." The brutal public assassination of the popular Socialist Party leader Asanuma Inejirō by a young right-wing extremist in 1960 shocked and alarmed the fourteen-year-old: "Just then in school we were learning about the attempted coups d'état of March 15, 1932, and February 26, 1936," which had helped put Japan on a course to aggressive war.

> I thought this was something limited to the past. . . . How could something like that happen in a time when we had such a Constitution? Using violence to kill people like that was wrong. People should find ways to solve problems by talking with one another without resorting to that. I didn't discuss this much with my family, but in a school speaking contest, I remember saying that.[19]

Yoshimi's excellence as a student gained him admission to Japan's most prestigious institution of higher education, Tokyo University, where he entered the literature department in 1965, eventually settling on history as a major. In Japanese society at large, in comparison with the tumultuous late 1950s and early 1960s, the period was one of increasing political quiescence. In the wake of the 1960 protests, the ruling conservative LDP party had moved to ensure its dominance and reduce political confrontation by focusing its energy and rhetoric on something all Japanese could presumably agree upon: economic growth. Benefitting from booming global markets, close cooperation between the state and big business, and strategic alliance with the United States, the policy was beginning to bear fruit.

Like students elsewhere confronted with similar Cold War inheritances, many of Japan's elite university students were restless regarding the conservative "normality" bequeathed to them by their elders. Growing material prosperity was associated with a sense of political and ideological narrowing. In Japan as elsewhere, this contradiction came to a head in the specter of the Vietnam War, which was supported by the Japanese government even as it eschewed direct involvement.[20] The Japanese normalization of relations with South Korea, seen as a further case of siding with U.S. imperialist interests against those of fellow Asian peoples—those of North Korea and China—was equally unpopular. "Just the year I entered college, 1965, was the year the [U.S.] bombing of Vietnam started, and the same year the Japan-Korea treaty was signed," notes Yoshimi. "The campus was in an incredibly active movement against these two, and I immediately entered the fray."[21] The activism of the student movements culminated in a year-long student strike at the Tokyo University campus in 1968–1969, bringing teaching to a halt and delaying Yoshimi's own graduation by a year. As the economy continued to boom, however, the Japanese public exhibited a decreasing sympathy with student activism, a situation that allowed the government to take increasingly aggressive measures against it. As in other places, participants in the student movements came to feel more and more isolated from society at large.

Like many of his fellow students, Yoshimi saw in the ongoing cruelties of the Vietnam War, and the domestic political and popular passivity in the face of it, the hypocrisy of an older generation that claimed to have learned from the mistakes of the past but appeared all too ready to repeat them. Looking to Europe in the same period, he witnessed "the 1968 generation" of Germans of his own age confronted with similar issues, who saw it as their moral obligation to conduct their own social reckoning of the past as a necessary prerequisite to achieving real social change in the present. "They asked their own parents, why did you cooperate with Nazism?" observes Yoshimi, "while in Japan we didn't have that. We didn't pursue our parents' responsibility."[22] Continuing into the master's program in history at Tokyo University against this background, Yoshimi began to delve into the social and political processes that had led to the collapse of Japan's prewar democracy and the wartime disaster. Under the supervision of Professor Itō Takashi, Yoshimi began by looking in a relatively conventional place: the experience of the leadership of the social-democratic political parties that competed for the popular vote in the first "mass suffrage" elections of the late 1920s and 1930s, whose eventual collaboration with Japan's military and bureaucratic elites was often seen as symbolic of the weakness of Japan's prewar democratic movement.

Yoshimi's advisor Itō was a specialist in political history known for his careful, detailed, well-documented research. He was also a political conservative whose cautious, source-based "positivist" approach represented a conscious rejection of the activist Marxist approach still dominant in the Japanese academy at the time. Yoshimi shared some of his advisor's skepticism regarding

Marxist attempts to fit history into a preconceived, overtly political conceptual structure.

> Marxism has a theory from the beginning and then tries to fit history within it, but real history [*genjitsu no rekishi*] is ever so much richer than theory—all kinds of unexpected things happen. For example, Katō Kanjū [加藤勘十, leader of the prewar Social Masses Party] was a socialist, but before he became one, he was a nationalist, a populist, everything mixed together, he had a complex personality. He could split into different directions, be a right-winger, a socialist, a communist, a fascist—the [interwar] was a period of such amalgams. And this sort of thing happens over and over. In *Grassroots* I think it's there too . . . the idea that there is a rich range of possibilities, you need to pay attention to that and not discard it. Professor Itô taught me to adapt to history's concrete reality. I think this was a great harvest for me.[23]

Yoshimi shared with Itō and many other postwar critics in Japan and elsewhere a frustration with orthodox Marxist narratives whose focus on impersonal structural forces and schematic social categorizations left little room for individual agency, experience, or nuance. As one critic of a bestselling Marxist history of the early Shōwa period wrote, "the military, politicians, and industrialists who compelled the war and the communists and liberals who opposed them and suffered suppression: it's only these two sides, while the strata of Japanese oscillating in between them are nowhere to be seen. In short, they've made a typology according to the abstract concept of 'class struggle.'"[24] For postwar progressives convinced that a politically informed and active role for ordinary people was essential to a democratic future, these narratives of the past "without people in them" offered little in the way of guidance or inspiration, seemingly confirming a national tradition of popular passivity. Marxism was also seen as constricting and reductive in its insistence upon a great divide between those portions of "the people" whose social position qualified them to fulfill a socially "progressive" historical role—the proletariat—and those, such as small landholders, businessmen, and others located socially within the category of the (petite) bourgeoisie, who were thereby condemned by default to a "reactionary" role.

Still, Yoshimi refused to follow his supervisor in rejecting Marxist tenets and concepts out of hand. Like many among his generation, he retained a respect for and identification with Marxist historical analysis and social critique and for the power of the theories behind them. For Yoshimi, conventional "positivist" political, diplomatic, and institutional history of the sort practiced by Itō offered little in the way of an alternative. The focus on elites, established institutions, and "official," "objective" documentation reflected a conservative worldview, confirming the status quo by failing to problematize it; the ambitiously broad social-structural conceptualizations and insistence on international comparability that defined the Marxist approach were replaced with topically and thematically narrow accounts stressing the particulars of each situation, strenuously avoiding adding up to any particular whole. "You can't have [history] without *some* sort of a framework," Yoshimi argues. "You can conclude that we need to look for something else, or rather that [Marxism] is insufficient but it has a meaning in it, that we need to reform it —in this sense Itō and I were of different opinions."[25]

Following the completion of his graduate education at Tokyo University, Yoshimi took up a position at Chūō University in Tokyo, where he has remained ever since. Here he began conducting his first research on the war period itself, specifically on the Manchurian Incident, at the invitation of war veteran and historian Fujiwara Akira, then head of the Contemporary Japanese History Research Group (*Nihon gendaishi kenkyūkai*) at Tokyo's Hitotsubashi University. In the vein of Yoshimi's advisor Itō Takashi, the general orientation of the group was "positivist," stressing the uncovering of new primary source material as central to the historian's craft. Between the mid-1970s and 1980s, Yoshimi and other members of the group devoted extensive time and energy to locating and publishing new primary sources on the war period. The results contributed much to what would eventually comprise the extraordinarily rich source base of *Grassroots Fascism*.

Yoshimi was struck not only by the increased quantity but also by the distinctive nature of new source materials then becoming available, allowing researchers access to a hitherto unavailable social panorama. "Happily, at that time a lot of material was appearing on war experiences," Yoshimi recalls. Many Japanese of the war generation "were just starting retirement, and their wartime experiences when they were young had been the most intense of their lives—when they retired, many wanted to write them down. . . . Just then word processors were spreading too. Even if publishers didn't accept them, they'd pay their own money and publish privately."[26]

To a remarkable degree, a large number of these documents were being produced by nonelite people whose literacy rates at the time of the war were comparatively high relative to Japan's objective level of economic development. In prewar Japan, Yoshimi notes,

> school education was widespread. Higher elementary school graduates had quite a high level of knowledge; those who graduated higher elementary school in the prewar period were probably better at writing than those who go on to university nowadays, and the proportion of graduates was also roughly similar—although very few at the time went on to university before the war.[27] They could reach the level of noncommissioned officers and they could write well. These were the people who had supported the building of postwar society for a very long time . . . and many were still in good health, so you could go and talk to them. In this sense the timing was just right.[28]

While many of these documents were memoirs written long after the fact, also surfacing in print were a surprisingly large number of personal records written during or just shortly after the war, assembled and published by the now elderly authors themselves, or—in the case of documents left behind by those who had perished in the war—by or at the behest of bereaved relatives who now too, for the first time, had the time and energy for the exercise. As reflected in *Grassroots Fascism*, many of Yoshimi's informants had increasingly come to share with him a concern that postwar Japan's peace and prosperity should not be allowed to encourage among the younger generation a dangerous ignorance of the lessons of Japan's recent history or a complacency with regard to the dangers of war. It is from these precious documents that *Grassroots Fascism* derives a remarkable immediacy and poignancy.

However, personal documents such as these can only go so far in accurately reflecting a wider sense of the complex and changing "popular mood" of the times. Equally crucial in enabling a study such as *Grassroots Fascism* was the collection of a large quantity of revolutionary new "official" evidence on the popular experience of the war by Yoshimi and his colleagues. The finds were made possible through a combination of dogged perseverance on the one hand and pure fortuitousness on the other.

> Two or three of us would go to government offices and archives in search of materials. This was very interesting. We found things in places we didn't expect. At the time there was no freedom of information law, so documents from government offices were rarely released. So we took part in a movement for such a law. This in itself was a big inspiration. There is research on farming, mountain and fishing

villages appearing in [*Grassroots Fascism*]: we got this from here and there during that process. That research was conducted by the (Cabinet) Planning Board [*ki-kakuin*]. [Later] it was donated to various libraries. The one with the most was Keiō University's library. In prewar Japan there were no opinion surveys, so it was difficult to know how to use the material. But before and during the war, as the suppression of speech became more severe, those in power too grew unable to tell what the people were thinking, and in the end they had to examine letters to the editor and postcards. . . . It seems it got serious after the Sino-Japanese War started. How could they get a grip on popular leanings? To the point that they directed their attention to letters to the editor, graffiti [落書き], et cetera . . . [29]

Like many other modern states facing the profound political, social, and economic crises of the interwar period, the Japanese state responded with increasing social intervention, including attempts to monitor and control "public opinion" to a hitherto unheard-of degree. The resultant archival material is testimony to the ominous, expanding reach of an increasingly authoritarian Japanese wartime state into people's daily lives—what many scholars see as a hallmark of fascism—but it is also, ironically, a revolutionary record of changing popular sentiments of a scale and scope unavailable to historians of any previous period.

Despite the group's historic strides in collecting source material, however, Yoshimi retained doubts as to whether the cautious "positivist" approach to this material favored by his colleagues in the Contemporary History Research Group could in itself lead to a richer understanding of the history of the war. "They were all Japan researchers and somehow the field of vision was narrow. The research was positivist and limited in scope," he notes. "It produced many researchers, who still continue today; this is significant. But concretely they have produced no books with a common theme." Participation in the group rather intensified Yoshimi's conviction that established approaches were insufficient.

There was a certain single pattern in the way the war was portrayed; I thought that if I simply did it that way—simply is a strange way to put it, but—if we accumulated our efforts in the same way, something would come out, but would that necessarily be meaningful, or would it be interesting? I had my doubts. I wondered if it couldn't be done in a somewhat different way. And where the war is concerned, if you just look only at the actions of the leaders—I had done that myself, when I was doing the research on the Manchurian Incident, I thought something might result from doing careful, detailed research using various new sources, but when I tried this I started to doubt it; I started to think maybe there's a *more* different side to it, a more different way to do it.[30]

In contemporary approaches to Japan's war experience, Yoshimi thus increasingly came to perceive a problem of narrowness in multiple dimensions: an ongoing, exclusive focus on social elites that left the role and experience of the mass of the population out of the picture, and in the work of his contemporary colleagues—who represented at that time the lion's share of Japanese scholarship on the war period—a focus on isolated topics that failed to add up to a larger whole. In the study of interwar history both in Japan and outside of it—at least among non-Marxist scholars—it was also a period of narrowing in the form of a trend toward a questioning of the international comparability of the interwar experiences not just of Japan and Europe but indeed among European societies and even between Italy and Germany, stressing the great domestic differences that lay behind the wartime façade of international fascist unity. The logical implication of this focus on historical specificities was to call the applicability of the term "fascism" itself into doubt.[31] Reflecting this trend, Yoshimi's former supervisor Itō Takashi joined Western scholars such as Peter Duus, Daniel I. Okamoto, and Ben-Ami Shillony in suggesting fascism to be a "failed concept" in the study of interwar Japan.[32]

Yoshimi and "positivist" colleagues such as Awaya Kentarō and Eguchi Keiichi in the Contemporary History Research Group continued to believe in the relevance of the term "fascism" to describe and analyze a fundamentally shared interwar experience in Japan and Europe, and they were not entirely alone. While continuing to argue for a fundamental prewar continuity in Japan's "absolutist" ruling regime that distinguished it from the mass-based regimes that implemented fascism in Europe, Ōishi Kaichirō nevertheless reflected the dominant view among contemporary Marxist scholars in asserting its unique "success" in "playing the role of fascism" by "mobilizing the mass of the people" for war on an unprecedented scale.[33] Attempting to move beyond debates over whether prewar Japan could be considered "fascist" despite its lack of strong mass movements comparable to those of fascist Italy or Nazi Germany, the innovative Marxist scholar Furuya Tetsuo meanwhile proposed a globally applicable definition of fascism centered on two fundamental characteristics: suppression and mobilization. As a form of dictatorship, he argued, fascism was distinguished by its "uniform organization of the masses at the level of daily life" combined with "the complete elimination of the roots of resistance and the mobilizing of the people in accordance with the wishes of authority."[34]

Particularly distinctive in Furuya's approach was his attention to Japan's situation as an *empire* in determining the specific shape of "Japanese fascism," a perspective lacking in conventional analyses on right and left alike, with their near-exclusive focus on fascism as a domestic phenomenon (be it Japanese, German, or Italian). Like those of Italy and Germany, Furuya argued, Japan's elites faced hostile revolutionary movements requiring a distinctly "fascist" mass mobilization and suppression in response. But unlike Italy or Germany, these threats came simultaneously from both within the metropole (relatively weak labor and tenant's movements, fear of which was heightened by a perceived threat of communist ideology from abroad) *and* from the colonial periphery (in the form of popular anticolonial liberation movements in China and Korea). This uneven challenge was met with a correspondingly uneven response: brutal and violent suppression of a nature and degree comparable to that seen in European fascism in the empire, combined with bureaucratically managed social mobilization and regimentation at home. The relative weakness of domestic left-wing movements, argued Furuya, meant that Japanese fascism did not require terror "at home" on a scale comparable to that of Nazi Germany.[35]

Yoshimi's use of the term "fascism" in the title of his book reflects a fundamental sympathy with interpretations such as these that stress a basic comparability between the European and Japanese experience and upon the ongoing value of such a comparison in connecting Japanese history to a wider global history. He confirmed this stance in a recent interview.

> Between the end of the First World War and the start of the Second World War . . . among the late-developing capitalist nations, which referred to themselves as the "have-not" nations, there arose systems that produced similar mass mobilizations and strong state control. . . . These got out of control to the point that the economy and the people's livelihoods were destroyed—I believe this is something they had in common. This is not simply military dictatorship, but something with a more profound content. Isn't it so that the shared qualities of fascism are born at that moment?[36]

Despite Japan's lack of a clear fascist movement "from below" that seized control of the state at an identifiable moment, Yoshimi questions the outward appearance of political and institutional continuity, arguing that Japan's experience shows that radical change in the direction of a fascist regime can also take place *within* state institutions rather than overwhelming them from without. "While the emperor himself remained in the same position without changing," he argues, "the nature of the emperor system changed greatly during that time." He emphasizes the wartime rise to institutional domination by a distinct generation of men with a radical, activist social outlook: in the bureaucracy, a generation of interventionist "reform bureaucrats," and in the army, middle-ranking officers.

> Within fascism, it's common that a fascist party appears and seizes power; in Japan such a thing did not happen . . . but I believe that the military played this role in its place. . . . At a glance, it appears there is continuity, but is it not so that its contents were in fact greatly changing? For example, if we think about the 1920s, the military did not have all that much power. It was no more than a department within the government, but starting with the Manchurian incident, the occurrence of the [February 26, 1936] incident, and amid the rush into a full-scale war, one thing is, the power of the military expanded remarkably, and the stratum that controlled the military also changed, with real power increasingly held by middle-ranking staff officers, field officers and the like—are those [who emphasize continuity] not overlooking that this sort of change occurred *within*?[37]

Like that of Furuya Tetsuo, Yoshimi's narrative of the unfolding of Japanese fascism is distinguished by his identification of the crucial role played by the interaction between the metropolitan center and the imperial periphery and the link between the increasingly brutal Japanese suppression of anticolonial resistance and fascist radicalization. This innovative perspective in turn emphasizes the historicity of the Japanese wartime regime as one evolving—and intensifying—in response to the perceived demands of total war. "Domestically there was not much of a crisis situation, but quite important in place of this was the great number of the people who were mobilized into the military and sent to the Chinese mainland, there having a crisis type of experience that played an extraordinarily great role in Japan's fascistization—this is my thinking."[38]

Yoshimi's centering of this China war dynamic in the making of Japanese fascism leads him to locate the critical moment of fascist consolidation at a time in which the savagery of the war and the tenacity of Chinese resistance prompted an increasingly radical Japanese response. He dates this moment to 1940–1941—precisely the period in which conventional, domestically focused scholars have identified a "failure" of attempts to consolidate a genuinely fascist regime in the political center "back home."[39] In turn, Japan's unexpectedly easy and dramatic string of victories against the Western Powers in Asia and the Pacific during the first months of the Pacific War that followed soon afterward imparted a deeper solidity and legitimacy to Japan's war, to the system supporting it, and to the sacrifices it demanded, its "success" virtually silencing all remaining domestic dissent. "Here, a true situation of wild enthusiasm had finally emerged," writes Yoshimi, "and emperor-system fascism had crystallized."[40] In this sense this experience can be fruitfully compared with similar developments in Europe in the wake of Mussolini's 1935 victory in Ethiopia and Hitler's unexpectedly easy defeat of archrival France in 1940, but for two reasons its impact was all the more broad and profound: militarily, it could not have posed a more positive contrast to the inconclusive and ongoing quagmire of Japan's war in China. Equally or more important was its matching of Japanese propaganda of "Asian liberation" with concrete and effective action. As Yoshimi observes in *Grassroots Fascism*, such a mission held an appeal not only for Japanese but indeed for peoples around the globe convinced of the illegitimacy of Western imperial domination, including Taiwanese, Koreans, and Southeast Asians.[41]

As indicated in the above citation as well as in the one with which this introductory essay begins, however, what ultimately sets Yoshimi's approach apart is his combination of an empirewide perspective with a focus on the rise of fascism from the "bottom up": the ambivalent role of ordinary Japanese not only as victims but also as agents and conduits of fascism. As he argues in the introductory portions of *Grassroots Fascism*, at least from the beginning of the twentieth century, ordinary Japanese people had consistently demonstrated both a fervent desire for greater democracy and support for imperial expansion; while popular imperialism was stimulated in the wake of the army's bold move into Manchuria in 1931 and the insecurity of the Great Depression, the period between 1931 and the outbreak of war with China in 1937 bore witness to the resilience of popular democratic sentiment in the form of ongoing support for parliamentary rule against military attempts to undermine it. Total war however brought a fundamental shift. In a dialectical movement between metropole and periphery, between battlefield and paddy field, between brutalization and brutality, and between visions of imperial prosperity and the grim reality of wartime deprivation, ordinary Japanese came to share with military and bureaucratic elites a desire for a transcendent resolution of the national crisis, producing indispensible mass support for a radical transformation of the relations of state and society along fascist lines.

In the Japanese countryside, Yoshimi says, at first it was "landlords and powerful landed farmers who were the core figures at the center of the system," reflecting a situation of social and political continuity since the Meiji period. But as the war escalated into total war, he argues, "many people were needed as supporters, and the central supporters [of fascism] become those of a slightly lower level—landed farmers and landed/tenant farmers."[42] For many, participation in the war effort was not simply the product of patriotism or pressure from above, but it also beckoned as a revolutionary opportunity for social and political participation and advancement in a time of crisis. From peasant recruits to small farmers to elementary school teachers to colonial settlers, we are thus confronted with grassroots fascism as an ambiguous, ambivalent product of oppression and ambition, hope and desperation, brutalization and brutality.

> These were the attempts of some men to find a way to live in the war's midst after the war had shattered their life prospects. It must be said, therefore, that soldiers were cornered into this situation. At the same time, we cannot overlook this aspect: that the desire to get as much profit as possible out of the war transcended their unhappiness at being conscripted and that soldiers supported the war in earnest.[43]

Such ambiguities are at their most striking in the case of rural women, for some of whom state-sponsored movements of mass mobilization represented an opportunity for social participation that was nothing short of revolutionary.

> In addition, as far as women, while their voting rights were not acknowledged before the war, the formation of the Ladies' Patriotic Associations advanced rapidly, allowing ladies in farming villages and cities to join the organization known as the Great Japan Ladies' Association, something heretofore impossible. And women who were only in the home up to then went out into society, entering society to support the war—this phenomenon occurs for the first time, and on this point it may be possible to speak of a social revolution.[44]

As noted above, prewar Japanese educational levels were comparatively high in relation to the level of economic development—a gap all the more dramatic in the relatively economically "backward" countryside—and this carried profound implications for the social mapping of fascism. Its greatest support came from those whose skills equipped them with the social potential and ambition to enter the middle class even as—or perhaps precisely *because*—their achieved social and material positions did not (as yet) match this potential. "Persons with the educational background to be in the Japanese middle class of the future," writes Yoshimi, "represented the core support of Japan's war. In contrast, among the lesser-educated graduates of elementary schools and higher elementary schools the relative level of sympathy was slightly lower, with that among elementary school dropouts and those who had never attended school a further level down."[45]

Yoshimi's empirewide and socially textured narrative thus produces a visceral and concrete sense of fascist radicalization and its connection to the imperial battlefield as few other studies; at the same time, it does not present or represent an explicit theorization of fascism as such. As the interview citations and passing references in the book's pages appearing here make abundantly clear, *Grassroots Fascism* was written with an eclectic and innovative notion of "fascism" in mind, but its theoretical and systematic explication is not the book's primary focus. In this sense the book is not so much a direct or revisionist counter to existing approaches but might rather be characterized as an attempt to illuminate precisely those aspects of the Japanese wartime experience that remain in the dark in these approaches: a history from the outside in and from the bottom up.

As such *Grassroots Fascism* can to some degree be located within a postwar historiographical tradition of "people's history" dating back at least as far as the early 1960s both within Japan and in the wider world. Frustrated with historiographical conventions of both right and left that excluded the mass of the population from what should be "their own story" according to progressive postwar democratic principles, scholars in many places sought from this time onward to pioneer more socially inclusive histories focused on the worldviews and experiences of ordinary people, representing them not simply as victims or abstract statistics but as active agents in their own history. This has however always been easier said than done: the basic qualities that can be seen to define ordinary, nonelite people—their relatively low levels of education and social status, their daily occupation with making ends meet, and thus their characteristic lack of time or energy for the recording of their experiences and opinions—have also made them an elusive and controversial subject for the writing of history. Attempts to piece together their lives and their worldviews demand the incorporation of new sorts of source material, including sources conventionally rejected as unofficial or uncorroboratable and therefore unreliable. Given the characteristically limited, fragmentary, and indirect nature of sources on "the people," it also demands an openness to creative extrapolation on the part of the historian not normally condoned within the "scientific" conventions of the discipline. Such research has therefore always held a potential for exciting innovation as well as profound controversy.

In English-language historiography, this trend was heralded by E. P. Thompson's profoundly influential *The Making of the English Working Class* (1963), in which he sought "to rescue the poor stockinger, the Luddite cropper, the 'obsolete' hand-loom weaver, the 'utopian' artisan, and even the deluded follower of Joanna Southcott, from the enormous condescension of posterity."[46] In Japan, a mix of related and distinctly local concerns saw the contemporaneous appearance of a school of history writing known as "People's History" (*minshūshi*), inspired by the potentials of "people power" revealed in the 1960 AMPO protests. Led by self-proclaimed antiestablishment scholars such as Irokawa Daikichi and Kanō Masanao, they too sought to reveal stories of forgotten, ordinary people as agents in their own history. But representing a generation of Japanese intellectuals who had also experienced wartime indoctrination firsthand as schoolchildren, theirs was also a distinctly national agenda that related directly to the perceived problem of a Japanese cultural heritage of popular passivity in the face of power.

Conventional interpreters of the early postwar era such as Maruyama Masao had blamed Japan's descent into totalitarianism and war on a failure to internalize notions of popular sovereignty and subjectivity, essentially depicting these as foreign imports into alien soil. Yet if this was really the whole story, the postwar political prognosis seemed little more promising. If political complacency was Japan's only indigenous popular political tradition, what was to prevent the return of authoritarianism in the future? The aim of the People's History scholars, therefore, was to look to the Japanese past in new and creative ways for signs of an indigenous popular democratic heritage that might in turn provide a sturdy historical foundation and precedent for the present and the future. This hope led these scholars to look back to moments when they imagined that Japan's people, left to their own devices, might have chosen a different course: "periods of possibility" before the people were overwhelmed by what these scholars perceived—and had themselves experienced—as the irresistible, oppressive power of the modern Japanese state. Logically, their primary focus therefore fell on moments in the prewar period in which the relative weakness of that state was seen to have allowed the people an opportunity, however limited, to envision a different political order: the early Meiji period (Irokawa) and the Taishō period (Kanō).

Their scholarship was both productive and influential. In a prominent 1978 essay, the American historian Carol Gluck described their output as "solid and vital—in many ways the most interesting work in the field in Japan today."[47] Irokawa's 1968 discovery of a popularly authored draft national constitution dating from the early 1880s in an abandoned country storehouse in Santama outside Tokyo was only the most spectacular of their finds.[48] Here was concrete proof of a popular democratic spirit dependent neither on foreign example nor input from the social elite, usually seen as the main actors in Japan's history.[49] Such rosy interpretations, however, faced criticism from established scholars across the political spectrum.

Those to the political right criticized the People's Historians—as they indeed regularly criticized Marxist scholars—for being overambitious, ahistorical, and presentist, selectively plumbing limited and unreliable data from the past for political ammunition to be used in the present. A historical narrative charting the trajectory of a path *not* taken: was this history or wishful thinking?[50] From the left too the People's Historians faced criticism, here for the vagueness of their social categorizations. Reflective of their perception of the distinctive problems of Japan's recent past, the fundamental social and political divide that the People's Historians defined—and which defined them—was that between "the people" on the one hand and "the state" on the other. This broad, binary scheme of social conceptualization allowed them the flexibility to include progressively inclined members of those conventionally seen as representatives of the social elite—sons of landlord families, for example—within the definitional bounds of "the people." This flexibility in a socially "upward" direction also allowed them to leap the nearly insurmountable empirical hurdle represented by the fact that subalterns—those at the social bottom of society—leave by definition few if any documentary traces of their experiences. But Marxists could hardly accept a definition of "the people" that included both peasants and landlords on the "same side" merely based on the fact that some landlord's sons sometimes had progressive political leanings; for them, the arrangements of Japan's socioeconomic system—the social "base" from which history's logic inexorably derived—positioned the landlords as a "parasitical" class in an antagonistic relation to the peasantry. The dark subsequent history of Japan's prewar "emperor system," they argued, had inevitably borne out this logic.[51]

Taking shape in the wake of the period in which "People's History" was highly influential, *Grassroots Fascism: The War Experience of the Japanese People* shares with the People's History scholars a basic focus upon the ideas, experiences, and historical role of ordinary people, defined as those without significant social power or influence, whose voices are therefore usually left out of the history books. In a similar spirit it too reserves special attention for the experience of the "forgotten" and disadvantaged people of rural Japan, who are seen to have paid the heaviest price for Japan's modernization.[52] It too is passionately concerned with chronicling a history from the bottom up in the face of what has heretofore too often been seen as an all-powerful state and a one-sided historical process. As a corollary it also shares a fundamentally binary conceptualization of society, defining and positioning "the people" against the powerful—the social, economic, and political elites who usually occupy history's center stage.

As such, *Grassroots Fascism* might also be held liable to similar criticisms from conventional right and left: From the right, for an excessively "political" and "presentist" concern with narrating history for contemporary social and political ends and for its ambitious and politically motivated attempt to document precisely those underrepresented in the conventional historical record. From the left, it can also be accused of presenting a broad and vague social definition of "the people" that is overly inclusive of all who are less than obviously elite, thus insufficiently highlighting what are for Marxists the all-important social fracture lines dividing the "progressive" and "reactionary" classes from one another—the landless peasant from the small landholder, the proletariat from the petit-bourgeois.

Asked of his definition of "the people" in recent interviews, Yoshimi responded,

> "What are the people?" is a fairly difficult one I think, but if I speak generally, there's the definition "not elite," and if you limit that a bit, in military terms, it's the strata of nonofficers, from ordinary soldiers through nonenlisted men; if you're talking about society, it's the blue-collar workers, white-collar workers below the level of section chief [課長]; in farming village terms, I think it's those who are not landlords—limited to tenants or part-tenant/part-landed farmers, or independent owner-cultivators. In terms of education, it's elementary school up to graduates of higher elementary school. Graduates of middle school might also be included among the people, but that's a bit dubious. Because the elite can also

be the semielite. That stratum of people, that is to say, those who lead but are not leaders, at the most local subleaders—I try to think of them tentatively as the people. . . . In terms of the book, there's the Tōhoku composition teacher who graduated from teacher's training school, so he stood right in between the leaders and the people—these sorts of people are difficult.[53]

Asked about possible methodological influences here, either Japanese or international, Yoshimi says he employed "no model in particular" to define "the people," but that

a special characteristic in the prewar Japanese military was that you had extremely excellent noncommissioned officers, and among them, they were mostly people who had graduated higher elementary school; moreover, these were the people who supported Japan's postwar high economic growth. In the factories, they were not the leader-level, but middle-level people who became those who supported the elite. So it has occurred to me that this becomes a certain model. And the generation that fought the war, in generational terms, most were born in the Taisho period, the 1910s and the 1920s . . . this is a certain "people"—not the lowest level of the people, but I think they make up the core of this book.[54]

Despite Yoshimi's disclaimers, the above parallels with the agenda, strategies, and challenges faced by the People's Historians might lead one to imagine that *Grassroots Fascism* was to some extent inspired by their work.[55] Still, Yoshimi maintains that the work of the People's Historians had little influence upon his own, at least at a conscious level. At first one might be tempted to attribute this to the fact that feelings of distance between the antiestablishment People's History scholars and the products of the Tokyo University establishment were often mutual. But a closer examination confirms a more fundamental difference in the basic scholarly problematic of *Grassroots Fascism*.

In the case of narratives of the experience of the war, it is not only the conventional elitism of scholarly approaches, a lack of source material, or assumptions about Japanese social "underdevelopment" that have kept "the people" off history's center stage. For here the issue of agency is infinitely more complicated—politically and morally—by the question of responsibility. Where the People's Historians sought to discover a popular light of democratic resistance against the encroaching darkness of the state—a storyline in which the notion of history from the bottom up inevitably carries a positive valence—an exploration of the active role of ordinary people in the war, and a resultant confrontation with the possibility of popular responsibility for the war, implies a loosening, if not an abandoning, of one of the most essential precepts of progressive politics itself. That is, the notion that ordinary people, by definition socially situated in a relationship of subordination to and domination by powerful states and elites, can never be held directly responsible for actions for which they are mobilized by ruling regimes and which are conducted by ruling regimes in their name. The more autocratic, hierarchical, and aggressive the regime in question—the more lopsided the power relationship between the regime and ordinary people and thus the more limited their subjective autonomy and maneuvering room—the more such a precept would presumably apply.

Such issues lead to further problematical questions both politically and methodologically. Even if we were to accept the controversial idea that ordinary people might bear a secondary if not a primary responsibility for, and agency in, the consequences of actions conducted by autocratic regimes in their name, how are we then to determine and represent the relative *distribution* of agency and responsibility between the regime and the people? And even assuming that this problem can be productively addressed in theoretical terms, there remains a political problem of research and narrative focus itself: presenting a narrative that focuses on the experience and role of ordinary people means, inevitably, that the deeds and role of the elites must remain relatively in the background and out of focus.

Despite the growing accumulation of source material on the popular experience of the war, for Yoshimi as for those who came before him there thus remained powerful reasons for hesitation and second-guessing—reasons, as he notes in his own afterword, that he "tended to leave off" the project in the decade between 1976 and 1985. "There are so many varieties of the people, sides to the people, there was the methodological question of how that can be analyzed," he says. But of all the critical comments posed by himself and others as he pondered his approach to what would eventually become *Grassroots Fascism*, the question most often raised—and giving him the most reason for pause—was "this political question: how can you focus on the people's responsibility, when the task of identifying responsibility among the elites still remains incomplete?" "Up till now," notes Yoshimi,

I had always written critical history, conducted historical investigation critical of the government, the leaders, power. . . . Taking ordinary people like us as my object, rather than people with power, the leaders, was difficult. . . . One reason was, it meant criticizing myself and criticizing those around me—my siblings, my parents, my relations. Another is, starting with the responsibility of the people, who should in fact have a lighter responsibility, even as the problem of the responsibility of the leaders is unclear: is this not the wrong order of priority? Should we not first clarify the responsibility of the leadership and then [only] after this take up the problem of the ordinary people whom they led?[56]

In the end, as Yoshimi himself notes, perhaps the impetus for such a bold, taboo-breaking project could only come with the help of *gaiatsu*, or "pressure from outside." To be precise, the pressure came from two sources. The first was a "push from behind" from an unusual, motivated group of scholars who came together at the invitation of Tokyo University Press editor Watanabe Isao to produce a series in "New World History" (*Atarashii sekaishi*) at the start of the 1980s. The second were two 1985 statements from a pair of German statesmen on the issue of war responsibility, the first a landmark of self-reflection and self-criticism, the second a statement sharply critical of Japan by comparison.

The New World History Series first convened in 1981–1982. As a whole the group represented a truly global spread of expertise, embracing Asia, Africa, Europe, the Middle East, and the Americas; Yoshimi was the only participant with a Japan specialization.[57] While "the subject or period were not decided in advance," he says, "the idea was to do something that wasn't from either a Marxist or a positivist position." In the view of the Americanist Yui Daizaburō as Yoshimi describes it, what the group shared was not so much a methodology as a critical attitude based on a shared formative context: "We were all of the Vietnam War generation, all in our twenties during the Vietnam War." In the end the methodologies chosen were different in each case, but all were united in the idea that "it was time for something new," that "if we kept doing it the old way, we wouldn't get any further." "Everyone got a very big result out of [the New World History series project], including me," says Yoshimi. "If not for this group, I might not have written this book." Yoshimi's first proposal to the group was to pursue a more conventional project: a "discourse on Japanese fascism" (*Nihon fashizumu ron*). But this was quickly voted down. "I was harshly told they thought this uninteresting." Sensing that he was onto something big—however controversial—they urged him to instead overcome his longstanding hesitation to explore the role of ordinary Japanese in the war.

This interaction with fellow historians from other regional specializations emboldened Yoshimi to tread a terrain of domestic history where no Japanese scholar had dared set foot before. But it also strengthened his conviction in the significance of this experience as a part of global history not only in terms of popular involvement in the rise of fascism but crucially also in terms of popular lessons learned in its ultimate downfall.

> If you go to a bookstore, it's interesting that my book is not in the Japanese His-
> tory section but the World History section. It's hard to find and that's a minus as
> far as selling lots of books, but I'm proud that it's in the World History section. . . .
> In doing research on the people's history of the war, I felt very strongly that theirs
> was a "world-history" experience. . . . I'm not an anarchist, but many people,
> ordinary people, realized that there's a positive meaning in the collapse of the
> state—I believe this [too] was very much a world-history experience.[58]

As he notes in his afterword, the mission and shape of *Grassroots Fascism* as a vehicle for bringing this experience to the attention of the Japanese public and to the world reached its full crystallization in response to the "challenge" posed by two German statements on the issue of war responsibility: President Richard von Weizsacker's landmark 1985 speech marking the fortieth anniver- sary of the Nazi surrender and former chancellor Helmut Schmid's subsequent public criticism of a lack of comparable "self-introspection" on the Japanese part in the same year. Yoshimi was particularly impressed with Weizsacker's "national-level acknowledgement of war responsibility" as well as the connec- tion drawn between the socially exclusive, murderous policies of Nazi Ger- many and the socially inclusive, open vision of postwar Germany embodied in the protection of minority rights. Schmid's speech identified a sharp distinc- tion between precisely such a German willingness to acknowledge and take responsibility for Germany's wartime crimes—thus fulfilling a prerequisite for the postwar reestablishment of friendship and trust with Germany's neighbors and former wartime victims—and a corresponding Japanese postwar failure on both scores.

Where the Japanese state was concerned, says Yoshimi, he could not but acknowledge the painful truth of Schmid's charges. But reading through the vast range of source material he and his colleagues had accumulated on the popular wartime experience and its aftermath, he was increasingly struck not only by the challenging complexity and ambiguity of popular wartime expe- rience itself but also by what he saw as a positive "bottom-up" inheritance: a spontaneous, broad-based, autonomous process of self-reflection and transfor- mation at war's end, and in the years since, that stood at a critical distance from the state.[59] "Among the various Japanese people's records and memoirs of the war experience, in the investigations and research of journalists, scholars, and the like, more than a few people were carrying out the self-examination that Schmidt was talking about," writes Yoshimi. Alongside a new understanding of the history of the war from the bottom up, Yoshimi's research had revealed "another discovery: Out of the experiences of battlefield and the rubble of war, ordinary Japanese people had come to rediscover the values of peace, freedom, and democracy."[60] The war experience from the bottom up had generated a powerful force for democracy from the bottom up. "This reaffirmed to me the great importance of the building of a peaceful Japan based upon the Japanese people's experience of the war."[61]

Born of such a purpose, *Grassroots Fascism* is an ambitious exercise in academic engagement, one driven by a combination of two agendas. On the one hand, it springs from an eminently scholarly commitment to a faithful and subtle representation of history's real-life complexity, nuance, and evolution—to letting the voices of history "speak for themselves"—across a wide, geographically and socially inclusive terrain. On the other hand, it is a humane vision of history as social compass, as a reservoir of lessons for a searching present. Critics in search of an illusory "objectivity" might see these aims as inherently contradictory, but it can be argued that such is the very essence of the historian's craft: Engaging with history is always and inevitably also an engagement with the politics of the present, history writing (and reading) an inherently selective and subjective act of representation and interpretation. Tensions between the disciplinary aim of maintaining distance and balance and the political aim of constructing a story of the past with a meaning for the present cannot be avoided. History and memory, past and present, inevitably adhere within each other; the best works of history seek not to overcome their tensions—in any case a methodological and political impossibility—but to embrace them and to strike a productive balance between them.

At its best, *Grassroots Fascism* is an extraordinary example of how the two agendas can work productively and synergistically, giving shape, power, and meaning to a narrative of the past that is all the more effective for its openness to ambiguity, nuance, and multiple valences. Any given strategy of imparting narrative and interpretive coherence to such a vast terrain of experience, however, brings with it both advantages and pitfalls. In seeking a balance between the multivalence of the past and the pull of the present—between the ambiguous diversity of historical experience and the retrospective homogenizing effect of memory—methodological dexterity must be paired with the most essential tool of the historian's trade: a wide range of representative, reliable, and complementary primary source material.

Rarely does the scholar of historical experience have the luxury of relying exclusively upon documentary evidence dating from the time in question, less so in the case of popular experience, still less so in a wartime setting. At the same time, in the case of documenting the experience of wartime—particularly that of a lost and *repudiated* war—the profoundness of the contextual change before and after defeat makes access to such material all the more urgent. In modern history there have indeed been few historical moments in which perceived realities changed more swiftly and decisively than at the end of the Pacific War, coming as it did so suddenly and so unexpectedly to so many people.

For better or for worse, up to the very end of the war, not only most Japanese but even many Asians did not seriously entertain the possibility of a Japanese defeat, let alone ponder its historical implications. The speed and seeming effortlessness of Japan's early victories in the Pacific War, combined with effective wartime propaganda of Japanese martial invincibility, had convinced many that defeat was out of the realm of possibility. Particularly in much of the wartime empire that did not become a battlefront—most portions of occupied Indonesia, for example—signs of impending defeat were limited and easily refuted or ignored. As vividly demonstrated in *Grassroots Fascism*'s second half, even for most Japanese in the mainland itself, where the course of the war was much more directly palpable, popular determination to fight on was strong enough to withstand years of dramatic shortages and, in the end, months of sustained, devastating aerial bombing throughout the length and breadth of a virtually defenseless homeland.

When it did come, in the starkest of contrasts, defeat was indisputable, total, and filled with an unheralded significance, its suddenness and unexpectedness only adding to the sense of a world turned on its head. Viewed in dizzying postdefeat retrospect, the desperation of the war's final stages now appeared with perfect clarity as indisputable confirmation both that defeat was inevitable and foreseeable and that resistance to it had been an exercise in futility symbolic of the "irrationality" inherent to Japan's prewar social and psychological system. Wartime overconfidence and dedication was now pathologized and explained (away) as "victory disease."[62] Once it opened up, this momentous chasm of discontinuity made narrative retrieval of the full ambiguity and complexity of experiences and sentiments left behind on "the other side" of the gap a near impossibility. Narratives of the war were now indelibly colored, refracted, and reshaped to the irresistible new reality and new demands of the postwar.[63]

In the face of this tremendous challenge, it is precisely where Yoshimi is able to bring to bear the full weight of his remarkable array of wartime source material—diaries, letters, government reports—that *Grassroots* is at its most compelling. What makes *Grassroots Fascism*'s reconstruction of the war experience uniquely persuasive and effective is its deployment of so many contemporaneous voices and archives that were frozen in their wartime authenticity, as it were, by circumstances (death in battle, filing away in a household dresser or a bureaucratic folder) before the postwar could tamper with or edit them. This is above all evident in its treatment of experiences on the Chinese continent and on the Japanese home front, where intimate, detailed, and often shockingly graphic accounts authored by (fallen) soldiers are supplemented with family diary entries, correspondence, and the like, along with more broadly suggestive data from internal government monitoring, to produce a startlingly textured and vivid canvas of wartime life. The evidence presented here is so overwhelming that it becomes impossible to see such phenomena as the Rape of Nanjing, for example, as an isolated "incident." The voices of Japan's own soldiers in the heat of action across wartime China provide indisputable evidence of how and why this "incident" was part of a much larger and more general and evolving, systemic pattern of radicalization and brutalization—evidence so overwhelming that *Grassroots Fascism* need not to take us to Nanjing itself to see it.

Where experiences in wartime Southeast Asia are concerned, in contrast, the availability of primary source material was and is, unfortunately, much more limited. In places like Indonesia, Vietnam, Burma, and Malaysia, the former Japanese occupiers often had weeks or months between the surrender and the arrival of Allied forces to destroy incriminating documents systematically. More was lost or destroyed in the chaos of the postwar transition and afterward, often on purpose. As an unusually forthcoming veteran of the Java occupation once acknowledged, particularly given how pleasant and peaceful the life of colonial occupier was for many Japanese there, feelings of guilt toward loved ones, the war dead, and fellow war veterans inhibited many from sharing their records or stories afterward.[64] To the extent that they were authored in the first place, very few personal accounts from the occupation period itself survive. Extensive documentary destruction also occurred in Japan and in other parts of the former wartime empire, but not with such overwhelming effect. "In the end," Yoshimi acknowledges, in the case of China, there are those who came back to Japan before the war was lost, and there was quite a good chance that what they wrote at the time survived as is. In the case of Southeast Asia, they were on site until the defeat, and when they returned to Japan, the material they had, one thing is they were afraid it would be confiscated, or they were afraid they might be indicted for war crimes, so they destroyed everything and there's nothing [left]. Therefore in this sense there's a very big difficulty—is [the story they tell] 100 percent the reality as is? There is a great concern that it may be a bit dramatized.[65]

Scholars seeking to document individual experiences of Japan's occupations in Southeast Asia are thus confronted with a stark choice: heavy reliance on memory documents filtered through the lens of postwar retrospect or—where available—resort to the suspect sorts of primary material that survived the war in larger quantities, government-approved, published "propaganda" media such as newspapers, films, and books. In *Grassroots Fascism*, Yoshimi chose the first of these two options, in line with his approach in the rest of the study. Well aware of the methodological problems involved, he relied to the greatest possible extent on documents of the wartime experience written as soon as possible after the moment of surrender, but these too were not always available. The result is that *Grassroots Fascism*'s narratives of Japanese experiences in Southeast Asia are more prone to a postwar emplotment than those of Northeast Asia, constructed with the surrender as teleological and meaning-filled climax. Here, at the mercy of its sources, it might be argued that *Grassroots Fascism*'s carefully maintained balance between the documenting of history and the revealing of its lessons is sometimes in danger of tilting rather too heavy-handedly in the direction of the latter.[66] Asked about this in recent interviews, Yoshimi acknowledged the dilemma.

From around the 1970s, there were many memoirs, and in things that were written twenty or thirty years after the war, postwar values are very much mixed in; this is certainly true. I do think you can say that there's a big problem here . . . in many cases we need to be conscious of the fact that things published in the 1970s are memoirs from the standpoint of the 1970s . . . there are also a lot of them that were based on things written not so long after the defeat, for example by people who came back from the Philippines. . . . Indeed it's best if the thing they wrote first survives, but many people threw that out thinking that now that they've revised it they don't need the old stuff. I do believe that there is definitely

a point of contention here. It's hard to know how to judge that, it presents a difficult problem . . . sometimes that's all there is—what should we do then? You can
reinforce it by doing interviews with the author to confirm things, and moreover,
if for example it's a case where they think the war was a holy war, then it's possible
to assume that their thinking didn't change much . . . and in so far as how they
remember what they experienced after the war, there's no mistake about how
they were thinking about the war at that time [the time of writing], and this we
can believe.[67]

At the same time, drawing upon the more well-known example of his landmark research on Japan's "comfort women"—and recalling debates on "subaltern history" in other contexts—Yoshimi argues passionately and persuasively
that such risks are inherent to all histories of the socially underprivileged and
undocumented and should not in themselves detach the historian from the responsibility to make the attempt.[68]

> The experience of plain ordinary people at that time probably went mostly un-
> recorded. This was a big debate at the time I was doing research on the "comfort
> women." As far as prewar sources on the "comfort women" go, there are only
> those from the side of the military and the state. The women themselves did not
> write anything or leave any written things behind. Because many of them could
> not write. And given that, what we can know is [from] meeting them now and in-
> terviewing them about what happened then. On that score, it becomes a question
> of which one is worth more, prewar and wartime sources from the government
> side or stories you hear today told by old ladies who were "comfort women," but
> it's not [a question of] which is more valuable; I believe they're the same, of equal
> value. Their value is determined by what it is you want to clarify—if you want to
> reconstruct what sorts of feelings those old women who were made into "com-
> fort women" lived with, there's truly no alternative to meeting them and hearing
> their stories. It's not so that this is meaningless; if you check these stories against
> other sources of various kinds from the time and it's impossible to say "it's not
> the truth," there is no choice but to acknowledge this as the truth. If not, you
> wouldn't be able to write about the shape of the women at the time—I feel that
> problem resembles this one [in *Grassroots Fascism*] a bit.[69]

A different but not unrelated historiographical issue has become clearer
in the light of contemporary retrospect: what one might call *Grassroots Fas-*

cism's narrative Japanocentrism. However critical and nuanced Yoshimi is in his documentation and analysis of his protagonists, however groundbreaking as well in the special attention devoted to minority groups at Japan's social margins, including Koreans and Taiwanese, the fact remains that the perspectives, voices, and histories of Asians not defined at the time under study under the general rubric of Japanese nationals (*kokumin*) are virtually absent from the narrative. In this as in all studies that focus on one side or the other of the imperial encounter, there were of course sound practical reasons for this: language barriers, lack of local expertise, the already ambitious scope of the endeavor. Still, as persuasively argued by a host of critical scholars and theorists in the period since the original publication of *Grassroots Fascism*, understanding the dynamics of the encounter between imperial metropole and colonial periphery requires equal attention to the view and experience on both sides and their mutual impacts.[70] A second and related problem, which might also to some extent be seen as a marker of the book's 1980s vintage, is its tendency toward a somewhat uniform and positive depiction of non-Japanese Asians as victims and resistors of Japanese imperialism. Social differentiation among Indonesians, Chinese, Burmese, and Filipinos was just as complex as that on the Japanese side, their political agendas and their experiences of the Japanese often ambivalent, complex, and contradictory.[71] While suggestively nuanced accounts of Okinawans, Taiwanese, and Korean experiences do make an appearance in *Grassroots Fascism*, such treatment does not extend far beyond the social boundaries of "the Japanese." As Yoshimi himself acknowledges,

At the time, I wrote in the awareness of this [problem] to a certain degree, but I wasn't focusing on Koreans or Indonesians, so it's abridged. I wasn't planning to clarify this to such an extent in this book. What was the case with the Japanese?— this was the issue. As you say, there is definitely this problem. It's complexly multilayered . . . this is something I am always conscious of. For example, Okinawans, they're Japanese like others, but they were discriminated against. When these Okinawans went to Southeast Asia or Taiwan, there's also the aspect that they became oppressors, as "residents of Yamato"—there's a hesitation whether it's necessary to go so far as to say this, and all the more so in the case of Indonesians, it's true one hesitates even more. And one more circumstance is, it's true that at the time my capabilities did not allow me to go so far as to explain such a complex structure to that extent. I think in the meantime research has progressed, making it possible to identify such a problem.[72]

The years since the publication of *Grassroots Fascism* have indeed seen progress and enrichment with regard to our understanding of the dynamics and nature of Japan's wartime experience. The voices of ordinary's peoples' wartime experience now made accessible for the first time here in English can be located within a genre of wartime accounts based on firsthand testimonies whose scope has since broadened significantly.[73] Sharing Yoshimi's longstanding conviction of a fundamental comparability between Japanese modern experience and that of Europe and elsewhere, an expanding group of scholars such as Andrew Gordon, Louise Young, and Harry Harootunian have meanwhile mounted a sustained challenge to established assumptions that Japanese experience was somehow different, "distorted," or "behind." In different ways they have sought to relate this experience to phenomena inherent to capitalist industrialization, nation and empire building and its attendant social mobilizations, of interactions between state and society in the shaping of these processes, and—particularly in the case of Young's landmark *Japan's Total Empire* (1998)—their dialectical interplay with imperial expansion and policy.[74] As revealed in the title of the last of a recently completed, high-profile, eight-volume series on the Asia Pacific War edited by a group of leading Japanese historians, this reflects a larger, ongoing contemporary trend to resituate Japan's wartime experience "within twentieth century history."[75] Here and elsewhere, as confirmed in the recent appearance of a pioneering collection of essays entitled *The Culture of Japanese Fascism*, attention is turning increasingly to previously overlooked or underestimated cultural aspects of Japan's wartime experience as part of a global modern experience.[76]

Such scholarship is informed by the increasing global dominance of critiques of Eurocentrism and Orientalism, part of a more general global interdisciplinary trend toward conceptual "border crossing" and scholarship "from the margins" founded upon a questioning of conventional cultural, social, and spatial categories and dynamics of identity and history, of the narrative forms in which they are presented, and of the power they express. Where Japan's war is concerned, scholars such as Oguma Eiji and Tessa Morris-Suzuki have sought in different ways to highlight the historical, negotiated, multiple, and contested making of categories of identity and allegiance across conventional boundaries.[77] Emphasizing the transnational workings of social and cultural formation in Japan's colonial encounters in a global context of empire and nation building, scholars such as Prasenjit Duara, Leo Ching, Hyun Ok Park, Jun Uchida, and Takashi Fujitani have sought to push beyond conventional categories of oppression, resistance, and "collaboration" alone to discover identities, interests, and processes that embraced people and institutions across the conventional boundaries dividing nation from nation and colonizer and colonized.[78] Yoshimi's own subsequent work on the "comfort women," along with his more recent scholarship on the Japanese army's use of poison gas, has also added significantly to our understanding of aspects of the war experience hitherto considered marginal to the "main story" but now seen to cast the "main story" in an important new light.[79]

Both within Yoshimi's own scholarship and in the study of the Asia-Pacific War more generally, the intervening years have thus seen *Grassroots Fascism*'s picture of the war experience supplemented by a number of important new angles and shades. Yet in the breadth, variety, and inclusiveness of its coverage in geographical, chronological, and social terms, in its connecting of battlefront and home front, and in its attempt to come to terms with issues of popular war responsibility, *Grassroots Fascism* remains not only Yoshimi Yoshiaki's most ambitious work but indeed one of the most ambitious accounts of the Second World War that we have in any language. As we work toward the development of more genuinely global understandings of this most global of conflicts and its border-crossing dynamics and legacies—beyond the conceptual, narrative, and political bounds delineated by the conventional centering of the nation-state and Euro-American experience—its relevance can surely only be expected to grow.

THE DESIGN OF THE BOOK

Grassroots Fascism is presented in the form of four chapters that trace out the rise and fall of grassroots fascism in chronological order: "From Democracy to Fascism," "Grassroots Fascism," "The War in Asia," and "Democracy from the Battlefield." In broad chronological and topical terms the first two chapters treat the period when the war was limited to China (1937–1941) and the last two the expanded Pacific War (1941–1945), with the text evenly divided between them. Yet reflecting the author's aim of transmitting and assessing a representatively diverse range of individual and group experiences "on the ground" across the broad geographical expanse of Japan's wartime empire, narratives within each chapter are largely structured in terms of diverse and specific geographical and social *sites*, with a corresponding multiplicity of microchronologies. Certain geographical terrains are revisited at different chronological points, as with the return to the China front at the end of chapter 3, which serves as a kind of bookend to the extensive China coverage in chapter 1. Socially too, certain individuals, once introduced, also make reappearances as the story progresses (in particular as the story returns to the home front), and nearly all of them reappear in its powerful conclusion. But overall, in chronological, spatial, and social terms, the narrative structure assumes the form of a collage, a distribution of vantages, making it by nature fragmentary. Analytically too, the experience, role, and responsibility of ordinary people in the wartime system is assessed primarily on the personal terms in which they themselves lived and perceived it: from the bottom up and the inside out, according to the specifics of individual experience.

Thus consciously eschewing the conventional, generalized, top-down view in favor of the multiple, diverse, and fragmentary picture from the bottom up, *Grassroots Fascism* correspondingly provides little in the way of an overview of the history of the Asia-Pacific War or a reiteration of conventional arguments, characterizations, or approaches to it. Readers unfamiliar with the basic facts, terms, events, and chronology of the Asia-Pacific War, as well as some of the major points of contention associated with them, may find this presentation challenging. The opening of the book—which immediately concerns itself with the nature and degree of democratic consciousness among ordinary Japanese people in the wake of the Manchurian incident and seeks its traces in a diversity of individual voices—is reflective of this larger challenge. Such a presentation assumes a familiarity with its scholarly counterpart: state-centered images and narratives of the history of 1930s Japan that locate the eclipse of an already fragile Japanese democracy and the rise of Japanese fascism in the Manchurian Incident of 1931 and its aftermath, including the end of party cabinets, crackdowns on the political left, the rise of the radical right, and increasing military influence in political and social life.

For the international reader unfamiliar with such particulars of historical and historiographical context, it is hoped that this introduction has helped fill in some of the gaps. For further assistance, throughout the text itself, this English edition of *Grassroots Fascism* has been supplemented with extensive new annotation, indicated by the translator's initials (EM), meant to provide substantial background information on important events, names, phenomena, and points of scholarly discussion and debate. For those seeking to go deeper, these annotations frequently include reference to related English-language scholarly works.

No single work of history can be expected to stand alone.[80] But it is hoped that this edition of *Grassroots Fascism* is hereby sufficiently fortified in its presentation to allow the international reader to proceed into the complex and fascinating terrain of Japan's war experience relatively unimpeded, and undaunted, by a lack of previous exposure to the subject—thereby positioned to discover a resonance and a relevance that extends far beyond the bounds of Japan and its former empire alone.

1
FROM DEMOCRACY
TO FASCISM

HOPES AND MISGIVINGS REGARDING THE WAR

GRASSROOTS DEMOCRACY

When the Manchurian Incident began in September 1931, support for war spread like a fever among the Japanese people, fueled by extensive media coverage of the conflict.[1] But the fever was a temporary phenomenon. Once the fighting subsided, people reexamined their lives. Agricultural depression continued in the villages, and inflation mounted in the cities, driven by military spending. By 1935, government attempts to overcome the Great Depression through military campaigns abroad were being reappraised.

"Imperialism externally, constitutionalism internally": It has been argued that these were the guiding principles of Taishō democracy, which took root following the Russo-Japanese War (1904–1905).[2] The popular demands for democracy that accompanied the democratic expansion of the Taishō period had not disappeared but continued to resonate in the mid-1930s.[3] In general, people demanded political and social liberation and improvement in their lives, to be actuated by the people themselves. Of course, insofar as it took the emperor system as a given, this thinking had an authoritarian aspect.[4] Its tendency toward an Asian version of the Monroe Doctrine was one indication of an "imperial" ideology prevalent in the Japanese nation as an imperialist latecomer. This popular framing of liberation in terms of "one sovereign for all subjects" (*ikkun banmin*) may be viewed as a grassroots imperial democracy consciousness.[5]

VOICES CRITICAL OF THE MILITARY

Through the mid-1930s, people continued to maintain this consciousness distinctive to post–World War I Japan, forcefully calling for social and political liberation and improvement in their lives. The startling military rebellion of February 26, 1936, occurred within this context, and amid the resultant turmoil, imperial democracy consciousness made an emergence onto the historical stage.

People felt a strong antagonism toward the young officers who had perpetrated the February 26 incident and toward the army authorities who used them in an attempt to secure hegemony.[6] Expressive of such sentiments in the wake of the incident, the family of a policeman who died in the line of duty defending a high-ranking government official was showered with condolence money and letters from all over the country.

On March 4, 1936, Vice President of the Asahi Newspaper Company Shimomura Hiroshi informed Imperial Household Minister Yuasa Kurahei of mass anger toward the rebel army.

> Every day I hear voices of righteous indignation and receive letters of anger and lamentation. Women are shouting that it was wrong to kill [Finance Minister] Takahashi [Korekiyo], and children are crying. Around Saitama [Prefecture] schoolteachers too have unexpectedly been telling their students, "after this sort of thing, you can't trust the army either." A growing number of people say, "if it's gotten like this, we can't send our boys out as soldiers." And at places like the Japan Club, even normally courteous elderly men are in quite an uproar.[7]

The large number of personal messages of encouragement, support, and sympathy received by Diet Representative Saitō Takao following his "purge the army speech" of May 7, 1936—in which he hammered upon the responsibility of the military authorities for the incident—revealed the people's genuine sentiments in opposing the trend toward military-directed fascism, yearning for the restoration of constitutional politics, and the realization of imperial democracy.[8]

Personal messages in the form of letters, postcards, and telegrams that Saitō received between May and June demonstrated the following variety of popular standpoints:

> Writing as "a loyal subject," one unnamed person called for an imperial politics of "harmony" (*wa*). "Killing a number of high-ranking officials and destroying capitalism," the person wrote, "will not make people's lives carefree just like that. Fascism, Nazism, communism—they're all the same."[9]

> Regarding the political maneuvers of the military authorities and the "young officers" who imitated Hitler and Mussolini, Kondō Tsugishige of Tokyo's Kanda Ward wrote, "We the Japanese people have been unanimously unhappy for some time." He urged the restoration of constitutional politics.[10]

> Demanding reform of "the capitalist economic system," another person in the name of "we, the proletariat of Tajima" wrote, "We register our admiration for your great speech, in which you said that the patience of the Japanese has its limits. We the proletariat have limits to our patience as well."[11]

Running through almost all of these personal messages to Saitō were expressions of gratitude for his strong reaction to and critique of the military authorities: "Mr. Saitō, thank you. You spoke well for us. Everything you said represents the voice of the people," read an anonymous letter. "I was thinking how regrettable it was that the people were unable to make their voices freely heard in the Diet, but you've said it well enough for us."[12] From this we must conclude that imperial democracy consciousness continued to survive at the grassroots.

Yet the people expressing this range of sentiments lacked the political power to come together into a movement that might have resisted the military authorities' fascism, and so their urgent appeals simply floated in space. That these sorts of expressions continued to represent a strand of public opinion again became clear, however, when an attempt to form a new cabinet miscarried in January 1937.

In the wake of this incident, in which former Army Minister Ugaki Kazushige was instructed by the emperor to form a cabinet but was prevented from doing so by army opposition, there was a strong popular reaction against the military.[13] "Among area residents" within the jurisdiction of the Sendai second division, warned division command and army reservist association reports, "there are those who criticize the army's attitude and act perversely for no good reason, while antimilitary thinking is on the rise. Strict precautions must be taken."[14] In Takata City in Niigata Prefecture, it was observed that "throughout the city and countryside, where public opinion is concerned, most people eagerly desire the formation of the Ugaki cabinet. . . . Commentary regarding the army's attitude ranges from discontent to indignation."[15] Within the jurisdiction of the Kanazawa ninth division, it was reported that "wherever local residents gather—in steam and electric trains, in the public baths, at the barber shop, et cetera—they never fail to discuss the issue of the change of government. What's more, there is a violent outcry against the military authorities."[16]

Despite this intense reaction against the military authorities, popular sentiment remained unable to transmute itself into a political force capable of stopping the move toward fascism. Stifled by the outbreak of full-blown war between Japan and China, popular views would end up changing dramatically.

TWO VIEWS OF THE WAR

When the Sino-Japanese War began on July 7, 1937, popular calls for "imperialism externally," a desire previously well buried, suddenly came to the fore. Along with limits on freedom of expression and the manipulation of public opinion, a number of other factors began to have a determining influence on popular consciousness. There was a manner of thinking along the lines of a fait accompli: "Now that the war has started, we'd better win it." There was a strong sense that Japan was winning the war. And by the end of 1937, Japan had dispatched some 770,000 troops, a reality that weighed heavily.

According to a national survey of thirty-eight municipalities conducted at the end of 1937 by the Cabinet Planning Board's Industry Section,[17] the attitude of people in farming, mountain, and fishing villages toward the war against China, summarized in terms of a single village, was divided between "the middle class and up," who "want the war to be pursued . . . to the fullest (to the point that [hostilities] will not flare up again)," and "the middle class and below," who "want it to be brought to as speedy an end as possible."[18]

Because their lives were comfortable, it can be argued that local people representing "the middle class and up" subscribed fundamentally and enthusiastically to the official war aims, to the ideology of a "holy war." In contrast, it may be said that "the middle class and below," who would pay a heavy price for the continuation of the war, were not so quick to absorb the whitewashed "holy war" ideology and strongly desired a quick end to the conflict.

Of course, there were those among the "middle class and below" who were enthusiastic, and attitudes toward the war varied considerably from one municipality to another.

At one end of the spectrum there was the following negative posture toward the war in Shizu'ura Village in Shizuoka Prefecture: "It may be assumed that the vast majority wish in their hearts that the Incident be brought to an end at the soonest possible moment."[19] In Aikawa Village in the same prefecture, the perceived mood was "There's nothing to be done about it," with residents desiring an early end to the war.[20] In Omoe Village in Iwate Prefecture, the general standpoint was "It would be good if it ends soon."[21]

At the other end of the spectrum were voices saying, "We hope that things are pursued thoroughly and are properly dealt with to prevent any reoccurrence." This view prevailed in more than half of the localities, including Kurotaki Village in Nara Prefecture, Wakasano Village in Hyōgo Prefecture, Nishishiwa Village in Hiroshima Prefecture, Kantama Village in Yamaguchi Prefecture, and Wakimisaki Village in Nagasaki Prefecture.[22]

A more ambivalent stance between the two extremes described above was probably closer to the general state of popular opinion.

GRASSROOTS IMPERIALISM

If we examine the calls for a speedy end to the war more closely—voices mostly from "the middle and below"—the following sorts of examples emerge with particular force.

- **A** "We hope that it ends quickly. (We hope that overseas development will be possible. There is only one person who does not want to leave the village and emigrate to Manchuria)."[23]
- **B** "In order to extend Japan's influence in northern China, we are planning to send out two or three of my boys."[24]
- **C** "To compensate for all the sacrifices the Imperial Army has made, [North and Central China] should be brought under the control of the Empire."[25]
- **D** "We hope that we'll be able to secure considerable rights and interests."[26]

Each of these statements represented a hope for a swift end to the war that went hand in hand with a yearning for concrete profits or rights and interests, clearly demonstrating that a "grassroots imperialism" ideology had begun to surge among the people. The people of Kawashima Town in Kagawa Prefecture were a representative example. Reflecting the complexity of popular attitudes, it was reported here that "if the war goes on for long it will be a problem—this is what people genuinely say. Yet on the other hand, people of all classes also say that we have to keep fighting until we win." Nevertheless, expressions like the following ones attributed to soldiers of the Zentsūji Eleventh Division— many of whom hailed from the same municipality and had fought in the two Shanghai Incidents of 1932 and 1937—were also on the rise.[27] One said that "it would be a waste meaninglessly to give back territory people have given their lives for." Another, in a viewpoint attributed "especially to the Eleventh Division," said, "The people will not accept it if we gain nothing—either land or reparations. We don't want to give back what we've already spent so much money getting for no reason. Northern China alone will not do. This is the second time we've shed blood in Shanghai."

As the Japanese Army moved deeper into China, there was furthermore a tendency to see a corresponding reduction among those seeking to emigrate to Manchuria (northeastern China). Among those from the "middle and below" who had been hoping to do so, "comments [were] ventured such as "Northern China would seem preferable to Manchuria.""[28]

By and large, people of the "middle and below" did not resist cooperating in the war effort either. From Wada Village in Kagawa Prefecture came the following report: "When military bonds are up for sale, poor folks come up with money to buy them, but the big capitalists don't. They're criticized for having little devotion to the nation. This is evident in Takamatsu City as well. If this is the situation, then it is in fact the middle classes and above that need to be targeted for national spiritual mobilization."[29]

Here, then, is the picture of a people who, in the midst of their difficult lives, earnestly desired to cooperate in the war because it was their "duty as Japanese," wishing simultaneously for a swift end to the conflict and to gain privileges from it.

COOPERATION FOR THE WAR AND
THE BACKLASH AGAINST IT

The Movement for Total National Spiritual Mobilization (*Kokumin seishin sōdōin undō*), initiated in September 1937, carried out campaigns for consumer thrift, the encouragement of savings, and the compulsory distribution of military bonds and the like. It was a movement for cooperation in the war effort that effectively centered on the reduction of standards of living to that end.[30]

In farming, mountain, and fishing villages, propaganda urging cutbacks in consumption met with strong opposition. In the aforementioned survey, statements like the following were representative: "Where farming villages are concerned, propaganda for consumer frugality and the like is pointless";[31] "Propaganda on the current situation appears convincing for the most part, but that on consumer thrift and such is rather met with antipathy";[32] "If farming villages limit their consumption more than they already do, the villagers' physical condition will deteriorate. There is no leeway for further economizing."[33] Resentment toward belt-tightening policies might be seen as natural, but there was more at issue.

Under the direction of the Aichi Prefectural Office, the Center for Spiritual Discipline (*Seishin tanrensho*) and the Shōwa Academy (*Shōwa juku*) in Nagoya City assembled a model menu for "making do with a minimal standard of living." But when the prefectural authorities promoted it, residents of Aichi's Midono Village, for whom the menu was "fancier than the finest treat," treated it with scorn.[34]

How did this sort of tragicomedy come about? City residents, for whom opportunities were relatively numerous, were beneficiaries of the war. In contrast, in each war since the first Sino-Japanese conflict (1894–1895), the people of farming, mountain, and fishing villages had borne great sacrifices. What was more, they had generally supported these wars with enthusiasm. In a report prepared after an observation tour of farming villages in the areas of western Honshū and Shikoku in September 1938, Navy Captain Konishi Tatehiko[35] described the situation: "Leaving Tokyo and setting foot in these farming villages for the first time, one is struck by the solemn atmosphere. Without the firmest of hearts, one cannot find the courage to speak of spiritual mobilization. In fact, when I enter a village, every now and then I have the feeling that it is rather my own national spirit that needs replenishing."[36]

Friction thus arose between the state and the people of farming, mountain, and fishing villages. What the state was preaching to the people was not an external war designed to maintain the current standard of living but rather the continuation of the war and a reduction in living standards.

Villages had joined in the war effort from an already low standard of living, prompting the strong reaction, "How dare you now ask for further belt-tightening?" Still, where material interests were concerned, the motive for popular cooperation in the war remained that of improving living standards. Since this was what villagers hoped the war was about, their grievances and discontent regarding the system that guided the war did not turn toward obstructing the war. Even the residents of Midono Village, who had experienced "the suffering of farming villages because of the depression in agriculture" since 1930, looked forward to the "favorable circumstances" they believed would come once the war was over.[37]

HARDSHIPS OF CONSCRIPTION AND GOING TO THE FRONT

In farming villages once again facing austerity just when recovery from the agricultural depression had finally begun, the first ones to be conscripted and sent to the front were farm households' primary laborers. Until they returned, their families would thus "sit idly by."[38] Concerned about the families they were leaving behind, conscripts left their villages with great reluctance.

On August 26, 1937—the day before he left for Shanghai—Private First Class Kamata Shūichi of Shiratori Township in Gifu Prefecture, aged twenty-three, wrote the following message to his mother from an inn in Hiroshima.

> Mother, I suppose you've already seen it in the papers, but among the soldiers who left from here the other day, August 19, they say there were more than a dozen casualties. We're also about to be sent into the fighting, so I don't expect to return alive. Please rest assured I'll do my utmost for the sake of the nation. There's no honor in dying. I'll give a good account of myself by returning home alive, so please wait for me. You must also be very busy with the autumn harvest. If I think about that I get worried, but there are plenty of people in the world more unlucky than we are, so Mama as you live on, please take good care of yourself.[39]

Although he believed that going to the front was necessary "for the sake of the nation" and a deed of honor, in latching onto the idea that there were other people more unfortunate—and clinging to the thought that he might not necessarily die—Kamata was trying to acknowledge how unbearable it was to be forced to leave his mother and younger brother behind in his home village, to abandon the autumn harvest, and to journey into the jaws of death. On October 12, at the height of the battle of Shanghai, he was killed in the fighting at Dachangzhen.

Takahashi Ichirō, a higher elementary school graduate from Fujine Village in Iwate Prefecture who was mustered into the Hirosaki 31st Infantry Regiment in September 1938 and died in battle in Shanxi Province in April 1940, was seen off by his family at Kurosawajiri Station on his way to the front. It was reported that he continued to clutch the hands of his newborn child even when the train began to roll, not letting go until the conductor, fearing an accident, restrained him.[40]

Ishikawa Tadashi had raised his infant siblings after his father's early death. On September 26, 1939, several months after being drafted, Ishikawa, then twenty-three, wrote his former teacher,

> Behind my happiness in being able to work as a soldier, I'm concerned about the life of my family. The lives of my aging grandfather, my mother, and my younger brother and sister in a family without a breadwinner, my responsibility to carry on in my father's footsteps—in tossing this aside, I can't deny feeling an acute responsibility. . . . Once again in times to come where my family is concerned, I humbly and sincerely beseech you to look after them.[41]

Ishikawa fought in northern China and in Southeast Asia and died in New Guinea in 1944.

On the home front, the thoughts of family members yearning for draftees' safety followed similar lines. Okamura Hideko, the mother of a Shizuoka army doctor serving at the front, wrote the following to her son on September 16, 1939.

> [When I heard of the ceasefire in the Nomonhan Incident,][42] tears just started rolling down my face. The sense of relief, the happiness that bursts from the bottom of one's heart—a family without someone at the front could never understand that. Whether they're a village headman or working people, it doesn't matter—so long as they don't have someone of their own at the front, they don't feel the slightest pangs of concern. . . . Even when they witness the sacrifice of tens of thousands of lives, they just put on a big, merciless smile and say, "this was only to be expected."[43]

Desperately hanging on, drafted soldiers fighting on the battlefield thought of their families at home, and families prayed for the safety of the soldiers in the field. As a result it was apparently all the more difficult for them to suppress their anger at the irresponsible behavior they observed in certain quarters of the home front.

THE PROFITS OF WAR

Yet for the soldiers and their families, conscription and deployment to the front did not bring only suffering.[44] An examination of letters from peasant soldiers who died in battle conducted by the Iwate Prefecture Farming Villages Culture Discussion Association (*Iwate ken nōson bunka kondankai*) makes clear that from the moment they joined the army, peasant soldiers were liberated from time-consuming and arduous farming chores. With "a daily bath," "fairly good" food, and "fine shoes," they led more privileged lives than they had in their farming villages. They received salaries that they could save or send to their families. They were able to enjoy "equal" treatment without regard to their social status or their wealth or poverty. They received education and were able to improve their social standing through their own talents.[45]

The army was also seen to afford peasant soldiers new prospects. If one became a noncommissioned officer—a corporal or sergeant—through service in the field, the road lay open to becoming a person of influence in one's village upon return. Soldiers were so eager to make the rank of corporal that teasing of those who remained privates sometimes led to incidents of assault.[46]

Soldiers perceived the colonies and the occupied territories as good places to "get ahead" after they'd been discharged. Abe Katsuo, a peasant cultivator from Iwayadō in Iwate Prefecture who fought in China's Shanxi Province, reported thinking to himself, "After this, for the sake of the development of northern China . . . they say you can find employment in a government office or a company, and if it's true you can earn as much as 150 yen per month, then maybe I'll try settling in China for a bit."[47] Sasaki Tokusaburō, the eldest son of an owner-cultivator from Tokiwa Village in Akita Prefecture, studied while in the army and hoped to take exams to become a forest superintendent in southern Sakhalin or to become a policeman there or in Korea or Hokkaidō.[48]

Tsuchiya Yoshio, the son of a track maintenance worker and tenant farmer in Saigō Village in Yamagata Prefecture, volunteered after the Manchurian Incident and was sent to Manchuria as a military policeman (*kenpei*). After his discharge he intended to "make a name" for himself (*hitohata ageru*) by finding employment with the South Manchurian Railway Company; when he later heard the announcement of the attack on Pearl Harbor, he pondered the possibility of becoming "even the master of some island in the South Pacific."[49]

Kimura Genzaemon was a former teacher at Tōmai Ordinary Higher Elementary School in Akita Prefecture. Aware that the Japanese official Tajimi Fumio[50] had argued for the establishment of Japanese girls' schools as part of his theory of "Long-Term Local Development" (*Genchi chōki kensetsu*), he entertained the following fantasies while taking part in the fighting in Shanxi Province in February 1939: "In the Girls' Schools they establish on the front lines [of local development], I wonder if they might let me teach Japanese . . . Japanese and Morals, or Religion. If it were Elementary Philosophy, I'd be just the man. Or Japanese History, that would be splendid."[51]

Serving a long term of duty in the field, "I feel unbearably miserable," wrote the officer-trainee Okamura Toshihiko, an army doctor from Odawara Township in Kanagawa Prefecture who was drafted soon after he started his practice. When he departed for the front, he left his mother and a sickly younger brother and sister behind. Thinking that his death in battle would at least bring them financial compensation from the government and thereby some guarantee for their future, Okamura behaved in a manner bordering on reckless.[52] At the beginning of 1938, realizing that he had no hope of repatriation any time soon, he was compelled to ask his mother to deal with his clinic. Beset by financial worries, he wrote to his mother from Shanghai:

> Even though I'm on the battlefield, I'm occupied only with this issue [of what
> to do with the clinic], and I'm really having a hard time. . . . After this there will
> be plenty of places to work on the continent, in places like Peking and Shanghai
> where a surgeon quickly earns three or four hundred yen. Looking to the future,
> I'm thinking it would be good to work on the continent—so not to be greedy, but
> if there's a tenant, please ask him.[53]

Fighting in southern China in July 1939, Sergeant Murata Washirō discussed with his underlings his plan of going into business in northern China upon his discharge and, if possible, managing a newspaper or hospital or organizing a resident's association.[54]

These were the attempts of some men to find a way to live in the war's midst after it had shattered their life prospects. It must be said that soldiers were cornered into this situation. At the same time, we cannot overlook this aspect: that the desire to get as much profit as possible out of the war transcended their unhappiness at being conscripted, and that soldiers supported the war in earnest.

TRENDS ON THE HOME FRONT

How was the situation in households that had sent out soldiers? As one example, let us closely examine the case of Abe Ta'ichi, a tenant farmer who lived in Ōizumi Village on the outskirts of Tsuruoka City in Yamagata Prefecture.

Abe Ta'ichi was born the first son of a tenant farmer in 1907. After graduating higher elementary school he took up agriculture, succeeding his father.

From 1931 to 1945 he cultivated an area that averaged eight acres,[55] in the category of petty farmer among the tenant farmers of his village. Regarded as a farmer of considerable excellence within the prefecture, he was selected in 1936 to serve for five years as farmer-bookkeeper of the Yamagata Prefecture Agricultural Management Guidance Farm (*Nōgyō kei'ei shidō nōba*) and was subsequently put in charge of the Ministry of Agriculture, Farming and Fisheries' Farming Management Research Rice Crop Section (*Nōgyō kei'ei chōsa inasaku bumon*) for three years beginning in 1941.[56] That said, the Abe family was of low social standing in its own village, and it was only in 1936 that it was able to procure membership rights in the village block association.[57] Abe thus pursued his daily tasks yearning for both economic and social advancement. When the Sino-Japanese War broke out, he was thirty years old; his family then consisted of his mother and father, his wife, four younger sisters (of whom one had married into another family), and two younger brothers (one of whom was working away from home as a chauffeur).[58]

Before the Manchurian Incident in September 1931, Abe had been influenced to some extent by the Marxism that swept through his village together with tenancy disputes.[59] Learning of the suppression of the Japanese Communist Party from the newspapers at the same time that he confronted firsthand the Depression-era suffering in the farming villages, Abe sensed that people had joined the party because of deep flaws in the contemporary social system.[60] He also nurtured doubts regarding the aims of the Manchurian Incident, viewing with sadness the spread of the flames of war.

Yet two months after the Incident, amid rising war fever, Abe was so enthusiastic he recalled tears coming to his eyes at the thought of the war. Again in 1936, when his younger brother Hiroshi enlisted, he felt this was something to be proud of and was overwhelmed with happiness. Still, Abe did not spend every day thinking about war. His passion was farm management, and until the outbreak of the Sino-Japanese War, the conflict was something that happened to make only a very occasional appearance from afar, unconnected to his daily life.

Examining Abe's diary entries for January 1937, we find that his rent payment was short as a result of the previous year's crop failure, and his thoughts were occupied with whether he might get a *sakubiki* (a tenant's rent reduction or exemption) or some leeway on the payment. One day he went about the village to collect money for the cooperative but failed to get a single penny. He wrote in his diary, "I quite understand the fact that the village, too, is extremely impoverished."[61]

Diary entries regarding the China conflict amounted to Abe's sending some dried seaweed to his younger brother Hiroshi's regimental commander in lieu of a New Year's greeting (as Hiroshi was then home on leave) and, in March, going out to salute the remains of two soldiers from the village who'd been killed fighting in a punitive expedition in Manchuria.

Preoccupied with thoughts of how he might escape from poverty, Abe determined to persevere, conveying his feelings in the song lyrics, "When I think of farming village revitalization, I live as one grain of wheat."[62] Accordingly, although his diary contained a short description of the general elections held in April 1937, there was no account of the outbreak of the Sino-Japanese war on July 7. Abe didn't have the time to think about the war, and he had little interest in it.

THE WEIGHT OF BEING DRAFTED

Like it or not, however, the war was drawing closer to home. On August 15, the first conscription notices were delivered in the village. On August 25, there was a great shock—Abe's farm horse was requisitioned by the army. On August 31, twelve men from the village headed for the front, and he accompanied them to the station. "It's nothing other than tragic," Abe wrote. On September 15, more soldiers from the village departed. After seeing them off, Abe described his fear of being drafted himself, however unlikely the prospect: "If by chance, if really by chance—coming home in a sweat, late, very late, what I really thought about was my elderly father, and then set against the Northern China Incident, how small, how truly insignificant my life is—I couldn't help but think about this."

If Abe were conscripted, the effect on his family would be terrible. On October 14, there was another call-up. The atmosphere in the village had turned grim. The son who was to inherit the household of the main family line received a draft notice and quickly held a wedding ceremony.[63] On October 27, Abe attended a lantern parade in Tsuruoka City in honor of the fall of Shanghai. In November, a festival of prayer for war victory and eternal fortune in battle (senshō/bu'un chōkyū kigansai) was held in the village. Abe's mother joined the Ladies' Patriotic Association (Aikoku fujinkai), paying the one-yen fee.[64]

The war was working its way to Abe's doorstep. On July 6, 1938, the remains of a soldier from the village arrived home. "Although they might say it was for the sake of the nation, I couldn't hear the news without shedding a tear," he wrote. The same month, it was decided that Hiroshi would depart for the front.

The four siblings journeyed to Yunohama Hot Springs and took a souvenir photograph—"this was not however meant as a last remembrance of this life," noted Abe. Abe's attitude toward the Sino-Japanese War was complex and ambivalent. Hiroshi had submitted an application for reinstatement to active duty in 1937; when this was denied and his discharge confirmed, Abe wrote, "There is nothing more that can be done. Where do we go from here? Thinking about it only breeds melancholy. I've fallen into disappointment."[65] With the expansion of the war, however, Hiroshi's discharge was cancelled. That the military now provided for his younger brother was a great financial boon to Abe's family, as was the military service assistance allowance they received with Hiroshi in the field. Regarding this "blessing," on August 13, 1937, Abe wrote, "This morning I went to the Village Office and received ten yen in military service assistance money. What a great help." Again on January 12, 1938, he added, "This is money I wasn't expecting, and so a great help." As the war extended, Abe thus came to hold a deep interest in it. When the China Incident One-Year Anniversary Festival of Prayer for War Victory and Eternal Fortune in Battle (*Shina jihen isshūnen kinen bu'un chōkyū kigansai*) was inaugurated under village auspices in July 1938, the Abe family was invited because it had a soldier in the field. Seeing the box of cakes, apricots, and good-luck charms (*omamori*) his father received, Abe exclaimed, "What good treatment!" On October 14, Abe managed to get a copy of Hino Ashihei's *Wheat and Soldiers* (*Mugi to heitai*) and read it in one sitting, writing admiringly, "I think this the best book in some time."[66]

DISCONTENT WITH THE SYSTEM AND SUPPORT FOR THE WAR

Still, Abe's daily thoughts continued to be dominated by farm management. He put his energy into improving the soil quality of a field where he cultivated peat, painstakingly blending fertilizer, and zealously guarding against the annually recurring rice blight, taking countermeasures when it did appear.

As for diary entries related to the war, by 1939 there were many references connected to returning soldiers, inflation, and shortages of goods. The Abe household was gradually becoming entangled in home front wartime controls. The prices of rice bran and wheat bran—feed for cattle and pigs—rose steadily, and items such as fertilizer, nails, and cement came under regulation, so that even repairs on the animal shed failed to progress as expected. The price of clothing also rose sharply. The entries suddenly piled up in Abe's diary. On February 19, 1939, he wrote, "The steady rise in rice bran prices has left me completely dumbfounded," and "I'm quite surprised at how expensive clothing has become." "There's no end to the high prices," he added on September 19. On the following January 8 he wrote, "The pigs have ended up a failure [because of high feed prices]. At this rate they'll probably make a law against profiteering." Four days later he complained, "Whatever I do there's a shortage of fertilizer, and with all the other material shortages, you can draw your own conclusion." The war was forcing sacrifices upon the Abe household, and he felt discontented with the contemporary system in many ways.

A look at Abe's commentaries regarding returning soldiers, however, reveals him to be a supporter of the war. Witnessing the return of the heir of the main family line on January 19, 1939, as his mother clung to him and exclaimed, "Thank god you're home," Abe was "filled with emotion." Yet at the same time he wrote, "What a shame he failed to make corporal—in truth even I thought this a pity."

On June 11 of the same year, Hiroshi somehow managed to return unscathed after narrowly avoiding death when a shell struck his metal helmet. In urgent need of employment, he searched for an opening on the continent, beginning with North China Transport (*Kahoku kōtsū*).[67] Allowed to take the policeman's service examination for occupied Manchuria (Manchukuo), he passed and, upon graduating the police academy there in December, was posted to the Kuanchengzi police station. Also in June 1939, Abe's other younger brother, Yasukichi, went to Tientsin in search of work and found employment with North China Transport. Both of Abe's brothers were taking advantage of war gains to make a living on the Chinese continent. The war was no longer someone else's affair.

THE PEOPLE'S WAR

THE WAR AND YOUNG MEN OF CONSCRIPTION AGE

The first half of 1940 represented a historical turning point. The Sino-Japanese War was turning into a quagmire with no end in sight, and the battered army was even considering a gradual reduction or withdrawal from the battlefront. Yet in comparison with the second half of 1937, popular opinion regarding the pursuit of the war had only grown more resolute. Even as support for fascism intensified, however, there remained a variety of thinking regarding the nature of the domestic system that supported the war.

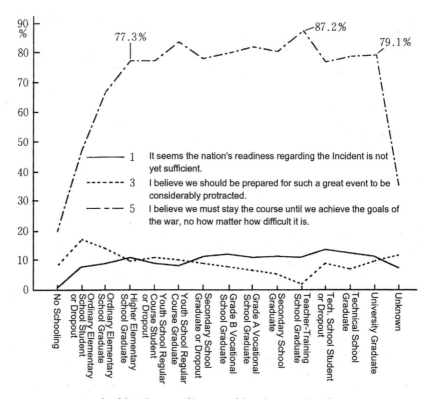

FIGURE 1.1 Graph of distribution of "Views of the China Incident."

In the first half of 1940, the Ministry of Education conducted a special opinion survey of *sōtei*, or young men of the conscription age of twenty, as they underwent the conscription examination.[68] According to this survey, 87.1 percent of men of conscription age answered either "No matter how difficult it is, we must stay the course until the objectives of the war are attained" (78.3 percent) or "We must be prepared for [the war] to be considerably protracted" (8.8 percent).[69] When asked what they thought of the effect on their daily lives, 72 percent of the young men said that they were prepared for a life of austerity, with 50.2 percent answering that they were "economizing" and another 21.8 percent answering that "it won't do to give up at this level [of deprivation]."[70] Even accounting for the bias inherent in the survey, there is no other way to see it: For the most part, these young men were firmly of a mind to endure the war's difficulties and continue the fight.

Examining attitudes according to educational background (see figure 1.1), graduates of teacher training schools (*shihan gakkō*)[71] were the most sympathetic to the war, followed by graduates of middle schools (*chūgakkō*), trade schools (*jitsugyō gakkō*), and youth schools (*seinen gakkō*).[72] These "persons with the educational background to be in the Japanese middle class of the future" represented the core support for the war.[73] In contrast, the relative level of sympathy was slightly lower among less-educated graduates of elementary schools and higher elementary schools and still lower among elementary school dropouts and those who had never attended school (broken line 5 on figure 1.1).

DISCONTENT WITH THE CONTEMPORARY SYSTEM

Those who responded that they did not "clearly understand" the aims of the war against China or were "uneasy because I do not know when the Incident will end" together comprised 1.0 percent of the total. The existence of considerable discontent with the war and the system that supported it was revealed in the fact that with regard to everyday inconveniences, 9.1 percent answered, "The nation is not yet sufficiently prepared"; 9.3 percent responded, "The way of imposing controls needs to be improved"; and 0.5 percent replied, "As it stands, we cannot make ends meet and are truly in difficulty." Among those choosing these responses were highly educated graduates of professional schools and universities deeply displeased with the way the control economy was being run (25.1 percent of professional school graduates and 40.5 percent of university graduates).[74]

Again with regard to everyday inconveniences, the fact that no more than 14.3 percent of respondents chose "We must work hard to produce many excellent goods"—the sole enthusiastic attitude expected by the Ministry of Education—reveals a passive attitude among "many young people who simply do as they are told, their attention stolen by the focus on economization," thus lacking in the will to produce necessary to increase goods production and quality improvement.[75] Discontent with the control economy and the weakening of the will to produce would eventually cause Japan's war system to collapse from the inside.

If we next consider the item "Hopes from current politics," a mere 7.5 percent chose "Things are fine the way they are," demonstrating that the majority were unhappy with the current system. Here, an overwhelming 69.5 percent chose such answers as "I would like a decisive foreign policy without concern for Europe and the United States" (36.1 percent) and "I would like a politics of strength" (33.4 percent), with no more than 1.3 percent selecting "Dictatorial politics are [a] good [idea]."[76] These were the voices of people being swept toward an approval of a distinctly Japanese "New Order," whose form they believed to be different from the "dictatorial" Italian and German ones, in sum a fascism under the emperor (emperor-system fascism).[77] Fascism and Nazism were not embraced as "dictatorial politics" as such by the Italian or German people either, but the Japanese people thought of these as "dictatorial politics," and they hoped for a "distinctly Japanese" system comprising "autonomous foreign policy" and "power politics," making the most of the strong points of "dictatorial politics."

Regardless of support for the war itself, there were still considerable differences of opinion on the running of the political system that supported the war. Criticizing bureaucratic self-righteousness, 10.1 percent responded, "I would like the voice of the people to be properly heard," and 6.9 percent responded, "Party politics is fine." These voices included those of people who were carried away by the "New Order," however.[78]

In what directions, then, did the sorts of dissatisfactions and differences of opinion described above point?

DISSATISFACTION TOWARD THE MILITARY AUTHORITIES

Around 1940, popular discontent flourished, and despite strict controls on expression, it was starting to seep out through rumors and other informal channels. In agricultural villages, laborers were expropriated by the military, and with additional people leaving home to work in the well-paid military industries, agricultural labor was in short supply. Horses too were drafted into service; agricultural implements, oil, and fertilizer became difficult to come by; and prices rose, with the result that food production fell short of expectations. In the cities too, goods were scarce, black market trading grew, merchandise declined in quality, and prices rose. Rice in particular tended to run short. By the end of February 1940, the number of personnel monitoring infractions of the various Control Laws had mushroomed to 3,030,000. In factories, conscription brought shortages of essential labor power, and shortages of raw materials and goods meant that peacetime industries and the consumer goods sector were gradually forced either to seek alternative lines of production or shut down.

Regarding the situation in the first half of 1940, the Eastern Army Command[79] attributed a tendency toward spreading "war weariness" and "cursing of the military authorities" to the economic downturn associated with the conflict. It located the causes in discontent over living conditions, an adverse war outlook, and the incomplete establishment of a "system of power through national unity" (*kyokoku itchi kyōryoku taisei*).[80] This was no exaggeration.

Yet such voices of weariness and complaint against the military did not grow into a force that might have brought a halt to the war. Some of them were suppressed, and others, in contrast, came to lobby for the establishment of a fascist system under the emperor. Regarding the reasons for this, let us now seek clues in the original voices (letters, postcards, and other personal messages) of people impressed by the February 2, 1940, speech of Diet member Saitō Takao concerning the prosecution of the Sino-Japanese War (the so-called antimilitary speech).

SYMPATHY WITH SAITŌ'S SPEECH

There is no question that Saitō's speech concerning the prosecution of the Sino-Japanese War gave voice to popular discontent about the aims of the war and the wartime order.[81] Saitō criticized what the government, the military authorities, and others referred to as a "holy war," the building of a "New Order in East Asia," the establishment of the Wang Jing-wei regime, and other war aims and directives, as confusing the nature of the conflict.[82] Rejecting the "holy war" ideology, he articulated an argument for power politics from a social Darwinist standpoint: Japan should hold to the law of survival of the fittest. And he insisted that Japan should bring about a speedy end to the war by entering into negotiations with Chiang Kai-shek based upon that principle.[83] Saitō was consequently expelled from the Diet, but there was sympathy for him among the many who could not hide their anger at the bleak war outlook.

With a few exceptions, most of the approximately seven hundred extant personal correspondences sent to Saitō between February and April 1940 more or less supported him in the name of preserving freedom of speech and constitutional politics. It seems safe to describe these as the voices of intellectuals and ordinary people with political attitudes ranging from support for imperial liberalism to support for imperial democracy.

However, opinions on Saitō's critique of the "holy war" were divided into two camps. The first group comprised people to whom the positive signifi-

cance of the "holy war" was plain but who were critical of how it had been implemented, viewing the problem in terms of how policy was put into practice.
"The objectives of the holy war and the building of a New East Asian Order are
shining and clear, but I believe we must allow for a thorough discussion and
critique of the actual policy [for their realization]," wrote a person from Ka-
makura named Godō (悟堂), who may be seen as a conservative intellectual.[84]
Yet those who acknowledged a certain value in "holy war" ideology could only
support the war, not oppose it. Thus, approving of the building of a New East
Asian Order, the owner of a grocery shop in Kumagaya City in Saitama Prefecture named Matsumoto Tadatsugu stated, for example, "It is my humble belief
that the New East Asian Order consists of a complete elimination of English
privileges from every corner of China."[85]

LOCATING THE CRITIQUE OF THE "HOLY WAR"

Important were a much larger second group who identified with Saitō's critique of the "holy war" as a conflict whose aims were unclear. In the face of
the cruel realities of the war and the sacrifices it demanded in daily life, most
of these people had come to entertain profound doubts about the "holy war"
ideology.

A woman living in the Hongō Ward of Tokyo City complained that her son
had died of an illness contracted at the battlefront. She wrote, "He was totally
unable to fathom the reason he was dying—saying this he departed this world;
as a mother what should I say to console [his spirit]? Should I pray at his tomb-
stone? We're completely at a loss."[86] Satō Kiyoshi of Ukyō Ward in Kyoto City
had lost his job because of the war. He wrote,

> They call it a holy war, [but] under the current situation it sucks the [word
> self-censored] of those Japanese apart from the prosperous classes, and cajoles
> people into sacrifice in view of the so-called survival of [words self-censored],
> with the figure already well nigh into the tens of billions; we're giving up our jobs,
> and it's getting to the point that more and more people are going without food—
> is this still something that can be called a holy war?[87]

Saiki Muneo was employed at the Great Wall Coal Ore Railway Company
in the city of Qinhuangdao in northern China. Noting among other things that
the local price of wheat flour had risen to roughly eight times its prewar level,
he lamented, "When the average Chinese has taken to wondering if this is what

Japan calls the New East Asian Order, then what result are we exactly after? We talk about pacification, pacification, but if there is in fact so little change in the hardship of making ends meet—and if all of China's people raise their voices in resentment of Japan—where indeed is the significance of a holy war?"[88]

Still, these sorts of criticisms of the "holy war" did not yield calls for an immediate ceasefire or outright opposition to the war. Among the nearly seven hundred personal correspondences, the single exception was from a person who called himself "a member of the Constitutional Party of Hakodate,"[89] who stated, "It's not too late to start over even now. If we reveal our sincere intentions by carrying out a withdrawal of our troops from all of China, then the suspicions of both China and the Powers will evaporate, peace will be established immediately, and East Asia will shine brighter than before."[90]

Two different perspectives broadly characterized those who were critical of the "holy war." First were those that maintained that it was necessary to improve the prosecution of the war. They attacked the military authorities' high-handedness and government officials' self-righteousness, pointing out flaws in the way the war was being directed, in the running of the controlled economy, and in the way the occupied territories were controlled.

Yamada Haruo, who lived in Tokyo, complained, "It is now such that there is money but nothing [to buy], with the only ones making great profits from the Incident and from the control [economy] being the heavy industrial sector, rayon companies, *sake* manufacturers and the like in collusion with disabled army leaders, many of whom are members of the upper class." Noting a "deterioration of popular sentiment and dissatisfaction," it was necessary, said Yamada, to devise "a policy now that has its roots a bit in reality."[91]

President of the Okayama Newspaper Company Yokoyama Kōta expressed doubts about the Third Konoe Declaration, maintaining that Chiang Kai-shek's popularity in China was greater than that of Wang Jing-wei[92] and arguing that as far as establishing a Wang administration, there was nothing more dangerous than the method of governance pursued so far, one that "seeks only to be free of the difficulties right in front of us."[93]

In the interest of ruling the occupied territories, the aforementioned Saiki Muneo of the Great Wall Coal Ore Railway suggested, "We should really and truly implement a benevolent government, taking into account the opinions and feelings of we who share our lives with ordinary Chinese and are familiar with the conditions of the people generously, and treating [the Chinese] in such a way as to make them think of Japan, in all sincerity, as God of the East."[94]

The second group opposed slogans professed in the "holy war" ideology such as "no annexation and no reparations," "respect for Chinese sovereignty," the "abolition of extraterritoriality," and the "return of the settlements."[95] Seeing the war as a campaign for survival of the fittest in which concrete fruits of battle such as territory and financial reparations had to be obtained to ease the pain of "Japanese sacrifices," these people gave voices to an increasingly strong grass-roots imperialist consciousness.

In a letter bearing the stamp of the Fukagawa Post Office in Tokyo City, a city resident complained, "Would the military authorities be there if not for us? If there are no territorial ambitions, no demands for compensation and whatnot, then why are we fighting this war? What of the people who've died fighting, what of the people working and paying high taxes to the point that goods are in short supply?"[96]

Under the assumed name of "a born patriot," a person from Iida in Nagano Prefecture wrote,

> More than one hundred thousand precious lives have been offered up, several hundred thousand officers and men have been wounded, more than ten billion from the national treasury spent, for their part the Japanese people have been forced to endure the suffering of material shortages, and what's the result of it all? If we don't seize land, don't take reparations, don't monopolize the Chinese economy, don't violate Chinese sovereignty or the rights and privileges of other countries, and in the end we withdraw, then the fruits of battle may as well be seen as next to nothing. . . . I don't want these huge, precious sacrifices to end in futility.[97]

In proportion to the amount of war debt and sacrifices accumulated over these three years, the feelings of people at the grassroots had sharpened and intensified.

Defining a "holy war" as "a battle" in which "the welfare of the entire race is assured" through the seizure of territory, Komori Hideo, a young man of twenty awaiting the conscription examination, quipped that if "no annexation and no reparations" represented a "holy war . . . does that make the [first] Sino-Japanese and the Russo-Japanese Wars, in which we gained Taiwan and South Sakhalin, unholy?"[98] Private Superior Class Takisawa Kazue, who had returned from the China front, was also indignant:

Although the army minister maintains that the rank and file understand the holy war and go gladly to their deaths . . . even when a soldier occupies only one piece [of land], it's as though the territory of Japan has been expanded by that much—he's fighting with that in mind, and that's the truth. When a man such as the army minister is telling lies to the nation, what is going on?[99]

These assertions that "we are waging war for the sake of territory" must be acknowledged as representing an honest expression of popular sentiments.

Rejecting "holy war" ideology as of benefit only to China—a country he likened to "a villain with many previous convictions"—one resident of Kōfu City instead argued for the advocacy of the notion that "Japan's prosperity means, in fact, true eternal peace in the East." Saitō Kingo and Saitō Kei'ichirō of Kyōgase Village in Niigata Prefecture signed a letter together in support of Saitō's Social Darwinist position, deeming it necessary to cancel the Konoe Declaration, to compensate for national sacrifices according to "the law of the survival of the fittest," and—for this reason—to "expel white people from the East."[100]

Although these voices were critical of the government and the military authorities, they revealed states of mind ranging from jingoism to support for a policy of aggression. Saitō's civilian correspondents were thus more straightforward than the government and the military authorities, who sugarcoated the true aims of the war. For many, the experience of several years of war had twisted and bent popular imperial democracy consciousness, resulting in a transformation. As every kind of reform had been shelved for the sake of the war, popular liberation consciousness had ended up transformed, with the "imperial" consciousness latent within it becoming manifest. We may see this as the wartime version of a transfigured Taishō democracy, one that had never been able to overcome the position advocating "imperialism externally" at the popular level. Rather than inclining toward a force capable of bringing peace or a system democratic or liberal, those who criticized the government and the military authorities for the toll of "more than one hundred thousand precious lives," "Japanese sacrifices," and the expenditure of "somewhere in the tens of billions from the national treasury" lay open to the seductions of a fascist system under the emperor and a new war. At a minimum, they inclined toward deployment as a force that could produce an order and a war of this sort. Of course, the popular experience of the three years that had spawned this shift was intertwined with the experience of the soldiers fighting in China—their experiences of the country and its battlefields.

ON THE BATTLEFIELDS OF CHINA

SOLDIERS' THOUGHTS AS THEY RETURNED HOME

On February 1, 1939—when the number of soldiers returning from the Chinese continent was beginning to increase rapidly—the undersecretary of the army issued to all relevant units the memorandum "Matters Pertaining to the Guidance and Control of Speech of Units and Soldiers Returning from the Area of the China Incident." There was a fear that graphic stories of war experiences related by returning soldiers would undermine trust in the "imperial army" (*kōgun*) and destroy home front "solidarity" (*danketsu*). A supplement to the memorandum, "The Situation of Units and Soldiers Returning from the Area of the Incident," recorded graphic accounts of the sort feared by the military and presented the behavior of soldiers overflowing with happiness at their repatriation as "examples of gross delinquency in the military discipline of an advancing army." Among the recorded cases were those who "have their wives hold their rifle while they hug their children as they march" or "hold the hands of their wives and children as they march," "who take food and alcohol from those who have come to greet them and eat and drink as they march" or "leave their ranks for no reason and engage in conversation with those who have come to greet them."[101] We can vividly imagine how these soldiers, overjoyed at the sight of their long-missed parents, wives, children, brothers, and sisters, broke with the strict regulations. What kinds of experiences did soldiers have in China, and what was on their minds when they returned?

THE BATTLES OF SHANGHAI, NANJING, XUZHOU, AND WUHAN

THE DREAMS OF FARMING VILLAGE YOUTH

Imai Ryūichi, a soldier on active duty from Higashishirakawa Village in Gifu Prefecture, departed Nagoya Harbor on board the battle cruiser *Haruna* on August 20, 1937, and participated in the battle of Shanghai.[102] He was born the oldest son of a farming family in 1915. After graduating from higher elementary school, Imai participated in the Youth Association (*Seinendan*) movement in addition to engaging in agriculture.[103] He enjoyed reading, and alongside magazines such as *Chūō kōron* and *Kaizō*, translated volumes of Gorky, Marx, and *The Works of Three Northern Europeans* could always be found on his desk. The New Testament was one of his favorites.[104]

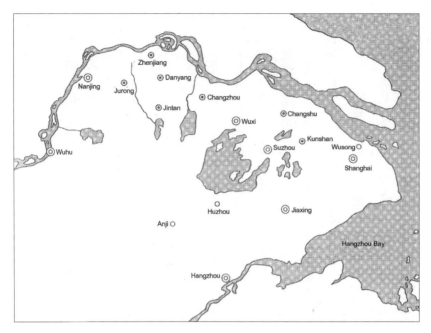

FIGURE 1.2   Map from Shanghai to Nanjing.

FIGURE 1.3   Imai Ryūichi's photo, taken the day before he was drafted, January 1937.
Source: Imai Ryūichi, *Tōkakan no jinchū nikki* [Ten days' camp diary].

Imai enlisted with the Gifu 68th Regiment in January 1937. The Sino-Japanese War began while he was in the midst of training, and he was sent to the front. During his training, he sent the following sorts of letters to his younger sister:

[On my days off,] eager to relax and listen to records—it being quite a while since I've done this—I go to a nice café called Minori. Eating fruit to the sweet melodies, I get into a very peaceful state of mind. At 11:30 I enter the Gifu theater, wanting to see a really good movie today. This is Gifu's only first-rate movie theater. They're showing Irie Takako's *When the White Rose Blooms* (*Shirobara wa sakedo*) and [Frank Capra's] *Lost Horizon*, set in foreign countries, and the scenes are quite beautiful.[105] The admission price is 40 *sen*! The pleasure of Sundays [the day of leave] is all the greater in comparison with the complete misery of the routine. (*Letter to Marui Miyo, August 1, 1937*)

You're probably not reading the Bible, but you know, Christ was truly a great man. He says things like love thy enemy and pray for he who hates thee, if struck on the right cheek then turn the other, and to those whose outer garment has been stolen, give your inner garment. I'm not capable of having the holy sentiments that Christ had, but I've reached the point of thinking that it is not such a bad thing, once in your life, to have the experience of being beaten by someone else. . . .[106] You must read a lot. The best thing is to read lots of good books.

(*July 25, 1937*)

In any case, I can't stop wishing I could return to a peaceful peasant's life, even tomorrow if possible. To work with all one's efforts at farming can't be all bad, and I daresay there's no place more beautiful and naturally blessed than our village. . . . We should enrich peasant's lives. Because they're so boorish. It need not be fancy, but they should have complete homes that are nice to live in; I think they should make much more use of means of amusement. When I return, I'm thinking of coming up with a new way of farming that's all my own. (*July 25, 1937*)

Imai was an exceptional young man, highly intelligent, with a great desire for learning and concerned for his younger sister. From the letter describing his day off in Gifu City, we gain a sense of his small but fully developed world. His second letter describes his experiences of Christ. The family were followers of Shintō, but reading the Bible made a deep impression. From the letter describing his postdischarge dream, we can feel the pleasure with which he looked forward to inventing new farming methods.

IN THE VORTEX OF THE BATTLE OF SHANGHAI

Once aboard the *Haruna*, Imai steeled himself for death, bidding farewell in his heart to his father, his mother, his younger brother, his older and younger sisters, and the girl he secretly loved, who had come to see him off at Gifu Station. On August 21, 1937, he went to the haircutting room and shaved his head and face for the landing. Refreshed, he thought, "Now I'm ready to die at any time." On August 22, eyeing such battleships as the *Mutsu* and the *Nagato* lying off the coast of Shanghai, he was generous enough to observe, "If you think about it, China is a country to be pitied." On August 23, he landed.[107]

From August 24 onward—the day Imai arrived at the front lines—casualties were suffered, and there were deaths as early as August 25. That day, he wrote, "In the space of a breath, the conscript Hotta was killed in action! Since we landed there has not been one day without casualties. In the end a man has been killed today too. I'm now writing in the shade of a house. A dead body lies less than two feet away from me. My whole body is filled with loathing for Chinese soldiers."[108]

This gentle, peaceful man had transformed into a soldier fighting to the death. On August 26, three more men were killed in action. "I've lost any understanding of what war is all about," he wrote. The next day, three more men died. "Oh, why does mankind wage war? As I stand guard over this village of death," he wrote that evening, "cold tears stream down—why I do not know."[109] On a field of battle more intense than he'd ever imagined, where life could be lost at any moment, battling hunger, heat, muddy water, lice, and the nauseating smell of death, and with the attack on the stronghold of Wusong coming the next day, Imai had a premonition of death: "In my family I've been blessed up until today. I have fine parents and older sisters, a kind-younger brother and sister . . . whenever I die it's alright. That my parents and everyone will grieve—that's the most painful thing. It's a shame there is no repayment I can offer . . . but it is for the sake of Japan."[110]

Imai sought to come to grips with death by acknowledging it as "for the sake of Japan." After two days' postponement, the attack on Wusong began on August 31. Savage bombing raids and naval bombardment reduced the city to "a gloomy state." Japanese army assaults left the city strewn with Chinese corpses, and the Japanese army's arson burned it down. Imai's platoon cornered between 150 and 160 of the enemy. Of the hour-long massacre that ensued, he wrote,

> We wiped off our blood-smeared bayonets in relief, happy that the battle had subsided for a bit. Oh, how many of them did I kill? Ten? Perhaps fifteen? Anyhow, this was the first time in my life I've taken the lives of other people with my own hand. Men who pleaded with their hands clasped together, men who came at us crazed with death! This was a place of nightmare.[111]

Although it could be said it was done in the heat of pursuit, the decision to massacre Chinese army soldiers who'd been cornered and lost the will to fight tortured Imai's conscience. From among the devastated buildings of Tongji University, he called out to his mother and younger sister.

> Mama, mama . . .
> Mama, I, your quiet son, have now become a terrifying frontline soldier, spending his life killing people and setting fires.
> I haven't had a bath for a week. Meals of crackers and a meager bit of rice, canned food, that's all we eat, mama . . .

> Little sister.
> Your older brother is well. Every day I wage war. How different this reality is from the life I imagined. Why do human beings make war? The other night in a dream, I saw the tear-soaked face of Christ. [Lying] on the green grass of the continent, with its shining stars!
> Every day your older brother is changing. Profound changes in my heart that seem to churn up from the depths of my soul. Whether this is a good or bad thing I do not know. . . . I do not wish to speak to you of this war that rages in the middle of [China's beautiful scenery]. Your young soul, I mustn't sully it just like that—that's my thinking.[112]

The intense unease of a young soldier driven into a vicious war, the bitter cries of his heart—it is as if we can hear them still. Imai's anguish continued as he was compelled to commit indiscriminate killing, arson, and destruction. He sought to overcome this spiritual crisis by deploying the achievement of "a permanent peace," sympathy for "the pitiable Chinese people," and a "China in decline" as justification. Thus as he watched the city of Wusong burn down, Imai wrote, "Oh China in decline, oh Asia's ancient history, for the sake of the pitiable Chinese people . . . I could not hold back my tears." The next day, he added, "A permanent peace, love—national character—solidarity!"[113]

While engaging in an enemy mop-up operation one kilometer to the west of Wusong on September 1, Imai suffered a bullet wound in the stomach, from which he died the following day. His dream of "coming up with a new way of farming that's all my own" had been cruelly torn asunder.

FROM SHANGHAI TO NANJING

Born into a farming household in 1913 in Yoshikawa Village, Fukui Prefecture, Yamamoto Takeshi was drafted in September 1937 and served in the battles of Shanghai, Nanjing, Xuzhou, and Wuhan as a member of the Sabae Infantry 36th Regiment. Until he was wounded on September 3, 1938, he fought mostly on the front lines as a foot soldier (first as a private first class, then as a corporal and sergeant).[114] Yamamoto graduated from the Fukui Prefectural School of Agriculture and Forestry in March 1931. During his period of study a number of incidents of suppression of the Japanese Communist Party drew his interest, including the mass arrests of March 15, 1928, and April 16, 1929, and he enjoyed reading related articles in the newspaper and proletarian literature.[115] After passing the military service examination with an A grade, being drafted in 1934, undergoing a rigorous training, and serving until January 1936 in the Shinkyo (in Chinese, Chanchun) garrison, Yamamoto became vice chairman of the Yoshikawa Village Reservist's Association.[116] As he took part in its meetings and training sessions, he came to believe that "one must wager one's life to the fullest for the sake of the imperial realm (君国) and quickly deliver a blow against the high-handed Chinese army."

Yamamoto landed in Shanghai on September 30, 1937. By the end of October, after unexpectedly fierce fighting, only sixty-four of his company's roughly two hundred men remained.[117] Only on October 20 did he see his first living Chinese prisoners. They were three soldiers, two male and one female, but even as he thought to himself, "Maybe we'll kill them for being detestable Chinese soldiers," he found them "still worthy of pity" because they were young, and one of them a woman.[118] On November 2, after crossing the Suzhou (蘇州) River, Yamamoto witnessed the platoon commander try out his sword on a prisoner's head. Failing to cut it off, he quickly showered the neck with blows, but the head still refused to fall. When the prisoner finally died, everyone was "relieved."[119]

On November 12, the order to pursue the enemy through Nanjing was issued. In the ensuing battle, Yamamoto had "no recollection of a single item" of food, such as rice, supplementary food, or canned food, "being supplied." Almost all rice, miso, soy sauce, and liquor was obtained through looting. On November 13, he once again witnessed the testing of a sword on a prisoner. This time the head flew off in one swipe, prompting "clapping and cheering" all around. On November 19, Yamamoto entered Suzhou. The next day, he and fellow soldiers went out for requisitions, seizing Taiwanese rice from a place resembling a wholesaler's, piling up bicycles from people's houses, and dividing up miso, soy sauce, liquor, and rapeseed oil to carry home. Seeing a special duty soldier[120] who had stolen half a bucket's worth of one-yen coins, Yamamoto searched for the bank but could not locate it. On the same day they were ordered to march for Wuxi, and when they left the encampment, they found the road strewn with large amounts of pomelo fruits. It appeared soldiers had stolen them and tossed them away. On November 23, they went to a village for requisitions, shot a pig, and brought the meat back with them. On November 24, Yamamoto took rice off a Chinese soldier killed in the fighting. Other soldiers seized such items as unhulled rice and a water buffalo.[121] On November 27, in the city of Wuxi, they requisitioned rice, miso, soy sauce, and pork in great quantities. The next day, with their heels getting sore from the march, they caught some Chinese men[122] and made them carry their rucksacks, duffle bags, gas masks, and other gear.[123]

On December 10, the unit was attacked near Nanjing, and two soldiers were killed in action. The next day they went on a village mop-up operation; the eight prisoners they caught were brought before the grave markers of the dead soldiers and stabbed to death. Thinking that the souls of his fallen comrades were probably also "pleased to have revenge taken for them," Yamamoto—who ended up taking the lead in the stabbing when the older soldiers recoiled from it—had a pleasant feeling of "relaxation in [his] chest."[124] On December 12, Yamamoto saw the sixth company bring in thirty prisoners, kill them, and bury them in a ditch. Just as he was thinking that this was a cruel thing to do, his own company also went out and captured twenty-six Chinese army soldiers and allotted these to the next unit, leaving their fate in their hands.[125] "No doubt . . . they got swords tried out on them," he thought.[126] On December 13, they entered the fortified city of Nanjing. On December 19, Yamamoto heard a story that at Xiaguan (下関) in Nanjing, the Kumamoto Sixth Division had "conducted mass killings, massacring those who had surrendered waving a white flag" with tanks and armored cars, raking them with machine-gun fire and shelling them. They had been rebuked by the army commander and were now carrying out the prolonged process of burning and disposing of the bodies—the place was in a wretched state.[127]

THE MISERY OF THE BATTLE OF XUZHOU

In the battle of Xuzhou, Yamamoto would personally experience this sort of brutal behavior in a more profound way.[128] On May 15, 1938, an order was transmitted from the divisional chief of staff stating that "since it is difficult to distinguish among ordinary residents, local rebels, and Chinese soldiers, kill them as you encounter them."[129] The next day his unit caught a large number of male civilians in a village called Hegua (河挂) and employed them as targets in a bayoneting exercise for the reservists, killing more than ten of them. Yamamoto wrote, "If they were soldiers I would not have anything particularly against this, but to kill ordinary residents is quite merciless and leaves a bad taste."[130] In the intense attack on Zhangerzhuang on May 18, his unit started fires upwind from a village and used "red candle" poison gas, inducing vomiting and sneezing. "To minimize our own casualties," he wrote, "it seems like there's no choice but this tactic."[131] On May 20, his unit left Xiaozhangzhuang and marched toward the Jinpū railway line. Along the way, Yamamoto witnessed the next unit setting a defenseless neighborhood alight, "starting a fire at the corner that made flames and black smoke arise from every hamlet." When asked why, members of the unit replied that it was to prevent the Chinese army from establishing a base there.[132] During the punitive fighting between June 23 and 26, staff and noncommissioned officers of the command squad did "things like going out and stealing money and items that caught their eye, raping Chinese girls (in Chinese *kuniang*, 姑娘), and murdering law-abiding people in towns we visited," and then proudly boasting about it. Yamamoto was indignant.[133]

At times when there was no fighting, Yamamoto viewed the people of China from a peasant's standpoint. Observing a farming village near Changzhou in Jangsu Province on July 14, 1938, he expressed frank words of admiration: "In the paddy fields along the roadside the stems are big and the plants are high, there's no crop damage from disease or harmful insects, and they're well cared for. The rice-growing methods of the peasants in this area are not in the least infantile—it's impressive." Although the peasants wore few clothes as they worked, Yamamoto had no disdain for them. Rather, he felt a sense of affinity, recognizing them as "overflowing with the toughness that is the hallmark of the peasant." Without thinking about it, he called out to them, "你的, 多々的辛苦辛苦" ("Keep up your good work"). Deeply emotional, Yamamoto wrote, "Not the faintest sense arises that they're our longstanding enemy."[134] As we have already seen, where Chinese army soldiers and prisoners were concerned, things were completely different. No mercy was shown to prisoners or soldiers who'd lost the will to fight. Nor was there a trace of remorse on the subject of the requisitioning of food and other items.

Relatively speaking, however, the killing of ordinary folk was something else again. The bayoneting of male civilians in the middle of the battle of Xuzhou (May 16, 1938) prompted Yamamoto to write, "How cruel and merciless a thing is war; if there ever was a hell, this battlefield must surely be it."[135] There was moreover an event in the battle of Xuzhou that Yamamoto proved unable to include in his memoirs.[136] Here is the description from the original text of his May 20, 1938, war diary entry:

> [We set fires in a certain village] and following orders, one after another, even though they're decent folk, we bayonet even women and children to death. It's the epitome of cruelty. Fifty or sixty people in one go, sweet young girls, innocent children, they cry and beg for mercy putting their hands together. It's the first time in my life I do something so cold-blooded. Oh how I hate war.[137]

YAMAMOTO'S EXPERIENCE OF CHINA

Yet Yamamoto—who heard his company commander tell the men to fight "for the sake of the imperial realm" and "in the aim of chastising a rebellious China" when he departed for the front—had already attained enlightenment before the landing.[138] He bore no grudge against the Chinese people, but he had to fight "for justice" without quibbling—that was his motto, which drove away any doubts. This was reinforced by an irritated sense that "the Chinese people are simply in awe of the Japanese army, yet they can only reminisce about the dreams of the old days of the Chiang regime—it makes me a bit angry";[139] he viewed them as "the people of a defeated nation, truly worthy of pity."[140] On July 1, 1938, Yamamoto was promoted to sergeant. Although worried about the upcoming battle for Wuhan, he was sincerely moved.[141] "The stars on my shoulder have increased by one. What a joyous thing this is for those who wear a military uniform. All my troubles up to now have been lifted from me, and I'm filled with a sense of superiority; that I'm the most right-wing of all the men promoted at the same time makes this feeling even more profound."[142]

On September 3, 1938, Yamamoto took a shell fragment in his left leg in the fighting at Yunxiyai and left the battlefront for the first time. On October 30 he was reinstated to his unit, and after guard duty in Jiujiang, Linxiang, and elsewhere, he was demobilized in July 1939.[143]

What Yamamoto had learned from the battles of Shanghai, Nanjing, Xuzhou, and Wuhan was that "the ravages of war are truly terrible." Of the 194 men who had originally accompanied him to the front, just a few more than twenty returned unscathed.[144] Yet so long as Yamamoto's worldview remained intact and he retained faith in a Japanese victory, this experience could not serve as a basis for antiwar sentiments. Returning to Japan, he "felt keenly the peace and prosperity, the vitality of Japan, matchless in all the world." Working to support the war through "increasing food production," he also became branch chairman of the village reservist's association, bustling about with the training of new recruits, the inspection of reservists, and village burials for the war dead.[145] When the Pacific War ultimately began, Yamamoto was "devotedly honing [his] efforts to meet the nation's goals with a grand conviction," and when the Imperial Rule Assistance Adult Men's Association (*Yokusan sōnendan*) was established, he became its vice chairman, "single-mindedly supporting its activities."[146]

BATTLES IN NORTHERN CHINA AND SOLDIERS FROM TŌHOKU

LETTERS FROM SOLDIERS FROM TŌHOKU

What were conditions like in northern China, at the center of the guerrilla war that began with the fight against the Chinese communist Eighth Route Army? Many soldiers hailing from the Tōhoku region in the north of the main island of Honshū, one of Japan's most impoverished regions, were sent to northern China. Let us begin by exploring these experiences from peasant soldiers' letters.

Katō Seiitsu, a peasant from Fujine Village in Iwate Prefecture, was a member of the Third Mortar Battalion. He departed Beijing on September 11, 1937, and was assigned to the 20th Division at Baoding. He was involved in intense fighting beginning with the battle of Jingxing on October 12. Yuci in Shanxi Province was finally taken on November 8. Katō described the situation during this period as follows.

> We march every day, kept alive on Chinese rock salt with millet and sorghum levied from Chinese households. Whatever sort of physique you had before, now you feel like you're wasting away entirely. . . . As far as food goes, sometimes we get one day's worth of rice every three days, but since every household in China has five or six pigs, we kill and eat these; when we have no miso or salt, we just boil it and eat it. . . . There are also lots of sweet potatoes (*satsuma-imo*) in China. There's sweet potato fields wherever you go, so sometimes I chew on a raw potato while walking along. . . . But it's disappointing there's no rice.[147]

This sort of requisitioning reached a sudden peak just after Katō's division entered Yuci. Eyeing the produce grown in the area, the peasant soldiers thought of home. Angry at the intensity of the fighting thus far and resentful at being unable to do the farming they wished they could, they went about looting, with the encouragement of the local Japanese army.

> Beginning when we entered Yuci, for we who had suffered badly from [shortages of] food and tobacco, it was a great windfall, so to speak. That is, we all requisitioned everything in the city. The rice was Nanjing rice, but here it was in endless supply.[148] We requisitioned sugar and soy sauce at every shop, carrying more and more of it. Tobacco too—we smashed open the monopoly bureau and took it all. The city's warehouses were all left empty. Soldiers entered every house and took rare items, everyone trying to be first. All Chinese were treated roughly. Doors, paper sliding doors, cupboards, we made firewood of all of these as we ran across them—it was truly a pitiful thing. No matter how nice the houses, we made stables of them, we made toilets of them. . . . Now we're nice and warm, carrying and wearing things like fur coats, knitted wool jackets and [other] clothing that we took from the Chinese. Items like futons too, we're taking turns getting new futons and draping these over ourselves. We take it all without paying a thing, so there's no holding back, and if we encounter something like a muddy stretch on the road we just lay them down and keep walking. If they were my own, each futon would be heartbreaking. The Japanese army is doing just what it pleases. It's truly absurd.[149]

While Katō saw this behavior as "truly absurd," among Japanese soldiers in general there was little self-reflection on this sort of looting. The only strong sentiment shared by Katō and his fellow soldiers was that "the people of a defeated nation [are] truly worthy of pity."

"THE PEOPLE OF A DEFEATED NATION ARE TRULY WORTHY OF PITY"

Many peasant soldiers recorded a sense of sympathy for the poor, pitiable Chinese people, but what was the nature of this sympathy? Takahashi Tokubei, a soldier from Fujine Village, revealed its true character in the following letter:

> Since the garrison before us went out to subjugate the area and burned people's houses down, these people make contact with the Chinese army and every night they come around to attack us. [But] we cannot be beaten. The food for Chinese is dwindling; they pluck tree leaves or pick young barley grains, rub them in their hands, and eat the bristle they cast off it. It's miserable to watch.[150]

The source of Chinese popular "misery" was the Japanese army to which these soldiers belonged, and lacking self-reflection, their sympathy lacked a sense of empathy; it was accompanied, rather, by a supremacist "we cannot be defeated" attitude.

Takahashi Takejirō, a peasant from the same village of Fujine who had also seen first-hand action years earlier in Siberia,[151] described a gruesome episode in Fangshang Prefecture in Hebei Province:

> Today I went out on a punitive expedition 3 *li* northwest of Fangshang Prefecture. We captured bandits and remnants of the defeated army as local souvenirs. They're fodder for tonight, or until tomorrow morning. The soldiers test their skills [killing people] with pleasure. . . . On November 10 the battalion suffered fatalities. Six killed in battle: One sergeant, one private first class, four ordinary privates. . . . On the punitive expedition, I too went to have a look. It was brutal. There were [dead Japanese] without eyes, soldiers without testicles, without ears and noses—my tears gushed out when I saw this. Bodies covered with bayonet wounds. . . . Negligence cannot be tolerated. . . . We need more fighting spirit than at the time of the Siberian Expedition.[152]

Their animosity growing, the soldiers carried out the execution of prisoners "with pleasure." Even Takahashi wrote that "Chinese people are to be pitied,"[153] but this sort of behavior was enabled by a sense of superiority and a contemptuous view of the Chinese people as having "less of a heart than the

Russians. If they get something [from you], the next day they don't say thank you. To that extent they're different."[154]

The aforementioned Abe Katsuo, a cultivator-peasant from Iwayadō in Iwate Prefecture, was also fighting in Shanxi Province. In letters addressed to his wife, not only did Abe show concern for her, his parents, his children, and the farming business; he also had the sensitivity to pay respects to people in the neighborhood. In January 1938, he wrote, "When this letter arrives it will probably be New Year's.[155] Among the men at the front from Iwayadō, there must be plenty whose families are unable to have a satisfying New Year's. Please give people like that some rice cakes (*mochi*) as consolation—any amount will do. Because the bitter taste is the same for everyone."[156] Yet this sort of consideration did not extend to the people of China. Abe referred to them with the derogatory term "natives" (*domin*), believed their resistance movement was "mischief," and maintained a sense of victimhood, angry that they interfered with his sentry duties:

> Even as enemy stragglers turn into bandits, we're unable to rest at night with any sense of security. When you chase after them they run away. When you come back they do some more mischief. They cut electric wires or destroy railroad tracks or shoot at trains, and it feels unforgivable that I'm unable to say that those of us keeping guard are fully meeting our responsibilities.[157]

> Last night too they made trouble by cutting electric wires, but since I can't be hard on each and every native, I give a few of them work in the aim of applying tender loving care, and then they take advantage of this to pretend they're natives, do mischief, and then walk off on us—it's really a nuisance.[158]

Within a mindset that perceived the Chinese people as "natives" and as mischievous "bandits," there was no room for the nurturing of a humane sympathy. Massacres of ordinary people were carried out under army direction. In the second of the above letters, Abe wrote,

> Since we can't tell which guys are making the mischief, it's getting so we can't be safe unless we take all the natives and tie them up or kill them (although we can't actually do that). . . . Recently, we went out to suppress communist bandits and guys in a village self-defense group called the Yellow Spears Society (*Huangqianghui*), and a number of these spear-carrying guys got away, but the twenty or thirty who were left, we killed them all.

Abe believed that "China's resources won't last for that long" and was prepared for repatriation. But on April 19, 1939, he was killed in battle in Shanxi Province.

A COMPOSITION TEACHER AT THE FRONT

Up to this point we've examined peasant soldiers' experiences through their letters, but how did the war alter the consciousness of soldiers from Tōhoku, and what was their thinking after repatriation? As an example, let us examine the case of a schoolteacher. Kimura Genzaemon, an instructor at Tōmai Ordinary/Higher Elementary School in Akita Prefecture, received his draft notice on August 25, 1937, and participated in numerous battles throughout northern China as a stretcher bearer in the medical corps of the 108th Division.[159]

Kimura was born in Nishitakizawa Village in Akita Prefecture in 1904. After his father was killed in an explosion at the Yūbari coal mine where he was employed, Kimura withdrew from higher elementary school and enrolled at a teacher's college while also working as a servant. Unable to pay the school fees, he left the college. He nevertheless continued his studies while juggling temporary and substitute teaching jobs, eventually passing the exam and becoming a licensed teacher. In 1933, he met up with Sasaki Takashi, leader of a progressive educational movement called Hoppō Education. Kimura became an exponent of the movement, enthusiastically improving his composition teaching at Tōmai Elementary School.[160] In this sense, in the first half of the 1930s, Kimura could hardly have been further removed from imperialism and fascism.

Before he departed for the front, Kimura recited a "speech on the world-historical and Japanese-historical significance of the [China] Incident." From this salutation, we may gather that he agreed with the war. Yet as he crossed over the Sanhaiguan Pass and entered Northern China on September 24, 1937, he offered the following calm, candidly pessimistic observation: "Those who would sincerely welcome the chance to go to the front are, in general, only the uneducated. Children, women, (uneducated) old folks. The intelligentsia are, in general, bystanders. Is the Japanese Spirit unable to hold its own against Culture?"[161]

As Kimura saw Chinese people made into refugees after defeat in battle, participated in their enslavement, carried out requisitions, watched prisoners murdered, and heard about the "shooting to death of all the village inhabitants" in a punitive expedition (October 14, 1937),[162] however, he came to believe sincerely in the "superiority" of the Japanese race:

When I think about the future of the Japanese race compared to the Chinese race I discover that I am all the more confident of our superiority, without a doubt. Of course among the ranks of Japanese youth an apathetic, utilitarian quality has recently been drawing attention, but at least so long as they retain their emotionalism, their obsession with cleanliness, and their yen for improvement, I believe it will be easy for them to overcome the animal-like prowess, the physical robustness, and the existential deep-rootedness of the Chinese masses.[163]

AMID A PEOPLE'S WAR

When it confronted the fierce resistance of the Chinese people, this sense of assurance turned into a powerful craving for retribution. Witnessing the burning down of a village near Dongyangguan (東陽関), where slogans such as "We Vow to Resist the Japanese to the Death" and "Army and People Working Together" were written on the walls, Kimura tentatively observed that the local people were probably not participating in anti-Japanese resistance and that being killed and having their homes burned down despite this was something "truly to be pitied." Yet at the same time, he wrote, "I find reducing things to ashes thrilling, and I even feel I wouldn't hesitate to help out" (February 15, 1938). Again on February 17, there is the following entry in which one senses a cold-blooded gaze—the brutal scenery notwithstanding:

In the neighboring village there is the usual anti-Japanese propaganda written on the walls in big letters. Only these houses meet the fate of being burnt to the ground. A Chinese mother and daughter are there crying and wailing as they cling to their father's dead body. Isn't that a bit sad? Wondering if more enemies are left behind, a fire is lit, and when the two of them come out of the house they're stabbed to death on sight.[164]

On February 18, Kimura's Kasuya unit entered Licheng-xian (黎城県) in Shanxi Province. They repeatedly fought with the Eighth Route Army in Shanxi, and the squads of Kimura's unit were gradually annihilated. Waged by a Chinese people whose solidarity extended to the elderly, women, and children, the fierce, relentless war against the Japanese far surpassed his expectations. Confronting this situation—one difficult to comprehend according to what had been Japanese popular "common sense"—Kimura found no means of overcoming his attendant spiritual crisis other than by abnormally ratcheting up his will to battle and his hatred of the enemy.

At the beginning of May, Kimura happened to read the March 1938 issue of *Nihon hyōron*.[165] In it was a record of Tokyo Imperial University Professor Kawai Eijirō's experiences in China titled "Beijing and Tientsin."[166] Kawai argued that Japan had taken on a heavy burden in occupying northern China and asked, "What are our chances of success?" Seeing this, Kimura was spontaneously indignant: "Among the people they call professors at the Imperial University, are there really such idiots as this?" he wrote on May 4. Since "our success is already concrete," it was "unacceptable to allow [Japan's young people] to think" that this represented a burden. Thus did he turn his thoughts to his personal role upon his return home.[167]

Kimura subsequently participated in several punitive expeditions in Shanxi, during which he had such experiences as "lopping off enemy heads without a second thought when the opportunity arises" (May 10, 1939) and "beheading one" prisoner while "submitting two more for vivisection" (August 11, 1939). He received a letter of commendation for his efforts in the campaign. Within this context, his view of China became even more warped.[168]

Regarding the trend of Chinese popular resistance to Japan, Kimura went so far as to entertain the counterlogical notion that "when they withdraw they leave their villages empty so they are laid to waste, they can't do any work and they can't earn a penny."[169] He further attributed "an exceedingly bad nature" to the people of Shanxi, who refused to submit to the Japanese army. To eradicate the resistance—"Is this not," he rhetorically asked, "the result of our pursuing half-hearted pacification and incomplete measures?"—he expressed the violent thought, "I believe we need to return to the very essence of the Sino-Japanese war, first wielding our mighty swords as necessary to bring the devil to heel, followed by pacification as warranted."[170] Thus did Kimura come to hold a unilateral view of the "Chinese race" as conservative, noisy, and passive and the "Japanese race" as hopeful, progressive, and active.[171]

KIMURA'S EXPERIENCE OF CHINA

On the battlefield, Kimura continued to ponder how he would put his personal experience of the war and of China to use in his teaching after his return home. In the intervals between hectic battlefield duties, he made repeated visits to observe classes in China's elementary schools. He taught children in local Korean cafés. He wrote out a "proposal for the promotion of instruction in manners" and sent it to his wife, who was working as a teacher in Akita. Deploring what he perceived to be a lack of true feeling in a collection of children's writings sent from his hometown as a gift for men in the field, he pondered proper writing methods. Surveying the results of his own efforts, he offered the following conceits:

> Having left teaching and looking back anew upon my own teaching, I've conducted many explorations into problems of method, and on top of that I've even sorted out matters that had remained unresolved trouble spots in my mind. . . .
>
> Presumptuous as it may be, I've expanded my thoughts to embrace the future of the nation and the race, pondering its reformation and its leadership principles. Because this is the source of an enthusiasm that surges anew from within me, and because, in dealing with the new-nation stage [of development], it is also necessary as a worldview.[172]

In August 1939, as he continued engaging in these sorts of projects, Kimura's return to Japan was decided. The Second World War began in Europe the following month, whereupon his views on the Sino-Japanese War became all the more extreme. Excited, he observed that it had been an "extremely dangerous adventure," but now that the global conflict had begun, the time had come for Japan to seize "the great initiative" in the aim of expelling British power from Asia, an initiative that could not be fettered by Euro-American might. "There is no need to hesitate," he wrote, for precisely this moment represented the best possible opportunity to eliminate all anti-Asian power from the Chinese mainland and fulfill "the mission borne by the Japanese fatherland."[173]

Yet looking back over the results of more than two years of battlefield experience on the eve of his October 30 return to Japan, Kimura realized he'd reached a point where a "spectacular idealism" had been conquered by an "extremely simple realism." His realism amounted to this: In order to construct an "East Asian Cooperative Body" (*Tōa kyōdōtai*)[174] and a "New East Asian Order,"[175] the "Japanese race" itself required a "renovation and reformation of its domestic style," but the gap between reality and what was needed was exceedingly wide, and overcoming this would be far more difficult than battling "millions upon millions of enemies."[176] Behind this thinking was a recognition of the fact that an anti-Japanese war of a truly popular nature was being waged, a recognition combined with a deep-seated fear. Thus Kimura ultimately hardened in his determination to see a New East Asian Order established: "No matter what the difficulties, so long as we cannot afford to evade it, we must continue to make solid progress toward it, step by step."[177]

On November 25, 1939, Kimura was reunited with his family at Akita Station, and from then on he would pursue his teaching in Akita Prefecture from the standpoint he had articulated on the eve of his repatriation.

ON THE BATTLEFIELDS OF SOUTHERN CHINA

THE WAR VIEWS OF A NONCOMMISSIONED OFFICER

Finally, let us examine the experiences of the battlefield and of China among soldiers on patrol in southern China. Born in Ushui Village in Fukuoka Prefecture on Japan's southern island of Kyūshū in 1903, Murata Washirō was called up in September 1937. He landed at Hangzhou Bay on November 5 and served as a noncommissioned officer (corporal and later sergeant) in the Fukuoka 124th Infantry Regiment.[178] Continuously on the front lines until he was hospitalized with malaria in November 1939, he fought on successive fronts in central China, later participating in the Guangdong campaign and engaging in defensive fighting in southern China.

Murata was a graduate of the Law Department of Meiji University[179] and was employed with the Mitsubishi Mining Company after repatriation, making him a member of the intelligentsia, with the highest educational pedigree of any of the soldiers described here thus far. He was thirty-three years old when he was called up, with a wife and children.

From the time of the landing, Murata's unit too engaged in the execution of prisoners, requisitioning of goods, and burning of villages, experiences about which he wrote. On November 15, 1937, Murata witnessed a warrant officer suddenly decapitate Chinese soldiers who had been pulled out of a shack next to a creek.[180] On November 24, he watched as approximately three hundred Chinese prisoners were "slaughtered and burned alive" in a situation he "could not bear to behold," trapped in a three-story family house outside the fortress of Huzhou that was burned to the ground.[181] While participating in a mop-up operation within the fortress the next day, "Private First Class Yoshimura shot and stabbed four members of the enemy to death. Private Superior Class Tanaka engaged in hand-to-hand fighting with one member of the enemy and slaughtered eight prisoners."[182] On another day, three young women who Murata encountered at the Huzhou fortress were "made to walk forward with the lower half of their bodies exposed. . . . They fervently pleaded with us to help them."[183]

In the punitive expeditions that began from February of the following year, Murata's Huzhou Garrison set fires on a regular basis. During the fighting on February 19, he wrote, "The town of Miaoxi was enveloped in black smoke, with flames licking out here and there like the tongue of the great king Enma.[184] They spread as we watched. I thought to myself this must be what's meant by a sight so spectacular it touches the heavens."[185] On February 21, "we set fire to houses in the entire area, and also set fire to the mountain we occupied, producing a great curtain of smoke as we moved southward." Undergoing such experiences, Murata evolved the following views:

> War begins with a bullet fired and ends with a woman. You surrender rice, you surrender your life, you surrender your virginity—the calamity of war. Losing means everything is stolen from you for a brief time.[186]

> *Defeat the arsonist, murderous Japanese robbers* [written on the wall of a house] is a near masterpiece. Just now, a soldier who came across a boat shouted that we should burn it. Japanese robbers, isn't that a good one? We keep on raiding people's houses, cooking rice, eating chickens, using beds and chairs for firewood. We don't show the slightest restraint. This is war. Arson, murder, and theft are normal.[187]

Murata viewed the war that Japan was waging with realism but also as a reality that offered no alternative.

CONTRARY VISIONS OF CHINA

Murata continued to be overwhelmed by what he perceived as the Chinese people's "racial qualities" that had never succumbed to European civilization, their "tenacious vitality" typified by an unconstrained and unrestrained fullness, and the "power of their great traditions." He feared that in their hearts the people might be laughing at the Japanese army. And he found it revolting that the peoples of the Japanese and Chinese nations, who held "no grudge or hatred whatsoever" toward each other, were killing one another.[188] He was also capable of imagining the indignation and resentment of the Chinese people, whose country had been stolen from them.

Yet observing Chinese people in the areas under Japanese control, on the other hand, Murata found them "individualistic" lazybones with no sense of nationhood. In China there was no shortage of wealth, but there was no "spirit" (*seishin*), and thus only Japan could expel Euro-American power from Asia and "rescue an enslaved China and India." Strengthened by "personal experience," this thinking, which ranged between Greater Asianism and an Asian version of the Monroe Doctrine, had become a conviction.[189] He wrote,

> Why have the Europeans and Americans been allowed to act high-handedly in Asia?—Japan is partly to blame, but China more so. Leave Asia to Asia—beyond doubt, this is how we should handle things from now on. There's no longer any need to hold back or make bones about it. . . . Though it be uncertain, Japan should join hands with China and expel Euro-American power on the basis of China's awakening. More than anything else, Asia needs to do a great deal more growing up.[190]

Just from the policing of the occupied areas, Murata was well aware of the insecure situation, and he felt a strong resentment toward the hard-line stance that was making an appearance in Japan proper: the naked argument for re-source acquisition.[191] Yet his reaction did not go beyond this, and by clutching at the idea of the construction of East Asia with Japan as leader, he sought to shield himself from the appalling reality of a war of aggression.

REARGUARD BATTLES IN SOUTHERN CHINA

As his tour of duty grew prolonged, Murata's sentiments underwent a remark-able transformation. He entered southern Chinese territory on October 12, 1938, and from then on there are an increasing number of peculiar entries in his diary. On October 17 he wrote, "It's the first time I've seen a dead body in a while—I feel deeply moved."[192] Upon witnessing a prisoner shot to death on November 11, he felt that he too would "like to try beheading" a prisoner.[193] On March 11, 1939, he came across a wood-engraved six-volume *kōkijiten* (Chinese: *kangxi zidian*) dictionary in a temple that had been abandoned as the Japanese army advanced and sent it to Japan with the idea that rather than leaving it to the elements, "even if it's only temporary, to be with a book lover is surely what the book itself would also wish."[194] After playing with a pet dog he found in the area on April 1, he revealingly remarked that, if only the Chinese people were like the dog, "there would not likely have been a war like this."[195] On May 1, viewing the remains of the village Lianhexu, to which the Japanese army had laid waste, he observed, "I think they did a good job of burning it. Like this, I don't think the inhabitants can return. And this way, I don't think it'll become an enemy army den either."[196] On May 6, he beheaded a Chinese prisoner and wrote, "After the cutting I felt exhilarated."[197]

As their tours of duty dragged on, many soldiers, like Murata, grew exhausted and desperate. This in turn amplified the brutality. On June 16, 1939, he wrote, "I've had it. Every day I'm at my wit's end. . . . There's no sign I'll be sent home."[198] His longing for a discharge upon completion of his tour of duty became obsessive, and he seemed ready to explode in frustration. On June 30, he felt he'd "like to try cutting off heads with my own sword to my heart's delight."[199] On July 21, after reading a piece by the war correspondent Hino Ashihei describing Japanese soldiers as having "grown tough" and "grand," he was indignant. Was it not so that the soldiers were all wasting away from food shortages? "Ashihei," he asked, "where are your eyes?"[200]

Murata's frustration grew into fury over the Japanese army's securing of no more than points and lines on the map, the worsening security situation of the occupied areas, the failure of pacification operations, and the deteriorating quality of supplies and soldiers brought in as reinforcements. He set down increasingly violent statements such as "Combat consists of smashing your opponent to bits" (July 26) and "If we don't get tougher in a bad sense, we won't be able to reach the final goal" (August 13).[201]

Murata subsequently engaged in "pacification" operations in the occupied areas and reconnaissance of anti-Japanese bases. To those members of the population loyal to the Japanese army, he was kind. To Chinese he judged to be anti-Japanese, however, he gave no quarter. He scolded a soldier stealing eggs in a pro-Japanese village, but in villages he judged as anti-Japanese he was completely different, adopting measures that were "tough in a bad sense," methods of "smashing the opponent to bits."[202]

VOICES CURSING THE WAR

From roughly the seventh month after his deployment at the front, Murata became consumed by the mortifying thought that getting drafted and coming to the front meant his "life had been snapped like a twig."[203] In September 1939, he recorded the following discontented commentary of soldiers marching on a punitive expedition:

It won't do for my descendents to be soldiers forever. Even though they're tired they all quietly say these sorts of things. Is there no God, no Buddha, they sigh. We're absolutely the only ones suffering this cruel treatment. Loyalty to the emperor and love of country (*chūkun aikoku*), I'll be damned if I'll be fooled by these words—some even say things like that. And there are those who say: We're being herded step by step into the gates of death, how can they be so cruel? Driving living human beings into hell while they're still alive. To bolster his own service record, [the unit commander] is competing with other unit commanders against the clock. . . . The end result is that they're quibbling over every minute, they don't let us eat or drink, we're driven into the jaws of death without a break.[204]

Murata was also seized by the thought that war was preposterous foolishness:

A full two years is a long time, but the actual amount of time I've spent under fire is miniscule. In order to get to places where the bullets are flying, we continue to use up great amounts of energy, make long marches, do without sleep or rest. Years of preparation, billions of yen, tens of thousands of people trained for something that takes a few minutes. Mustn't we agree that war is an absurd act of folly?[205]

Murata wished to be released from this folly, to be free and return home as soon as possible. This realization held the potential to yield a new way of thinking. Yet so long as Japan remained undefeated, this potential could not bear fruit.

MURATA'S EXPERIENCE OF CHINA

What was Murata's experience of China during his long term of duty? For the sake of "building East Asia" (*tōa kensetsu*), he was beginning to believe that many more young, outstanding Japanese should take up the task of continental administration: "Younger people, members of the intelligentsia, should participate in the administration of the occupied areas," he wrote on September 27, 1939. He added on October 12 that when it came time for young Japanese teachers to enter the fray, "this ignorant China will surely be brought back to life through a fair and proper Japanese culture."[206]

Murata had become aware of the shallowness of Japan's policy and practice of "forcing its way with a spear and a rifle in front while trailing selfish profit seekers in its shadow." He also had an inkling of the profound shortcomings of the "Japanese spirit" (*Nippon seishin*) that had engendered such a situation and of the inflexibility of the Japanese people's insistence on uniformity (*kakuitsu shugi*). He was dismayed at how Japanese residents in Guangzhou lived hand to mouth, how they were preoccupied with the sense of working far from their true homes, and their corresponding inability to put down local roots. Murata consequently believed that the Japanese should take a lesson from the European and American missionaries, teachers, and doctors who had risked their lives to make China their permanent home. In this interest, "spiritual research, spiritual training, the remaking of the Japanese, this [was] the highest-priority task":[207] Here Murata was developing an approach unprecedented in its aggressiveness—and even more of a tall order.

Yet while he claimed that "Japanese culture" would resuscitate China, on matters of culture and civilization there coexisted in Murata an ineradicable sense of inferiority vis-à-vis the West and superiority vis-à-vis China. A closer look at his ideas of "Japanese culture" and the "Japanese spirit," meanwhile, reveals them as surprisingly empty. He had an authoritarian consciousness of rank and of levels of development—the Western individualist form of life, the Japanese single-generation family system, the Chinese permanent, extended family system—and a sense of values in which "the difference between primitive and civilized countries lies here: Where there is no individual awakening, there can be no unified nation."[208] He consequently believed that as fellow Asians, the spreading of Western "civilization" in China was a fitting mission for the Japanese: "The world is constructed with Europe and America at its center. If China is to raise its standard, it must depend on Europe and America. As a result, Asia must first unite and rise up through Asia alone. In the end, the Sino-Japanese incident too must be pursued with this goal in mind."[209] For China to achieve a modernization along Western lines, Japanese cooperation was paramount. The war, too, was for this purpose. So concluded Murata, who subscribed to the Japanism and Greater Asianism born in the midst of modernization.

In April 1940, Murata's return to Japan was decided. He recorded his thoughts on demobilization: "Upon my return . . . many matters of the gravest importance await me . . . rapid strides are necessary. Flying high and far is the most important thing."[210] Hearing shouts of *banzai* from Japanese who had come out to greet returning soldiers at Jilong Bay in Taiwan on his way home, he was unexpectedly moved to tears, boasting that "one day our descendents where we fought, in middle and southern China, will thank us too—when I thought of that, there arose in me a feeling that I'd been allowed, in some small way, to carry out a promising task."[211] On April 16, he arrived back at the Fukuoka Regiment; of his impressions at that moment, he wrote simply, "The little flags flutter like rain. I can't hold back the tears."[212] He too arrived home with a new determination and conviction to fight on in a war of aggression whose end seemed far away.

———————————

From 1939 to 1940, Japan not only expended more than ten billion yen and suffered more than one hundred thousand deaths in battle. It also absorbed several hundred thousand repatriated soldiers who had accumulated raw experiences of China and its battlefields, who had developed a deep fear of the Chinese resistance that involved the country's entire people, and who had hardened in their determination to fight on.[212] The Japan of this period was thus a Japan different from before. One by one, people returning from the battlefield—along with people at home who had been supporting the war—were becoming earnest and beginning to give it their all.

2
GRASSROOTS FASCISM

THE ROOTS OF FASCISM

POPULAR DISCONTENT

VOICES OF DISSATISFACTION IN THE CITIES

Beginning in May 1940, as news of Germany's blitzkrieg victories circulated throughout Japan, a considerable change in popular consciousness became apparent. Among urban residents, including white-collar and factory workers, small- to medium-scale merchants and nonmilitary manufacturers, discontent over inflation and war-related shortages intensified; at the same time, demands increased for a speedy "resolution of the [China] Incident" (*jihen kaiketsu*), to be realized through a "politics of strength" (*kyōryoku seiji*).

At the end of 1939, rice supplies grew extraordinarily tight in Tokyo, Osaka, Kyoto, and other large cities, leading to major social unrest. In May 1940, the Conference of Economic Prosecutors (*Keizai jitsumuka kaigi*, convened by the Criminal Affairs Bureau of the Ministry of Justice) launched an investigation of the problem. Participating prosecutors cited an incident in which people had stormed the entrance of an Osaka rice shop and another in which a large number of people had broken into a rice shop in Kyoto in the middle of the night and demanded, "Sell us rice!" In the case of Osaka—with just a fifty-day supply of rice remaining in stockpiles and merchants holding only five day's worth—they reported that within rice-trading circles word had circulated that "given that the most serious problems with rice will arise between the end of this coming June and the first half of July, this should be seen as a hazardous period." The investigators added, "We cannot help having an uneasy feeling, not knowing when or what sort of ominous event could happen."[1] In July, the Yamaguchi Prefectural Prosecutor's Office reported that in every urban area of the prefecture, rice shortages had resulted in stocks so low that they could "barely cover the amount consumed in two to three days."[2]

Among the ruling class, the situation fostered a deep sense of crisis. On May 1, 1940, Mitsui *zaibatsu* chief Ikeda Seihin worried, "It seems to me the rice crop interval of June and July will be the most dangerous in the end."[3] In a late August cabinet meeting, Agriculture Minister Ishiguro Tadaatsu stated,

> At this moment when our countrymen are waiting out the situation on the assumption that once the New Order comes, a variety of things will likely get easier and their livelihoods guaranteed to some degree, a variety of worrisome problems are arising—by roughly the end of this year, fuel problems will flare up again, and I don't know what will happen with the rice problem either. When things do get more serious, our own resolve will be of the utmost importance . . .

. . . whereupon the entire cabinet fell deathly quiet.[4] On September 17, the former ambassador to England (and future postwar prime minister) Yoshida Shigeru wrote to Prime Minister Konoe Fumimaro, "Want of goods, shortages of rice, industrial decline, difficulties making ends meet, etc.—these social aspects threaten city dwellers, and on the streets and about town there are many voices of discontent, dissatisfaction, and deep resentment; it's truly a trying situation with little parallel in recent years."[5] As urban discontent smoldered, it turned in the direction of the New Order Movement, a Japanese-style fascist movement.

EXPECTATIONS OF "THE NEW ORDER" AND "POLITICS OF STRENGTH"

According to "Voices of the Lower Middle Class During the [China] Incident" and "Workers' Thought Tendencies During the [China] Incident," two reports from the Tokyo Prosecutor's Office issued in July 1940,[6] Tokyo's white-collar workers, factory workers, day laborers, and small- and medium-scale merchants and manufacturers were deeply distressed by extreme declines in product quality and shortages of items such as rice, charcoal, underwear, socks, work clothes, and raw materials. According to the former report, people were complaining that rice was mixed with undesirable foreign rice, that rice substitutes such as bread and noodles were all but sold out, that clothing, underwear, shoes, and socks were expensive and quickly wore out, and that work clothes, work gloves, shirts, and split-toed socks made with rayon were particularly shoddy.

The report also summarized opinions on the prosecution of the Sino-Japanese War:

❶ Among white-collar workers, many wish for "a quick war with a prompt conclusion," via a German-style blitzkrieg.

❷ Among small- and medium-scale merchants and manufacturers, many say the appearance of a "strong cabinet" (*kyōryoku naikaku*) should set things straight and that "Chiang Kai-shek must be thoroughly defeated."

❸ Among factory workers and day laborers, many also hope for "a quick war with a prompt conclusion."[7]

What was the nature of these popular sentiments demanding "a quick war with a prompt conclusion"? These were divided between the sort that admired Hitler and Mussolini, saying things like "party politics, a dictator, anything is fine, we need someone with the power to pull along the entire nation," and those who did not hope for a Hitler in Japan but deemed it necessary that the nation "become as one body united in cooperation [*kyōryoku itchi*]." Hardly anyone said that a speedy peace should be reached with China.[8]

The opinion that the war needed to be pursued all-out prevailed among both the white-collar and laboring classes. Many shared the view that, as a local official put it, "we should also occupy the Netherlands Indies and Hong Kong, go all the way down that road to get things taken care of,"[9] and, in the words of an employee of the Kojima Printing Company, "for four years the Incident has continued and even now there's no end in sight; this is because while German and Italian blitzkriegs have steadily been yielding results, our government's China policy remains lax. We should occupy the Netherlands Indies and French Indochina in one fell swoop, cutting off Chiang's supply route."[10]

The latter report further confirmed that those who yearned for a "quick war with a prompt conclusion" did not want "peace no matter what."

[Where workers are concerned,] a wartime consciousness attained after living through well-nigh three years of holy war, the development of the Industrial Patriotic Movement (*Sangyō hōkoku undō*),[11] changes in the European situation and the like have made a slowly deepening recognition of our nation's current difficult position apparent. While there are voices demanding an early resolution to the Incident, those who speak of an indiscriminate early resolution as in bygone days are extremely rare; the rising trend is one in which an early fix is seen to consist of a thoroughgoing resolution to the Incident, and there is an insistence that a breakthrough in the international crisis must be struck through national unity (*kyokoku itchi*).[12]

Among those small- and medium-scale merchants and manufacturers— apparently relatively numerous—who hoped for a "politics of strength" and a New Konoe Party (*Konoe shintō*[13]), some had become resigned toward the Sino-Japanese War and wartime controls. The following sorts of opinions, recorded in "Voices of the Lower Middle Class During the [China] Incident," were representative:

I hope for a quick end to the Incident. Up until now there is no way to know when this will be achieved. In the current mode where the people don't understand the objective, a resolution will be difficult. There is talk of the construction of a New Order in East Asia (*Tōa shinchitsujo*), but under the present situation I have my doubts about whether this can be achieved. If Japan is a powerful nation then it needs to come out forcefully. (A dealer in Western-style apparel and accessories)[14]

Regarding a resolution to the Incident, many are already brimming with feelings of hopelessness. The government's actions on every problem are timid. I call upon it to get stronger. (A dealer in kimono fabrics)[15]

We've already resigned ourselves. This is what comes of the inadequacy and inconsistency of the control system, along with skyrocketing prices and maldistribution of goods. For a successful finish to the holy war, we need to get the nation's power in order first. (A hardware vendor)[16]

Here was an ambivalent mentality, combining a sense of resignation toward the war's unpredictability, skyrocketing prices, and goods shortages with expectations of economic recovery and a "profitable" resolution to the war based upon a "politics of strength."

The New Order Movement was borne along by this popular discontent and expectation. In October 1940, the Imperial Rule Assistance Association (*Taisei yokusankai*) was formed, and with the inauguration of the New Economic Order (*Keizai shintaisei*) the following year, imperial fascism was established.[17] Yet although this imperial fascist system (the "New Order") was capable of sustaining the popular sense of expectation, because it was completely powerless to end the war, tackle inflation, or reverse goods shortages, it was unable to address the people's fundamental dissatisfaction. Wartime profiteers and people connected to military-related industries were the only exceptions.

SWELLING DISSATISFACTION

In April 1941, a system of rice rationing was implemented in Japan's six largest cities. With a rice deficit estimated at fifty million bushels (equivalent to the annual consumption of ten million people), the aim was to tide over the shortage through allocation restrictions according to age and occupation. According to a Justice Ministry investigation, the new system fueled popular discontent, "work evasion and a mood of deliberate idleness," an exodus to cities without the rationing system, and rampant rumors. "This will generate a situation requiring concern for security," stated the report.[18] Their stomachs empty, workers detested night shifts and overtime work and changed jobs or moved to industries and areas where the amount of [rice] allocations was high—"whether or not there will be rice to eat" became a crucial factor in job searches.[19]

Lower-class urban residents, unable to fill the rice gap (30 to 50 percent of demand) with rice substitutes, were the hardest hit by consumption restrictions. In Osaka, "demands for reform regarding quantity increases, for a balancing of supply and demand for alternative foodstuffs, and for changes in the standard [rationing] quantities are turning into feelings of anger." Among longshoremen, who normally ate large quantities to maintain their strength, Korean longshoremen were hit particularly hard and extremely dissatisfied. Osaka's roughly eight thousand longshoremen were allotted only 50 percent of the amount they required, and with the costs of substitutes such as rice cakes (*mochi*), steamed buns (*manjū*), and *udon* noodles reaching levels they "cannot by any means manage to afford, they complain most vociferously, and moreover there is a trend toward a great exodus of those seeking to move into other lines of work."[20] On April 2, approximately three thousand Koreans gathered at the Miki *udon* shop in Osaka City's Shikitsu neighborhood and demanded, "Sell us dried noodles!"[21]

Insecurity and dissatisfaction among small- and medium-scale merchants, manufacturers, and workers were made all the more acute by the National Conscription Ordinance (*Kokumin chōyōrei*), problems of unemployment, changes of occupation, wage controls, and prohibitions against the movement of workers ensuing from the implementation of the National Mobilization Law (*Kokka sōdōin hō*).[22] Because of a decline in real wages, most workers were forced into "a life of insecure days and nights" with "suppression of the freedom to pursue profit as before." "A tendency toward increased negativity among a portion of the workers" was observed as a result of the combined effects of inflation and goods shortages.[23]

Middle-aged and older self-employed businessmen, with little choice but to become laborers, were bewildered by work to which they were not accustomed. "The majority are living in extremely tight circumstances."[24] Among those who received conscription orders, many at first "respond[ed] enthusiastically to the draft," believing it an honor to answer the call, but they soon lost their enthusiasm, and the number who deliberately failed to respond gradually rose to the point that "each time a draft order is enacted, there is a no-show rate of 20 to 30 percent."[25]

Among workers and the lower middle class—among whom the proportion of those profiting from the war was relatively high in comparison with people in farming, mountain, and fishing villages—dissatisfaction and unrest grew. Among workers in the civil industries being sacrificed to the war, many were "hoping for a speedy handling of the Incident on the assumption that prosperity will not come without an end to it."[26]

"DISTRESSED THAT THINGS AREN'T SHARED EVENLY"

Yet many people were not simply demanding a straightforward resolution in the form of a sufficient supply of scarce goods and relief from difficult living conditions. On the contrary, they revealed an understanding of the reasons and causes that compelled such an existence, and as they endured a life of frugality, they expressed frustration with the failure to make it work. Analyzing correspondences concerning the control economy addressed to the Kyoto Prefecture Economic Peace Preservation Department between July 1938 and May 1941, a report from the Kyoto Prosecutor's Office observed the following:

Examining the psychological attitudes of those submitting letters, leaving the so-called "suggestion fiend" practical joker-types aside, the trend is toward earnestness along with a general acknowledgment of the need to strengthen controls, with opposition or dissatisfaction toward strengthening limited; instead there are many acting on the notion that "I'm not distressed that there is not enough [to go around], I'm distressed that things aren't shared evenly," and thus more than reports on infringements [from small- and medium-scale merchants and manufacturers concerning their competitors], there are many [from consumers] concerning supply et cetera, earnestly leaning toward "minding my own business first."[27]

Between the end of 1941 and the beginning of 1942, dissatisfaction regarding inflation and shortages grew more intense. Discontent over food shortages was particularly severe, thus "giving rise either to speculation, or to absurd superstition. Since around the end of the sixteenth year of Shōwa [1941], an expanding area has seen the circulation of rumors of the sort requiring attention, to an increasing degree."[28]

Unrest was also spreading from the cities into farming villages. Seeking to secure rice stocks in the face of the rationing system, peasants took a variety of measures that in turn amplified urban unrest. Even in Niigata Prefecture, a rice-producing area, there were complaints about shortages of supplied rice: "If rations of rice for eating are not increased, I'll have no choice but to kill myself." "With the shortage of rice for eating as it is now, it's natural that peasants hide rice."[29] In February 1942, the work rate among miners at the Beppo Pit of Pacific Coal's Kushiro Mine fell to 65 percent because of food shortages.[30] On February 28, an incident occurred at the Nakajima Aircraft company dormitory in Gunma Prefecture, in which approximately one hundred conscripted workers rioted over food problems, throwing tableware and trays. Amid the unrest that spread with the rice shortage from the end of 1939 onward, administrators responsible for public order, fearing a repeat of the 1918 rice riots, took frantic countermeasures.[31]

WILD ENTHUSIASM OVER PEARL HARBOR AND SINGAPORE

The popular view of the Sino-Japanese War as a winnable and just one, along with expectations about the new war, served to suppress an explosion of popular unrest. The wild enthusiasm that accompanied the Pearl Harbor attack on December 8, 1941, and the occupation of Singapore on February 15, 1942, was a clear expression of this. The writer Itō Sei recorded the mood of the population—and himself—in the following terms: "Today everyone is cheerful, with a pleased look. It is the very opposite of yesterday. This is the result of the destruction of a number of American warships in Hawaii."[32]

> They say that in [South]East Asia, there's rubber and sugar in abundance. There's nothing like lots of sugar. This war is cheerful. If you read Carossa['s *Romanian Diary*], in the middle of World War One, Germans and Austrians are both dreaming incessantly of peace. This is not like that. . . . More than before the China Incident, the feeling that the nation is sharing equally in the joys and the sorrows is surely what's making the country cheerful. And the gloominess of the period just before the Greater East Asia War is also gone. This war is truly good. It's cheerful.[33]

The sort of reaction was not limited to intellectuals tormented by a sense of inferiority toward Europe and the United States. On December 9, 1941, the Department of Peace Preservation at the Ministry of Home Affairs was able to boast that the nation was excited by military gains, that "there is a deep sense that the system of national unity (*kyokoku itchi taisei*) is strengthening more and more," and that "nothing unusual is observed—where public peace is concerned there is no unrest." Here a true situation of wild enthusiasm had finally emerged, and imperial fascism had crystallized. What sorts of people were supporting this system on the home front?

THE AGENTS AND RECEPTORS OF FASCISM

A FORMER TEACHER AND RESERVIST'S ASSOCIATION BRANCH CHAIRMAN

Takahashi Minejirō (b. 1883), a resident of Fujine Village in Iwate Prefecture, became branch chairman of the Fujine Imperial Reservist's Organization in 1932. He looked after bereaved families and kept his former trainees up to date on the situation in their home village by sending them copies of the branch bulletin *Shinyū* (真友, lit. "true friend"). In 1938 he received a decoration from the prefectural governor for his work on the home front.[34]

In support of an effort to build an army airfield in the village at Gotōno in 1938, Takahashi ran about carrying twenty or even thirty canteens for the Construction Service Association, giving rise to rumors that he was "soldier crazy" (*heitai baka*). Yet he was not a simple "militarist"; he had spent years as a dedicated schoolteacher, deeply involved in youth groups, Boy Scout activities, and the like, forming strong attachments with the children. He was furthermore distressed by the widespread poverty in the Tōhoku region and passionate about his home village. He served as member of a temporary arbitration committee on financial dues and a local welfare committee and was a part-time instructor at a Youth Training Center (*Seinen kunrensho*).[35] In 1941 he became a member of the Iwate Prefectural Committee on Juvenile Reform and devoted himself to local welfare and guidance. Takahashi described his activities as school teacher and as branch chairman of the reservist's association in a book he wrote, *A History of Fujine, Our Native Village* (*Fujine kyōdoshi*).

> I was employed at a school in Fujine from Meiji 39 [1906] onward. . . . I was always unable to forget the cruelty of the [Russo-Japanese] War.[36] Even when there is peace, you never know when war will break out. From the time they were children, I aimed to raise [my students] to be strong, brave, and righteous, and I assisted in the development of youth groups and the Boy Scouts as well as leading the Youth Association and the Veteran's Association; in the end war came again, so I looked after [them] with more and more passion. I did such things as recommending young men to volunteer for the army, sending off and looking after soldiers entering and leaving the ranks, and going around to homes of families to make sympathy calls; I also issued the branch bulletin, providing [them] encouragement and keeping in contact—because of this everyone called me "soldier crazy," and it even happened that I was asked if I was out of my mind.[37]

In the Sino-Japanese War, many young men from Fujine Village were sent to fight in Shanxi Province and other parts of northern China. Takahashi maintained such an intimate bond with soldiers from the village that he received as many as seven thousand military postcards and letters from his former students in reply to the *Shinyū* bulletin that he sent out. For example, the *Shinyū* recipient Senda Zenpachi wrote to Takahashi on October 23, 1941, "My tears flow. I am grateful and the tears flow. At the heart of Gentleman Takamine,[38] which remains unchanged forever, my tears flow. I read Takamine's newspaper from cover to cover, over and over. And I cry tears of 'thank you, thank you.'"[39]

The war situation slowly worsened, and the number of men from the village killed in battle rose from the previous one or two per year to five in 1942, thirteen in 1943, and a combined total of 106 in 1944 and 1945. Around the middle of 1942, "in an extraordinarily agitated state," Takahashi "went to the station to see soldiers off and continued to go around visiting and encouraging bereaved families in the village."[40]

By bringing together people of this sort—who had for many years devoted themselves to the locality and were intimately attached to the people—imperial fascism anchored itself at the local level.

HOME-FRONT SUPPORT FROM A BANK EMPLOYEE

Born in 1882, Uchida Yasuke was an employee at the Chita Bank in the town of Utsumi in Aichi Prefecture. He began sending a monthly mimeographed booklet of roughly thirty pages, "News of Our Hometown, News of Our Brave Warriors" (*Kyōdo no tayori, yūshi no tayori*), to soldiers at the front on October 7, 1937. He continued to do so every month for eighty issues until May 1944, after a police warning that it be halted.[41] There were eighty copies of the first edition, a figure said to have reached four hundred at the periodical's height. In the first half of each edition the goings-on in Utsumi were related in diary format; communications from soldiers at the front appeared in the second half. From the eighth edition onward, hometown photographs were included.

Uchida had served in the Russo-Japanese War as a private. He had taken a bullet in his right arm, and he remembered the hardships of the front and the intense training of recruits. He came up with the idea of sending them something that would comfort and console them and show "profound gratitude from the bottom of my heart for their strenuous efforts of loyal service" (first issue).[42] The fourth issue onward was placed under police censorship, and from then on the section containing letters from soldiers in particular was "cruelly erased." Yet when he read a newspaper article that said that "there is nothing that pleases soldiers at the front more than correspondence from their home town. Even just an envelope will do, they want you to write them," he decided to keep publishing after "giving it some thought": "No matter how worthless it is, it's better than nothing" (fourth issue).[43] Uchida's doctor had forbidden him from engaging in strenuous activity because of heart disease, an aortal aneurysm, and diabetes, but "even if my illness gets worse," he wrote in the fifth issue, "I've made up my mind that since I'd be laying down my life for the brave warriors, I cannot presume to spare myself." Ignoring the [doctor's] prohibitions, he got on his bicycle and rode around to the homes of families with soldiers in the field to gather information for *Kyōdo no tayori*.[44]

Uchida was an ordinary townsman who believed in the "holy war" and that Japan was compelled to keep fighting because China was being high-handed and rash. But concerning himself with "mail-order patriotism" and enthusiastically promoting support for the war on the home front, he played a role that went beyond the bounds of the ordinary townsman—he came to support the order of imperial fascism on the local level.[45]

In 1938—just after Prime Minister Konoe Fumimaro declared his "refusal to negotiate with Chiang Kai-shek"[46] and as the war was turning into a quagmire—Uchida wrote to his hometown's soldiers, "While you're at it, please bring the stubborn army of Chiang Kai-shek to heel, along with the hated bandits. We too are girding ourselves up to strengthen the defense of the home front" (sixth issue).[47]

In 1940, Uchida encountered dissatisfaction among the people of Utsumi, who were "pondering how far away we are from a successful finish to the holy war, how the strengthening of the control economy is gradually bringing us into tight circumstances, worrying about family members in the army, etc." In this context he welcomed news of the conclusion of the Tripartite Pact with Italy and Germany. "It is truly such that I cannot contain my delight," he wrote. "There is no difference between the battle front and the home front; it is truly a time demanding a great, all-or-nothing readiness" (38th issue).[48]

Again in January 1942, when he heard reports of victories in various battles against the Americans, British, and Dutch, he was wildly enthusiastic: "As far as offering words of thanks appropriate to the officers and men of all ranks, I cannot even begin to express my joy, there are only tears of gratitude. . . . My satisfaction, like iron and steel congealing over the heads of the red-haired Anglo-Saxons, a tight fist that's pounded them, is truly an intense pleasure that relieves the accumulated grudges of years in an instant." At the same time, Uchida reaffirmed his determination that the home front would need to "assume responsibility for a total war lasting a long time" since this was going to be a war of economic endurance, and "a war of economics is a war of the home front" (53rd issue).[49] To the limit his body allowed, Uchida visited bereaved families and participated in sendoff ceremonies for soldiers, monthly festivals of prayer for eternal fortune in battle, and burial ceremonies for those killed in combat.

At news of subsequent victories by the Japanese army, Uchida's "needless anxiety vanish[ed] like vapor." This sense of relief was reflected in a *haiku*: "Flags of occupation increase by the day—[like] mist over the map" (55th issue,

March 1942).[50] In the Imperial Rule Assistance Election (*yokusan senkyo*)[51] in April, he voted for the recommended candidate, Nakano Hanzaemon, "as the heart of the hearts of soldiers at the front" (57th issue).[52] Thus, by the middle of 1942, Uchida felt at relative ease.

Yet, from around that time, illicit trading among Utsumi farming families spread, and there were reports of the loss of warships. "I wonder if this will do, can we prevail in such a situation?" Uchida wrote (64th issue).[53] At the end of 1942, his own son was mustered up. In response Uchida once again affirmed his commitment to "postal patriotism" (*tsūshin hōkoku*). He went around preaching "selfless" cooperation regarding labor service and metals collection as well.[54]

A BRANCH CHAIRWOMAN OF THE LADIES' PATRIOTIC ASSOCIATION (*AIKOKU FUJINKAI*)[55]

Itō Matsuo was born in Natsuta Village in Iwate Prefecture in 1894. After graduating from the women's section of the Iwate Teacher's Training School, she became an elementary school teacher. She married in 1915, and the following year she transferred to a teaching position in the neighboring village of Oyama.[56] There, she wrote, young women who graduated from elementary school dealt with "the strenuous ordeal of service as daughter-in-law, with an existence worth less than that of the family horse." To comfort and aid these women, Itō established a "mothers' and sisters' society" and a "maiden's society." She then "sacrificed every Sunday and winter holiday" to advising those with problems and courses in self-improvement (practice in the abacus, writing the Western alphabet, and food and clothing knowhow). Her subsequent involvement in the Ladies Patriotic Association was rooted in this concern with the hardships of farming women, in particular those of new brides. Itō keenly felt the necessity to "raise the status of farming village wives," all the more as she herself had suffered as a new bride, running away from home and wandering about on the verge of death.[57]

In 1936, Itō's husband, who had been working as a deputy village chief, was appointed village headman. Itō—who had quit her teaching job to farm in 1931—was obliged to become branch chairwoman of the local Ladies' Patriotic Association. There were fewer than thirty members from the village, but for those who could not afford the one-yen annual fee, Itō gained approval from the organization's leadership for a system of associate membership whereby "although they couldn't pay the membership fee, the entire village would band together as one in performing service." When the Sino-Japanese War broke out, Itō quickly succeeded in bringing the membership to over six hundred.[58]

At the time, the Ladies' Patriotic Association, under the direction of the Home Ministry, was in fierce competition over cooperation in the war effort with the mass-based Great Japan National Defense Women's Association (*Dai Nihon kokubō fujinkai*), which was supported by the military authorities and quickly expanded. There was also another organization known as the Great Japan Alliance Ladies' Association (*Dai Nihon rengō fujinkai*), which was linked to the Ministry of Education. In Oyama, Itō became chairwoman of all three organizations. She purchased only ten National Defense Women's Association sashes and decided to have the same people switch sashes and mobilize together.

> Thinking back to those times, yesterday we'd be the Ladies' Patriotic Association, today the National Defense Women's Association, and tomorrow the Great Japan [Alliance] Ladies' Association; we'd exchange the three different-colored sashes, or we'd wear one sash over each shoulder, and we'd head out, leaving behind empty houses. Even though the aim [of each organization] was one and the same. Working with one hundred million hearts beating as one, aflame with sincere love of country and loyalty to the emperor (*chūkun aikoku*)—there were none who declined it.[59]

Itō led the members of the Ladies' Association with "the pride of making frantic efforts to confront the national crisis," journeying every day as far as Orii Station in the neighboring village to see off soldiers and receive their remains. She further carried out "such deeds as labor service toward families on the home front, the preparation of comfort bags (*imonbukuro*), the daily dispatch, without fail, of a letter of comfort to soldiers at the front (three hundred in all), the consolation of bereaved home front families, and sympathy calls to the army hospital." She participated in scrap recovery efforts and the contribution of items such as pickled plums, wool scraps, and hardware sponsored by both the Ladies' Patriotic Association and the National Defense Womens' Association, and she directed that the Ladies' Association carry out tasks for farm families whose chief breadwinners had been called up. She writes, "With the pride of farmers of the Empire, the ladies took over for men in all sorts of jobs. In the meantime looking after horses and cows."[60]

In the war's closing stages, Itō took in evacuees. Amid material shortages she improvised such things as *sakujipan* (bread made of rice bran) and steamed pumpkin dumplings and came up with ways to prepare the nuts of Japanese oak and horse chestnut trees. She slurped rice gruel and ate rock salt after rationing it between herself and her horses and cattle.[61] She recalls her thoughts at the time.

> I would like to reveal to you my heart. My bosom that swelled with the sincere blood of "selfless service" (messhi hōkō), of "love of country and loyalty to the emperor." . . . We who assumed responsibility for the times were truly in earnest. Selfless service . . . is it not so that we perform selfless service nowadays too, in our homes, for the sake of our husbands and our children? For us in those days, the spirit with which we thought of the nation and of our homes was one and the same. The fact that the members of the Oyama Ladies' Association became as one and confronted the national crisis—to this day even, it's something I feel proud of.[62]

To a profound degree, such spiritual devotion served to buttress the war against China and Asia.

RECEPTORS OF IMPERIAL FASCISM

How did the supporters and receptors of these sorts of popular mediators of imperial fascism respond? Let us examine this issue by making a division between the generation born in the 1900s and in the prime of life during the war—who had been influenced by imperial democracy in their youth—and the younger generation of people born after the First World War who had had little exposure to imperial democracy, having turned twenty after the Sino-Japanese War began.

ABE TA'ICHI'S "WAR"

Beginning with the generation in the prime of life, let us once again examine the case of Abe Ta'ichi (b. 1907), a tenant farmer in Ōizumi Village in Yamagata Prefecture.[63] Beginning around the middle of 1940, farmers in the village were compelled to deliver rice because of a severe rice shortage. In June, the former Agriculture Minister Sakai Tadamasa, a representative of the Wartime Food-stuffs Patriotic Drive Corps (Senjika shokuryō hōkoku suishinhan), traveled around Tōhoku pushing for the fulfilling of rice delivery quotas.[64] When he came to Ōizumi Village on June 8, the village headman and others complained of shortages of feed and fertilizer and petitioned for a reduction in the prices of several products expensive relative to rice. Abe reacted coolly, writing in his diary, "In the industrial union (*sangumi*),[65] they said there should be two hundred sacks of delivered rice from Hakusan Village,[66] but I wonder how much [actually] went. I'm thinking of giving it to [the rice merchant] Genji." Abe felt compelled to sell some of his rice for a high price both because his younger sister's wedding was imminent and because of the steep rise in prices for other goods; under the circumstances this was an inevitable measure of self-defense. With the national control of rice beginning on November 1, Abe hastily sold some fourteen bushels of glutinous rice a day earlier.

In the same month of October 1940, the opening ceremony of the Imperial Rule Assistance Association was held in Tokyo; in Ōizumi Village, an opening ceremony for its branch office followed on December 9, and Abe became a member of its economic corps (*keizaihan*).[67] His role was to determine the allotments of rationed items such as fertilizer, work gloves, matches, charcoal, fish, and squid. From the beginning of 1941 on, the distribution of rationed goods kept him extremely busy. He wrote in his diary, "Issues occupying the economic corps are innumerable" (March 4). "In the morning there are rationed goods from the economic corps. Fertilizer, little presents, over and over like this; it's not helping me any" (March 13). Abe came close to predicting the start of the war against the United States and Britain. The "Special Maneuvers of the Kwantung Army" in July 1941 and the large-scale mobilization in preparation for the invasion of Southeast Asia and the Pacific caused a stir in Ōizumi Village—many men were conscripted and horses seized for military use.[68] On July 12, Abe wrote, "It seems something big is going to happen."

On the day Abe heard the war had begun, he wrote, "At last it has started. I feel my body stiffening sharply" (December 8). On December 10, when the results of the attack on Pearl Harbor were announced, he took the afternoon off from work and spent half a day "reading the newspaper from cover to cover." In January 1942, Abe missed the formation ceremony of the Great Japan Assistance Men's Corps (*Dai Nippon yokusan sōnendan*, abbrev. *yokusō*), but he became a member.[69] He attended the drill meeting of the *yokusō* that began on February 15, and the passionate speech of the social education director "made a very deep impression." The following day, he heard "the expectantly awaited news of the fall of Singapore" on a newly purchased radio. On February 18, there was a parade through the village celebrating the fall of Singapore, with marchers waving flags. Abe also greeted the April 30 Imperial Rule Assistance

Elections (*yokusan senkyo*) with deep emotion: "At last today was the day."[70] On the same day, he became head of the economic corps.

Thus was Abe integrated within the village system that supported the war and imperial fascism. He cooperated zealously, yet his posture was one of cooperating and agreeing with the grand scheme of the war effort while harboring deeply negative feelings toward what was going on in his immediate vicinity. This is well-reflected in the following diary entries: "I am made to go and join [in the members' meetings of the *yokusan sōnendan*]. Somehow the *sōnendan*'s manner of working is disheartening. From my point of view I'm forced to make too many sacrifices. It's vital that I keep right in step" (December 5, 1942). And upon hearing the address by the head of the *sōnendan*, Andō Kisaburō, to mark the one-year anniversary of the beginning of the Pacific War: "A tear-jerking voice, I guess you could call it that. I was moved to tears. The truth touched my heartstrings. Standing before the radio, I participated in the national rally honoring the first anniversary of the Greater East Asia War by grant of Imperial Rescript" (December 8, 1942).

In Abe's immediate vicinity, the most urgent issue was meeting rice delivery quotas. According to his diary entry for March 19, 1943, "The people of the village gathered at the school to discuss rice deliveries. Mr. Nagase, Tagawa Regional Office Director, sternly ordered us [to deliver rice]. I am entirely at my wit's end." Further meetings on this problem followed. On April 21, he wrote, "It now appears certain we have to deliver rice in our personal possession meant for family use." Peasant families were now to deliver all their rice at once and receive an allotment for personal consumption (returned rice or *henkanmai*) afterward.

As time went on the rice delivery policy grew harsher. The coercion of the rice yield deliveries of 1943 bring to mind the requisitioning going on in the battlefields overseas. "This evening, on the subject of rice deliveries, some big shots—the village headman, the manager of the Tagawa office, and prefectural officials—came and demanded 'turn over your rice' in words that would draw blood. There was no rationed rice in return, not even a pittance. All of it for delivery. The village managers had a simple dinner. What with this and that, I didn't get any sleep the whole night" (February 7, 1944).

The amount of rice delivered that year amounted to 95.7 percent of the Abe household's total production.[71] Yet amid all this, even as he confided his dissatisfaction to his diary, Abe faithfully cooperated in the war effort, assisting with goods distribution, cooperating with rice deliveries, seeing soldiers off to the front, purchasing Patriotic Bonds (*hōkoku saiken*), and attending regular village and *sōnendan* meetings where the goals of government, prefectural, and central organizations were presented.

A JAPAN STEEL PIPE EMPLOYEE COOPERATES IN INCREASING PRODUCTION

Mori Shintarō (b. 1908) was employed at the Japan Steel Pipe (*Nihon kōkan*) shipyard in Tsurumi. Pondering the "ongoing decline in people and things" in the five years of all-out war since the start of the Sino-Japanese conflict in his diary entry for August 21, 1942, Mori wrote of daily unhappiness—of a "feeling of sadness and frustration."[72] Over the course of that month, he worked without missing a day, but he felt weary and departed "for work, as ever, on the fence about whether to go or not" (August 22).[73] "In the community and at work, life in my surroundings is (inevitably) so intense," Mori wrote, "that every so often I have the feeling I'm suffocating." He added, "Drink, travel, the theater: I very often have an urge for spectacular enjoyment. But I don't have the budget for it." (September 1).[74]

When Mori heard news[75] of Japan's defeat in the second battle of the Solomon Islands—an aircraft carrier was seriously damaged and a destroyer sunk—he wrote, "I feel surprised; at the same time I think it's a real shame" (August 27).[76] At his workplace he labored every day in support of the war, unloading pig iron, delivering gas pipes from the warehouse, and taking cement deliveries. On September 2 there was a lecture regarding "planned shipbuilding" in which the audience was urged to "work hard for the sake of winning the war." "They're really right," thought Mori. On the other hand, he felt, "If we work hard without getting status, compensation, a break, or anything else—and all they do is make demands—what's the point?"[77]

In January 1943, Mori was designated a company employee,[78] and his support of the war effort grew more ardent. On February 1, when "the sea battle off the coast of Rennell"[79] was reported as a "military triumph," Mori was joyous.[80] He purchased one Bullet Stamp,[81] thinking, "We too should resolve ourselves to a full wartime life, answering the bravery of the officers and men of the Imperial Armed Forces." "First," he swore, "I'll start by not smoking, and then comes a life of making do." (Mori failed to stop smoking.) On March 2, canned crab was distributed. It was a rare treat, moreover attractively priced, and Mori felt "a bit excessively eager" for it, but he then reconsidered and held back "because everyone wants it."[82] At news of the shooting down of the plane carrying Commander of the Combined Fleet Yamamoto Isoroku on May 21, Mori was astonished, "feeling how extraordinary this fight is." At the same time he declared, "We must decisively destroy England and America." On June 27, he went to his wallet for a twenty-yen war bond. Mori thus sought to support the war with enthusiasm.[83]

Yet from July 1943, when Mussolini fell from power in Italy, a sense of weariness took hold of Mori. "It may be wartime, but I'm fed up, fed up with the company," reads the entry for August 30. When he heard that Italy had surrendered on September 9, he wrote, "There is gloom in my heart. It's detestable, this Badoglio administration that sells out the fatherland. . . . I distract myself from my anger by eating rationed sweets."[84]

In 1944, Mori cut short the New Year's holiday, returning to work on January 2.[85] Heeding the instructions of the company president and the office director to "take no days off," "work two or three times more," and "combine forces and cooperate together harmoniously," he "resolved to hang in there and not miss work this whole year." He was also motivated by the feeling that he would otherwise do the troops in the field a disservice.[86]

Keeping the troops at the front in mind, although he was deeply discontented by galloping inflation and the rapidly worsening shortages of foodstuffs and other daily necessities, Mori sought to help in increasing production, proclaiming, "If we can go on eating, that will be enough in the end." Around the middle of 1944, however, there was a great increase in call-ups of midlevel staff and factory workers. Mori received a draft notice on June 13. Now he himself would be forced to take part in the fighting.[87]

We have seen how people of the generation influenced by imperial democracy supported the war with enthusiasm even as they expressed dissatisfaction regarding its effect on their immediate circumstances. Their attitude was distinguished by a certain broad-mindedness (*kokoro no yoyū*). In comparison, how was it with the younger generation?

A LACQUERWARE MAKER RESPONDS TO LABOR AND MILITARY CONSCRIPTION

Mori Isao (b. 1922) followed in his father's footsteps as a lacquerware maker (*nushiya*) in Furukawa Township in Miyagi Prefecture, in northern Honshū. After graduating from higher elementary school in 1937 he became a lacquerer for the family business, the Mori Lacquerware Shop. As he was acquiring experience in making trays and bowls and lacquer-coating wardrobes, tables, and the edges of *fusuma* (thick-papered sliding doors), hostilities opened with the United States and Britain.

Mori believed in the chastisement of China, the so-called aim of the Sino-Japanese War, but he "did not know whether to be happy or sad" about the progress of the conflict, which seemed likely to compel the sacrifice of the business his grandfather had begun, a business "unconnected with national policy" (*hikokusakuteki*).[88] Apprehensive, he sometimes gave in to the urge to shout "You stupid fools!" (*bakayarō*), but "what instead came out of my mouth was only the frustrating '*banzai!*'—I found this irritating."[89] It was in this context that Mori heard news of the outbreak of the war against the Allies, and in his diary can be found the statements "This has become something dreadful" and "Now that it's come to this, I feel like this is the point of no return as a Japanese."[90]

Yet when the fall of Singapore was reported and a celebration event was held in his town on February 16, 1942, Mori wrote in his diary that he rejected the pessimistic view expressed by a worried friend. "I'm convinced of an inevitable victory. . . . Seeing as we're really achieving these sorts of glorious military gains, to worry about this and that in the future is no more than needless anxiety." Mori had come to believe wholeheartedly in the idea of "The Eight Corners of the World Under One Roof" (*hakkō ichi'u*).[91] When he was classified as a Grade B no. 2 in that year's draft examination and thus unable to become an active-duty soldier, he moreover cried "tears of regret in spite of myself."[92] "Unable to become a soldier, I lack the makings of a youth of today"—a thought that was difficult to bear. In comparison with this disappointment, his concern about the strict discipline to which he would have been subjected in the army barracks was negligible.

Yet for Mori too a military call-up notice suddenly arrived at the end of the year. "It's not [out of] girlishness," he declared, but he realized that the blood had drained from his face, and when he placed his signature and his seal on the document his hand was shaking.[93] After three months of training, he was discharged in April 1943.

Upon his discharge, Mori was ordered to join the reservist's association. When he wore his uniform during branch events, he later recalled having the feeling that he'd become a "man of power," with "the military" behind him and no more fear of police or "bad guys" (*yotakō*), "a perverted feeling that in this

Japan there was nothing to be frightened of."[94] He was prepared for another military call-up, but that November he was startled to receive a labor draft notice instead.[95]

> Based on my normal approach to life I should be truly happy at being drafted, but no matter how much it may be a duty to the nation, when I think of the family business I've inherited from my ancestors, I somehow have a painful sense of impoverishment, and I also can't help feeling a failure. The words "drafted laborer" also have a cold ring to them. . . . I have a certain fear of factories. Maybe my preconceived fear is the influence of a proletarian novel I read once about a gloomy factory struggle. [96]

Mori had managed to prepare himself to welcome a conscription notice, but he resented being drafted for labor service. He was placed at the Nakajima Aircraft Company's Ojima Factory in the town of Ojima, Gunma Prefecture, and put to work glazing the interior and exterior wing frames of Navy aircraft.[97] Assigned to the workplace on January 9, 1944, he reconsidered and remained employed there until the end of the war, thus supporting the war from below, notwithstanding continued occasional discontentment.

CHEERING ON THE HOME FRONT: A RAILROAD EMPLOYEE

Konagaya Saburō, born in Hayakawa Village in Kanagawa Prefecture in 1918, was working as a switch operator (substitute train dispatcher) at Takashima Station in Yokohama City when the war against the United States and Britain began in December 1941. He greeted the news with quiet emotion and a sense of liberation. "The moment we received the news from the station manager, our feelings were instantly released from the sense of idleness we had until yesterday. A feeling of being relaxed as one should be relaxed. At the same time, I can't help being prompted toward an irrepressible new spirit" (December 8, 1941).[98] This sense of relief combined with raised spirits was not something unique to Konagaya but was shared to a considerable degree with the younger generation and intellectuals, who had a strong inferiority complex regarding the West.[99]

Konagaya greeted the fall of Singapore and the surrender of the Netherlands Indies with a sense of wonder; at the same time, he also became obsessed with the following sorts of preoccupations: "To forever busy myself with [train]-coupling as a *yōnin* [one rank below a regular employee] in a train world facing increasing shortages of manpower—as a male subject of the empire, as a young person, this is truly an act of infidelity [to the emperor]" (December 13, 1941). Upon visiting the Meiji Jingū Shrine, "I can't help feeling ashamed of the narrow, selfish existence I've led up to now (January 7, 1942)." In the conscription examination "I was classified a C Grade—it's truly a pity that I can't serve on the front lines. I should be overjoyed at our great war gains, but the greater they are, the smaller I feel" (March 12, 1942).[100]

Konagaya had more than ten brothers and sisters, and he hoped that at least one of them would die in battle and so become a "Yasukuni God"—that at least one would take part in the "holy war." And because he himself desired to step forward and head to the front, when he heard that the station manager had failed to publicize the arrival of an appeal for civilians to work in military employ on the railroads in Malaya, he was indignant—the manager thought only of protecting himself, he wrote, and was averse to having his underlings transferred (March 24, 1942).[101]

Konagaya was just 148 centimeters tall and weighed a mere forty-five kilograms, but he took secret pride in the possession of two physical strength badges, signifying that he had passed the Hayakawa Village Youth Association (*seinendan*) physical strength examination. He was proud, as well, that the station manager recommended him to the fourth squad leader of the Takashima Station Youth Corps[102] third platoon, formed on November 3, 1942. He was moreover deeply moved when promoted to regular employee on April 18, 1943, writing, "I must do my best more and more, must make great efforts."[103]

Yet when a draft notice arrived for his older brother, Konagaya "felt a tumult in my breast that made it impossible to relax" (May 20, 1943). A draft notice for his brother-in-law followed on May 23. With the war thus drawing close to his own family, he wrote, "I must keep all the more steady."[104]

Beginning in the second half of 1943, Konagaya's friends headed to the front one by one. As the only one in his circle who was left behind, he could not suppress his loneliness. When his friend "N" was killed in battle in May 1944, hypotheses and rumors about the manner in which he'd died made the rounds. Konagaya wrote, "It's in any case an honorable death. I'm even envious of his happiness as one who lives in eternal righteousness."[105]

Waiting impatiently to be conscripted, Konagaya thus desperately lent his support to the war on the home front, his inferiority complex providing extra motivation. On June 14, 1944, he was Takashima Station's sole recipient of a "good deed award."[106] Startled by news of the "honorable defeat" at Saipan on

July 18, he decided to make his diary into a "personal testament."[107] These sorrowful lines appeared on the first day following this decision: "Dying while defending transport for the decisive battle—I believe this the highest glory. Even if I do not become a Yasukuni God, my spirit will always protect the imperial land."[108]

This sort of thinking among members of the younger generation—who had barely encountered imperial democracy—represented forceful support for both the system of imperial fascism and the war.

THE SITUATION OF JAPANESE IN THE OCCUPIED AREAS

LIKE A FLASH FLOOD: THE INVASION OF JAPANESE

What was the situation of Japanese in occupied areas of China? Let us consider Beijing, Shijiazhuang, Taiyuan, and Qingdao.

In Beijing, the population of resident Japanese at the end of 1939 was 21,477 men and 13,784 women, for a total of 35,261—an increase of 17,000 over the previous year.[109] Most numerous were company and bank employees and shop clerks, followed by railroad employees, *geisha* (along with prostitutes and barmaids), and public officials, in that order. Nightclubs (including brothels), cafés, restaurants, bars, hotels, and boarding houses were doing the best business, and it was also reported that the private construction industry was making considerable inroads. The number of Koreans had reached 9,969, and Taiwanese 186.

In the city of Shijiazhuang, roughly three hundred kilometers southwest of Beijing, there were no Japanese in residence before the war's outbreak.[110] But in October 1937, in tandem with the invading Japanese army, there was a sudden influx of workers employed by nightclubs, restaurants, inns, cafés, general stores, and the like, with "merchants in the service of the army, geishas, and barmaids at the head of the list." By the end of 1939, their numbers had surpassed ten thousand. Thirty percent of these were Korean, many of whom operated restaurants and general stores, although roughly half were seen as black market traders.[111] As if chasing after them, Japanese big business followed, dealing in such wartime-controlled goods as cotton, wool, and steel.

In Taiyuan too there was a flood of Japanese just after the army invaded in November 1937. The majority had the army as a client—people in service establishments such as nightclubs, cafés, restaurants, and inns, including geishas, barmaids, hostesses, waitresses, and maidservants, were all said to be possessed by a "frivolous front-line-type pleasure-seeking mood." There were more than a few opportunity seekers with dreams of getting rich quick and smugglers who dealt in banned substances such as opium and morphine. As the security situation stabilized, employees and technicians of army-operated factories and the Northern China Transport Company, along with their families, entered in numbers that surpassed those in the service industry. Resident's associations were established, followed by the opening of schools for Japanese, reservists' associations, fire brigades, and branches of the National Defense Women's Association—this is how the foundation of the "development of Japanese nationals" (*hōjin hatten*) was laid. In February 1940, the population of resident Japanese nationals had reached 8,143 Japanese, 1,673 Koreans, and three Taiwanese.

CHINESE RESPONSES

This flash flood of Japanese nationals meant the seizure of factories and institutions; many Chinese lost their jobs and were driven from their homes. As a result, the consular police observed, "it seems there is a trend toward [Chinese] privately harboring relatively ill feelings towards Japanese nationals."

In Qingdao, the state of Chinese sentiments toward Japanese was reported in detail. Here it was said that among Chinese officials in every government office, many nursed dissatisfaction about being "used as message boys, just like robots" for Japanese advisors. Among those working in education, "large numbers [were] seen to be anti-Japanese," with those of high rank particularly critical of Japan. Most factories were bought up by Japanese or semicoercively put under joint management, and controls on raw materials drove those that were not either to scale down or go out of business. Trade fell into such a crisis, because of currency controls, import-export restrictions, interruption of trade with villages, and the advance of Japanese traders, that "speech and behavior regarding Japan [was] not inclined to be mild."

In farming villages, because of drought and war, the harvest was no more than 60 percent of a normal year's. Inflation rose, and people got caught in the disparity between the competing northern puppet government–sponsored *lianyin* (聯銀券) and nationalist-sponsored *fabi* (法幣) currencies, circulated in areas under the control of the Japanese army and anti-Japanese forces respectively. This resulted in "the appearance of deep resentment and even an antiwar trend that blames this distress on Japan's aggressive war against China."[112]

Runaway inflation in staple goods, to between two and four times their prewar prices, was driven by "goods shortages thanks to deteriorating public order in the hinterlands"—there were liberated anti-Japanese districts on the outskirts of many towns—and hoarding by irresponsible traders. "A trend toward strikes and revolt" was observed among workers.

THE WORDS AND ACTIONS OF RESIDENT JAPANESE

These sorts of trends among Japanese residing in China appeared to unsettle the Japanese army. The following text paraphrases observations from *Sources for the Education of Countrymen, Observed from the Words and Actions of Overseas Japanese* (draft manuscript), assembled by the Imperial Headquarters Army Research Squad in May 1940: In China, civil officials and employees of national policy corporations and private enterprises are earning high salaries and many are abandoning themselves to "the pleasures of food and drink"; things are the same among construction contractors and lower-class merchants, and this is generating resentment among the soldiers.[113] In dealing with Chinese people, there are "not a few who act insultingly toward Chinese out of a pointless, misplaced sense of superiority, inviting their resentment." There are those who get a thrill from seeking exorbitant interest rates in doing business with Chinese, and deceiving their customers. There are those who treat all Chinese as coolies. The ill treatment of servants, coolies, and rickshaw drivers is "ubiquitous." There are those who walk away with merchandise after handing over only one-half or one-third of the price asked by Chinese merchants. There are those who get into rickshaws and then do not pay the fare or pay only part of it.[114] The majority of self-employed Japanese "dream of getting rich quick and out of selfishness pursue any means fair or foul."[115] From all parts of Japan come large numbers of sympathy-visit groups and people on inspection tours making "observations for business purposes," moves to gain privileges and the like. Those inspecting the actual front lines are few. There are those who "sing loudly, etc., making an idiotic racket" and "behave as if on a pleasure jaunt."[116]

JAPANESE IN "MANCHUKUO"

The Imperial Headquarters Army Research Squad report continued: "In Manchukuo . . . rivalry and friction between the Japanese and Manchurian races" is extreme, and furthermore, "most of the blame lies with the Japanese side."[117]

Antagonism between officials is caused by "the arbitrary actions of Japanese officials, discrimination in wages as well as contempt toward Manchurian officials."[118] Relations between Japanese policemen and the Chinese people are poor because of a "sense of oppression." During a dispute, for example, they "take inappropriate measures such as twisting a story where Japanese are at fault and [instead] reprimanding and punishing Manchurians, and such things as slapping Manchurians in public are also not uncommon." This is giving rise to antipathy among the people.[119] In factories, there is strong resentment against Japanese employees' "ruling class–type attitude or acts of violence based on contempt" toward Chinese employees. Japanese merchants' political oppression of Chinese merchants and "harsh and rude" attitude toward customers severely injures the feelings of Chinese people.[120]

The colonists represent a threat to Chinese people's control over their lives, and their immigration from Japan has thus provoked a "considerably sharp" reaction among the local population. Because the colonists' education has pumped them with "national pride" as national policy emigrants, they are contemptuous of Chinese people, who face "beatings and assaults that in severe cases extend to killing" and who feel oppressed and persecuted "all the more given that this occurs in group format." On an everyday basis, disputes and violent incidents between colonists and Chinese people "arise out of the lawlessness of many colonists."[121]

The majority of Japanese newcomers to Manchuria come in a "makeshift mood," the report continued, passing the time in a lighthearted frame of mind. People in positions of power such as officials, members of the Concordia Society (*Kyōwakai*),[122] and employees of government-related corporations take the lead in "provoking rivalry and wandering around drunk, exposing the Manchurian people to a shameful sight."[123]

"SHORTCOMINGS IN THE JAPANESE NATIONAL CHARACTER"

The Imperial Headquarters Army Research Squad sought the causes for the situation it thus described above in "shortcomings in the Japanese national character," whose sources it analyzed. Excepting those obviously erroneous or overly specific, they can be paraphrased as follows:

The majority of Japanese that had emigrated to China "entertain the prejudice that" Chinese people are "people who have lost the war, conquered people. . . . They are haughty and hold them in contempt." This idea has been cultivated ever since the [first] Sino-Japanese war (1894–1895); even Japanese children at play shout things like "Chinky-chinks, they're the ones who lose and run away," and "Chiney-Chineys from China lose the fight!" Adults similarly use such expressions as *chankoro ga, chanko ga,* and *chankō* in any public setting.[124]

Newly resident Japanese generally fall into a "sojourner mentality" (*dekasegi konjō*), and since they have no desire to settle permanently, their behavior embodies the adage "travelers know no shame." Given their narrow-mindedness and exclusivity, Japanese as a rule prefer not to live or work together, and they sink into loneliness. Most merchants have no capital or managerial abilities, and because they don't cooperate with one another, they're unable to compete with Chinese merchants, who endure a frugal existence, cooperate with one another, and possess a wealth of managerial genius. In their powerlessness they dream of getting rich quick, taking "illegal and improper measures of desperation."[125]

In conclusion, the Research Squad saw the problem as "having an inseparable relation to the character of Japanese from the homeland and their attitude toward the holy war."[126]

Although it had reached the disturbing conclusion that Japanese did not correctly understand the "aims of the holy war" and that emigrant Japanese were "essentially lower-class people of inferior character," the Imperial Headquarters Army Research Squad did not follow up on its investigation.[127] Even the unit itself—which did claim to "understand correctly" the "aims of the holy war"—considered the Chinese as "people of a defeated nation" (*haisen kokumin*), and since they accordingly believed that the "culturally superior" Japanese should stand above the Chinese and "cooperate" with them "from a leader's position," their outlook was ultimately not much different from that of the uncomprehending emigrants.[128] It was in this context that the Asia-Pacific War[129] began, and even larger numbers of Japanese flooded into China.

DEPARTING FOR AND JOURNEYING TO THE FRONT IN THE ASIA-PACIFIC WAR

A SAILOR'S DEPARTURE FOR THE FRONT

Nonomura Taizō, a stoker (機関兵) from Shiratori Township in Gifu Prefecture, boarded the SS *Nippon-maru* and departed the Kurile Islands on November 26,

1941, to make the sortie for the surprise attack on Pearl Harbor. The day before, he wrote the following in his diary:

> Although I rest well, when I remember this is my last night, I somehow think of my mother and father back home. My deceased parents and my brothers, sisters, and near relatives. In the hammock, I think of my wife, and when I ponder my daughter Kazue's future—I don't begrudge my own death, but when I think of Kazue's future a gloomy feeling comes over me. No, no this will not do. My body has already been set aside for the sake of the emperor, for the sake of the Empire. Is this any time for reluctance? . . . Kazue, when your father has gone, heed what your mother says, live big and bright. I'll always be watching over you.[130]

It is a diary that vividly conveys the feelings of a soldier on his way to die, who casts aside irrepressible thoughts of his kin by thinking "for the sake of the emperor." In the end, Nonomura returned from the Hawaii campaign unscathed. But he would meet death in the battle of the Philippine Straits in November 1944.

In a letter home from the battle lines in the South Pacific (date unknown), Nonomura wrote, "No matter what, we must gain victory in the Greater East Asia War. So that our children, grandchildren, and succeeding generations can be happy—we sacrifice ourselves to construct that peace." In heartbreaking fashion, he laments, "When I see the far-off moon, I recall my child Kazue, busying herself in the garden."[131]

Yet as earlier seen in China, during the early stage of the Asia-Pacific War, it cannot be denied that among soldiers' acknowledged incentives for going off to fight, issues of national "profit" and personal "profit" were persistently tied together. For Nonomura, profit of the exclusivist racial variety—"so that our children, grandchildren, and succeeding generations can be happy"—was a part of the bargain. Let us now examine several other cases.

A PRIVATE'S DEPARTURE FOR BATTLE IN THE PHILIPPINES

Tsubokura Junji, who was drafted on October 3, 1941, joined the Fukuchiyama Regiment and was assigned to the 20th Infantry Regiment, 3rd Battalion, 10th Company. He would join the attack on Ramon Bay in Luzon in the Philippines in December 1941.[132]

Born in Yasaka Village in Kyoto Prefecture, Tsubokura assisted with farming tasks after graduating higher elementary school. While on active duty as an enlistee in the late 1930s he fell ill and was relieved from military service, after which—alongside farm work in his native village—he was employed as an instructor at a youth school (*seinen gakkō*).[133] Upon receiving his draft notice in September 1941 he was so happy, he wrote, that he unthinkingly shouted "Terrific!" to himself. Conscription meant relief from a difficult situation: His compensation for being relieved from military duty was an annual salary of only forty yen plus a year-end bonus of seven yen, for which he was obliged to work two hundred days annually at the youth school. The "unendurable pain" of doing farm work alongside this service made him feel trapped.[134] Further-more, his farming family was extremely poor despite plowing a sizable amount of arable land.[135] He wrote, "If I'm enlisted the family's economic situation will be much the better for it, even though the daily salary of a Private First Class might only be twenty-one *sen* [0.21 yen]." Surveying the field of battle upon arrival, he wrote, "If I recall how things were when I was in the village . . . this is far more pleasant."[136]

THE CASE OF A GUARD SOLDIER IN THE PHILIPPINES

After his squad leader and four other comrades in arms were killed fighting guerillas in the final stages of the war, Itō Seiichi, an army sergeant from Toyo-hashi City in Aichi Prefecture who served at the Tarlak garrison on Luzon, de-scribed his feelings in a chronicle addressed to his wife.[137]

> The [Filipino] natives, I don't even want to see the faces of the natives. I [now] have a feeling of revulsion toward they to whom I felt so close until yesterday, whom I even dearly loved. . . . But it's true this consciousness was already grad-ually weakening. What's the lesson of this reality? In the China Incident, the Japanese have killed many Chinese, and yes, innocent people. How do the Chi-nese, in whose [veins] flows the same blood, feel about this reality? The children, younger brothers, and wives whose fathers, older brothers, and husbands have been killed: How could they not hold a grudge against the Japanese? [Yet] the Japanese have continued to fight for righteousness. Moreover this has brought sacrifices. Many Philippine Island natives have also probably lost their lives on the Philippine front. Doesn't this matter to the natives? [138]

Capable of putting himself in the shoes of the Philippine people, Itō still did not go so far as to entertain doubts about Japan's war. This was because he was possessed with the idea that "Japan, as Asia's leader, must bring them political and economic stability and happiness," and moreover because he had served on the battlefront, "making me keenly aware of the weightiness of the mission that Japan and the Japanese bear in the East."[139] While Japanese were talking of saving Asians, however, in reality they were killing them. To overcome this contradiction, the only strategy that Itō could think of was to acquaint all Japanese with "a sense of atonement" and "a truly blood-sacrificing love dedicated to [Filipinos]" in the manner of Jesus Christ. "Being here, I feel as if I well understand how Christ felt on the cross. To make up for the sins of the [Filipino] people who have killed the lord's martyrs [the Japanese], the Christian spirit of sacrificing one's own life is surely the last and the only thing that shall sublate[140] the Japanese spirit."[141] Ensnared by the cause of constructing a "New Order in Greater East Asia" while sincerely desiring to interact with the Philippine people: Itō's remarks exemplify a heartrending mental cul-de-sac.

LETTERS OF SOLDIERS FROM YAMAGATA PREFECTURE

Where soldiers from farming villages were concerned, the tougher life on the home front became, the more complex their emotions upon departure for the front. Nakagawa Shizuo—a peasant draftee from Takahana Township in Yamagata Prefecture—was sent to Manchuria in June 1943, leaving his wife and one-year-old son behind. He promised to send his wife pressed Manchurian flowers and wrote her in anticipation of their reunion.

> I think the army is a really good place to be. There are plenty of treats—Glico candy, Glico Balls, Kachidoki,[142] rice cakes (*mochi*), etc. Yesterday I bought some and made some visits at the hospital, but owing to circumstances I brought it back with me. I treated a barrack soldier to it, he was happy. . . . Yesterday liquor was distributed for the first time in a while, and for the first time in a while I got drunk and was apparently even singing songs. But it seems like I've gotten able to drink more and more liquor. This is only encouraging.[143]

Nakagawa was hardly the only soldier to be impressed at the sight of a variety of sweets and liquor rarely to be found anymore in farming villages. He proved an excellent noncommissioned officer in battle and was decorated with a Golden Kite medal.[144]

Kamakami Han'ichi, a peasant from Nakayama Township in Yamagata Prefecture, left behind a pregnant wife when he was called up. In June 1944, he wrote letters to her from Yokosuka in which he expressed his worries about the upcoming autumn harvest, the impending birth of their child, and the battle area where he'd be heading. Among them appears the following passage:

> You know yesterday was the great festival at the Yasukuni Shrine. I was the company's representative, and I took the train to Tokyo and visited Yasukuni Shrine and the Imperial Palace. Afterward I did some sightseeing in Tokyo and returned to my Yokosuka company at seven thirty. I'm entirely blessed (*mattaku kōfuku desu*). It's much better than life at home, and there's no excuse for it whatsoever. The day before yesterday they also handed out winter clothes; they're brand-new wool and warm, and I was thinking about coming home on leave wearing them.[145]

Sightseeing in Tokyo while sporting new woolen attire in the autumn of 1944, as the war situation was deteriorating—this would have been mind boggling even for someone who wasn't a poor peasant. Military censorship and a desire to avoid worrying his family no doubt played a part in how Kamakami chose to portray things, but we would seem obliged to acknowledge the sincerity in his declaration "I'm entirely blessed."

Many soldiers found military service better than they expected; if we assume this reaction represented support for the war at a profound level and then add to this a sense of mission of the sort evidenced in the following excerpt, a soldier's perspective on the war grew into something unshakable. Suppressing the desire to see his infant first-born son, his wife, and his parents, Saitō Yoichi, a noncommissioned officer from a Yamagata peasant family, sent his wife a letter from Manchuria:

> More than you think, I can't wait for that day [when I'm discharged]. A warrior who says effeminate things might be laughed at. But I suppose this is the human nature of a husband, and between a father and son. I think everyone has these instincts. Casting these away and consecrating everything to the emperor without reluctance—that is the nobility of the Japanese, who lives on the path of loyalty.[146]

A CIVILIAN IN MILITARY EMPLOY

Abe Yūgo,[147] who volunteered as an army administrator, with the status of civilian in military employ (*gunzoku*), and journeyed to the Philippines in April 1942, wrote the following to his wife: "Thus I've come out to the front lines, and the part I'm directly playing in the middle of the Greater East Asia War is a small one, but it's the highest of honors that I've been able to take part, and we can also say that my accompanying the army has served a purpose."[148] Abe was straightforward about being proud of taking part in the war as "the highest of honors." Two years later, in April 1944, he wrote his wife about promotions, pensions, and medals.

> Thanks to my having accompanied the army, by around this month there should also be a pension included. And come August or September, I should be able to get a medal. Whether I'll be here that long I don't know, but at the end of September, if things go well, it's not impossible I'll get a pay raise. If that happens it'll be like *Obon*[149] and New Year's all at once, but as you might imagine it would be even better if the day of my dreams[150] were close at hand. The people here from Tokyo seem to be worried about things; the homes they left behind are being evacuated to the countryside. Even on that score I don't have anything to worry about, and as far as going along with the army, there couldn't have been a better time.[151]

None of these aspirations were realized; in July 1944, Abe was killed in battle.

A COLONIST GOES ABROAD

As the bombing of Japan by the U.S. Air Force continued in 1945, Yamazaki Seiji, who had emigrated to join the Shūshin colonists' association (*kaitaku-dan*) of Keshan Prefecture in northern "Manchukuo," sent a letter to his sons in his hometown of Shiratorichō in Gifu Prefecture on May 29.

> If Masa'aki, Kameo, and Yoshiharu all grow up to be big peasants, they should come [to Manchuria]. The land is wide, and anything is possible. The sun rises from the plain and sets in the plain, and the days are truly long. . . . As far as food, there are countless things I can raise myself, and I get a high price if I sell them. This year each house has three *cho* [roughly 7.5 acres] planted. Next year it'll be four *cho*. You can raise pigs or chickens—there are any number of occupations. Whatever you do, you can do it big. If you feel like coming over, I'll come [to Japan] and fetch you after the autumn.[152]

The letter evokes Yamazaki's excitement at receiving a large amount of arable land and becoming a "big peasant," enabled to pursue a variety of worthwhile occupations. Like many other colonists, he did not consider whose arable land it might have been and whether Japanese might have stolen it from Chinese.

That various places in Japan were being reduced to ashes and that defeat was approaching in the battle of Okinawa, he had not the slightest idea. As Japan was being driven into a corner, Yamazaki was still cooperating in the war effort. Thus did the Asia-Pacific War evolve, swallowing up dreams such as these as it went.

RANKING THE PEOPLE

LESS THAN AN ARMY PIGEON

Following the establishment of the structure of imperial fascism, the Japanese people's consciousness of rank grew extremely intense. Hamano Kenzaburō was on Luzon as a contracted employee of the Philippine expeditionary army's Department of Information. On April 6, 1945, he wrote the following in connection with a struggle over sweet potatoes that occurred between Takunan students (students of the *Takunan juku*, a school established in the name of Southeast Asian "development") and soldiers:

> For them [soldiers], even if they're only a private second class, they're still a soldier. The *trusted retainers* of the emperor. The class called *gunzoku* (civilian employees of the military) who've come over here are as wretched as any. Privates second class—military horses—military dogs—military pigeons—*gunzoku* . . . : in sum, our existence has become less than that of a pigeon. What's more, even among *gunzoku*, Takunan students are the lowest-ranked employees. So even if they're in the right, they could never win against Tsukihara, an active-duty lance corporal.[153]

Discrimination, the making of hierarchies, and mobilization involving Japanese or people considered to be "Japanese" in areas under Japanese control (Japanese subjects) was truly harsh. In concert with the establishment of the Imperial Rule Assistance Association in Tokyo in October 1940, the system of imperial fascism sought to mobilize as many people as possible throughout the empire, as first illustrated by the formation of the National Korean Mobilization League (*Kokumin sōryoku chōsen renmei*) in Korea, followed by the Imperial Subjects Service Association (*Kōmin hōkōkai*) in Taiwan, the National Service Association (*Kokumin hōkōkai*) in southern Sakhalin, and the Micronesian Imperial Rule Assistance Association (*Nanyō guntō taisei yokusankai*).

PEOPLE OF OKINAWA PREFECTURE

NAME-CHANGING

Japanese rank-consciousness was bluntly expressed in policies of assimilation (*dōka*) and imperialization (*kōminka*), along with the denial of the cultural specificity of every area outside the "Japanese mainland."[154] In February 1937 the Okinawa Education Association's "Committee to Investigate the Revision of Surname Pronunciation" (*Sei no koshō kaisei i'inkai*) announced a list of eighty-four "names whose readings should be altered," thus initiating the Movement for Name Revision (*kaisei undō*).[155] This evolved out of a movement begun by the Okinawa Prefecture educator Shimabukuro Gen'ichirō in the 1920s that sought to spare Okinawans from discrimination and from being perceived as a different ethnic group by mainland Japanese because they had names peculiar to the island.[156] According to the list of "names whose readings should be altered," this movement sought, for example, to change the reading of *agarijō* (東門) to *higashikado, aragusuku* (安良城) to *araki*, and *gushichan* (具志頭) to *gushikami*.[157]

As for changes in written names, the following method of circumventing the family registration law (*kosekihō*) was proposed. In the Edō period (1603–1868), in order to show off to the shōgun the fact that it ruled a "foreign land," the Shimazu (Satsuma) domain in neighboring Kyūshū had forbidden Okinawans to bear "Yamato-style family names," forcing the changing of the standard Japanese 船越 (Funakoshi), for example, to the nonstandard 富名腰, and 下田 (Shimoda) to 志茂田.[158] It was thus advocated that Okinawan names be changed under the rationale of restoring them "back" to the original (復姓, *fukusei*). The changing of characteristic Okinawan female names such as *kamii* and *ushii* was also proposed.[159]

This movement progressed during the Sino-Japanese War. In Okinawa it had formerly been customary to change one's surname each time one was bestowed new land. Since surname changes were approved for those genealogically verified, "Yamato-style surname restorations" of the above sort were also approved through a special dispensation from the prefectural authorities. With the adoption of "the aim of changing all names" peculiar to Okinawa, changes in as many as three thousand names were estimated.[160] In the context of the Asia-Pacific War in 1942, requests for name restoration and name changes—

until then decided by the governor—were simplified and instead put under the discretion of assistants to heads of local offices.[161]

This policy of assimilation, which denied Okinawa's culture, was also promoted as the Dialect Extermination Movement (*hōgen bokumetsu undō*). In 1938, Okinawa Prefecture Social Education Director Yoshida Tsugunobu published an "Outline for the Promotion of Standard Japanese Language."[162] This policy was approved by the Committee for Total National Spiritual Mobilization, and thus began the Dialect Extermination Movement. In 1939, Okinawa Prefecture decided upon an "Outline for a Prefectural Subjects' Movement to Enforce Standard Japanese," calling for "thorough enforcement among students, children, and young men and women" and "penetration into family life." Posters were put up that read "Crystal-Clear Standard Japanese All the Time" and "Standard Japanese for the Whole Family." In elementary and middle schools, Standard Japanese encouragement associations were established, with committee members (teachers) and "officials" (students). Enforcement of the affixing of "dialect badges" as punishment for children who spoke in dialect was also strengthened.

Yanagi Muneyoshi visited Okinawa at the invitation of the Prefectural Department of School Affairs in January 1940. He criticized the department's excessive pursuit of dialect suppression, arguing that unless those of other prefectures respected Okinawa's distinctive culture—and unless Okinawans themselves took pride in it—it would not be possible to conquer discrimination.

> I am not against the use of standard Japanese, but we must not neglect the language of the Ryūkyūs for this reason. I have traveled widely and know from what I've seen that there is no place where standard Japanese is spoken with such proficiency as in this prefecture. In [other] places [in Japan] like Aomori and Iwate, teachers and students are using the local language. In sum, we mustn't get so carried away encouraging standard Japanese that we adopt an ethos of neglecting local languages.[163]

In response to Yanagi's critique, the Okinawa Prefecture Department of School Affairs offered the following counterargument on January 8, 1940:

> Hailing the profoundly significant 2,600-year anniversary of the Imperial Era, we cannot but respectfully support this historic, divine undertaking, decisively executing reforms and improvements truly embracing all aspects of the life of

prefectural subjects united as one.[164] Above all the strict enforcement of standard Japanese is now at a point that it is steadily reaping results as a great prefectural subjects' movement involving the entire prefecture. . . . It was only five or six years ago that newly arrived children were instructed in mixed local dialect, but now from the moment they enter school, even in isolated islands and places however remote, standard Japanese instructors are elevating their educational efficiency. [We now see] old country folks who answer in clear standard Japanese even when you ask directions to your travel destination; the lucid, fully confident manner in which young men and women reply; the recent crowds of emigrants working away from home [on the mainland], who send news of gratitude at being saved from derision and discriminatory treatment thanks to the encouragement of standard Japanese; powerful letters of thanks and encouragement regarding this movement from newly recruited soldiers! [And there are] the views of the military authorities, wherein opinions voiced on common defects among soldiers from the prefecture are suddenly turning in a favorable direction! Here we feel an unlimited sense of reassurance, as if we have been provided a signpost as to the basis of this prefecture's advancement.[165]

At the root of the problem was discrimination against Okinawans by narrow-minded "mainland" Japanese, who could not acknowledge cultural diversity and rejected different ways of life. While the prefecture's stated objective was to pursue cultural unification in order to conquer this discrimination, its efforts were colored by the government and military policy of assimilation (*dōka seisaku*), which aimed to turn Okinawans into "imperial subjects" (*kōminka*) and thus produce more "loyal" (*chūryōna*) soldiers.

On this point, Baron Ie Chōjo, a nobleman from Okinawa, stated, "At a time when Japan must gird itself up to rule as leader of East Asia (*tōa no meishu*) with the 2,600-year anniversary of the Imperial Era as its moment and with Okinawa shouldering responsibility as our southern lifeline, it must be deemed exceedingly natural that we reform its customs and embark upon eliminating its local dialect" (January 29).[166] Responding to Yanagi, who had told him, "I don't think there is any harm in the proper use of both standard Japanese and local dialect," Okinawa's governor Fuchigami Fusatarō too advocated the abolition of dialect to support the assimilation policy, stating, "On the contrary, seeing the situation in this prefecture as the same as that in other prefectures doesn't work. In this prefecture, things are such that at the time of the Sino-Japanese War [1894–1895], there were people who wanted to side with China."[167]

How did the people of the prefecture react to this debate? More than a few agreed with Yanagi's propositions, but many voices were also raised in opposition. Matsuo Kiyoto, for example, who had once been in the Kurume Cavalry, supported the prefectural policy from the standpoint that standard Japanese was needed for military duties. He wrote, "[Before] we were made to repeat things dozens of times because [people from this prefecture] could not speak proper standard Japanese; even now I can't help recalling vivid memories of these scenes of strenuous effort. In the cavalry we served as messengers, so standard Japanese was particularly necessary" (January 25).[168] In a text under the heading "To the Eminent Gentlemen" (*erai katagata e*), a woman named Ōgimi Umeko offered a refracted critique of Yanagi: "It's fine if the baby's kimono gets respect,[169] but taking [the baby's] hand so that it quickly learns to walk, and giving it a scolding—these are the things we appreciate the most" (January 31).[170]

THE STRUGGLES OF SOLDIERS FROM OKINAWA

As exemplified in the Movements for Name Revision and Dialect Extermination, the Movement for Total National Spiritual Mobilization in Okinawa was stricter than in other areas and prefectures, and policies of assimilation and imperial-subject-making were pursued to a degree not seen elsewhere. What was the effect of these policies in Okinawa?

Maehara Nobuo from Tomigusuku Village on Okinawa's main island joined the Third Company of the Kumamoto Western 16th Unit as an active-duty soldier in December 1940 and was dispatched to Yongji Prefecture in China's Shanxi Province.[171] He took part in numerous battles in northern China, central China, southern China, French Indochina, and Thailand and witnessed many atrocities.[172] While he was in Bangkok in early August 1945, news of the ghastly battle of Okinawa was passed along by Allied prisoners of war, putting soldiers from the island on tenterhooks.

> Among the soldiers from Okinawa there are men anxious about the well-being of loved ones, and they go on half-crazed rampages, seeking to shoot their superior officers, drawing their swords and shouting and the like; I had trouble quieting them. In fact everyone from Okinawa is feeling similarly uneasy. So when they screamed, "What's to become of Okinawa!" and "Send us back to Okinawa right away!" one of the things I thought was: it's good of you to say that for us.[173]

Amid ongoing discrimination, Okinawan soldiers' discontent exploded at their people being driven into a merciless war and at the fact that Okinawa itself would now be offered up in battle. Tomishima Yoshimatsu,[174] who joined the Aircraft Maintenance Unit at Kumamoto on March 1, 1942, serviced aircraft in Manchuria and northern China as a member of the 207th Airfield Construction Unit (later the 301st Unit).[175] Assigned to a maintenance unit for suicide squads (*tokkōtai*) from the end of 1944, Tomishima was in Daegu, Korea, when Japan surrendered; he was repatriated to Kumamoto in October 1945. Hearing that Okinawa had met with annihilation (*gyokusai*) and that it would be better not to go back, he stayed on in Kumamoto for a while. In December 1946 he returned home, landing at a Naha City in ruins. He was struck powerfully by the feeling that "in this war it's Okinawa that got it." He learned from a cousin that his father, wife, son, younger sister, elder brother's wife, and five nephews and nieces had died in the fighting and that his daughter had died of measles; of his close family members who had remained on Okinawa only his mother was still alive. His older brother had been drafted and taken prisoner in Taiwan—the ones who had gone to the front were the ones who had survived.[176]

Kiyan Kyū-ei[177] was drafted before the battle of Okinawa. When he returned from being mustered up, as ward headman he was ordered by the Ishi and Take units[178] stationed in his village to deliver items such as pigs, potatoes, vegetables, bamboo, and rope "in a manner of treatment amounting to coercion." Once he was punched in the nose by a soldier extorting deliveries.[179] In 1944, Kiyan's oldest son was dragged by a Japanese army truck and broke a bone. The family was repeatedly thrown out of the village air-raid shelter by the Japanese army, and his third son was injured in the naval bombardment after being chased out. His father was hit in the leg and died after suffering shock during the retreat. While searching for the air-raid shelter in the middle of the night, Kiyan stumbled into a military kitchen, was taken for a spy, and nearly killed. He also witnessed other residents shot and killed as suspected spies.[180] He described his thoughts at the time: "Combat is a thing where you never know who's going to do the killing, it's like that. There's no such thing as soldiers from your own country or enemy soldiers, you know. You kill your own refugees because they're suspicious! That's war."[181] In the Japanese army's failure to protect the population, Kiyan recognized this ultimate aspect of war. He was eventually discovered by American soldiers and taken prisoner.

Matsukawa Masayoshi, a substitute teacher at a youth school (*seinen gakkō*) from Ginowan Village on Okinawa's main island,[182] took his physical examination for the draft and joined the 13th Independent Infantry Battalion in 1944. Shortly thereafter the battle of Okinawa began, and he was assigned to the machine gun corps, joining the fighting at the Kakazu front. There were only two machine guns per platoon and "no opportunity to fire" given the danger involved; the American army showered anyone who shot at them with concentrated mortar fire.[183] Matsukawa and his comrades dug foxholes in which they hid, risking their lives hurling jerry-built grenades when tanks approached, but this strategy turned fruitless when American infantry and tanks began to advance together. On April 19, 1945, part of Matsukawa's right upper thigh was blown off by a mortar as he headed for his foxhole.[184] Afterward he was repeatedly shuttled between the army's field hospital and nearby caves. One day, he heard a story about severely wounded soldiers being poisoned to death when the Haebaru Army Hospital withdrew, and he wrote: "After that, we were all full of resentment. 'Over there [at the hospital] they killed them, but we're just left to ourselves. . . . This is unacceptable, why doesn't the hospital director do us the favor of killing us?' we asked. It was frustrating because we wanted to be poisoned to death. . . . As a result we even felt hatred toward that branch hospital director."[185] "Rather than regrettably leaving an Imperial Army soldier to the enemy," he thought, he'd reached the point that he would rather be dead. In the middle of June, Matsukawa was abandoned in a cave, and he was in and out of consciousness, on the verge of death, when he was discovered by the U.S. Army.

Ōshiro Eizen from Kitanakagusuku Village on Okinawa's main island took part in the battle of Okinawa at age nineteen, having taken the conscription physical two years earlier. He joined the 15th Battalion of the Ishi Unit in February 1945 and was wounded in the leg and the back of the head in the battle of Urazoe Village.[186] He then withdrew. Along the way he took custody of a five- or six-year-old boy, the only surviving male member of a household that had been wiped out. Because the child continued to cry for his father, Ōshiro was ordered by Lance Corporal "T," who was wounded and unable to move, to kill him. When Ōshiro pretended not to be able to hear him, "T" instead gave the order to a medical orderly from another prefecture and had him killed. Ōshiro found this "atrocious," but there was nothing he could do.[187] The lance corporal subsequently chased an elderly man and woman out of a cave.

Afterward, the cave was destroyed by a U.S. tank gun. Standing at the entrance, the medical orderly was killed, but Lance Corporal "T" miraculously survived. Ōshiro was unhurt. In consultation, in dialect, with several women from Itoman who were also on the scene, he decided to make a run for it. As he fled from the coast he was spotted by an American soldier, and he searched for the hand grenade he thought he had, reluctantly seeking to kill himself. It seemed he had lost it somewhere along the way, however—it was nowhere on him. Thinking "whatever happens, happens," he lay face up and closed his eyes, but the American soldier led him away and attended to his wounds. At this he thought to himself for the first time, "My goodness, how kind they are."[188]

THE AINU

ASSIMILATION POLICIES TOWARD THE AINU

From the Meiji period onward, the Ainu people of Hokkaidō had their land and their hunting and fishing rights stolen from them. They were also forced to abandon their traditional culture, including tattoos and earrings. The family register reform (*Koseki hensei*) of 1873 (Meiji 6) obliged them to take Japanese surnames, and according to the Law for the Guardianship of Hokkaidō Former Natives (*Hokkaidō kyūdojin hogo hō*) of 1899, their status was made that of "former natives."[189] At first, the coercion of Japanese names did not always extend to given names. As late as 1900, for example, two Ainu active-duty soldiers with the names "Oyamada Inaoanreki" and "Nakagawa Katsukoresai" were "petitioning" to change their names to the Japanese "Hiko'ichi" and "Katsutarō."[190]

Where military service was concerned, the same draft regulations were applied to the Ainu as to the Japanese of mainland origin (*wajin*) of Hokkaidō,[191] and the first recruitment of Ainu took place in 1898. In the Russo-Japanese War (1904–1905), sixty-three Ainu were deployed to the front; eight died in battle or of diseases contracted at the front, and three were decorated with the Golden Kite medal.[192]

The education of Ainu children was carried out in "former native elementary schools," "former native's classes," and the like, established under the Rules for Former Native Children's Education of 1901. There were periods in which the minimum attendance on Hokkaidō was a mere four years and periods in which children began school at age seven, with half-day classes. The use of Japanese was standardized; Ainu language, history, and culture were the objects of scorn. In the early 1930s textbook *Ordinary Elementary School National History*, for example, there was a description of the "subjugation of the Ezo"[193] by Yamato Takeru and Saka'no'ueno Tamuramaro, and the fifth-grade *Ordinary Elementary School Japanese Reader* included a description of Princess Ototachibana.[194] At the time it was assumed that the "Ezo" were the Ainu, and Ainu children were subjected to lessons in which they were scolded as descendants of "traitors" who had not submitted to the emperor's rule.[195] When "former native elementary schools" were abolished and integrated with schools for ethnic Japanese (*wajin*) in 1937, Ainu children became subject to open discrimination from *wajin* teachers and students.

Discriminatory attitudes consequently spread among the Ainu themselves, who in turn scorned Koreans. According to the bitter childhood memories of Washiya Sato, "While we were despised as 'Ainu! Ainu!' on occasion I also saw these same Ainu make fun of Koreans as *senjin* or *hantōjin* [lit. 'people of the peninsula']."[196]

THE AINU SOLDIERS' WAR

As the Ainu were thus coerced into an assimilation that denied them equal rights and acknowledgment of their distinctive culture, they were meanwhile mobilized for a war that their neighbors the *shisamu* [mainland Japanese, lit. "neighboring people"] had started in their own interest.

Teshi Toyiji, an Ainu born in the town of Teshikaga in 1923, was drafted and joined the Asahikawa 7th Division on February 8, 1944. He was sent to Dong'an in Manchuria a week later.[197] Teshi had been attending the Kutcharo Former Native Elementary School. When this was incorporated into a Japanese (*wajin*) elementary school in 1937, Teshi felt the pain of discrimination as Japanese children in his new school taunted, "Hey, there's a dog here."[198] Teshi withdrew from the first year of the higher elementary school curriculum because of family circumstances. After working some time at the post office, he was wandering Hokkaidō as a woodcutter when he turned twenty and underwent the conscription examination.

Teshi went through basic training in Dong'an and was made a private first class in a selection conducted after six months, subsequently receiving training as a communications soldier. His unit (Yama 3476) was incorporated into the 32nd Army, and he was dispatched to the main island of Okinawa in August 1944.[199] Here he became an orderly for the First Battalion commander.

From January 1945 onward, Teshi departed daily from the Yoza and Nakaza Headquarters in the southern part of Okinawa's main island, heading for the military emplacements. After the American army landed, he became a runner (*denrei*) for the battalion headquarters and participated in the Battle of Shuri. In the unit's full-scale offensive that began on May 4, the battalion commander was killed.[200] Teshi wrote of how once, when he was a first-year soldier and it was his turn for cleanup duty, he said he'd prefer to clean up with warm water as the weather was extremely cold. "What should we do with such a slack spirit?" a superior scolded him. "You've been an insolent one ever since you joined the Kwantung Army!"[201] He was beaten so viciously that his face swelled up. While serving as a foot messenger during the battle of Okinawa, he performed a variety of memorable deeds: bringing in for treatment a badly wounded child of around ten years old who was clinging to his dead mother, caring for an infant that was crying beside its dead mother before entrusting it to two women escaping to the south, and convincing a group of nurses who were intending to commit group suicide not to go through with it. As the final battle approached between June 10 and 19, he says he returned the bodies of thirteen members of the defense units whose hometown was near the caves they occupied to their homes on his own authority, treating them as war dead.[202]

There was a deep connection between this sort of behavior and the Ainu culture that Teshi embodied. He behaved very spontaneously and felt close with Okinawans, having been raised in an Ainu society where "the sense of cooperation [was] strong"[203] and where it was natural to treat all people equally. In such things as the tattoos worn by elderly women he also discovered a culture similar to that of the Ainu. In an emperor's army in which the abnormal had become normal, however, his spontaneous behavior stood out.

In the decisive battle that began on June 13, Teshi's unit was annihilated. A friend from Teshikaga had his upper thigh blown off by a mortar and was quickly put out of his misery with poison. "Taught nothing other than how to die,"[204] Teshi wandered in the mountains. Discovered by an African American soldier in October, he finally surrendered two months after the war's end.

THE UILTA AND CHAMORRO PEOPLES

THE UILTA

Dahinieni Gendanu, a member of the Uilta minority group, was born in 1926 in Sachi on the outskirts of Shiska (Poronaysk) in southern Sakhalin (Minami Karafuto). He received a call-up notice from the Shiska army secret service organ[205] in August 1942.[206] The minorities of southern Sakhalin went through a period of "Japanese-Russian cohabitation," becoming "Russians," subsequently "Japanese," and then "Soviets" after Japan's defeat, their extremely unstable position at the mercy of the "Great Powers."[207] In 1905, when southern Sakhalin became Japanese territory, the Japanese government did not assign family registers to local minorities. The Sakhalin Native Population Regulation,[208] the Native Population Report Regulation,[209] and Matters Regarding the Execution of the Law of Nationality and Four Other Issues[210] were applied to the island's minorities.[211] Because the Uilta, Nivkh, and others were not assigned family registers, although they held Japanese nationality in a broad sense, they were made registerless "Japanese." Again, "native education centers" were constructed for the Sakhalin Ainu in 1909, but the establishment of these for other minorities lagged behind. The establishment of the "Shiska Native Education Center," combined for use by minorities other than the Ainu who had been forced to move to Otasu, came much later in 1930. The Uilta, Nivkh, and others were treated as "natives" (*dojin*), a level lower than the Ainu.

When he turned nine in 1934, Gendanu started attending the Shiska Native Education Center. Its classes combined the first through sixth grades. Gendanu realized for the first time that his name was being changed to "Kitagawa Gentarō" (北川源太郎) after he was made to write it many times over in *katakana*.[212] Around 1930, the Native Affairs Office Shiska Branch had assembled a Native Name Registry to keep tabs on the local inhabitants, in the process changing their names to Japanese ones. The Shiska Native Education Center took "the cultivation of national sentiment" (*kokuminteki jōsō no kanyō*) as its primary objective. Gendanu commuted to the center every day, learning Japanese and taking pleasure in his contact with Japanese people.[213] He enjoyed his classes in morals (*shūshin*), and when he heard that the emperor was "the most exalted of gods in all the world," he felt "glad to be living in the land of the gods." He was furthermore "inexplicably deeply moved" at stories of Japan's victories in the First Sino-Japanese and Russo-Japanese wars and "at soldiers' heroic stories of punishing China, which is now giving offense to the emperor of Japan."[214] Instruction to make "natives" into imperial subjects (*kōminka kyōiku*) was also carried out at the Native Education Center. Thus, says Gendanu, did he learn to dislike shopping in town with his mother, Anna, who wore Uilta clothing, and in time he developed an unbearable feeling of fear and self-loathing.[215]

After he graduated from the Native Education Center in 1940, Gendanu was hired by the Shiska Government Branch Office and became a ticket puncher (later ship's captain) on the steamship connecting Shiska and Otasu. When he received a draft notice in August 1942, he says, "I ran about blindly with the postcard in my hand in an excess of joy" at becoming a Japanese soldier.[216]

Having been hunting societies for many centuries, the northern minorities excelled in marksmanship and hiking the tundra. As spies for the secret war against the Soviet Union, they became guerilla soldiers (*yūgeki senshi*) trained in both basic military skills and in intelligence and espionage by graduates of the Army's Nakano School.[217] The Imperial Instructions for Soldiers[218] and the Code of Battle[219] were beaten into them, and they were told, "Come on, don't let the Takasago race[220] outdo you in the Southern Regions, fight as secret warriors on the northern front!" After four months they were "discharged," but in June 1943 they were once again "called up" and assigned to Yokunai on the western coast of Sakhalin.[221] Gendanu's mission was to gather information as a spy. During this period he heard a report of the death in combat of a fellow trainee named Washka but was also told minority casualties were treated as if they had died not in battle but of illness.[222] The group was dissolved in November but once again "called up" in May 1944.[223]

In April 1945 Gendanu was assigned to the Shiska secret service. On August 10, ignorant of the opening of hostilities with the Soviet Union two days earlier, he and the others were sent to the Asase temporary military station at the border under the leadership of Sergeant "S."[224] It seems this was a deployment aimed at death in battle with the Soviet Army. On August 17, having somehow made it back to Shiska unharmed,[225] Gendanu and his comrades were informed of Japan's surrender by the director of the Shiska Government Branch Office of Native Affairs, and Sergeant S. quietly escaped.[226] There was a debate about their postwar fate, but they "persuaded one another of the idea that we were all Japanese and so should withdraw to Japan." In the end "withdrawal"—everyone back to Japan—was the decision taken.[227]

On August 23 Gendanu become a Soviet prisoner of war. He was court-martialed in the Toyohara (Yuzhno-Sakhalinsk) Prison and sentenced to eight years of hard labor for the crime of assisting in espionage.[228] He eventually spent seven and a half years in the "lager" (concentration camp). Fellow detainees Manjirō, Igarainu (Nivkh), and the Heijirō brothers died; Gendanu was paroled in the spring of 1955.[229] Because he'd been a "war criminal" and submitted to Soviet law as a "Japanese," he felt inferior and hesitated to return to his hometown—now in Soviet territory—going instead to stay with his older brother in Hokkaidō. This older brother had also been made a member of the secret service and had crossed over to Hokkaidō after his internment in Siberia. Thus not

only was Gendanu's family dispersed between Sakhalin and Hokkaidō, but he
himself concealed his Uilta heritage and came to live in fear of discrimination.[230]

THE CHAMORRO

Phillip Mendiera (Japanese name Menjō Kyūkichi), born on Rota Island in the
Mariana Islands in 1911 as son of a village headman who was a Chamorro im-
migrant from Guam, was sent to Guam as a civilian employee of the Japanese
military secret service in April 1944.[231]

Under Spanish control from the seventeenth century, the Marianas, with
the exception of Guam and several other islands, had become German territory
in 1899. The Japanese military had occupied them during World War I, and in
1919, along with the Marshall and Caroline Islands, they became the Japanese
mandated territory of Micronesia. After graduating from the Saipan Islander's
School Rota branch in 1922—the year such facilities were renamed "public
schools"—Phillip continued in the two-year Saipan Public School supplementary course.[232] Elementary school for Japanese people lasted six years, with an
additional two-year supplementary course, but public school for the local population was limited to a three-year course. In his three elementary school years,
Phillip had received a thoroughgoing education in becoming an imperial subject (kōminka), every day raising the Japanese flag, bowing in the direction of
the imperial palace, and singing the Japanese national anthem, "Kimigayo."[233]

After finishing the supplementary course, Phillip worked as a translator for
the South Seas Government. He then became a translator for the South Seas
Development Corporation (Nanyō kōhatsu kabushiki kaisha), helping the company, which was involved in the sugar industry, with the leasing of local residents' land.[234] In 1934, while he was working as a translator, Phillip traveled to
Japan as "South Seas representative" of the "Second Pan-Pacific Young Buddhist's Convention" and wrote the following for the first issue of the Buddhist
magazine Daihōrin (October 1934): "I truly realize that there is no country
grander than this [Japan]. . . . For myself I have the idea that I must imitate the
Japanese, that the more I imitate them the more I will advance. . . . We would
like to become Japanese soon, and also have a go at becoming soldiers."[235]

As a result of his education in becoming an imperial subject (kōminka
kyōiku), Phillip had become a consummate "Japanese." After working for seven
years at the South Seas Development Company, he retired. His status was still
no more than that of apprentice to a company employee. He subsequently

worked as a manager of a sugarcane field. In 1941, with the outbreak of war between Japan and the United States imminent, he agreed to a request to became an assistant for the South Seas police. In February 1944, as the Americans prepared to land, he had little choice but to obey an appeal from his boss, the section manager, to become a civilian staff member of the secret service's special squad and make the crossing to Guam.[236]

The majority of Guam's inhabitants were Chamorro like himself, but because the island had been American territory since 1898, anti-Japanese sentiments were extremely strong when the Japanese occupied it on January 12, 1942. Phillip's duties included monitoring local "anti-Japanese" Chamorro, searching for hidden weapons, detecting people sending information to the American military, and tracking down escaped prisoners of war. He walked about the island in civilian clothes, inspiring trust by speaking ill of the Japanese military in Chamorro.[237] In July 1944, under American naval and aerial bombardment, the Japanese army slaughtered residents in the village of Matsuyama (Merizo/ Malesso). The infuriated population killed Japanese in revenge, and Phillip investigated these incidents as well.[238]

Shortly thereafter, on July 21, 1944, the U.S. Army landed. After fleeing to the jungle, Phillip was discovered by local inhabitants as he headed for the home of an uncle on his mother's side, and it appeared that he would be put to death as a "Japanese spy." But through the intervention of a relative, a Catholic priest— who argued that "the war is something between the Japanese and American armies; it has nothing to do with us local people"—his life was spared.[239]

Taken prisoner by the American army, Phillip concealed his identity and maintained that he was a translator for the South Seas Development Company. He thus avoided execution and was released. But when he got out of the POW camp and tried returning to Rota Island after the war, it turned out that because he'd crossed over to Guam in secret, he'd been suspected by the *Japanese* police as an American army spy. His wife had been thrown into detention despite being pregnant and had died after being drafted and forced to perform heavy labor upon her release.[240] His older brother Thomas had been working as a translator for the Lota Island garrison. Suspected as a spy for the same reason, he'd been arrested and likely executed.[241] His younger brother[242] had been adopted by the chief Buddhist priest of Saipan's Honganji Temple, acquired Japanese nationality, and attended school in Japan, but in 1944 he'd been drafted and sent to the Burma front. After the war he returned to Rota Island, but he "just kept on drowning his cares in drink, regretting that Japan had lost to America."[243]

陸軍兵志願者訓練所

FIGURE 2.1 Propaganda images of the special army volunteer soldier training station (*Rikugun tokubetsu shiganhei kunrensho*) for Koreans.

Source: Government-General of Korea, Information Section, *Atarashiki Chōsen* [New Korea] (Seoul, 1944), 41.

KOREANS

THE ENACTMENT OF THE SPECIAL ARMY
VOLUNTEER SOLDIER SYSTEM

Koreans were also placed in an inferior position, one even lower than Okinawans and Ainu. When the Sino-Japanese War began, the Korean independence movement was suppressed more violently, and Koreans were forcibly mobilized as soldiers, laborers, civilian military employees, and "comfort women." The Korean masses saw themselves as bystanders to the Sino-Japanese War, and they refused to cooperate with the colonial Government-General based on a widespread opposition to Japanese domination that wrought havoc upon their daily lives.[244] Within this context let us examine how the Korean people were treated, focusing upon the volunteer soldier and draft regulations.

On February 22, 1938, the Special Army Volunteer Soldier Edict (*Rikugun tokubetsu shiganheirei*) was promulgated. Among Korean males aged seventeen and over, those in good health would be trained as Japanese soldiers to be sent to the front or used for Japanese ends in colonial Korea.[245]

The Army Ministry and the Government-General of Korea publicized the volunteer soldier system as an honor and a favor toward Koreans, but there could not have been many eager to throw their lives away for the colonial ruler. In fact, the "volunteering" was coerced by the Japanese authorities. Even those Koreans inclined to accept the propaganda of "Japanese and Koreans as One Body" (*naisen ittai*)—a notion that took colonial rule as a prerequisite—were dissatisfied with the volunteer soldier system because of the absence of measures that might improve Koreans' status, however slightly, such as a mandatory education system, the granting of suffrage rights, better treatment of Korean officials, or the liberalization of household registration.[246] Still, there were Koreans who sought in the volunteer soldier system a means toward obtaining a mandatory education system and suffrage rights.

As shown in table 2.1, beginning in 1940, the number of volunteer soldiers increased sharply, but the proportion of those found eligible decreased with each passing year. Few of those desired by the Japanese—young people from the middle class and up—volunteered; most who did were elementary school graduates and below. Many could not speak Japanese or say the "Imperial Subject's Pledge" (*kōkoku shinmin no seishi*),[247] and few volunteers became

TABLE 2.1   Special Army Volunteer Soldier Recruits (Korea), 1938–1943

YEAR	NO. OF VOLUNTEERS	NO. OF VOLUNTEERS ENTERING TRAINING CAMP	PERCENTAGE ADMITTED
1938	2,946	406	13.8
1939	12,348	613	5.0
1940	84,443	3,060	3.6
1941	144,743	3,208	2.2
1942	254,273	4,077	1.6
1943	303,294	6,300	2.1

Note: The shift to a draft system occurred in 1944.
Source: Naimushō, "Chōsen oyobi Taiwan no genkyō" (July 1944), cited in *Taiheiyō senka no Chōsen oyobi Taiwan*, ed. Kondō Ken'ichi (Tokyo: Chōsen shiryō kenkyūkai, 1961), 33.

imperial subjects (*kōminka*) in the way the Korea Army hoped. Of those who qualified in 1938 and 1939, 80 to 90 percent were tenant farmers, and most of the volunteers were forced to apply as a result of the wretched condition of the country's farming villages, brought into sharp relief by the Great Korean Drought of 1939.[248]

THE SITUATION OF THE EARLY VOLUNTEER SOLDIERS

Yet the Korea Army made a very high assessment of those volunteers who qualified early on and were sent to the front in northern China as active duty soldiers. In the case of the 20th Division, the first volunteers were assigned in May 1939, roughly twenty to each regiment.[249] In the case of the Heijō (Pyongyang) 77th Infantry Regiment, the volunteers were seen as "surpassing [Japanese] soldiers of the same age in excellence," with "a positive bearing that sets an example for other soldiers." Some described them as "unreliable with regard to independent messenger duties" because of "unclear language" or "generally lacking in . . . quick-witted action and behavior," but in general they had a good reputation.

   Of the twenty-four volunteer soldiers assigned to the Ryūzan (Yongsan) 78th Infantry regiment, the assessment said that nineteen of them were superior to Japanese soldiers; of the five judged inferior, one was reprimanded for taking shelter from the battlefield. The assessment concluded that "with the exception of a small minority, they represent a great hope for the future of the Imperial Army, calmly minding their primary duties, applying themselves with industry, their spirits full in taking the initiative in the assault and in proceeding toward the place of death."

Of the twenty-two men assigned to the Taikyū (Daegu) Infantry 80th Regiment, nine were promoted to private superior class and thus qualified to be candidates for noncommissioned officer. As a whole, "their battlefield record" was rated "in general extremely good. . . . In fact they serve as a model for the rest."

Amid these positive assessments, only that of the Ryūzan Infantry 79th Regiment stood out in contrast. With the exception of a few superior soldiers, here half of the Koreans were rated as on par with average Japanese soldiers and the rest as inferior. Although their battle record was "recognized as passable," it was said that they were in need of additional training and "cultivation of Imperial Army consciousness."

Thus while there was some dissatisfaction, on the whole the volunteers assigned to the 20th Division were rated highly.

Korean volunteer soldiers were compelled into front-line service by the Japanese army, suffering injury and death while made to bear a "sense of responsibility as the first volunteers representing the [Korean] peninsula." They were forced to speak Japanese on the battlefield and even among fellow Korean volunteers. Placed as victims at the very front of the front lines, they were at the same time placed in the position of victimizers with regard to the people of northern China.

Fighting in the mountainous eastern region of Yicheng in Shanxi Province on July 7, 1939, I Hiyansu, a volunteer in the 80th Regiment, "fought a brave fight, consistently in front." Having "offered himself up amid the enemy," he suffered a bullet wound through his neck from a rifle round, fell unconscious, and died as he was being sent back.

Prior to this, on June 22, Private First Class I Inseok of the 79th Regiment died during the fighting near Wanshan Village in Shanxi Province. As his was the first death of a Korean volunteer soldier, it was publicly declared that he was "the embodiment of the Japanese spirit."[250] Yet the report from the 79th Regiment coldly chronicled that when he was wounded, "the extremely tense battle situation notwithstanding, he cried '*aigo aigo*,'[251] lost all fighting spirit, and entered a state as if blind to victory or loss in battle." Just before he died, however, he said to his comrades, "Keep your spirits up," and then "chant[ed] 'Long Live the Emperor' (*tennō heika banzai*) three times in a soft voice."[252]

After his death, I Insoku was exploited as an "inspiration" to young Koreans. His story was told as one of loyalty and bravery in newspapers and magazines, and he was awarded the Golden Kite in 1940. In that year, the volunteer and acceptance rates from his home district of Okcheon in North Chungcheong Province were the highest in Korea.

It can be assumed that the military quality of Korean volunteers changed little as time went on. Through June 1942, approximately seven thousand men finished training and entered the Korea Army either as active duty soldiers or as first reserve soldiers; roughly 60 percent of these were eventually promoted to private superior class.[253] Discharged men were forced to participate in the Movement for the Making of Imperial Subjects (*Kōminka undō*),[254] becoming members of the National Total Energy League of Korea (*Kokumin sōryoku chosen renmei*) or promoters for the Patriotic Squad (*Aikoku han*). In 1944, the Inspectorate General of Military Training (*Kyōiku sōkanbu*) emphasized their excellence.

> Although the quality of [Korean volunteer soldiers] is annually declining relative to that of first-rate volunteers, they may still be seen as high quality among people of the [Korean] peninsula, and their unit records are generally good. On the battlefield, furthermore, the number of those who have accomplished glorious fighting deeds or have met death in battle with honor continues to grow.[255]

These sorts of "achievements" lay in the background of the Conscription Law in Korea in 1944. The situation of volunteer soldiers, however, was not simple. It is said that when a farewell party for Korean student soldiers attended by the governor-general was held in the Seoul Public Hall (Keijō Fuminkan) around 1943, a number of students stood up and shouted, "We shall go. We shall sacrifice ourselves. But what will you do for Korea after that? Will you grant it independence?"[256] The Japanese government and colonial Government-General, however, never gave a thought to recognizing Korea's independence. Failing to associate "Japanese-Korean integration" (*Naisen ittai*) with "Japanese-Korean equality," they also failed to abolish discrimination.[257] According to the above source, furthermore, the General Directorate of Education was anxious that the volunteer soldiers' notion of the "national polity" (*kokutai*)[258] stopped at the level of abstract knowledge and had not become a conviction. Although they worshipped at Shinto shrines, it appeared they had trouble grasping the notion of a Japanese-type god, imagining instead something like a demon, Christ, or Kishi (Kija: an ancient Chinese ruler of the northwestern Korean peninsula). They lacked the backbone inherent to the Japanese sensibility, in which one "considers one's death as nothing and lives eternally in righteousness." When discriminated against, it was feared that they took "to having very bad feelings, spreading the bad influence of an alarming nationalist consciousness."[259] The army had no choice but to recognize that the assimilation and spiritual incorporation of Korean volunteer soldiers was fraught with problems and that discrimination within army units was becoming a cancer. The conscription system was forcibly put into practice within this context.

THE IMPLEMENTATION OF THE CONSCRIPTION SYSTEM

The conscription system's implementation was announced in May 1942, and promises of mandatory schooling and suffrage rights were shelved.[260] This was odd given that from January of that year onward, Prime Minister Tōjō Hideki repeatedly proclaimed that Japan supported the "independence" of the Asian peoples. Granting no rights, Japan enforced only the duty to march to the place of death, deeming this an "honor."

The announcement of conscription brought a complicated response not only from among the Koreans at whom it was aimed but also from among Japanese. In the Japanese homeland, those who welcomed the development were in the minority—strange for a people in a dominant position. The words of an elementary schoolteacher in Hiroshima Prefecture were representative of this group. He described the announcement as a matter for congratulations to the Japanese nation and Koreans, citing four reasons. First, among Korean schoolchildren, "two or three out of ten are extremely excellent." Second, Koreans were cooperating enthusiastically in the war. Third, having them as soldiers was very apt "from the standpoint of human economy." Fourth, because the enactment of the conscription regulation was in touch with the core of "universal brotherhood" (*dōhō*) that was the "great spirit" of the emperor, it bespoke the great success of colonial rule by the Japanese race (*yamato minzoku*). Thus, while he advocated that all young Koreans of superior quality be driven into the war on the basis of "human economy," the teacher then turned this around and claimed that their conscription derived from the emperor's "great spirit" of treating Koreans equally. Moreover, he did not abandon his suspicion of Koreans, advising that it would be necessary "skillfully to direct" the conscripts' passions, keeping an eye on "problems of thought" and working to make them identify as Japanese.[261]

Against this was the majority opinion that saw conscription as being implemented "too early." Doubtful about how well the policy of making imperial subjects (*kōminka*) was working, many feared Korean independence and secession. "We need to be very careful about giving them weapons at the present time—the world knows that the fact that India has not yet enjoyed independence up until today is because politics without weapons does not work well," argued a company employee in Kōbe. A village headman in Shimane Prefecture stated, "There is also the view that one reason America and Britain both suffered heavy losses in the Greater East Asia War was that they deployed large numbers of soldiers from their dependencies at the front."[262]

Japanese living in Korea were overwhelmingly opposed. They believed that conscription would encourage the "insolent attitude" of Koreans, make Japanese lives difficult, and be taken advantage of by Koreans as an opportunity to demand rights such as political participation and a mandatory education system. A merchant living in Kōshū (Kwangju),[263] for example, had the following to say:

> Nowadays there are even Koreans who blurt things out to me like "Who in the world made your fortune for you, wasn't it thanks to us Koreans? So each of you all should donate a share." . . . If you talk about Japanese-Korean integration, they immediately demand the same rights as people on the mainland. If by some chance the Greater East Asia War pans out in favor of England and America, they might cooperate with the enemy.[264]

Japanese colonizers evidently thought that if Koreans used the conscription system to improve their standing even a little bit, this would immediately put their own positions at risk. Their colonial location amplified both their nationalism and their sense of crisis.

THE SITUATION FOR KOREAN SOLDIERS

The first physical examinations for the military draft were held between April and August of 1944. According to Utsumi Aiko, more than 209,000 men were mobilized for the war as a result of the volunteer and conscription systems, and among army soldiers alone, more than six thousand died in battle.[265] What was the situation like for these soldiers? One barracks receiving new recruits from northern Korea in the autumn of 1944 found that the share of those who could not understand Japanese was increasing. When the recruits came in, a piece of paper instructing in the most basic Japanese—the five vowels "a-i-u-e-o"—was hung up within each unit, and the barracks was reported to be "like a nursery school," frantic with instruction in Japanese.[266]

Beaten on a daily basis even as the aims of the war remained unclear, many deserted.[267] Once they left the barracks they were surrounded by sympathetic fellow Koreans, and most were never caught.[268] Tamura Sadakichi, a veteran of the 134th Independent Infantry Battalion, stationed in China's Shuyang in June 1944, writes that more than thirty college- and university-educated Korean volunteer soldiers responded to an opening for staff cadets—but that when two-thirds of these were rejected, most deserted.[269]

What of those who completed their training and did not desert? In what position did they find themselves?

Born in 1920 in Chinnampo Pyongan-namdo, Kim Sangpil (Japanese name Yūki Naosuke) volunteered upon his graduation from a Christian private school and from Yeonhui (延禧) vocational school in Seoul. He matriculated at the Kumanoshō branch of the Tachiarai Flight School in Kumamoto Prefecture (special cadet for pilot, first graduating class).[270] After passing through the (Suizhong) 13th Educational Flight Unit and the (Donhua) First Independent Flight Unit, Kim, now a second lieutenant, was placed in the G (Makoto) 32nd Flight Unit of the Second Squadron in Shinkyō (Changchun) on February 11, 1945. This was a sixteen-plane suicide squad composed of Type 99 Intruder planes, and Kim commanded the Fifth Formation.[271]

On April 3, Kim took off from Ni'itabaru Base and crashed into an American warship at Okinawa. Before this, on March 14, he'd met his older brother at Shinkyō for the last time, and his brother had encouraged him to desert. Kim was said to have replied, "I represent Korea. If I deserted or something like that, my fatherland would be scoffed at. Many of my compatriots would be forced to bear further insults."[272]

Gwak Gwi-xun was drafted while studying at a teacher training school in Chonju and joined the 77th Infantry Regiment in Nanam on September 9, 1944.[273] Arriving in Hiroshima on September 20, he was assigned to the Seibu Second Unit Second Machine Gun Company. Among recruits of the same class some could not understand a word of Japanese, and in other units of the Hiroshima 224th Division some committed suicide, unable to endure the agony of the resultant maltreatment. After finishing the first-term inspection, most of the soldiers were assigned to the front lines, but Gwak stayed behind as a staff cadet and was reshuffled into the Seibu Second Army Chūgoku 104th Unit Cavalry Squad.[274]

With "completely unbearable" feelings, Gwak observed how Koreans in Hiroshima were treated like thieves or less than human. He endeavored to serve as a model for other soldiers in every aspect of his life and behavior in the unit. "We can't be outdone by Japanese": this thought never left his mind.[275] At one point, Gwak was granted a ten-day leave by the company commander, which he used to visit his hometown. He wrote, "I'd be returning to my home-town again, able to see people dear to me. And then when I thought of how I'd be crossing the sea of Genkai with an army corporal's insignia on my staff cadet washer,[276] I was so happy I couldn't sleep."[277] Despite his dismay over the treatment of his fellow Korean soldiers, Gwak was conceited about being a staff cadet of the Hiroshima Division, one of the Japanese army's elite units, "the core that moves the core unit of the Japanese army."[278] On August 6, 1945, Gwak would be injured in the atomic bombing of Hiroshima.

Oh Rim-jun grew up in the city of Kōbe after crossing over to Japan from Kyongsang-namdo Masan Cheongup-myon with his mother and father in 1930. After finishing elementary school he worked as an assistant at a bookstore, a blacksmith's, and a general store. He was eventually hired as an apprentice drill operator at an ironworking company thanks to the wartime shortage of skilled workers.[279] Having lost hope of realizing his long-cherished dream of becom-ing an artist, he took the conscription examination in the faint hope of improv-ing his circumstances, half voluntarily and half coerced by an officer attached to a youth night school.[280] He was eighteen years old at the time. He passed as a Grade A and was ordered to report to Kyongsang-namdo in late September 1944.[281]

Daring to answer the call-up despite his mother's fierce opposition, Oh wrote the following about his mental state:

> The sight of my distraught mother is certainly a heavy blow, but if I were to die, at least the Japanese would probably treat us differently from the way they have up to now. They'd likely treat us a bit more *equally*. . . . If in being added to a Japa-nese army unit as a Korean sacrifice (*chōsenjin no sute'ishi*) I can learn a bit of that esoteric thing marksmanship—something we've not even been allowed to get a peek at up to now—there will likely come a time when that knowhow will come in handy in some small way.

Oh also wrote, "I wanted to be promoted to a Japanese. The Japanese-lan-guage-only world was everything [for me], body and soul."[282] Yet when he was assigned to the Kurume 12th Division at Laoheishan in Dongning Prefecture on Manchuria's eastern border, he was subjected to one extreme punishment after another in the barracks. The words of his Japanese lance corporal, who dished out the beatings, led him to recognize his error: "The peninsulars [*hantō*, a derogatory term for Koreans] still aren't worth a damn."[283]

Oh was subsequently transferred to the Ryūzan 120th Division, in which he was serving at the time of the Japanese surrender.[284] Many Korean draftees went home the same day, but he had no hometown to return to, and in order to get back to his mother and father in Japan, he had no choice but to stick with his unit. Just then, his unit was ordered to participate in the suppression of the Korean independence movement, and he was stuck blocking the way of his Korean comrades—who were shouting "Independence forever!"—with a Type 99 infantry rifle. "What the hell is this! Koreans shooting Koreans. Will there ever again be anything so absurd, such a paradox?" By this time, Oh wrote, he had reached his "wit's end."[285]

TAIWANESE

REACTIONS TO THE SINO-JAPANESE WAR

When all-out war between Japan and China began in 1937, Japan had ruled over Taiwan for forty-one years. Yet most Taiwanese people neither wished for a Japanese victory nor believed it would happen. From public statements to graffiti to letters to the editor, expressions of hope for a Chinese victory and a Japanese defeat were ubiquitous. Predicting a Japanese defeat, people withdrew their savings from banks, credit associations, and post offices. The following details give a glimpse of the Taiwanese people's attitude toward the war.

Anonymously polled about the words and actions of their parents or other guardians regarding the Sino-Japanese War, Taiwanese sixth graders in the four public schools Murayama (Cunshan), Sachi (Xing), Akebono (Shu), and Jushikyaku (Shuzijiao) in Taichung City yielded the following results:[286]

❶ Those who predict a Japanese victory and have a favorable opinion of the Japanese army: 300.
❷ Those who predict a Chinese victory and incline positively toward the Chinese army: 145.
❸ Other: 30.[287]

Since it is likely that a substantial number of these sixth graders did not respond honestly out of fear of causing trouble for their elders, it can be assumed that the number of parents who foresaw a Chinese victory was far greater than shown by the poll. Even the children themselves, who had been receiving Japanese education ever since they had started to understand what was going on around them, were not necessarily confident of a Japanese victory. A survey of fifth and sixth graders at the Tainan City Minato (Gang) Public School yielded the following results:

❶ Regarding the causes of the Incident and who was to blame for it, the respondents were utterly ignorant.

❷ A number feared it appeared as if Japan would lose.

❸ To the question "Are there points on which you think the Chinese are in the right?" as many as fifteen responded, "Song Zheyuan is right, he is a person who keeps his promises."[288]

From these results, Taiwan Army Headquarters drew the following conclusion: Since the outbreak of the war, the Taiwanese people had held rallies and social gatherings, declaring their determination and feverishly making donations to [Japan's] national defense, but it was too soon to take this to mean that they possessed an "imperial subject consciousness." They "trusted too much" in the capabilities of China and saw China as their fatherland; those who hoped for Taiwan's return to China upon a Chinese victory were in the majority. Taiwan's imperial-subject-making (*kōminka*) efforts were "in a deplorable state," a situation that did "not allow pause for relaxation" from a defense standpoint.[289]

In Taiwan as in Korea, then, the policy of making imperial subjects, which began with the changing of family names and mandatory use of Japanese, was compelled by force. The reaction of the Taiwanese people, however, was complicated.[290]

When 1,350 Taiwanese were conscripted as military porters in September 1937—coinciding with the mobilization of the Taiwan Army (all of whose soldiers were of course Japanese)—it was an extraordinary shock. Among them were some who answered the call-up without prompting, but many were anxious about leaving their families behind and going to the battlefield, fearing they'd be killed by Chinese soldiers—their fellow countrymen—at the front. There was thus a steady stream of people who gained exemptions from service as military porters by making donations to national defense and many others who sought to avoid conscription on the basis of illness, the family business, or the condition of their relatives. There were also those who deserted on the way. And, thinking that fluency in Japanese would ensure future conscription, there were also those who withdrew their children from public schools or themselves stopped attending local Japanese language training centers (*Kokugo kōshūsho*).[291]

Faced with this situation, at the same time as it promoted the Movement for Total National Spiritual Mobilization, the Government-General of Taiwan cracked down on the expression of pro-Chinese sentiments. As a consequence, the speech and conduct of Taiwanese people soon became "markedly reserved" (*ichijirushiku senkōteki*). False obedience was becoming the norm.[292]

On the other hand, Taiwanese also participated in the war effort. When the Government-General posted job openings for one thousand men in an agricultural volunteer group that would be growing vegetables in the neighborhood of Shanghai to supply food for the Central China Expeditionary Army in March 1938, twice as many men applied. This was partly the result of the skillful Japanese exploitation of Taiwanese people's desire to make personal inroads in China.[293]

Those most heavily influenced were students in public, vocational, and middle schools. According to one account, during the Asia-Pacific War, Japanese instructors ridiculed students at an elite Taiwanese middle school who could not pronounce voiced consonants well and mixed up the pronunciation of "de" and "re." "The Chinese are hopeless," they would say. "For them to properly pronounce the language of a superior race like Japanese is hardly possible." Or "Chinks are useless fellows. No matter how much you teach them you can't get rid of their Chinese accents." In due course, the students boasted of their ability to speak Japanese well, even among themselves, not only "being ashamed and making fun of the strangely accented Japanese of their parents' generation" but not wanting to speak their own mother tongue.[294]

MOBILIZATION AS MILITARY PERSONNEL AND CIVILIAN MILITARY EMPLOYEES

Their mother tongue was not the only thing they lost. Let us examine the cases of some uniformed and civilian military employees. In Taiwan, the Army Special Volunteer Edict was enacted in February 1942 and the Navy Special Volunteer Edict in August 1943 (see table 2.2). The conscription system was put into effect in January 1945.

TABLE 2.2   Army Special Volunteer Soldier Recruits / Recruits Admitted (Taiwan)

YEAR	NO. OF VOLUNTEERS	NO. OF VOLUNTEERS ENTERING TRAINING CAMP	PERCENTAGE ADMITTED
1942	425,961	1,020	0.24
1943	601,147	1,008	0.17
1944	759,276	2,497	0.33

Note: For 1942, the number of recruits admitted includes forty members of the (aboriginal) Takasago people; for 1944 the cited number of volunteers includes those for the army and navy combined, and the cited number of recruits admitted includes reserves (*yobi'in*).

Source: Naimushō, "Chōsen oyobi Taiwan no genkyō" (July 1944) , cited in *Taiheiyō senka no Chōsen oyobi Taiwan*, ed. Kondō Ken'ichi (Tokyo: Chōsen shiryō kenkyūkai, 1961), 34.

Awi (whose Japanese name was Matsuoka Tsuneo) was born in 1925 in the Pāran shrine of the Taiyal people (one of the Gaoshan peoples, the aboriginal inhabitants of Taiwan). After graduating from a "barbarian (*banjin*) public school,"[295] he worked in agriculture. In 1943, at the age of eighteen, he applied for the sixth installment of the Takasago Volunteer unit and volunteered to be a naval civilian employee.[296] Although the process was called "volunteering," there was in fact a forced allotment from each village. Awi's father had been killed by a Japanese policeman during the Wushe Rebellion of 1930,[297] but having "absorbed the Japanese spirit" as a result of his four-year Gaoshan public school education, it could not be said that he was resentful about this.[298] After four months of training and assignments in the Philippines and Rabaul, he was sent to Bougainville Island, where he was reassigned to the army. The shock troops were reorganized, and the Gaoshan people were always made the advance party, attacking with woodman's hatchets while carrying hand grenades and land mines; many of them died in battle.[299] That the Japan they'd been told would certainly win could ever lose—this was truly unthinkable. Returning to Taiwan in April 1946, both upon boarding and disembarkation from the repatriation vessel, items of clothing and other possessions were taken from them, leaving "everyone weeping in spite of their manhood." Exploited to the maximum by Japan during the war, they were discarded afterward.[300]

Born in 1929 in Taipei Prefecture, Lin Jinming was conscripted while attending middle school in Taipei and assigned to the Taiwan 13,863rd Unit in March 1945.[301] Lin's mother, father, siblings, and many of his relatives were teachers. His parents were supporting Japanese efforts, his father as a member of the Imperial Subjects Service Association (*kōmin hōkōkai*) and his mother a member of the Ladies' Patriotic Association (*aikoku fujinkai*). Even for such a family, the Government-General's enforced assimilation policy took a heavy toll. Those who did not change their full names were unable to enter public middle schools or girls' schools, so his father unhappily had him change his name to "Hayashida Akezō."[302] Few Taiwanese had been eager to take up arms on the Chinese mainland, but with the outbreak of the Asia-Pacific War there was "a sense of discovering a kind of salvation" now that the fighting against the "fiendish Americans and English" was justified in the name of "Asian liberation." When the volunteer system was inaugurated in 1942, it was almost entirely coercive, but when it turned out that those who passed the examination were highly regarded by Japanese, genuine volunteers emerged. "By the time the conscription system was enacted," Lin noted, "I was no longer particularly surprised."[303]

Lin's older brother volunteered and died in battle in Manila. Lin himself was drafted and went to Jiaoxi in Taiwan. Of the moment when he heard of Japan's surrender, he wrote, "I did not immediately believe the news that the war had ended. I believed in immortal Japan [*shinshū fumetsu*, lit. 'eternal land of the gods'], that the one time it faced a great crisis in 2,600 years [of imperial history] the 'divine wind' would intervene. Somewhere along the way I'd become completely Japanese."[304] Following the surrender of the Taiwan Army, Lin was repatriated as a private first class, but he still feared being unmasked as a traitor. In March 1962, he would make an escape from Taiwan to Japan.[305]

Kō Sheng De was born in 1921 in Dajiajie Township in Taichung. Upon graduating from Changhua Vocational Business School he applied to join the Imperial Subjects' Service Association Southern Industrial Colonization Fighters' Training Center (*Kōmin hōkōkai takunan kōgyō senshi kunrensho*).[306] His father had run a business, but tiring of Japanese discrimination, he had gone off to Java in 1927 and amassed a considerable fortune cultivating coffee and cotton in Malang. When the Pacific War began in 1941, he was arrested by Dutch police as a resident Japanese and forcibly relocated to a prison camp in Canberra, losing everything. Kō applied to join the second installment of students at the training center in the hope that he might be able to go to the Netherlands East Indies where his father was.[307] Even if he could not be a volunteer soldier, he also wanted to accompany the army as a civilian in military employ for the sake of "the nation."[308]

During six months at the training center, Kō studied architecture and learned Malay. At the end of his term, he immediately received a conscription order as a military employee. On the day he was mustered out, Kō was ordered to change his full name to a Japanese one; he chose "Isomura Kazuo."[309] He was assigned to the New Guinea First Research Unit (Minoura Unit) of the Navy 101st Fuel Depot and arrived at Ambon Harbor on New Year's Day, 1944. But the boat was sunk in a torpedo attack just before entering the harbor, and twenty of his one hundred fellow second installment students lost their lives.[310]

At the end of February, Kō reached the Kashimu Base (Minoura Unit Headquarters) at Berau Bay in New Guinea. He went to work felling trees for architectural lumber, a dozen-odd local inhabitants working under him. Situated at the outermost reaches of the Japanese army, Kō was at the same time set up in a dominant position over the local population.

While in the naval hospital in Ambon suffering from fatigue, malaria, and beriberi-related heart problems, Kō heard news of the last-ditch defeat at Biak Island. All of the Taiwanese civilians employed by the Minoura Unit, he wrote, had just been sent to Biak.[311]

After leaving the hospital at the beginning of October, Kō was reassigned to the 104th Naval Facilities Unit in Ambon, where he heard the announcement of the surrender on August 15, 1945. When ethnic Chinese came around to sell sugar, cigarettes, and foodstuffs in the Ambon prison camp, he was surprised at how his mother tongue, the banned Fujian language, came out "entirely naturally."[312] He reawakened to his Taiwanese identity, but he knew that if he returned to a Taiwan under Chinese government control he would be despised as a soldier of an enemy nation—and depending on circumstances, he might be executed as a traitor. There was no use going to Japan either. Transferred to a prison camp on Seram Island, Kō escaped and led a nomadic life within the local ethnic Chinese society. In April 1947, he left Ambon in the company of nineteen Taiwanese former civilians in military employ, arriving in Japan in May.[313] For some time, he could not make up his mind whether to stay or return to Taiwan. Thinking that his history of Japanese service might put his family at risk, he decided to remain in Japan. He went to live with his younger brother, who—having been drafted for labor and transferred to Japan—was then in Tokyo's Kamata district.[314] Having lost his homeland, Kō described the chagrin of being used and then discarded by Japan.

> After the war, the nationalist government in Taiwan received lots of aid from the Japanese government. As a condition for this, I heard they agreed that Taiwanese who'd been conscripted by the Japanese army would not demand damage

compensation. In the war, people from Taiwan were sacrificed for Japan. I never dreamed that we would also be used as collateral for nationalist government loans. It's often said that the weaker you are the sooner you're sacrificed, and that's the truth.[315]

The order of imperial fascism was built upon the blood sacrifices of many people who suffered discrimination and oppression. How the Japanese people themselves seek to deal with this issue is consequently of great significance in determining the nature of postwar society.

3
THE ASIAN WAR

THE ILLUSION OF INDONESIA

FROM TRANSPORTER TO THE YOKOSUKA HEAVY ARTILLERY UNIT

A TRANSPORTER'S DEPARTURE TO THE FRONT

Nitō Seikichi (b. 1906), who managed a shipping company in Tokyo's Ōmori district, was called up in July 1940 and joined the Yokosuka Heavy Artillery Unit.[1] He was an untrained reservist at the rank of private second class.

After withdrawing from higher elementary school, Nitō had worked selling crystal radio sets, as a finisher at a body company, and as a driver-in-training at a company called Meika Garage. In 1931 he opened a transport company with a single one-ton-capacity used Model T Ford. It was hard going at first, but by the time he was called up he had five trucks and twelve employees and was profiting from the war to the tune of three thousand yen per month.[2] The Heavy Artillery Unit needed a professional driver, and thus Nitō, who had three children, was conscripted at age thirty-five. His company continued to operate under his employees' management, so he maintained a decent income, and with his savings he was at no loss for money even at the battlefront, where he was known as "New-rich Nitō." Under a subsequent business reorganization, however, his agency was absorbed by a subsidiary of the Tōkyū Group, and when he was repatriated in 1946 as a sergeant, he had nothing but his remaining savings.[3]

In August 1940, Nitō journeyed to the front at Bao'an in China's Gwandong Province, where he took part in the campaign to cut off the "Chiang Supply Route"[4] in the vicinity of Hong Kong. He witnessed the summary execution of men caught carrying commodities without so much as interrogation, and he raided towns and villages on his own initiative, participating in the requisitioning of such items as liquor, sugar, chickens, and pigs.[5]

On December 7, 1941, the heavy artillery line that had until then been facing the Chinese army turned toward Hong Kong. The next day the war with the United States, Great Britain, and the Netherlands began, and Nitō participated in the capture of Hong Kong, setting foot on British territory for the first time. Since there were no military police at the front line yet, he heard that those with free time in other units "went out on the loose, looting all night long." He too looted a soft feather quilt, underwear, and Western-style clothes and wrote of searching in vain for jewelry.[6]

ENTERING FORTRESS SINGAPORE

In February 1942, Nitō's unit hastened to the battle of Singapore as reinforcement. They entered Johor Baharu on February 9, and he described his experience there as follows:

> In the vicinity of the Johor Baharu artillery emplacements there were many overseas Chinese-owned mansions, and given this was a perfect area for private requisitioning I believe some among the artillery unit's soldiers and noncommissioned officers got quite some spoils. . . . I too thought the British army must have thrown away a considerable amount of stuff, and when I searched around in something like a small chicken coop . . . there were twenty [empty] oil cans of roughly eighteen-liter capacity piled up pell-mell, so I filled as many as eight cans with looted cigarettes, powdered milk, and sugar and piled them into the car I was charged with driving. . . . When I went into a house with about ten rooms there was a beautiful ethnic Chinese girl of about twenty who'd been slow to escape and was crouching down, and she asked for help; I pointed her in a direction where there were no Japanese troops and she was delighted and ran off, saying "*duoxie, duoxie*" [many thanks, many thanks]. There was a lot of that sort of thing in Johor Baharu, including some people who seem to have committed rape.[7]

Nitō's unit entered Singapore on the night of February 13. In the middle of the night a British artillery shell landed next to the truck he was driving, and he missed the explosion by an instant. In Singapore too a considerable amount of looting took place. Nitō acquired a taste for seizing liquor, raisins, corned beef, and the like from British army provisions storehouses: these soon came under military control, and his attention turned to British army vehicles, of which he requisitioned two—an automobile and a touring car. "Plunder-type requisitioning became the fashion" in the unit. On one occasion Nitō and his comrades seized a dump truck, a vehicle not yet familiar to Japanese, from the municipal roads department. After piling it up with cooking implements, they put it in gear; its bed rose up, and two or three people were thrown off.[8] The truck was eventually returned by military restoration order.

THE DREAM OF MANAGING A PLANTATION IN SUMATRA

Afterward, in June 1943, Nitō's unit (the Tomi 9380 Unit First Company) crossed to Sumatra. Here their main duty was to defend fifteen cannons on the Straits of Malacca near Banda Aceh. Without the tools necessary to dig emplacements for the guns, Nitō resourcefully cut train rails to make such things as a stone chisel, a *baran*,[9] and a sickle. He also handcrafted parts that could be substituted for such items as automobile shocks.[10]

As for the heavy labor of making covered trenches, however, Nitō drafted inhabitants from nearby villages every day "at cheap wages. . . . I worked them very hard, with pay in military scrip." By the time he withdrew, shortly before the surrender, he consequently feared being attacked by the local residents.[11]

While out on an official trip, Nitō observed the splendor of Dutch-run hemp plantations south of Medan and the apparent prosperity of trading companies run by overseas Japanese. He was seduced by the zest of colonial management:

The hemp plantation of Rarasa sprawls roughly twenty kilometers in every direction. . . . There were eighteen mechanized vehicles that extracted the raw materials from the hemp, about five hundred trolleys of roughly two tons each that piled up the harvested hemp, a hundred long, partitioned tenement houses serving as accommodation for peasants and laborers; there were umpteen thousand employees, and also a market set up especially for the plantation as well as a hospital and a maternity ward. When I first witnessed its grandeur I was surprised. . . . I was fascinated with the splendor of the Dutch-managed plantations. . . . I thought

if I were sent to the Southern Regions as a civilian in military employ and engaged at the Rarasa hemp plantation or a Medan trading company, as a civilian
in military employ treated as a noncommissioned officer . . . that would be a lux-
urious life.[12]

Nitō began to "dream of getting a local discharge in Sumatra and managing a
Sumatra plantation if Japan wins the war."

The effect of the "comfort stations" (*ianjo*) on relations with the local people cannot be overlooked. According to Nitō, the roughly five hundred members of his unit made frequent visits to the "comfort station" the Japanese army
had set up in the town of Shiguri, where local Chinese, Acehnese, and Batak
women were made into comfort women.[13]

NITŌ'S EXPERIENCE OF THE SURRENDER

Nitō's unit pulled out of the area in May 1945 and moved to temporary lodgings
behind the Shōnan Shrine in Singapore. Here the imperial surrender decree
was communicated by the unit commander. Nitō was shaken by the news but
relieved as well, "because of the prospect of being able to live on and repatriate
to Japan proper." He also wanted to participate in Japan's reconstruction.

After it was disarmed by the British, Nitō's unit entered a "self-administered
prisoner-of-war camp" on Rempang Island and returned to Japan in June 1946.
He went back to Tokyo in the spring of the following year, bought a used truck,
and started his transport company anew in January 1948.[14]

FROM LOCAL JAPANESE RESIDENT TO EMPLOYEE IN A
BRANCH OF THE SUMATRA MILITARY GOVERNMENT

THE STRUGGLES OF A JAPANESE RESIDENT OF SUMATRA

Ida Masakichi, a dentist in the Sumatran town of Lahat, departed Batavia on
the last evacuation boat to Japan in November 1941, on the eve of the Pacific
War.[15] Born the son of a railroad worker in Kumagaya City in Saitama Prefecture in 1911, Ida had found employment at Kumagaya Station after graduating
from higher elementary school. He was dissatisfied with this job, and when he
heard that Sagawa Michiya, a dentist who ran a clinic in Sumatra, had briefly

returned to Japan to look for assistants, he made a personal solicitation and journeyed to the city of Pagar Alam in December 1930.[16]

Pagar Alam is in southwestern Sumatra, in a renowned coffee-producing region. In the vicinity were five large Dutch-operated coffee plantations with several thousand laborers.[17] Including Sagawa's dental clinic there were approximately ten resident Japanese in the city, one with a combination general store/photo studio and one with a pawnshop, along with a woman—a former elementary school teacher—who was married to a local man.[18] Along with the usual duties of his practice, in which he saw Dutch, Indonesian, and Chinese patients, Sagawa sharpened the teeth of the daughters of the Pasemah people and placed gold crowns on six of their upper teeth, a custom called *dabon*.[19] Over a "dizzying three years," Ida was rigorously instructed in the principles and clinical practice of dental medicine; at the same time, he learned Malay.[20]

On January 13, 1934, Ida was entrusted with Sagawa's branch clinic in Lahat. He split it into a combination dentist's office, pharmacy, and family medicine shop and "was able to live days of responsibility and fullness." As in Pagar Alam, Lahat had around ten Japanese residents, among them two hotel owners, a barber, and two dentists. There was also a Taiwanese-run photo studio. Ida began to study Dutch, and he was retained to handle dentistry for the Dutch-managed joint hospital at the Pagar Alam Plantations.[21] He also received permission from the Dutch authorities to practice dentistry independently.[22] Mohammad Ahmad, the regionally influential headman of the village of Merapi, invited him to attend the wedding ceremony of his eldest son, Noh.[23] Ida was thus building a solid status for himself in Lahat.

THE OUTBREAK OF WAR

With the Japanese occupation of northern Indochina in September 1940, however, Ida and his fellow resident Japanese began to experience "uneasy, somehow restless days":

> Doubts about why I'd made efforts up to now, the invisible destination toward which we were steadily headed—I had a foreboding to the point of being deeply anxious about how we might manage on the [Japanese] mainland if the time came that we were forced to withdraw to Japan. Yet on the other hand I lived my life with all I had—I'd been able to make a contribution to the local society, even

if only a small one, without anyone second-guessing me behind my back. Looking back at this, I told myself this was enough. That said, those living abroad like this were caught right up in the wave of those changing times, and I had a persistent, sharp feeling of confronting the danger of being forced to pay the price with every bit of my livelihood.[24]

The breakdown of Japanese-Dutch trade talks in June 1941 brought major changes to Ida's circumstances. All Dutch males carried rifles and started attending battle training on a daily basis, and a de facto warning from the Japanese consul-general in Batavia to withdraw to Japan was printed in *Jawa Nippō*, the Indies' sole Japanese-language newspaper. Ida eventually resolved to begin preparing for this, though he was still unable to relinquish the idea that "it might not end up being such a big thing."[25] Having achieved some small measure of success, he wrote, "the truth of the expression 'it's difficult to make a name for one's self' hit me all the harder."[26]

Japanese on the mainland largely greeted the outbreak of war against Great Britain and the United States with wild enthusiasm, but among those who returned to Japan from overseas, there were those, like Ida, who met it with feelings of chagrin.

SELF-SACRIFICE AS A MEMBER OF THE SUMATRA MILITARY GOVERNMENT

Serving later on the staff of the army's military government in Sumatra, Ida sought to put his ten years of experience on the island and the language skills he had acquired to use. In December 1942, a lieutenant colonel from General Staff Headquarters asked him for information about Palembang; "I responded quickly to this military request," Ida wrote, "and fulfilling this duty with a document, I cheered up, conscious of what one must call a feeling of superiority at being one of the Japanese selectively chosen."[27] He reported no sense of contradiction in participating wholeheartedly in the same war that had stolen the basis of his livelihood.

Ida had departed from Hiroshima's Ujina Bay on May 25, 1942, exhilarated that he was returning to his long-time home as one of roughly twenty members of a Sumatra team.[28] On May 30 their transport ship the *Takachiho Maru* was sunk in a torpedo attack. Ida sustained a serious injury and was forced to spend three months in an army hospital in Taiwan. He finally reached Palembang in August, where he was employed as a translator in the Military Police Department of the local branch of the military government. "I'd gotten the good post I'd hoped for, and with this in mind" he swore he would "expend every ounce of my energy."[29]

In November 1942, the "Operational Essentials of the Sumatra Military Government" (*Sumatora gunsei jisshi yōryō*) were put into effect, and a new civil administrator was appointed.[30] In the Military Police Department, Akiyama Masami and a person referred to by Ida as "M" from the Kyoto police arrived and became section chief and department head, respectively. Ida had two Indonesians from Palembang attached to him, lower-grade employees of the old city government. He lived together with three colleagues in the mansion of the former head of the Department of Industry and was appointed joint director and auditor of the Palembang City Public Tobacco Monopoly Corporation—established to sell seized enemy goods to the local population—thus guaranteeing his livelihood for the time being.[31] When the emperor's younger brother Prince Takamatsu came to make an inspection, Ida became so emotional at his words of appreciation that he "felt a lump in my throat."[32]

Realizing that many local policemen desired to study Japanese and taking advantage of the language allowance for local employees, Ida held classes in the police department for two hours every evening from Monday to Friday. They were extremely popular, with approximately sixty people attending each day. He next opened classes for civilian employees of the military government, which were attended by roughly one hundred people daily. Eighty percent of these were Indonesians, of whom eight out of ten were government officials; the remaining 20 percent were overseas Chinese. These classes continued for six months until they were cut short by the "Su" Operation Incident.[33]

SUPPRESSION OF THE INDEPENDENCE MOVEMENT

The "Su" (Sumatra) Operation Incident, at the beginning of 1943, involved suppression of a popular independence movement in which Palembang's "half-castes" (of mixed Dutch/Indonesian descent) and Indonesians played a central role.[34] When responsibility for the incident was sought after the war, "M," the former military police commander, received a death sentence from a Dutch military court. Ida threw all of his energy into the wartime investigation, whose command was assumed by Lieutenant "I" from the Army's Nakano intelligence/counterintelligence school. By the time it was over, wrote Ida, "my head was fuzzy and my physical strength drained . . . as if in a state of collapse."[35] He was tasked with translating the reading of the judgment of Higher Court Judge "S," a job he considered sacred—transmitting the words of a judge, comparable to the voice of God. Feeling "a vivid excitement and responsibility I'd never felt before," he observed the spectacle of defendants turning pale upon hearing not the judge's voice but his own.[36]

Because the Japanese army had at first been welcomed by Mohammad Abdul Nabib, the powerful district chief (*gunchō*) of Kayuagung, Ida was not conscious of being a conqueror.[37] He thought highly of the army-sponsored State Advisory Assembly system,[38] which he saw as advancing the local population's aspirations for independence and demonstrating to influential figures the value of cooperation with the military government.[39]

After the "Su" Incident, Ida perceived that the security situation had become more unstable; with a sense of crisis he pursued his duties with extra diligence. To protect the Japanese armed forces, Homeland Defense Auxiliary Army (*Kyōdo bōei giyūgun*) units were established, local people were engaged as soldiers' auxiliaries (*heiho*), and an officer's training school was set up for the sons of the elite.[40] Alongside his work as a Japanese instructor, Ida devoted himself to assembling a three-thousand-word Japanese-Indonesian dictionary titled *A Collection of Administrative Terms*.[41]

LOCAL CONSCRIPTION

In early 1944 Ida underwent a conscription examination—he had never taken one before being posted overseas—and passed in the second or "B" classification. He was conscripted on the spot and made an army medic.[42] "With the moment of truth of the motherland that had given me life staring me in the face, offering up my life for the sake of the nation in this difficult situation was truly what I, as a man, had long desired," Ida wrote.[43] He was thirty years old.

After three months of training, Ida joined the Tomi 10499th Unit (the southern army's 17th Army Hospital) in Bukit Tinggi, West Sumatra, and was assigned to the dental ward. In 1945, the training was limited to desperate assignments including how to mount suicide attacks against enemy tanks with armor-piercing charges in hand.[44]

IDA'S EXPERIENCE OF THE SURRENDER

On the afternoon of August 16, Ida's superior, an army surgeon, told him of the surrender announcement, "an announcement that I could not even begin to believe. . . . I doubted my own ears, slipping into such an absentminded condition that I could hardly remain standing where I was."[45] His unit had seen no actual fighting with the British army, and it was difficult to swallow the reality of the surrender.[46]

In Bukit Tinggi, the Minangkabau people's independence movement came out into the open at the time of the surrender—Japanese flags were burned, and the handover of military equipment and food was demanded.[47] The Japanese army did not comply with these demands, and under the circumstances the British army did not disarm the Japanese.[48] Three months later, Ida's unit moved to the internment camp at Payakumbuh, where they set up a plantation. Relations with the local residents were not good; among several incidents, an entire cooking squad was attacked and killed by the inhabitants of a village they'd entered in search of provisions.[49]

At the end of April 1946, after dumping all their weapons in the straits between Sumatra and Malaya, Ida and his comrades arrived in Singapore. When Ida, by then a private superior class, threw his short sword into the sea, he "felt an inexpressible feeling, acutely conscious that this was my final parting with the Japanese army."[50]

In Singapore, he was searched and interned for a week at Changi Prison before returning to Japan on a liberty ship.[51] He was not interrogated in regard to the "Su" Operation Incident. Walking past the homes of overseas Chinese in the Singapore suburbs, his eye was drawn to laundry hung out to dry and fluttering against the blue sky, prompting thoughts of the "happiness of life and the preciousness of peace." After returning to Japan he would read the new constitution and identify with its declaration, "The Japanese people forever renounce war as a sovereign right of the nation"; this reaction was profoundly connected to the realization he'd had in Singapore.[52]

Ida returned to Kumagaya around May 1946 and learned of the city's destruction in the last U.S. air raid on August 14, 1945. He was also informed that his own house had burned down and that his younger brother had died in battle in Burma. Without a license in Japan, he could not open a dental clinic. He at first found work making packing rope out of rice straw and then opened a paint shop.[53]

INTO THE IMPERIAL GUARDS CAVALRY REGIMENT
BEFORE CROSSING TO SAIPAN

A NONCOMMISSIONED OFFICER OF THE IMPERIAL
GUARDS REGIMENT AT THE FRONT

On March 12, 1942, Ishii Masaharu, a sergeant-paymaster of the Imperial Guards Search Regiment, landed under enemy fire at Labuhanruku on the northwestern coast of Sumatra Island.[54]

Ishii was born the son of a settler-farmer in Sapporo in 1916.[55] After graduating from middle school in Kushiro family circumstances forced him to abandon his studies. It was planned that he would work at his uncle's agricultural experiment station on Saipan Island,[56] but before making the crossing he volunteered for active duty to complete his military service. Thanks to his excellent record he received recommendations from his middle school resident officer and the branch chairman of the army reservists' association. He was assigned to the Imperial Guards Cavalry Regiment[57] in January 1936, but with a future on Saipan still in mind, he did not volunteer as a staff cadet and enlisted instead in the accounting department, becoming a sergeant in 1938.[58]

In December 1939, Ishii was assigned to the Imperial Guards Mixed Brigade and sent to China's Kwangtung Province. While stationed in Chungshan Prefecture in December 1940, he was assigned to the newly assembled Imperial Guards Search Regiment (*Konoe sōsaku rentai*) and promoted to sergeant major. He also entered into a paper marriage with a woman on the Japanese mainland whom he refers to as "K." He participated in the occupation of southern Indochina in July 1941 and headed for Sumatra after taking part in the Malaya and Singapore operations.[59]

"LOCAL LIFE" IN MEULABOH

After mop-up operations in Sumatra ended, the regiment relocated to Meulaboh in Aceh State on Sumatra's northwestern coast in October 1942. Meulaboh, with a population under five thousand, was the only commercial harbor in West Aceh, shipping rubber, coconuts, gold, and platinum. Ishii would spend the next seven years here.[60]

Around Meulaboh the regiment constructed defensive obstacles, tank traps, bunkers, and a cave encampment, accumulating weapons, explosives, and provisions. A huge amount of manpower was needed for this purpose, and under the name of "labor service," the military government rounded up local residents and overworked them as *rōmusha*. Overseas Chinese shopkeepers and others who'd never worked as manual laborers dreaded this toil.[61]

Afterward, instructed to promote "conditions of self-sufficiency," Ishii resolved to employ overseas Chinese to produce goods for daily use, seasonings, and the like. Among other necessities he made salt by pouring sea water into a large cauldron stoked by burning coconut shells and soap by extracting oil from coconut palms and adding salt and soda. For soda, he poured water on the ashes of coconut shells and skimmed it from the liquid. He made miso and soy sauce by mixing a bacteria called *ragi*, meant for use in home brewing, with beans in place of yeast. He gave official military authorization to illicitly brewed liquor made by an overseas Chinese named Zeng, regulating its price. He built a cafeteria for military use and had Zeng run it. He began raising ducks to make salted duck eggs (*enzō tamago*), but this ended in failure: ducks are big eaters, and the feed ran out. He also established a toilet paper recycler along with a pig sty and factory for tanned leather. The overseas Chinese on whose cooperation he relied nicknamed Ishii "Dr. Know-it-all" (百暁, Bai Xiao), suggesting that he was proficient at everything but unable actually to accomplish anything.[62] For Ishii, however, it was apparently the discovery of a reason for living. He wrote,

> Before it had been enough just to share provisions forwarded to us; making and distributing these things myself kept me many times more busy, but precisely in the fun of putting ideas that came into my head into action one by one, my dreams kept growing bigger and bigger, all the more so because it was something worth doing, and something everyone appreciated.

As the war situation worsened, each unit was left to provide for itself, but Ishii proudly wrote that his unit "was totally unaffected," having already made sufficient preparation.[63]

THE DEFEAT AND THE INDONESIAN INDEPENDENCE MOVEMENT

Ishii was stunned when his unit was informed of Japan's surrender by the regimental commander on August 17; it was something he had not even dreamed possible. Having been involved in no fighting, it was difficult for him to even visualize defeat.[64]

Given his extensive contacts with the local inhabitants, Ishii was called upon to deal with the massive quantities of goods the regiment had accumulated. To avoid these being "stolen" by the starving people—or their confiscation and redistribution for public relations purposes by the Allied forces—Ishii decided to auction off the goods. Conducting the auction in (now worthless) Japanese military scrip was also a responsible way of removing it from circulation. After five days, he had sold enough to reacquire all of the military scrip. On September 5, leaving a single platoon behind, his unit pulled out of Meulaboh.[65]

The regiment moved to the outskirts of Shantaru,[66] where Ishii made contact with an overseas Chinese acquaintance and began selling rice on the black market for the benefit of the regiment. When a crisis arose in relations between the guard unit and the inhabitants in Meulaboh, however, Ishii was ordered to return—this time by the Allied forces, who sought to use the Japanese army to suppress the Indonesian nationalist movement.[67]

In Meulaboh, Ishii told people he'd left the army and become a merchant in army service, wore *ben'i* (the same civilian clothing worn by the local inhabitants), took up residence in a Chinese household, and traded army-held fabric for food. As the independence movement reached Aceh, residents surrounded the Japanese guard unit, demanding guns and explosives. Ishii was summoned by the town's wealthiest person, Haji Daud,[68] held captive, and made to go to the guard unit to negotiate. An allied repatriation ship had arrived, but with no guarantee they could safely board it, Ishii went back to Haji Daud's place for further negotiation. On December 12, they agreed to a ceasefire, and the unit was safely repatriated, but Ishii was taken prisoner and left behind alone.[69]

The withdrawing unit had poured gasoline on their rice stores and destroyed their rifles. On top of this, during the occupation members of the Meulaboh district nobility had been executed by the Japanese army as pro-Dutch. Ishii was consequently treated as a criminal—members of the same nobility were among those promoting the independence movement. Zeng, whom Ishii had earlier employed to make liquor and run the cafeteria, gave Ishii food, but the townspeople held him in contempt as a result. Ishii wrote that one night he dug a hole for his own execution, but the person in charge lost his nerve and failed to carry it out.[70]

THE PAIN OF SEPARATION FROM THE UNIT

Ishii subsequently became chairman of the board of the expatriate Japanese "Welfare Friends Association" (*Fukushi tomonokai*). According to a classification system he devised, Japanese who had became separated from the army and navy at the time of the surrender fell into the following major categories:

❶ people who feared being pursued for war crimes: those connected with the military police (*kenpei*), military intelligence (*tokubetsu jōhōhan*),[71] the POW camps, and the police;

❷ people who'd had their weapons stolen by Indonesians and feared being called to account by Allied and Japanese forces;

❸ people who'd served as instructors for the volunteer army (*giyūgun*) or at youth training centers (*seinen kunrensho*),[72] who, out of both duty and sentiment, felt it impossible to abandon Indonesians seeking independence because they'd encouraged the dream of independence in their training;

❹ people who were pessimistic about any future for them in Japan, believing they'd lost their homes and their families in the devastation of war—or, as in Okinawa, that their entire home towns had been lost—and discovering a new dream in the independence movement;

❺ people in remote mountain areas who had their way blocked by the inhabitants, failed to make contact with their units, and were left behind; and

❻ those who joined the independence movement in a brief moment of excitement.[73]

At the time of the defeat, Indonesian antipathy toward the Japanese army was strong, and their experiences of mounting attacks against Japanese to obtain weapons added to this. Indonesians were also killed in Japanese army counterattacks. The Dutch and the affiliated Indonesian nobility viewed the Japanese as their bitter enemy. Japanese separated from their units were therefore in an extremely precarious position. Only men in category 6 ended up returning to their units after a short time; the rest did not. Or could not.[74] This was the case for Ishii, whose incarceration lasted until January 1946, when the Indonesian Army Command was established at Kotaradja. Assigned to an Indonesian unit upon his release, Ishii now returned to Meulaboh for the third time. All the overseas Chinese who had cooperated with Japanese forces during the occupation were labeled traitors and ostracized, and Ishii, who had not cooperated with the independence movement, suffered harassment as well. Unable to rely on Zeng's kindness alone for support, he began to repair shoes, subcontract chains for necklaces, and make leather at the leather tanner's that he used to manage. Having lost the backing of the Japanese state, Ishii finally stood on his own, and despite "numerous handicaps," he began a true, flesh-and-blood association with the Indonesian people.[75]

Around this time, on the recommendation of Zeng's wife, Ishii married their daughter. As far as his Japanese wife, "K," was concerned, he had abandoned the idea of returning to her, having heard that a report of his death in battle had been issued. He adopted the Chinese name Huang Demin (黄德明) and the Indonesian name Mohammad Amin, using one or the other depending on the situation.[76]

PARTICIPATING IN THE INDEPENDENCE WAR

During the Second Independence War[77] in February 1949, Ishii was forced to serve as a military porter, carrying explosives and provisions. His advice regarding reconnoitering and operations, based on his old army experience, proved useful, and the independence army began to view him positively.[78] Returning in triumph to Meulaboh after the armistice two months later, the soldiers proudly spread stories of meritorious deeds, and before he knew it, Ishii was "promoted to hero," his honor restored.

Indonesia became independent at the end of 1949, and Ishii retired from military service in 1950, after fifteen years in the Japanese and Indonesian armies. He was subsequently interred at a camp in Kotaradja along with roughly one hundred other Japanese by a central government fearful of the Aceh independence movement (he was elected head of the camp's Japanese Association). Ishii gained Indonesian citizenship on March 12, 1964, and after managing an iron works and serving as head of the Kajima Trading Company in Surabaya, he established a sandal-making company in 1970.[79]

Examining such experiences of Japanese soldiers who came to support the Indonesian independence struggle, it seems the foundational moment of this support came when they were completely separated from the Japanese military and decided to make Indonesia their home.[80] The Japanese military itself was either uncooperative or hostile to the independence movement and was furthermore under Allied orders to suppress it.

THE JAPANESE PEOPLE'S EXPERIENCE OF INDONESIA

Having outlined the experiences of three people, one conclusion I believe we can reach is that so far as the Japanese people's understanding of Indonesia was concerned, the depth or shallowness of one's intercourse with the Indonesian people was decisive. In Nitō's case, he certainly believed that Japan should make up for the crimes it inflicted upon Southeast Asia.[81] Yet at the same time, he also believed that Japan should carry out his long-treasured aim of developing agriculture and forestry, securing a source of food for Japan so he and his companions' "journey to the front would not have been in vain."

Behind this was the thought that "through Japan's Southeast Asian occupations, a huge area of the world became independent nations, escaped from colonization, etc.," and that "Japan's crimes at the time of the Second World War were great, but Japan's achievements were greater." This perspective would seem to be related to the fact that Nitō had only limited interactions with local people.

In contrast, as a dentist in Sumatra and through his work with the military government as a translator and Japanese-language educator following his return, Ida had a much richer experience with the local population than did the average soldier. Yet the nature of his interactions was completely different across the two periods. As a dentist, they were direct and personal without state involvement. He was of use to the local people and led a full life; looking back on that time, he saw no reason for regret.

During the second period, however, his relations with ordinary local people were bitter. He now largely interacted with notables and pro-Japanese officials such as Mohammad Nuh (a student at the officer training school and postwar commander of the South Sumatra Defense Army), H. A. Bastari (a student in the Japanese language school, military government police department chief, and postwar South Sumatra governor-general), and Raden Hanan (an employee of the Department of Military Government and postwar governor of Palembang State).

Ida himself remained ambivalent: He felt there was a significance in his own war experience as well as in achievements of the military government in creating the State Assembly system and the Volunteer Army for the Defense of the Homeland. Yet in the end he did not feel himself in a position to make a judgment about the ultimate reason for the war. His reflections are touching:

> Looking back now as I finish writing, I feel my experience itself had its own meaning, but on the other hand, what was the point of the war?—to this day I do not know the correct answer regarding its nature. It was a war that slaughtered and brought suffering to many people, intensified mutual mistrust among

nations, and ended up destroying the global environment. No matter what grand label you might want to put on it, after all it's nothing but foolish man's desecration of God. This is my conclusion after having gone through it myself.[82]

Because Ishii chose to live Indonesia, he saw what others did not—the Japanese army as victimizers of the Indonesian people. Certainly he too stated that the soldiers on the front lines were spiritually pure. In his case, however, he did not stop here, but said that "love of country, love of one's countrymen—what bound this up with ideas of territorial expansion was the ideology of rugged warriors of a warlike nation." Ishii pointed clearly to Japan's "aggressive" nature,[83] pleading that the tragedy of the sort of aggressive war it waged in Indonesia should never be repeated.[84]

BURMA'S METEOR SHOWER

FROM FREE LABORER TO THE BURMA DEFENSE ARMY MOBILIZATION BUREAU

FROM SOUTHERN CHINA TO BURMA

Born in Narumi Township in Aichi Prefecture in 1918, Katō Mifumi took part in the campaign to capture Burma, going as far as Lashio. After the campaign ended in the middle of May 1942, he was removed from the military roster.[85]

The youngest of thirteen children (six boys and seven girls), Katō left home for Tokyo after graduating from higher elementary school, planning to earn his way through middle school. He worked at various jobs, including newspaper delivery and construction. He took the military conscription examination when he turned twenty and joined the Third Company of the Toyohashi Engineer's Regiment as an active-duty soldier in January 1939.[86] In April he was sent to the Chinese city of Guangdong. In the fall of 1941, while Katō, now a corporal in the Third Company of the 20th Independent Engineers' Regiment, was stationed on the outskirts of Guangzhou, guerillas stole ten guns on his watch.[87]

Katō's company commander suggested that he should prepare either for seven years' penal servitude or an honorable death in battle. Putting his life in the company commander's hands and in full expectation of being killed in combat, he joined the Hong Kong, Malay, and Burma campaigns. He was always

FIGURE 3.1   Map of Burma.

posted on the very front lines, in sea landings, suicide squads, and the storm-
ing of enemy positions in hand-to-hand assaults in which the Japanese soldiers
were referred to as "human bullets" (*nikudansen*). "Every time I saw the company commander, he looked to me as if to say, 'Are you still alive?'" he wrote.
"It was so rough I couldn't stand it."[88] Fortunately the campaigns ended before
he was killed, and Katō's efforts were recognized: while in Pegu, Burma, he was
promoted to sergeant.

Katō did not get off scot-free, however. In July 1942, soldiers who had
started their service the same year as he were returned to Japan from Burma,
but he was ordered to join the 15th Army Command in Rangoon and become a
Burma Defense Army instructor as a contracted employee (*shokutaku*).[89]

On his own in a foreign land, Katō consoled himself with the ambition of
overcoming his poor reputation and becoming, with luck, a father of Burmese
independence—he "resolved to find [his] grave in Burma." Upon arriving at the
Army Command, he was assigned to the Personnel Service and Mobilization
Bureau of the Burma Defense Army. He "felt the blood in [his] whole body
seethe with excitement"[90] when he learned of his duty: to recruit young men
for what would be a ten-thousand-strong Burma Army under the command
of General Aung San. His fellow contracted employees included the translator
Kondō—who had lived in the United States—and another man he refers to as
"K," who like Katō himself had risen from the lower ranks to sergeant. Katō
held the status of a junior official (*hanninkan*) and wore the peacock insignia of
a Burma Defense Army instructor on his chest. On the advice of Kondō, who
had been appointed earlier, he went out "furniture thieving" in broad daylight,
bringing back tables, chairs, lamps, and the like for his lodgings from a mansion
whose former occupants were presumably English. To learn Burmese, he did
his best to go out in the street and practice everyday conversation with stall
holders.[91]

THE DUTIES OF THE MOBILIZATION BUREAU

The Burma military government was inaugurated on June 3, 1942, and on August 1, the Burma Central Administrative Office was established with Ba Maw
as chief administrator. Katō could not help seeing its false nature:

> The Burma Administration Office, established after so much trouble, was also no
> more than a name. It was compelled to submit to the directions of the Office of

the Military Commander when undertaking anything. The Office of the Military Government was itself under the thumb of army dignitaries, and the government officials sent from Japan, the so-called imperially appointed higher officials, were also unable to enact any policy as they might. Day and night witnessed the silliness of 150 *geisha* aimlessly embraced, of gay voices and boisterous dancing on the new tatami mats of the fancy restaurants [*Suikōen*, 翠香園, catering to senior officials]. And the trading companies that turned up from Japan put their energies into making money, keeping busy gathering raw materials but not taking any measures [for the sake of] production.[92]

The Personnel Service and Mobilization Bureau began by constructing a factory for the production of uniforms. Many Burmese girls were employed as seamstresses. It then turned to recruiting soldiers, for which Katō served in a unit under a Major Tenwen, guarding a safe box that held thirty thousand rupees. As the unit moved around the Hinthada, Bassein (Pathein), and Prome (Pyay) regions of southern Burma, the major successfully urged village chiefs and other influential figures to help achieve Burmese independence by borrowing the sword of Japan and assembling young men to wield it.[93] Recruiting in Bassein, Katō went to have a look at a "comfort station" and wrote that all of the "comfort women" there were Korean.[94]

While the young Burmese recruits received Japanese-style military training, Katō was put on cooking duty and became discouraged. His enthusiasm also cooled as he observed the bribery that flourished between noncommissioned officers of the Mobilization Office and trading companies. Once a Burmese recruit told him, "The slapping, I just can't bear it. I've never gotten this kind of punishment from my parents or from English people. Are the Japanese savages?" Katō was at a loss for a response.[95] During this period, he fell in love with a woman named Maē who worked at the sewing factory, and he began to visit her home often. On the day of Burma's biggest annual event, the April Water Festival, they poured water over each other in a public acknowledgment of their romantic relationship.[96]

DISCHARGE, MARRIAGE, AND MAKING DRIED POTATOES

In the middle of June 1943, all contracted employees of the Personnel Service and Mobilization Bureau were summarily fired. Katō was angry at the army's cold treatment, but there was nothing he could do. The army did not provide passage for its ex-employees back to Japan, so even if he'd wanted to return, he could not. In his position, moreover, returning to Japan would be unacceptable: Even if he returned he would not find employment, and he was embarrassed at the idea of returning before compensating for his past failures through success in Burma.[97] With few employment options, Katō took work at a Japanese-run Rangoon market dealing in food for the army. His salary was three hundred rupees—just enough to survive as a bachelor—but with the strong encouragement of Maē's parents, they were married. The new home he'd just rented, however, was burned down in a British army air raid. Katō sought a wage increase but failed and was forced to quit the market.[98] Together with Maē, he began making and selling ice cream to the Japanese army, but this too did not go well.[99]

Katō subsequently headed to Kalaw at the invitation of "K," who was now purveyor to the Nakajima Unit branch freight depot in Kalaw City, the advance base of the 33rd Division. "K"—who had two Burmese mistresses, a mother and daughter—had taken possession of a formerly British-owned holiday house in the village of Roiyam; "K" and Katō used this house as both residence and workplace, employing local people to make dried potatoes and combine water with quicklime to make slaked lime (calcium hydroxide) for military use. Saying no matter how much they made it would never be enough, the paymaster handed out military scrip unsparingly, and their desperate production efforts continued as 1943 drew to a close.[100]

Not everyone in Roiyam was cooperative. Among the most prominent villagers, on Katō's side were the headman, Konniyu; his wife, Mrs. Mashiyabi; the elderly Afghan Shiromat; and the Filipino Porisutan, former manager of the holiday house. But the Afghans Esaku and Hatsukan—who had their own connections with the Japanese military— kept their distance.[101]

In 1944, as Japan's eventual defeat grew more certain, someone poisoned Mrs. Mashiyabi. When the nearby Anban airfield was bombed by Allied forces that summer, the number of workers under "K" and Katō was halved; those who remained insisted they be paid from rice stocks rather than in military scrip, which had fallen in value. When the rainy season began it became difficult to dry the potatoes, and production dropped sharply.[102] "K" washed his hands of the business and moved to Kalaw City to manage a distillery he had bought from a Korean named Lee.[103] On his own in the large holiday house, Katō set his mind to "making a name for myself beginning now." But for these men whose lives and livelihoods in fact depended on the military, the withdrawal of the Japanese army brought unseen danger in its wake. Ominously, Katō's associate Porisutan was attacked and robbed even of his pots and pans.[104] Around this time, Maē's uncle paid a visit in a truck. Katō took the opportunity to send his wife back to her parents.[105] But her mother told her that a married couple must be as one until death, and Maē was back with Katō a month later. Moved to tears, he wrote, "I'd be happy to die with this woman." Hatsukan, who had opposed him, was kind enough to advise him to get away as soon as possible, but Katō replied that with so many soldiers at the front lines fighting and dying for the emperor, he could not run. Hatsukan replied, "Having a king is a tough thing, isn't it?" Katō wrote that he was envious to no end of Hatsukan's home country of Afghanistan, where everything was said to be decided through consultation among village elders.[106]

BOUND BY THE HEAVY BURDEN OF THE STATE

In January 1945, Katō was subjected to local conscription along with all other Japanese residents in Shan State. Contemplating the sacrifice of his life to the army in this final hour, for Katō "being Japanese had become completely detestable." At the call-up location of Taunggyi, he discovered that he was the sole Japanese there.[107] With the unit headquarters in disarray, he made up his mind to return home.[108] Afterward, "K" took advantage of a field hospital unit with which he had connections and fled on his own. In March 1945 Katō left Maē with a "native ruler" and did the same. He would never see his wife again.[109]

After escaping as far as Rangoon, Katō nevertheless purposely went to army headquarters and asked to be conscripted. Even having come so far, he could not separate himself from the army. When his request was refused, he slipped in among the soldiers, crossed the Sittoung and Salween rivers, and arrived in Moulmen. Here he again went to army headquarters, where he happened to encounter an officer from the Nakano School. Declaring that he could speak Burmese, he was hired by the "Zelkova Organ" (*Keyaki kikan*), an espionage unit.[110]

While in a village in the vicinity of Kawkareik working to unmask the anti-Japanese Sokū organization, Katō learned of the defeat from leaflets scattered by Allied planes that read "Japan Surrenders Unconditionally."[111] The cessation of Allied bombing raids seemed to confirm the defeat, but the unit commander said it was an enemy trick and transmitted a purported order from Army Minister Anami Korechika to fight to the last man. However, when a Sokū group turned up backed by the local population, everyone in the unit fled to Moulmein. Katō went to the army headquarters there and received a dismissal from the rolls, then fled to Thailand. In Bangkok he received a certificate of Japanese nationality and spent approximately one year in the camp of Banbūton.[112]

According to Katō's observations there was conflict in the camp between those who believed that "democracy" was good and sided with the victors and those who stubbornly wished to destroy the enemy, as well as between penniless refugees from Burma and "well-off" residents of Thailand. Katō had himself lost all his money, but still found life in the camp "enjoyable," having keenly experienced the fetters of the state. He wrote of meeting the surrender with the feeling, "It's finally come. The bell of liberation has rung. I'm not going to die anymore, I'm going to make it back to the Japanese Islands alive."[113] On July 3, 1946, he landed in Kagoshima. After working as a stall holder, a factory laborer, and in the real estate business, he ended up as a boiler technician.[114]

KATŌ'S EXPERIENCE OF BURMA

Speaking the Burmese language and marrying a Burmese woman, Katō was able to experience the tenderness and kindness of the Burmese people at first hand. While Katō and his wife were on the way from Rangoon to the front lines at Kalaw in 1943, for example, a stranger put them up in his home. Given the climate of unrest, with train robberies and the like, Katō feared having his money stolen and throat cut. Mae chided him, saying "what are you talking about? There are no Burmese as bad as that. If they did such a thing, for starters the priests (*ponjee*) would never allow it." The next day he offered the generous sum of ten rupees as repayment, but this was absolutely refused. When he heard that "putting up travelers in need for a night is only natural" in the predominantly Buddhist country, he thought to himself, "the people of Burma are truly kind," and felt ashamed to have doubted it.[115]

Yet in the sense that he lacked skills and was unable to make a living apart from the Japanese army, he lived apart from the Burmese people. He later reflected, "I too, who boasted that I would find my grave in Burma" when parting with Mae in March 1945, "was after all a Japanese. . . . Having cooperated however meagerly with the Japanese army, how much had I done to benefit the Burmese?"[116] In light of this statement, it can be said that his old view of the world had collapsed. When he got news in the camp that Mae was in good health, he was exceedingly happy, but he did not seek to meet her again.[117] One consideration, no doubt, was that because he'd been associated with an intelligence agency that worked to suppress the anti-Japanese movement, even if only for a short time, there was no way he could live in Burma after the war. But stronger than this was the keen reflection that he'd been of no use whatsoever to Burma. In Katō's memoirs, there is not the slightest posturing to the effect that Burma got its independence thanks to Japan. Having been close to the local people, he had been liberated of that groundless notion.

FROM ACCESSORY MERCHANT TO THE 114TH INFANTRY REGIMENT

A HABERDASHER'S DEPARTURE TO THE FRONT

In the spring of 1940, Miura Tokuhei, who had an accessory shop in Iizuka City in Fukuoka Prefecture, was called up and joined the Kokura 114th Regiment. That summer he was assigned to the Seventh Company of the regiment's Third Battalion and dispatched to China's Guangdong Province.[118]

Born in 1918 in Ashiya Township, Fukuoka Prefecture, Miura graduated from Iizuka City Vocational School. At his conscription examination in 1938, he was given a B grade and exempted from military service. When the call-up notice he thought would never come arrived, he gave his employees a leave of absence and closed shop. Most of the men with whom he was called up were also B grade—slightly built men including a dry goods store clerk, a tailor,[119] and a watch salesman. According to Miura, the older barracks soldiers commented, "How in the world will these guys be of any use?"[120] Nonetheless, he would return from the front as a sergeant.

Miura's unit landed at Songkhla, Thailand, in January 1942 and fought in the Malaya and Singapore campaigns. In April they landed at Rangoon and participated in the Burma campaign, and in the autumn they were posted to guard duty in northern Burma. In advance of this posting, Miura was chosen for education in the Burmese language.

INTERACTION WITH THE BURMESE PEOPLE

In the village of Lonton, where Miura was first garrisoned, the Japanese mobilized residents to build a road for military use. They were, however, given the impression that they were building a road for the sake of the Burmese people themselves, with Japanese cooperation. In the vicinity were abundant forests of teak, which was used to make bridge girders and posts. During the period of British rule, the unauthorized felling of even a single teak tree was punished severely, and thus—as if to dispel their accumulated resentment—the inhabitants let out "a big cheer every time they cut down a tree."[121] Miura "felt the Burmese people warmly welcomed the Japanese army occupation and were sincerely devoted to slogans such as the 'Greater East Asian Co-Prosperity Sphere.'"[122]

After four or five months, Miura's platoon advanced to the small village of Ebomy and took up a reconnaissance assignment. The inhabitants did not see the Japanese army as their enemy; by contrast, in early 1943, while in the middle of conducting a search, Miura encountered an inhabitant dangling the freshly severed heads of two Englishmen. Several months later, when he departed the village, the inhabitants were so sorry to see him go they took forever bidding farewell. "Although we didn't understand each other's words very well," he wrote, "even today I still recall a warm feeling that seemed to go through us both."[123]

On May 28, 1943, Miura's unit took up guard duty in Kyaukme along the Lashio railway line, and he assumed the function of supply officer at the rank of corporal. While carrying out air surveillance duties in the neighboring village of Hsenwi, he grew close to the local peasantry, engaging with them in rice-planting competitions and teaching them such techniques as straight-row planting and rice-paddy weeding. Upon his departure from this village, he again received a send-off from a large crowd of people, from the village headman on down.[124]

In the summer, Miura's platoon was sent to Mong Mit with an assignment to recruit assistant soldiers (*heiho*). One day, the platoon captured two Gurkha soldiers from the Wingate Penetration Force.[125] He wrote that the platoon leader, loath to endure the annoyance of coordinating with garrison headquarters in Kyaukme, killed the prisoners.[126]

THE BATTLE OF MYITKYINA

In March 1944, Miura's unit assembled at Myitkyina and ended up in battle with the Wingate paratroopers. The British forces, who had constructed a base at Mawlu, were of a much higher caliber than the British troops at Singapore and Bukit Timah, and the Kokura Regiment, which had confidently prided itself on its strength, was ignominiously defeated. In several hours of fighting on March 22, one of the regimental battalions suffered seventy-eight dead and 155 wounded, its battle strength cut by two-thirds.[127] Miura writes that as reported by Corporal Takesada, who had escaped a British encirclement near the airbase at Mawlu in the battle, British soldiers tied the hands of a number of Japanese they'd taken prisoner and "bayoneted them one by one."[128]

Afterward Miura's unit carried out numerous attacks, but they were unable to capture the base. Around May 2, the unit exchanged places with another one and escaped the killing fields. At that moment, he wrote, there welled up "a feeling of having been saved" and "the happiness of having been liberated."[129]

The unit headed for Myitkyina, but along the way the British army made an appearance at Namkwin. The unit launched attacks on May 14 and was again defeated, eventually leaving the battlefield in order to relieve Myitkyina. The Third Battalion, with over 430 men, arrived in Myitkyina on May 24, and the Japanese troops were soon surrounded by allied forces. Miura and his fellow soldiers were unaware of the general war situation, but they all believed that reinforcement units would doubtless arrive and they would go on the offensive. Yet as the rainy season began, the Japanese army was in a hard fight. Miura wrote,

> The soldiers of the encampment stayed wet, their rashes never healing. A sour stink came off their bodies. When the rain stopped, their body heat dried them; when it rained, they got wet again. No one had a raincoat or anything like that. We bailed and bailed out the foxholes but the water kept collecting. The soldiers guarded the encampment like roosting chickens, on perches[130] that stuck up in the middle of the trench. A small round hole was their living space as well as their place of burial. When you died in the hole, your comrades-in-arms would cut off your little finger and cover you from above with earth. Everyone had fastened together a bunch of dried little fingers and hung them around their necks—they looked like comma-shaped jewels (*magatama*).[131]

With no medicine, the "field hospital" fastened the wounded to rafts, gave them rice balls and canteens, and sent them down the river at night. It was three days to Bhamo and the local Japanese army headquarters, with guerilla attacks and rapids en route, and no one seems to have survived. The attack units were completely annihilated. On the ashen battlefield, the only things that eased Miura's boredom, reminding him of his home village, were the Japanese lettering on leaflets dropped by British planes—the leaflets were also useful as toilet paper—and British army broadcasts of such songs as "Kage o shitaite" ("Longing for Your Presence"), "Sake wa namida ka tameiki ka" ("Is Wine Tears, or a Sigh?") and "Yoimachigusa" ("Evening Primrose").[132]

THE SLAUGHTER OF VILLAGERS

At one point when the garrison found itself surrounded and in a hard fight, an enemy heavy machine gun detachment suddenly penetrated deep into the Japanese encampment. Somehow they were wiped out.[133] The regimental commander subsequently issued an order to punish the local inhabitants, concluding that the enemy unit, with horses pulling heavy equipment, could not have penetrated without their guidance. As a noncommissioned intelligence officer, now Sergeant Miura was ordered to gather all the inhabitants together, informing the village headman that each inhabitant, including infants, was to be given a jar of rice and a can of salt. Suffering from a shortage of food, the villagers—all twenty-seven of them—gathered in the trench with smiles on their faces.[134]

The unit first pulled out five people and shot them to death. One man who realized what was happening fled the trench; they fired on him, killing him as well. They next threw a hand grenade into the trench, and shot dead the two or three people who managed briefly to escape with a light machine gun. Miura was stunned: It had never remotely occurred to him that he was rounding up the inhabitants for mass murder. He had participated in the execution of prisoners before, but this was the first time he was complicit in the killing of local inhabitants with no hostile intentions. Recognizing that he had been made complicit in a systematic atrocity, he wrote,

It was too much; I got goose bumps over my entire body. Up to now we'd cut off POW's heads, blown enemies in the base to bits with hand grenades, put bayonets through the chests of enemy soldiers begging for mercy——. But these were all things that happened in the confusion of battle. These were things that arose only between friends and foes, commonplaces in times of combat. . . . Because if you didn't, you'd lose your own life. But this time is different. It goes against everything. Now we would see people killed who have no hostility and harbor no hatred, who've committed no crime. Unresisting as they are, with no clear reason. Yet now that things have come to this there's no way to stop it. Without doubt I can be counted among the cruel soldiers. . . . You could say I was not fully aware of the scheme they'd concocted, but as the one who rounded up the local inhabitants with sweet words, my guilt is very great. An indescribable feeling pounded in my chest.[135]

That it was necessary to kill enemy soldiers and prisoners begging for their lives in order to survive is a dubious claim. But like most of his fellow soldiers, as the battle raged on, Miura was cornered into a psychological state in which there seemed no other choice, alienated from the burden of conscience.[136] Even so, the massacre of ordinary civilians was something that could not be justified at all, either rationally or emotionally.

WITHDRAWAL AND SURRENDER

At the end of July 1944, the garrison commander made the decision to abandon Myitkyina. Miura, who was prepared for an honorable death, thought to himself, "I've made it, I won't die!"[137] His battalion, which had numbered 430 upon arrival at Myitkyina, now numbered little more than forty.[138] Of these, only just over twenty managed to get across the Ayeyarwady River.[139]

In October, Miura's unit returned to Kyaukme and then headed for Mong Mit, aiming to stop the advance of Allied forces there after the failure of the Imphal Campaign.[140] Already "worn out" from the fighting, Miura marched slowly forward, thinking this time he would surely meet death—no point in hurrying to it.[141] After surviving fierce British assaults on his unit from March 1945 onward, he learned of the defeat while at Sittaung and returned to Japan in July 1946, landing at Ujina.

MIURA'S BATTLEFIELD EXPERIENCE

At times when there was no fighting, Miura's encounters with the Burmese people were friendly. This was probably a significant factor in his coming clean about the mass murder in which he played a pivotal role. While many of Miura's comrades—whose thoughts repeatedly turned to their parents and wives and children in their hometowns—died overseas, most of the army generals, division commanders, staff officers, and regimental commanders—who expended the lives of so many officers and men—repatriated safely. Simultaneously aware of the cruelty of the Japanese army, the British army's "entirely unspeakable and unwriteable" brutality toward Japanese prisoners and wounded (from March 1945 onward), and the Chinese army's "certain amount of atrocities," Miura developed a strong repugnance for war.[142] Reflecting on the vast number of soldiers who died in the conflict's final stages, Miura wondered, "Why did the emperor, who was ultimately responsible, not decide to end the war sooner?——Why was he unable to do that?"[143] His feelings are summed up in the following simple observation—written as accounts of the Nazi slaughter at

Auschwitz, of the barbaric acts committed by the Soviet army in its invasion of northeastern China, and of the Nanjing Massacre, which he learned of only after the war, added to his own experience: "Even units of the British army, which championed the cause of humanity and peace, underwent this sort of transformation on the battlefield. . . . War distorts the humanity of all races, completely obliterating it. . . . For this reason, I despise war. —Forever."[144]

FROM NITTSŪ TRANSPORT AGENCY CLERK TO RETSU CORPS COMMUNICATIONS UNIT

FROM CENTRAL CHINA TO BURMA

On March 21, 1941, Sakimoto Takashi joined the 13th Telegraph Regiment of the Central China Expeditionary Army, then in Hiroshima, as an active-duty soldier.[145]

Sakimoto was born in Komenotsu in Kagoshima Prefecture in 1920. Upon graduating from the Kumamoto Technical College Training Department, he was supposed to be employed at Japan Nitrogen (*Nippon chisso*) in Korea, but because of illness he was unable to join the company and worked instead in his family's affiliate of Japan Transport, Komenotsu Transport. In his 1940 conscription examination, Sakimoto qualified as First (A) Class. He never forgot his father calling out to him as he set off to join his unit, "Takashi, can't you get a little larger-sized uniform?"[146] Sakimoto went to the front as a private second class; by the time of his repatriation he was a corporal.

Assigned to his regiment's Fourth Company, Sakimoto underwent training at Pugi in central China in April 1941. In February 1943, he was reassigned to the 26th Brigade and sent to Ipoh in Malaya. In May of that year the brigade was rechristened the 31st Infantry Group (Miyazaki Detachment) Communication Unit and headed for Burma, but Sakimoto was delayed after catching malaria along the way and reached Kawlin only in July. According to his impression at the time, the Burmese people were "sociable and kind."[147]

Accompanying a mid-August inspection tour by the infantry commander as a member of the wireless squad in preparation for the Imphal Campaign, Sakimoto enjoyed friendly treatment from the local population everywhere he went. He "believed wholeheartedly" in the Greater East Asian Co-Prosperity Sphere "as precisely the national policy" and believed the Japanese army was assisting Aung San in "finishing off the British" in order to "make Burma independent."[148]

THE IMPHAL CAMPAIGN

In the second half of February 1944, Sakimoto's unit left Naguddo and headed for Penpapa. Their diet consisted primarily of bananas, salted papaya juice, and edible jungle weeds, and despite the many bottles of Wakamoto Digestive Enzyme in their rucksacks, cases of jungle rot and diarrhea from malnutrition were rampant.[149] They first heard word of the Imphal Campaign at the Chindwin River crossing in early March, and when it was explained that the campaign would rely entirely on weapons, ammunition, and food captured from the enemy, Sakimoto could scarcely believe it.[150] The plan called for Sakimoto's 31st Division (the Retsu Division) to occupy Kohima.

On March 15, they crossed the Chindwin River and headed for the Arakan mountain range. When Sakimoto grew tired, he had local inhabitants carry his equipment, paying them in military scrip. They were accompanied by members of the Indian National Army, who were extremely pleased when they reached the India-Burma border. After they penetrated into India and reached Chamu, they found flour, butter, dried vegetables, and canned goods in an abandoned English barracks and trench.[151]

In the second half of March, a fierce battle was fought at the village of Sangshak. Though five hundred Japanese soldiers were killed, they occupied it in the end but failed to prevent a British withdrawal.[152]

In pursuit of the British, Sakimoto's unit headed toward Kohima. Here British bombardment destroyed the wireless unit's radio. From then on, Sakimoto's duties shifted repeatedly, from wire communication to construction of an interim track maintenance station, transportation of the wounded, base construction, and combat service.[153] On May 7, a fierce British assault began. Having already handed over the fifteen shells from his cavalry gun to his unit, Sakimoto had no choice but to fight with his remaining fifteen bullets and two hand grenades. That day, a corporal and a private superior class were killed, and Sakimoto was wounded.[154]

During this period, Sakimoto went to villages looking for rice, goats, and other foodstuffs to requisition. One day, a soldier who had gone off requisitioning came back with a large elephant tusk, from which Sakimoto made a pipe and a seal (he later wrote that he still retained both and that the seal was officially registered).[155]

On June 1, 1944, against the orders of 15th Army Commander Mutaguchi Renya, Retsu Division Commander Lt. Gen. Satō Kōtoku issued an order to withdraw from the outskirts of Kohima to spare many of his underlings a pointless death. But the seven-hundred-member Miyazaki Detachment—an infantry group—was singled out to stay behind and block the road between Kohima and Imphal, facing an enemy that even the full force of the division had failed to check. Despite pressure among war veterans to refrain from these sorts of recriminations, Sakimoto criticizes General Satō for sacrificing the Miyazaki Detachment,[156] saying "it was not in our power to understand his thinking."[157]

WITHDRAWAL

After resisting for five or six days, the Miyazaki Detachment pulled out. Sakimoto became a member of a unit transporting wounded, carrying a stretcher as he withdrew along a road that had turned into a muddy quagmire. They sensed that the local population, warm toward them as they advanced, now viewed them coldly. For mutual protection, they now went in groups of four or five to requisition food.[158] Sakimoto buried the wireless unit in the mountains, and, unable to communicate, they withdrew in complete isolation from their command. Along the way, many soldiers fell by the wayside; the master sergeant distributed hand grenades to those who could not walk, ordering them to kill themselves.[159]

The road from Ukhrul to Fumine was strewn with countless bodies of those who had died of starvation. The soldiers came to call it the "bleached skeleton highway."

The entire bodies of soldiers who'd died of hunger or disease were draped in black by bluebottle flies, the countless eggs that came out of their rear ends turning instantly into maggots; you grew horrified at the sight of them crawling around, but you encountered them everywhere. As a result the heads became like skulls in an instant, some of them with hair and beards still attached. Their limbs were covered only with leather, with each one of their bones minutely visible. Their clothes were covered in mud—it was a completely hellish vision. Hundreds, thousands of soldiers were dying like this. If the dead had even the smallest thing that might be of use on them—be it an undershirt, underpants, boots—it was stripped off. At one point I witnessed an officer pulling off boots. I swore to myself, "Even if it means my death, I'm not going to do that."[160]

Sakimoto was able to make it through this difficult withdrawal by summoning the memory of his father calling to him as he left for the front.

As the retreat continued, British airplanes scattered leaflets with provocative texts: "While you're all engaged in a bloody fight the guys from military headquarters are sleeping with girls and indulging in merriment in the May-myo scenic resort area." Although they didn't believe it, the soldiers were more than a little shaken, with everyone cursing "that goddamned Mutaguchi!"[161]

Around July 16, Sakimoto finally arrived at the Retsu Division headquarters at Tanan in Burmese territory. The men of the communications unit "all embraced one another, together celebrating our safe return."[162] Sakimoto immediately separated from the unit, having contracted a virulent strain of malaria and amoebic dysentery. He was able to cross the Chindwin River using the army engineers' Daihatsu, but as he marched along in bare feet, he apparently came down with a brain infection that caused temporary insanity, and he retained no memories of this period.[163]

After pausing at the supply depot at Wuntho, Sakimoto reached Kanbalu Station by train at the end of September. Accompanied by a man who was badly wounded, he sought to get back on the train, but a lieutenant turned them away, saying that since the train was flying an army flag, "I can't have soldiers who look like beggars like you riding along." Sakimoto was indignant: "Why in the world have we been fighting this war?" he thought. In all his long days as a soldier, he wrote, he'd never felt such intense disappointment.[164]

Sakimoto somehow managed to catch up with the infantry group communications unit—following the Imphal Campaign, a unit that had 240 men at the time of the advance now had forty-eight.

Among those who made it back, a large number had thrown away their guns. Sakimoto had been taught that if he lost his gun he would be confined to the guardhouse and that it would be a stain on the family register, so he never let go of it no matter how bad the situation. Those who came back without guns, however, were issued new ones without any trouble, whereas the rust on his rain-beaten rifle remained, and he was scolded each time there was a weapons inspection. "Is this what they mean by 'honest guys finish last'?" he wrote.[165]

SAKIMOTO'S EXPERIENCE OF THE DEFEAT

During the second half of November, Sakimoto was assigned to the 58th Infantry Regiment in Kanbalu and participated in the battle of Ayeyarwady (the Ban Campaign). The British forces advanced swiftly, and the Japanese army fell back repeatedly. The 58th Regiment too continued to retreat, withdrawing from Sagaing Hill in early February 1945 and from Kalow on April 27. Over the seven hundred kilometers from there to Pa-an there was no more fighting—nothing more than the Japanese soldiers taking to their heels.

First hearing of the defeat on August 17 via a telegram from the Retsu Division, Sakimoto comprehended it more fully when he saw the text of the emperor's surrender decree on leaflets scattered by the British army the following day. The hope he felt was mingled with the confusion of not knowing what to do next and anxiety that he might be put to work like a slave or killed.[166]

From September 28, 1945, until April 15, 1947, Sakimoto lived in British prison camps. Around the middle of January 1946, at the Zematoe Camp, he attended a lecture on democracy. He wrote of the experience:

> The one giving the lecture was probably a university professor. The contents were along the lines of "*minshūshugi*[167] is the translation of democracy, meaning that the people hold political power, and thus different from monarchical rule, in which power is concentrated in the hands of a single person. . . . It is the realization of freedom and equality. In Japan, democratization is moving forward based on the Potsdam Declaration." It was the first time I'd heard this; in part I was surprised, while in part the emotion of hope that welled up when I returned home was all the deeper.[168]

Even within the prison camp, Commander "N" of the communications unit recklessly beat his underlings, appropriated staple goods they had earned through their own labors, and redistributed them in a self-beneficial manner, provoking disgust among the unit's members, who referred to the system as "N-communism."[169] In May 1947 the unit arrived in Sasebo, and when the repatriation ceremony was over, many soldiers moved toward Commander "N" to settle accounts with him. One announced, "Only those who want to settle things with the unit commander should stick around." This way of sorting things out—just the men with a score to settle with the commander staying behind—was extremely refreshing. Sakimoto did not take part in what ensued.

When he later cooked food for "N"—who returned after getting a beating—the commander hung his head and said, "*You* remain kind to me to the end." It was then, wrote Sakimoto, that "I felt I was witnessing the pitiful end of the military clique."[170] One might say that the members of the unit went their separate ways after putting democracy into practice for the first time.

Reflecting on the war, Sakimoto felt that although the military might have ordered it, "there was no question that we'd trampled other countries underfoot" and that he "would like to advance the building of a peaceful nation, without war."[171] Komenotsu Transport, the family affiliate, had been amalgamated into Japan Transport on August 1, 1945, and so he went to work at the Japan Transport Izumi branch, automatically becoming a union member. In 1954, at the urging of the All Japan Transport Union, Sakimoto was elected to the Izumi city parliament.[172]

IN THE PHILIPPINE COUNTRYSIDE

FROM CREWMEMBER ON A MOTORIZED SAILBOAT TO THE SECOND TANK DIVISION ENGINEERS

THE DIARY OF A SOLDIER COOK IN THE ENGINEERS

On August 2, 1944, Yano Masami of the Second Tank Division Engineers Fourth Company in Boli, Manchuria, departed for the Philippines.[173]

Yano was born in Niugawa Township in Ehime Prefecture in 1920. After graduating from higher elementary school, he worked as an assistant in the family marine transport business and on the crew of a motorized sailboat. He was drafted on March 10, 1941, joined the Seibu 37th Corps, and trained with the 11th Engineers Regiment then in Hulin, Manchuria. Fed up with the freezing cold of Manchuria, Yano was excited to hear of the outbreak of war with the Allies—he looked forward to the prospect of being transferred to the south. He was eager for a quick discharge after completing his tour of duty and did not aspire to make noncommissioned officer.[174] Choosing not to volunteer for the parachute corps or the military police, he was still a private first class when he was transferred to the newly organized Tank Division Engineers in September 1942.[175]

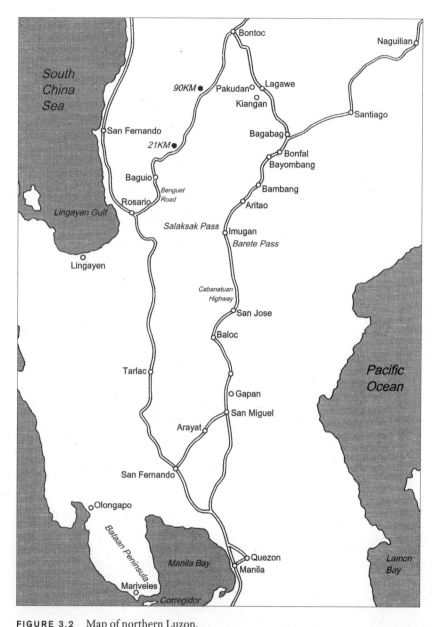

FIGURE 3.2   Map of northern Luzon.

After four years of active duty, Yano was finally promoted to private superior class in 1944, despite repeatedly skipping maneuvers and slapping other soldiers. He often talked with fellow veterans about the finish of their tours of duty.[176]

AT THE GAPAN AND SAN MIGUEL MARKETS

When he departed Boli, Yano was appointed the company cook (*kyūyogakari*, lit. "provisioner"), which became his principal duty.[177] The boat that carried his company, the cargo ship *Eiji-maru*, was sunk by a submarine off the Taiwanese city of Kaohsiung. The next cargo ship they boarded, the *Shiranesan-maru*, barely managed to reach Laoag on Luzon. From there Yano and his company went by motorized sailboat to San Fernando, arriving in the town of Gapan on September 28, 1944.[178]

Wishing to make the acquaintance of the town's female population, Yano promptly began to study Tagalog. As provisioner, he regularly went to the market to make purchases and soon became conversant. With his natural cheerfulness, Yano became a favorite among the local women—who might primarily have been interested in his ability to buy them things.[179] He received love letters from a girl named Ojia, and in San Miguel he learned Tagalog from a girl named Bunshin; they grew intimate, and she gave him a copper coin to commemorate it. He described this period: "For meat I buy one pig, I buy up fish directly as well, and I also go out to the farmer's to buy vegetables, so the bill gets fat. The inhabitants are kind, and me, I'm as happy as if I were in heaven" (October 23, 1944).

> With Hirose along I go to the home of Lushīn [whom he elsewhere described as the most beautiful girl at the market]. Several village girls gather around shouting, "Yano, Yano!" A guitar is produced and my comrade Hirose strums it. . . . As I softly hum [the song *"Kage o shitaete"*][180] Lushīn says, "Please sing for me." When I begin to sing, a suffocating feeling seizes my breast, maybe because this song has an especially sad tune. I'm caught up in emotion, feel I'm about to cry . . . I want to be free, I want to be a native.[181]

When Yano's company left San Miguel, by his account the inhabitants were reluctant to see him go, and cries of "Yano [and his girlfriend's name], Bunshin" arose like a chorus from among them. Afterward he grew close with the manager of a radio shop in Karanban; visiting the man's elegant home, he mused that once he finished his local tour of duty he would like to marry the daughter of such a family.[182]

REQUISITIONING, FIRE SETTING, EXECUTIONS

Relations between the Japanese troops and the people of the Philippines, however, were not always so peaceful. There was an incident in which two soldiers were attacked on the road between Gapan and San Miguel, and in retaliation the company raided a village at the foot of Mt. Arayat. On November 9, 1944, they burned the village to ashes; from a neighboring village, with thirty to forty houses, they requisitioned rice, potatoes, and pigs, even pulling the clothing from a chest of drawers and piling it on an armored vehicle.[183] They also captured two men who were harvesting rice (the two men would be stabbed to death on December 13). On the orders of his warrant officer, Yano stabbed to death an old woman who was too slow to get away.[184]

On January 9, 1945, as American forces landed at Lingayen Bay, the company left Gapan and headed for the mountains. After passing through San Jose, the soldiers went over the Barete Pass on February 4. Japanese military scrip lost its value, and as making purchases grew impossible, they came to rely solely on requisitioning. Day after day, the company's soldiers, with explosives strapped to their backs, died mounting attacks against tanks.[185] To provide the best possible food for his soldier comrades waiting for enemy tanks in foxholes, Yano went to a village to make requisitions, confiscating pigs, chickens, and turkeys in return for useless military scrip—he wrote that he took what he needed and no more.[186] While making requisitions on January 23, he confronted the scene of a woman being raped as she clutched a suckling baby.[187] Returning from attacks on January 28, Yano was treated to rice at the home of an elderly couple; afterward the warrant officer accompanying him stabbed them to death.[188]

WANDERING IN BARETE AND SALAKSAK

When they went over the Barete Pass, the company, 124-strong when they departed Manchuria, had already suffered 40 percent casualties. They had no tanks and a total of just six armored cars and trucks.[189] Joining an attack platoon on March 31 in an attempt to recapture what they called Tennōzan Hill in the vicinity of the Barete Pass, Yano suffered a severe wound in the back from a hand grenade. On April 2, he was carried by stretcher to the company base;

told that he could not be delivered to their next destination, he walked toward a field hospital in the rear leaning on a cane. "Wearing a raincoat and carrying a duffel bag, no matter how you see it I cut the figure of a beggar," he wrote. "How miserable I am!"[190]

On April 5, Yano arrived at Aritao Hospital, later moving to another one. On April 29, an order was issued to leave the hospital, and he returned to what was left of his unit at Inaban on April 30. From his company six men joined this unit, most of these suffering from malaria. His wound was gradually improving, but afraid to return to the front, he insisted that he was in bad shape.[191]

As the stands at both Barete and Salaksak had been broken, Yano and his fellow soldiers withdrew, departing Inaban on May 31. On June 10, en route to Kiangan, five patients including Yano were pushed off the truck—discarded. "If you can't survive on your own then kill yourselves," said the quartermaster-sergeant as he abandoned them.[192] On June 15, as they scattered to escape gunfire and bombing from Lockheed P-38s in the mountains, Yano lost track of three gravely ill comrades. The next day, Yano arrived at Kiangan with one colleague, a private superior class named Tokura. The Allied bombing raids were fierce, so he left the town on June 22 and went in search of his unit along a road lined with dead bodies.[193]

The marching was tough. On June 26, Tokura got his rucksack stolen, losing a precious liter of rice. That evening an associate went off to settle the score and returned with someone else's stolen rucksack.[194] Even fellow Japanese soldiers could no longer be trusted. On July 3, Yano got close to the unit he belonged to but chose not to rejoin it, assuming he'd probably be obliged to do onerous chores. The words of the quartermaster-sergeant—"If you can't survive on your own, then kill yourselves"—still rang in his ears.[195] On July 7, Tokura died of illness. As an epitaph, Yano wrote, "Here lies former Army Lance Corporal Tokura Otokichi," promoting him by a rank.[196] During this final march, Yano thought time and again about surrendering and becoming a POW. Leaflets scattered by American planes specified times for surrender and said to approach the sentry line carrying a white flag. But when push came to shove, he writes, as a Japanese soldier this was impossible.[197] On the contrary, Yano chose to keep after his original unit, wishing to "die a meaningful death." On July 10, the day after a sergeant in his group killed himself, he wrote, "I think about returning to my old unit, going with my comrades to the front, and locking swords with the Americans in mortal combat. To collapse and die on this roadside, or to die by suicide—neither is of any use to the nation."[198]

On July 15, Yano stole the rucksack of a Japanese resident who came asking for shelter. On July 22, an associate killed a medical sergeant who appeared to be a deserter, and they all grabbed his rice, potatoes, work socks (*jikatabi*), clothing, and blanket. Yano wrote of taking his new noncommissioned officer's sword and, later that night, eating his flesh.[199] On July 25, he was attacked by a Japanese soldier and barely defended himself.[200] His body swelled from malnutrition, and on August 11 he had a relapse of malaria. With his willpower ebbing, he at last determined to kill himself, thinking that he would like to die on August 23—the fifth anniversary of his older brother's death from an infection contracted at the front in Shanghai.[201]

YANO'S EXPERIENCES OF THE PHILIPPINES AND DEFEAT

Yano learned of the defeat from American leaflets on August 19. Allied shelling and bombardment had also ceased, and when he heard from an orderly that the Japanese army had issued a cease-fire order, he concluded that it was true. His "tears kept overflowing," he wrote, and he was so overjoyed that he could not sleep.[202] He arrived at company headquarters on August 29, was disarmed at Kiangan on September 14, and entered an American POW camp on September 20. There were fourteen survivors from his company.[203] In the camp, he set down his thoughts on the future of Japan now that the war was over. Referring to Murakumo, a civilian journalist employed by the military named, he wrote, "Murakumo is discussing the nation after we return to Japan. The soldiers are thinking of [making] Japan one of the states of the United States. I don't know but that would probably be good. We've had enough of war, and if I look at the U.S. Army's equipment and their soldiers' standard of living, I get the feeling that would be better. They're big-hearted and seem to have freedom" (November 7).[204]

In the camp, for the first time, Yano became aware of the repulsiveness of the Japanese state to which he'd been fettered. He yearned for the generosity, freedom, and economic prosperity that the United States of America represented and that he now saw Japan as lacking. After Filipinos shouted "Thief!" and "Die!" and pelted him with rocks as he boarded a train following the repatriation order, he wrote, "If I consider everything we've done to the inhabitants of the Philippines ever since landing at San Fernando, I can't stop thinking about the vastness of our crimes. Murder, arson, robbery, rape—we've committed every sort of crime again and again. It was not meant to be a war against them—so why did we do them so much harm? Why did we come and fight in this far away land? . . . No doubt we are truly criminals" (December 10).²⁰⁵ Over the course of one year, Yano—whose only images of the Philippines before he landed had been palm leaves and native girls—had arrived at this perspective through the experience of defeat and the collapse of the Japanese nation to which he'd been fettered, along with his experience of the Philippines that encompassed both intimate association and intense animosity.

Upon his return to Japan, Yano discovered that his parents' shipping business had folded because the military had taken away their four boys and that his oldest brother was managing a factory that baked earthen pipes. For several years, he engaged in black market activities, and then in 1951 he began dealing in earth and sand for construction work, making use of a transport boat.²⁰⁶

FROM MANILA JAPANESE ASSOCIATION STAFF MEMBER TO HOUSEWIFE

A DESIRE FOR SELF-RELIANCE

In May 1943, Kumano Aya, who was then learning typing and shorthand, answered a job advertisement seeking staff for the Manila Japanese Association and headed for the Philippines.²⁰⁷

Kumano was born into a sake wholesalers' family in Kumamoto City. After her father died, wartime enterprise consolidation forced the family to abandon the business, and her mother ran a lodging house with Kumano and her younger sister. For a young woman who desired to be self-reliant, the job in the Philippines was extremely attractive. She made the trip thinking, "Of course I want to go to Manila and discover a new world. Even as a woman I can probably be of use in some way." She'd convinced her mother that if she could earn a salary of 150 yen—as opposed to around twenty-five yen in Kumamoto—she could send approximately fifty yen home and thus allow her mother and sister to live comfortably.²⁰⁸

A BLESSED LIFE IN THE PHILIPPINES

Life in Manila was even more enjoyable than Kumano expected. Observing people gathering in the evenings in Luneta Park to sing accompanied by guitar and harmonica, she wrote, "When they speak of paradise, are they not speaking of this country?"²⁰⁹ Her chronicling of how she spent her first pay earned from shorthand work brims with happiness: "I get a salary of 150 yen in military scrip. Imagining my mother's smiling face, I send fifty yen of that from Yokohama Shōkin [Bank]. For my little sister I send red shoes costing seven yen fifty sen, ten yen worth of Western fabric, and a box of candies that you can't easily get anymore in Japan. It's embarrassing to be wearing shoes worn down in the sole in this town. I'll get some new ones."[210]

On October 14, the Philippines became "independent."[211] Kumano was relieved that Tagalog was designated the sole official local language, because now it was necessary to learn only one new tongue. On September 5, Kumano married Ni'imi Hiroki, a graduate of Kumamoto Commercial School employed at the Hitō Kinka Meriyasu Company (Philippine Kinka Knitwear Company),[212] and took his family name. After moving into her husband's home, she grew friendly with the Filipino family across the way via sign and body language. On July 24, 1944, her first daughter was born.

Around that time there was a major spike in inflation; a single banana, for instance, could cost as much as ten yen. Ni'imi would carry a basket full of military scrip to the market and would refill it with what she was able to buy. The dollar began to come back into circulation,[213] and there was also growing guerilla activity. "Why must people fight with one another?" she wrote. "Can't we solve our problems through discussion, without killing one another?"[214]

On September 21, Manila was bombed from the air for the first time. Yet things remained calm. Her husband played mahjong with friends, and when the bombing started, they lightheartedly bet that the first person who ran away had to pay a thousand yen. Ni'imi too remained optimistic, pondering how she would like to have her mother witness the beauty of the Manila sunset once peace had come: "When she sees the trees, grass, and houses appear to change into seven different colors, Mama will surely put her hands together and be thankful, saying that this must be what they mean by the Pure Land (*jōdo*)."[215]

THE BEGINNING OF "THE WAR"

In October 1944, almost all of the Kinka Meriyasu Company's employees, including Ni'imi's husband, were mustered into military service. He gave her a pistol with two rounds in it, to kill herself and her daughter Junko should the need arise. When she went to visit him at his base, she dressed Junko in her best Western clothing, dolled herself up in a lace dress, and traveled in a horse-drawn cart. Her husband, however, remained in civilian clothes, and she was moreover surprised to see him sporting a hand grenade at his waist. For the new conscripts there were not even any uniforms; as for the hand grenade, this was for use in a suicide attack.[216]

Her husband soon went to battle at Olongapo. Ni'imi decided to return to Japan on a combined cargo and passenger ship, but it made an emergency landing at Olongapo during an air raid and was sunk. Without an alternative she returned to Manila, where Japanese relations with Filipinos had so deteriorated that it was impossible to buy things even with money. When she sought conversation with Filipinos they turned their backs.[217]

After December 20, the elderly, women, and children were evacuated to San Jose on the instructions of the Japanese consulate. When Ni'imi and the others in the group she had journeyed with arrived at the San Jose base, however, a colonel rebuked them, asking why they had come when it was said the Japanese were hanging on in Manila.[218] San Jose itself was soon subjected to aerial assault, of which Ni'imi wrote, "No matter where I go it's air raid, air raid, why must we wage war?—Myself I don't understand it. It might have been a war started to expand Japanese territory for living, but isn't it possible to talk things over without fighting to the death? Even if it hadn't been a Japanese possession, I would have been able to live fine in Manila up to now." Her reflections did not extend to the question of why and how so many Japanese, military and civilian, had come to be living in Manila in the first place.

Trailing behind the army, Ni'imi and her companions reached Bonfal at the end of January 1945, where they organized a cooperative settlement named Mizuho, whose headman was a member of the consular staff. As the provisions supplied by the consulate were insufficient, they got food from Filipinos by trading military scrip, shirts, clothing, blankets, watches, and rings. When they ran out of things to trade, the consulate supplied them with vegetable seeds, which they took the liberty of sowing in Filipino-owned fields.[219]

The individual settlement members soon sought to requisition their own supplementary food, and they began to steal sugarcane, guanabana fruit, potatoes, and vegetables. Ni'imi was unable to obtain milk or rice to make gruel, and her infant daughter grew thinner by the day. At nine months she still could not sit up, and if laid down on her side she would stay that way indefinitely. Ni'imi herself also grew gravely weak. "Win or lose, it doesn't matter. This war cannot end too soon for me"—this had become her prayer.[220]

WANDERING IN THE MOUNTAINS

When the Japanese withdrew from Bonfal, Ni'imi was among a number of ill people who were meant to be left behind. But thanks to the good will of a doctor she knew, she was allowed to get on a truck. She wrote, "Shall the two of us, Junko and I, stay behind and turn ourselves over to the American army? I hear they line you up and flatten you to death with their tanks. That's frightening. Anyway I don't want to put up my hands and ask for help. When all is said and done I want to escape as much as it's possible to escape. To go as far as I can go, and if I have to die, then to die."[221]

Eventually forced off the truck, Ni'imi and her companions wandered in the mountains. The soldiers departed, saying, "Make sure you don't make a nuisance of yourself for the army." Hiding in the brush to avoid being seen from the air, she got separated from the others. She trudged along, heading for the consul station that was supposed to be at "kilometer point 318," between Bagabag and Lagawe. No matter how much she begged, passing military trucks refused to let her aboard. Even in villages where Japanese had assembled, she was refused entry into houses because the residents didn't recognize her. She was saved from starvation when she happened to run into the wife of the Kinka Meriyasu section chief, who gave her some rice. She was also given meat by a soldier who had just slaughtered a cow. From a Filipino household, she stole some precious brown sugar and garlic.[222]

After much pleading, Ni'imi was finally allowed to stay at a house where soldiers were boarding, but when she went to wash diapers, her rice, raw and salted beef, salt, brown sugar, and garlic were stolen. The soldiers professed ignorance, and she had no one to turn to. Finally she reached kilometer 318, only to find there was no consul station here. Claiming she was getting in their way, soldiers forced her onward toward Kiangan.[223]

When she reached Pakudan after passing through Kiangan, Ni'imi was able to get rice from the consulate. Shortly thereafter, she entered the mountains and wandered about the valley of the Ashin River. Her rations exhausted, she stole sweet potatoes from the local Igorot people and even ate the vines and leaves. She caught snails and consumed snakes and grasshoppers she received from passers-by. For her baby, she made soup out of rice husks left behind from soldiers' meals.[224] In early August, the child died. Ni'imi dug a hole with a woodman's hatchet and buried her in Western lace and a cardigan sweater, writing "Here lies Ni'imi Junko" with a pencil on a wooden grave marker. She

FIGURE 3.3   Ni'imi Aya and her daughter wandering on a mountain road in Luzon. Painted by Ni'imi Aya.

Source: Ni'imi Aya and Yoshimi Yoshiaki, *Firipin sen tōhikō* [Journey of escape at the Battle of the Philippines] (Tokyo: Iwanami Shoten, 1993), front cover.

decorated the grave with rocks and pink-colored orchids from a dry riverbed nearby.[225]

NEWS OF THE DEFEAT

Ni'imi learned of Japan's defeat from leaflets scattered by U.S. planes. Allied leaflets were treasured as fire starters and toilet paper and so were customarily hidden and hoarded without discussion, but one day a leaflet reading "Japan Surrenders" came down. Resident Japanese who had managed to survive now gathered together. Confirmation of the surrender came by way of a soldier claiming to come from military headquarters who ordered everyone to ready themselves for suicide because Japan had surrendered. Talk of suicide stopped after opposition from the resident Japanese, but someone from the consulate declared that anyone who acted on their own would be barred from the repatriation ship, so they remained in the mountains for more than ten days.[226] During this period, many people died of hunger. An order to move was issued on September 5, and Ni'imi arrived at the Canlubang POW camp on September 20. She landed back in Japan on November 1; the following year, 1946, she was informed of her husband's death in battle.

NI'IMI'S EXPERIENCE OF THE DEFEAT

What had sustained Ni'imi as she wandered in the mountains clutching her baby was the conviction that Japan would certainly win and that, because she was Japanese, she could not surrender. When her will was on the verge of breaking, she recovered by imagining that Japan would not lose. After the defeat, she learned of a group of Japanese, known as the "banzai group," who had surrendered without fleeing to the mountains. When told by a female camp inmate from this banzai group that things had turned out badly for her because she'd fled hastily to the mountains despite knowing Japan was going to lose, Ni'imi reacted strongly: "I don't want to hear it. How could a person who's forgotten the Japanese spirit (*Nihonjin no kokoro*) understand how I feel? Even if we lost the war I'm still Japanese. This lady doesn't understand the feelings of people who fled into the mountains."[227]

With this in mind, we can say that Ni'imi's tragedy was amplified by the imperial state's binding power. The state continually trifled with her earnest faith in it. Yet although we can say it came far too late, even she perceived the loss of the war as good news. Although taken aback when she saw the American leaflet, Ni'imi thought, "If the war has really ended, I'm saved. . . . I can return to Japan, I can see my mother."[228] Only now was she finally liberated from state control.

FROM WHITE-COLLAR WORKER TO THE
SUGA CORPS ARTILLERY BATTALION

A WHITE-COLLAR WORKER'S DEPARTURE FOR THE FRONT

On June 17, 1944, following his second call-up, Fujioka Akiyoshi joined the Shinodayama Field Artillery Regiment.[229]

Fujioka was born in 1915 in the Osaka Prefecture village of Sugawara. After graduating from Osaka Commercial College, he was hired as an accountant by

Osaka Machine Works.[230] Called up for the first time in 1940, Fujioka was assigned to the Osaka Infantry 37th Regiment Infantry Artillery Company (the unit that served as the model for Noma Hiroshi's *Shinkū chitai*)[231] and took part in battles at Yichang and Changhsa in China. Confronted with the reality of the war in China as a war of aggression, he wrote, "What in the world have we come here to do? Is this what you call 'the Imperial Army's holy war'?"[232] He subsequently fell ill while participating in landing exercises for the capture of Bataan and Corregedor in the Philippines in December 1941 and was repatriated in November 1942. Fujioka chose not to enlist as a staff cadet—a privilege granted to graduates of middle school and above—in the belief that "tasting and enduring together the hardship and sorrow endured by the majority of Japanese soldiers [was] the right way for a person to live." He returned home a private superior class.[233] Mustered again into active duty in 1944, Fujioka was sent to the Philippines. His unit embarked from Moji on July 1, 1944, with the ship so full there were men sleeping in the toilets and on the staircases. At least a third and perhaps twice that many of the ships in their convoy were sunk en route by American submarines.[234]

Fujioka arrived in Luzon on July 17 and was assigned to the Independent Combined 55th Brigade (Suga Brigade) Artillery Battalion. In Bongabon, on the outskirts of Manila, his unit spent days and nights practicing for close-range attacks on tanks. Although he was an artilleryman, Fujioka had neither his own gun nor a cannon assignment, and he shouldered only a bamboo spear. He sometimes went to Manila, but goods were in short supply in town, and soldiers received threatening looks from Filipinos. He wrote,

> Hardship, antipathy, and the withdrawal of everything civilized is the true shape of Philippine independence and the advancing Greater East Asian Co-Prosperity Sphere that the Imperial Headquarters boasts about. Drinking one cup of coffee paid for with this worthless paper, this military scrip that's stolen everything of this country's wealth, what a big deal. The eyes of Filipinos reveal a limitless animosity, my heart suffers every time I look at them. But whatever my thoughts and however my conscience may be troubled, how does this change the reality that I'm one of the tools of imperialism?[235]

At least as far as Luzon and China were concerned, Fujioka was painfully aware that he was an aggressor.[236] Able to view things from this standpoint, he was better able than other soldiers to see the rotten nature of the Japanese army.

On October 4, Fujioka's company arrived on the southern Philippine island of Jolo bearing only three months' worth of provisions, three field guns, and three mountain guns.[237] The island's Moro, or Tausug, inhabitants, followers of Islam, had a history of bravely and boldly resisting foreign occupation, including that of the United States before the war. So it was only natural that they resisted the Japanese army, which landed six thousand soldiers on the island with very few provisions for the sole aim of confronting the American army.[238] In advance of their own landing the Americans supplied the inhabitants with effective weapons; their Japanese opponents were short on equipment. The Moro specialized in close-range fighting in the jungle, excelling in surprise attacks with woodmen's hatchets and shooting at close quarters, and even the Japanese soldiers with combat experience got flustered and fell into disarray at the inhabitants' sudden point-blank attacks, to which they succumbed in great numbers. Fujioka wrote that dead soldiers had their weapons, clothing, gold teeth, and raw livers plucked from them. Thus did he come to regard the Moro people as "a fiendish race" of "natives" (*dojin*).[239] In under a month after the landing, nearly one hundred soldiers were killed by the Moro, and a raid on their stronghold of Maimbung was repulsed.[240]

Around March 1945, Fujioka became a lance corporal. On April 9 the American army started to land. Having fled to Tumatangas Mountain, the Japanese army withstood fierce, concentrated attacks from the American army for two months. Having decided to fight to an honorable death as soon as American forces landed, the Japanese troops had thrown away much of their provisions and medical supplies. As a result, there was frequently terrible conflict among them, directed especially against the units responsible for the remaining provisions; the rucksacks of the ill and wounded were frequently plundered as well. On Tumatangas, many succumbed to malaria. Most of the soldiers had their hands full just staying alive, and the ill and wounded were abandoned, including a chronically tyrannical superior officer.[241]

THE BATTLE WITH MUSLIM GROUPS OF THE MORO PEOPLE

Afterward, most of the American forces moved on from Jolo, leaving behind a smaller mop-up group. The Japanese soldiers went out to requisition cows, rice, sweet potatoes, and other vegetables, but this meant plundering Moro property, and they suffered violent counterattacks. As the number of wounded and malaria sufferers increased, hostility among the soldiers grew, and a few at a time of those still healthy, and those who got along with one another, came to break away and lead an independent existence; ultimately each man ended up on his own.[242]

When the Americans subsequently began hunting for remnants of the defeated army, the Japanese moved to Shiroman Mountain, twenty kilometers distant. During the difficult march, subjected to repeated attacks by the Moro, Fujioka dreamed of slipping away and surrendering to the Americans, but circumstances did not allow it.[243] Of his company's 135 men at the time of the American landing, eighty-two remained when they left Tumatangas, and by the time they reached Shiroman Mountain, their number had been reduced to thirty-five. Of the six thousand total Japanese army and navy personnel deployed to Jolo, just 350 were left.[244]

Finding food on Shiroman was extraordinarily difficult, Fujioka wrote:

> The day we arrived we raided a native's house and got only one cow, and from the next day on the natives mounted counterattacks. When we went out to make requisitions we got ambushed; the number of victims only mounted with each day, and hunger came upon us. On top of this . . . when it rained you couldn't light a fire, and when you'd sleep just soaking wet like that your belly got cold—disease was rampant. . . .
>
> The unit leaders held a meeting and the outcome was that if the units went on this way there'd be nothing left but for everyone to starve to death, so that night we'd raid native homes at the foot of the mountain. The order came down that we were to go out to the edge of the jungle until nightfall and then each unit would launch a surprise attack, taking advantage of the twilight. . . . Coming out of the jungle or not, each unit ran toward their designated house. It was dark all around us and the houses were further away than we thought. . . . In our Tanigawa Unit too, the headquarters in the vanguard went in firing a light machine gun, but the native house was just a shell, there was nothing inside. The cattle had been withdrawn too. As we loitered around bewildered, natives came shooting at us from below.[245]

After this incident it became impossible to raid people's houses, he added. When Japanese soldiers went into the fields at night and "got distracted plucking grain," the Moro fired on them from all sides.[246]

As they roamed about in the jungle, many soldiers died of battle wounds, malaria, starvation, or took their own lives.[247] They noted the arrival of August

15 as the day of the Obon festival, but they had no way of knowing this was also the day of the surrender. A week later, Fujioka's new best friend joined the dead.

Soon afterward, U.S. planes began to scatter leaflets. Having had a premonition of the defeat, to which he looked forward, Fujioka says he picked up a leaflet and "could not suppress my heart's palpitations in the joy of having my hopes miraculously come true."[248] The majority opinion in his company was that it was probably true, but officers picked up the leaflets and threatened that any soldier found secretly holding onto one would be hacked to pieces.[249] One by one, men Fujioka was particularly close with—Sergeant Major Toki, Navy Petty Officer Sugawara, lance corporals Takeuchi and Yamada, and Private Superior Class Nishida—dropped out of the ranks.[250]

Although frightened both by the possible consequences of having committed the crime of desertion and the prospect of a Moro attack, Fujioka made his way to an American army barracks. When he saw American soldiers waving hats and a white cloth, he was speechless, his lips trembling with joy.[251] Just before they passed through the camp gate, he and his comrades washed their dirty faces "for the sake of the honor of the Japanese army." Fujioka's sense of caution vanished as he saw that the American troops lacked any trace of hostility, and he "got choked up on happiness at being saved."[252]

Afterward, Fujioka went along to bring in remaining Japanese soldiers, but convincing the unit headquarters about the surrender was not easy. Only after a 14th Army staff officer paid a visit did everyone finally lay down their arms. The original Jolo contingent of six thousand men was now down to eighty,[253] and it should be said that most of those survived thanks to Fujioka and his compatriots, who had deserted in desperation and thus opened the way.

Fujioka and his fellows were soon moved to the Zanboanga POW camp on Mindanao. The remaining American army also withdrew from Jolo. In the camp, Fujioka continued to ponder the meaning of what he had been through.

If we first examine things from the standpoint of his Philippine experience, he was already well aware that the Japanese army was a victimizer, conscious from early on that he was "one of the tools of imperialism." This is reflected in his deep sympathy with the following words of a certain sergeant, spoken in admonishment of a navy chief petty officer who had punched a simple-hearted Taiwanese volunteer and called him a "damned Chink" (*kono shinajin me*):

> Do you know whose fault it is we've reached the point that Filipinos—nay, all the peoples of Southeast Asia?—can only call us "fools"? What we've called "Greater East Asia" and "The Eight Corners of the Earth Under One Roof" (*hakkō ichi'u*):[254] Have you ever given a thought to how shallow they are when you don't even have the capacity to embrace such an innocent Taiwanese?[255]

In contrast, however, Fujioka had difficulty perceiving himself as a victimizer of the Moro. What is evident in his writing vis-à-vis the Moro is an overwhelming sense of fear; on the surface at least, there is no recognition that Japanese forces had ruined their lives. His view of the Moro as "natives" and "a fiendish race" did not change after the surrender.[256] Fujioka's experience of the surrender and its aftermath was particularly intense. In the POW camp, defeated Japanese soldiers who had been wandering in the mountains unaware of the surrender came in every day. Fujioka wrote,

> The one who entered camp today didn't know the war had ended either. After his unit broke up he'd been moving in a group of six, but all of them died off and he was alone, and in the end, finally at a loss for food, he surrendered himself to a native family, and had spent about a half a day babysitting and running errands. When he was brought here, he thought he was going to be killed. He was using a false name.[257]

> The two men captured this evening had wrapped themselves in jute bags, they weren't even wearing loincloths. When they were let off the truck at the camp office they clasped their hands together begging for their lives, and they clung so hard to an American soldier he was surprised and ran off.[258]

Feeling as if the American soldiers right in front of him were concretely demonstrating the freedom, equality, and benevolence that he'd learned as ideals in his college days, Fujioka cross-examined himself: "Is being defeated in war really such an unfortunate thing? Is winning a war really such a happy thing?" He reached the following conclusions:

> I don't think so. At least not for the ordinary masses. Win or lose, war is something that brings bitterness and sorrow to the people. In that sense, this defeat is

surely "divine grace" for Japan. This defeat is what has provided the Japanese—who believed they would certainly win whenever they fought, and convinced that what was theirs was the best, and their spirit and power were absolute—a chance to reflect and criticize.

They say Japan was defeated by science. Everyone thinks so. But the majority have either forgotten or do not know that the basic method of science is critique. . . . This time, Japanese are being given an opportunity to be critical, the nation of Japan has gotten a chance to reflect. Japan is blessed.[259]

With this conviction in mind, Fujioka returned to Japan in January 1947 and soon resumed employment at the Osaka Machine Works.

BACK ON THE CHINA FRONT

FROM GIRLS' HIGH SCHOOL TEACHER TO FOURTH MORTAR BATTALION

THE DIARY OF A MORTAR UNIT SOLDIER

Ōnishi Katsumi, who was born in Kurodashō Village in Hyōgo Prefecture in 1909, was called up in January 1941 and joined the Second Company of the Fourth Mortar Battalion in Shanghai that February.[260]

Following graduation from the Tokyo Physics College, Ōnishi had become a middle school and girl's high school teacher. He was employed at the Osaka Ikuno Prefectural Girl's High School when he was called up as a private second class. Of his complicated emotions as he prepared to report for duty, he wrote,

The night before, [my wife] Tokiko and I were wrapped in serious conversation. Both of us even cried. I asked her to please take care of everything afterward. To be filial to my father, to live in harmony with [my older sister] Minami, to look after [my younger brother] Gi'ichi, to raise [our oldest son] Taka'aki to be strong without fail, and I too strongly swore that I would wholeheartedly do my best in my service, that at a minimum it would be at least two years, and that in that time I too would not commit any disgraceful infidelity against her.[261]

Ōnishi's artillery unit had originally been a poison gas attack unit; except for the fact that it frequently used poison gas shells, it was not particularly different from other units. Ōnishi did not apply to be a staff cadet, thinking that if he did his return would be delayed, and also because he was physically weak. His time

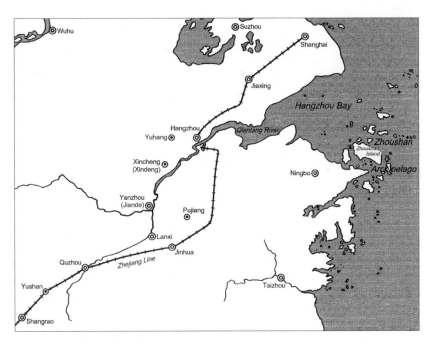

FIGURE 3.4   Map of the Zhejiang Campaign.

would be tougher as a result.[262] Still, he was lucky to be good at the math and science tasks required by the mortar unit, and he was always the top spotter in his group.[263]

THE ZHEJIANG-JIANGXI CAMPAIGN

Learning of the opening of hostilities with America, Britain, and the Netherlands from a mimeographed news bulletin posted on the board of the command group on the day of the event, Ōnishi grew melancholy. His diary entry that day reads, "A heavy atmosphere. I can't write anything."[264] His first combat experience was to be in the Zhejiang-Jiangxi Campaign, which began soon afterward. On April 18, 1942, Tokyo, Yokohama, and other cities were bombed for the first time by American planes.[265] Fearing another bombing raid, Imperial Headquarters ordered the destruction of the Chinese nationalist airfields in Zhejiang Province and Jiangxi Province that had been used for the American landing. When he saw the advance of the regimental banner at the front on May 15, Ōnishi wrote, "The colors move impressively forward. The banners reflecting the setting sun, the gallant standard bearer, the unit continuing on, the expected battle progress. For the first time, I revere the soul of the soldier. I lose myself in it, and I feel a sort of firm determination."[266] Looking toward his first battle, he felt ready in his heart. But he did not anticipate how cruel and merciless the campaign would be.

On May 7, Ōnishi's company arrived in Hangzhou. He spent the night at the library of the Zhijian College literature and science faculty; as he watched, a veteran soldier "went through pages of a photo album, tore out and stole the good ones like a thief on the prowl." Ōnishi was indignant. "It's a national shame. The valuable record is touched for a moment by an evil claw and reduced to waste paper."[267] Descriptions of requisitioning began to appear frequently in his diary. In a village in the vicinity of Yūhang on May 13, "they requisition pots and vegetables and put the residents to work; I pluck lots of green peas in the field in front."[268]

On May 16, the fighting began. The Second Company carried out a surprise attack with "red shells," containing a poison gas that produced vomiting and sneezing, against the Chinese army at Fenghuang Mountain.[269] Red shells would continue to be employed repeatedly, but perhaps because the effects of the gas were temporary, it seems from his diary that Ōnishi had no pangs of conscience about it.

On May 17, the soldiers seized and ate green peas and a pig for lunch. That day Ōnishi wrote, "We destroy houses along the side of the road, many doing more violence than necessary." He sought to intervene at one point, saying "that's overdoing it," but his comrades restrained him. On May 18, they triumphantly entered Xindeng. Of breakfast that morning he wrote, "Some go out requisitioning nappa cabbage and sugar, some wait and make *zenzai* [sweets made from beans]; they're fit, strong is what soldiers are. My squad is even more high-class . . . they run along with cheeks filled to bursting with sweet bean (*adzuki*) cakes made on the spot."[270] As he marched on May 20, he watched the town burn:

There was a bustle over the fire, but in the other units they didn't forget to requisition rice. Some soldier says the city's inhabitants gathered in great droves on a small hill far removed, dazed and wailing bitterly at the flames—their cursing [of us] was something fearful. My unit rerequisitioned the rice [others had] picked up and tossed away again; I wonder if there's ash and sand mixed in. In any case I fastened it to the saddle. . . . We walked about the hill and took a break in a pavilion, talking about things like how to set the roofs of straw-thatched houses alight.[271]

That day a soldier from the battalion column commandeered a resident and his cow. Seeing the man's relatives cry and wail, Ōnishi was possessed by a feeling for which "the word grief doesn't say enough." On the way he saw a "coolie" (a commandeered resident) who had been stabbed in the head and belly with a saber and tossed below an embankment, groaning and covered in blood. "I don't know what this is all about," he thought, "but it's awful, awful."[272]

On May 21, lacking rice for the following day, all the men went out to make requisitions and seized a large quantity of sweet potatoes. In fierce fighting the next day, the company showered the village of Liantang with red shells. On May 23, they used the poison gas again in the vicinity of the plateau southeast of Baifoshan. On May 24, they seized chickens, cucumbers, eggplant, and bamboo shoots. The following day, they entered Jiande. The military police (*kenpeitai*) had already confiscated goods there, but Ōnishi "was quite pleased to find a small quantity of rice, rice flour, and candy."[273] On May 29 it rained, so they commandeered inhabitants and forced them to carry rice. They entered a prosperous village and each unit took high-quality fabric and shoes, making the "coolies" change clothes. They also wrapped the trunks and necks of their pack cows in widths of fabric, "their rumps in red cloth, their necks wrapped in green, made to carry big *futons* in flower patterns." It looked "like a procession of baggage at a wedding, or a great festival at the Myōken Shrine,"[274] and everyone in the company roared with laughter. On June 1, they requisitioned great quantities of pastries, sugar, and pastry flour from a large store.[275]

From the June 3 launch of the Quzhou Campaign onward, Ōnishi's descriptions of savagery grow numerous. Amid "impacts like a thunderstorm falling on a pond," he transported projectiles ceaselessly on the campaign's first day. After an intense battle that resulted in five men being badly wounded, two men hiding in the attic of a house who seemed like soldiers in mufti were dragged outside. They begged for their lives but were beaten with a sword and a piece of wood, and then beheaded. On June 4, the company took accurate artillery fire from the Chinese nationalist army near the Quzhou provincial castle; soldiers argued that this was likely thanks to a Chinese informant. Ōnishi wrote, "Voices calling 'kill all Chinese' are clamoring. 'Dump a bunch of them in the pond.'" They attacked the castle the following day, with orders to use red shells.[276] Japanese planes bombed the fortress's interior while Ōnishi's company conducted a coordinated barrage with other artillery units. "A magnificent, jet-black plume of smoke stretches far and high into the heavens," observed Ōnishi during the fierce assault. "It's an intense funeral pyre." He saw a young Chinese soldier who had been hiding in a pillbox receive a blow to the head with a cross-hoe and get kicked into the rice paddy. "On the way back I observe the death of an old woman. Some soldier's cruel, atrocious prank."[277]

In the requisitioning on June 7, along with chickens, they seized children and girls; along the way they sent them home again. On June 9, Ōnishi wrote,

> In the requisitioning there are those who look for money and valuables—that is, to steal money. The requisitioning spirit should be something limited to what's inevitable for the execution of the campaign, it should be kept to an absolute minimum. You shouldn't make profits or cart things off. And you shouldn't kill or injure Chinese just because you feel like it, without basis. And yet, albeit under intense circumstances, there's been a lot of beastly, cruel behavior the last few days, and there's no way to express my righteous indignation.[278]

On June 11, the men who went out for requisitions returned with "great fruits of battle," and everyone gathered to portion out the goods. Ōnishi thought to himself, "I don't want to go out for requisitions, and I don't want to receive anything besides staple food."[279]

Yet it seems that Ōnishi, too, conducted not only "public" but also private requisitions. On June 15, he wrote, "At Sergeant Watanabe's invitation we crossed the river and went to look for things. We bring back eight pomelos and a large, eccentrically lettered and illustrated scroll of rare beauty from a big house."[280]

THE EXPERIENCE OF THE SEKKAN (ZHEJIANG-JIANGXI) CAMPAIGN

After the destruction of the Quzhou airfield and a month spent requisitioning provisions for men and cattle, the unit retreated via Lanxi, Pujiang, and Hangzhou, returning to Nanjing at the end of September. During this phase of the campaign, Ōnishi witnessed countless incidents of arson—perpetrated, we can only assume, by the Japanese army. Along with again commandeering local residents for use as "coolies," Ōnishi and his fellow soldiers requisitioned such items as hulled and whole rice, pigs, chickens, ducks, sweet potatoes, ginger, sugarcane, peaches, green tangerines, pomelos, coal, fabric, and straw sandals, as well as straw for their horses. These requisitions obviously caused great hardship to the Chinese. The following entries in Ōnishi's diary draw a picture of the situation:

> 0400 [hours] departure for requisitions, a squad of eight men. . . . We split up right and left and requisition coolies; the sight of them running for their lives and scattering into the mountain recesses is also a bit of entertainment. . . . We return with one soldier driving on several of them with their hands bound behind them. Like cattle being driven to a market in Taishō times. . . . Our squad's chinks [*nii*, lit. Chinese for "you"] are marked by blue cloth tied around their arms—we caught fourteen of them. . . . We cross the river with the chinks carrying us. The arch-shaped stone bridge that one sees in pictures—the Imperial Army has laid waste to this quiet village too, there's nothing left.[281]

> Out this morning to requisition unhulled rice. Recently most inhabitants have returned to the village, harvesting and threshing by moonlight and fleeing to the mountains with the unhulled rice at first dawn. Yesterday on patrol we caught four people harvesting. It amounted to a kitful of new rice, and we made a porridge of it. It was delicious.[282]

Devastating towns and villages, plundering food and even the inhabitants themselves—this was truly the definition of an aggressor army. Ōnishi, sensitive to the anger of the Chinese people, was himself driven to anguish. On September 9, finding a "statute book" smeared with waste and lime below the command unit's office shelf, he saw a Chinese poem on the cover that read: "From the aerial bombing everywhere, there is no end to the property reduced to ashes, and not a soul who can bear parting with it—oh witnessing such tragedy, there are no words for it" (飛機到処的轟炸　財産焚焼無計数　人民到処感流連　目睹惨噎無限). He had "the feeling that the hands of the people's anger are strangling me in the dark." It felt "unbearably frightening."[283]

For his part, Ōnishi attempted to deal humanely with the Chinese "coolies" around him. So long as they did not try to run away, he interacted with them in a spirit of "shared pleasures, shared hardships" (同甘共苦), and he did not commit acts of cruelty. He was impressed by "coolies" who kindly helped him with his baggage, who were considerate, who held his hand as they climbed, and so forth. "Could these be our enemy?" he wrote on May 21.[284] After joining a group of "coolies" in the task of separating unhulled rice from requisitioned rice plants, he wrote, "Japanese farmer's sons and Chinese farmer fellows lined up together like old friends. We are thankful for the harvest of the Zhejiang fields."[285]

Yet such sentiments alone solved nothing. Ōnishi sensed a profound contradiction between the good cause for which Japan claimed to be fighting and the behavior of the Japanese army in China, but he sought to reconcile himself with it as a reality he could do nothing about. On September 19, he heard from the company commander that "the army is full of contradictions. First setting yourself against this, second accepting this, and third feeling like it can't be helped—these are the usual changes [you go through] with time." Ōnishi thought to himself, "I'm in tune with my resignation and it's pleasant. . . . In any case, I shall do my best."[286]

He subsequently took up policing duties in Nanjing. On September 3, 1943, on the basis of his excellent performance, he was selected as company representative for a ceremony to transmit the imperial will (*seishi dentatsushiki*). His "heart pulsed and legs quaked with satisfaction at the greatness of the honor and the smallness of myself." Ōnishi did not participate in the Changde Campaign that began shortly thereafter. Now a lance corporal, his status meant he was pampered to the extent that "in the command squad recently, the looking-after virtually extends to washing my feet; they do things like taking off my lace-up [boots] for me and making up my blanket while I'm taking a pee."[287] Having resigned himself and closed his eyes to the contradictions of the Japanese army's behavior, he had become a successful junior noncommissioned officer.

THE THROUGH-THE-CONTINENT CAMPAIGN (*TAIRIKU DATSŪ SAKUSEN*)

In May 1944, Ōnishi, who had now attained the rank of sergeant, participated in the Through-the-Continent Campaign (at first the *Shōkei* or Xiangjiang-Guilin Campaign) as leader of the Second Company's Fourth Squad. The soldiers advanced southwestward through the provinces of Hubei, Hunan, and Guangxi near to the Guizhou border, then turned sharply and progressed eastward through Guizhou, Hunan, and Jiangxi. The total length of the march was two or three thousand kilometers. Fearing American retaliation, the army leadership had forbidden the unit to use poison gas in this campaign and ordered that poison gas shells be turned back in. Counterattacks against requisitioning forays grew more frequent, but because supplies were extremely poor, requisitioning efforts did not abate despite the heightened risk.[288]

On May 19, the soldiers departed Wuchang. Over the course of their march, in addition to commandeering residents, they requisitioned a vast range of items: rice, tobacco, *chirimen* (crepe) shrimp, onions and spring onions, Chinese noodles, salt, pigs, cows, chickens, vegetables such as sweet potatoes, pumpkins, eggplant, cucumbers, soybeans, beans in the pod, daikon (white radishes), amaranth, and spring onions, bananas, liquor, sugar, preserves, pastry, clothing, shoes, *xiexi* (low shoes), blankets, towels, soap, and books. Leather, sewing machines, record players, and records were seized as souvenirs. Some among the soldiers also went on the hunt for women and for valuables such as *fabi* currency and watches.[289]

Alongside food, Ōnishi obtained Chinese books, notebooks and other items, such as the ones listed in his June 30 entry:

> Today it's the battalion commander's inspection. . . . I've arranged it nicely inside. . . . The teapot and the teacups are all painted in gold leaf, on the podium in front is that fancy [requisitioned] mantel clock, and on the side of the Shintō altar in the back there are posters of beautiful women and the two hanging [calligraphy] scrolls we brought back from the elementary school the other day. . . . It's really turned into a nice room.[290]

Regarding the "coolies," Ōnishi's feeling of "shared pleasures, shared hardships" did not change, but it was not necessarily absolute either. On September 7, in the area of Changning, for example, he released inhabitants seized in You (攸) Prefecture when they pleaded to be allowed to return home, but in return he had them capture local people as replacements.[291]

Perhaps because he had grown accustomed to the battlefield, Ōnishi apparently lost his distaste for the countless requisitions. On the way to Liuzhou on November 29, for example, he wrote about a house he and his comrades took over for a barbecue:

> There's lots of rice at the back. I take a seat and have lunch. There are plenty of chickens. There's Chinese noodles, shoes, lots of toothpicks. . . . Nakajima and others [who went out to requisition] return and say there's quite a lot of stuff— they come back with dress shirts, shirts, fabric, leather slippers, sugar, raw sugar, candy, cream, and assorted other items. Warrant Officer Ishizashi also comes

back smiling with the soldiers. Because the *kantsū* [*kansoku tsūshinhan*, or spotter communications squad] got plenty of sugar in block strips. They treat us to candy. We had the coolies change their tattered clothes too . . . they could take whatever they liked. Shoes and the like lay all about. I got a [short-sleeved] wool jacket too. I heard Ishizashi's and Shimizu Shigeo's detachments requisitioned horses when they crossed the river.[292]

In the context of the fall of Saipan and a war climate where "the spirit of self-sacrificing attack" (*tokkō seishin*) was being emphasized, soldier's feelings continued to fray. A regimental commander appeared riding a palanquin and waving a fan as he directed troops, and the marching discipline of the advancing mortar regiment was seen to be loosening.[293] Ōnishi wrote, "I deeply realize that our battalion, among others, is really a slipshod unit with loose military morals." Descriptions of taking pleasure in the hardships and misfortunes of fellow soldiers began to appear in his diary: "To be honest I really enjoy [hearing about] big problems in other detachments; it's fun."[294]

MEMORIES OF LUANSHAN AND LIU VILLAGE

At the end of 1944 Ōnishi took up guard duty in the village of Luanshan (巒山, Jp. Ranzan) in Guangxi. Here he had his most intense experience of the Through-the-Continent Campaign. Holed up in a mountain cave, the villagers were mounting resistance, and in February 1945 a sergeant was killed when soldiers who went out to requisition building materials for a bathhouse entrance were attacked.[295] Further casualties followed. The First Company sustained thirteen dead in combat. After a "battalion suppression" operation failed, the resistance finally subsided in March when a "divisional subjugation," involving tanks and flamethrowers, blocked up the cave entrance.[296] Captured inhabitants were subjected to such cruelties as "putting hot coals between their toes." "The old soldiers could torture [the women] as they wished," Ōnishi wrote, reporting that he heard of women being tied up and burned at the stake. After the counterinsurgency operation was over, whole rice was requisitioned from the uninhabited village.[297]

Ōnishi was subsequently posted to guard duty in the village of Liu (六村, Jp. Rokuson), but soon thereafter the troops were pulled out with the aim of making them available to engage the U.S. Army.[298] On May 19, 1945, some of the men in his unit conducted requisitions in Niuwei (牛尾, *gyūbi*) and Bama (巴馬,

haba), "pacification villages" (*senbu buraku*)[299] where requisitioning hitherto had been prohibited. Ōnishi described his bitter feelings at the time:

> In both of these villages up to yesterday—nay, even now—the fact of our depar-
> ture is kept a secret in what should be the company's pacification village, and
> after we leave we show them no gratitude,[300] no one cares how much we lose
> face, how much trust in us is damaged, or how much the residents are troubled or
> confused. This is the attitude of the entire Japanese army in China. How can true
> pacification be achieved, let alone Sino-Japanese cooperation?[301]

It's as if it we can hear it: the deeply sorrowful voice of a noncommissioned officer who could only despair at the Japanese army's heartlessness even as he held faith in Sino-Japanese cooperation. Ōnishi's unit departed on May 20, setting fire to six villages already laid waste by a unit that had previously passed through.

THE WITHDRAWAL MARCH

Requisitioning continued during the withdrawal. According to what Ōnishi heard from a person who appeared to be the head of a pacification village, "We also have to collect military provisions and horse fodder for passing units . . . and given the lawlessness of [these] passing units, pacification is also quite difficult."[302] In the sectors under Japanese occupation, Chinese people came to purchase items the Japanese had requisitioned, including clothing, fabric, and silver coins.[303] Upon entering resource-rich Hunan on June 24, he wrote, "The fire of greed" began to "burn in our breasts. . . . [Soldiers shouted,] 'From here on there's piles of stuff!' "[304] When he arrived that day in a populous village with many inhabitants, Ōnishi was inspired.

> Many residents come out on the street and enthusiastically make way for us. Dusk
> is near and there are also many Chinese girls (*guniang*); standing there with their
> fans, they look beautiful to these eyes that have gone so long without. I haven't
> seen so many inhabitants—girls who really talk with the garrison and the like—
> since we departed Wuchang; there's really a feeling of life restored to peaceful
> ease, I'm happy to view the true shades of [what] casting out the barbarians[305]
> [has achieved].

This sort of "peace" based upon the Japanese subjugation of China was Ōnishi's ideal, but the fact that he had not once seen such "peace" in the excess of a year since he had left Wuchang shows how limited it was. Everywhere he went for requisitions he was reminded of this reality. During requisitions on June 30, residents who spotted the Japanese soldiers all ran away at once, and there was nothing in their houses. Having had so much already stolen from them, the residents could think of no alternative but to hide everything, except a single day's necessities, in a distant location.[306]

Yet while he acknowledged that the Japanese army was laying waste to China and tormenting its people, Ōnishi too had grown unable to suppress entirely the feeling that requisitioning was fun. Seeing residents running about trying to escape the requisitions on June 30, he felt "an amusement that truly defies description."[307] After he passed through a town in Jiangxi's Yichun Prefecture on July 21, he wrote,

> To my surprise, the businesses were still intact. A fair amount of articles of every kind are still on the shelves, quite scattered about. When I asked, they said the residents were unaware of anything and just minding their daily business when, just like that, an advance detachment of one unit came in. I wonder what sorts of things there were—it must have been fun. Even now there are still plenty of Chinese noodles and such, and we seized a few buckets of sugar. For the time being we attached it to a confiscated horse and an army horse (*kan'nami*) with some difficulty. The *kan'nami* is incredibly swollen thanks to the Chinese noodles.[308]

FROM SURRENDER TO THE RETURN HOME

On August 11, Ōnishi heard of the Soviet entry into the war and thought, "This puts Japan in danger too. I really can't stand the anxiety."[309] But when he heard rumors of the defeat at Lushan on August 15, he didn't believe it—he opined with disgust that soldiers shouldn't spread that sort of rumor.[310] Ōnishi learned of Japan's unconditional surrender on August 17 from the company commander. Although he had overcome great hardships with the faith that they were for "the sake of the great fight that we cannot lose" or "peace and prosperity after victory," he was now stupefied, feeling as if he had been hurled down into a deep, pitch-black pit. He experienced a sense of futility—that the war had all been no more than "froth on the water"[311]—the confounding recognition of surrender without having suffered defeat on the China front and the chagrin of being compelled to recognize that "the nation assembled through the tremendous sacrifices of all Japanese since Meiji has come entirely to nil. China, Manchuria, Korea, Taiwan, southern Sakhalin—all are [now] foreign countries."[312]

Ōnishi's unit was subsequently disarmed by the forces of the Nationalist government. "When I add together my abuse of prisoners working at the Quzhou airfield and the crimes I've committed in the recent *Shōkei* campaign,"[313] Ōnishi wrote, he had "a truly frightened feeling above all," but he avoided investigation.[314]

As the unit's members ceremonially bowed toward the Imperial Palace on New Year's Day, 1946, the unit commander instructed, "This year we should all safely complete our repatriation together and apply ourselves to the reconstruction of the motherland." Hearing this, Ōnishi was deeply affected.[315] The difficulties and dangers of the military campaign were gone—and as he realized this the pain of POW camp life dissipated as well. "These are, in any case, days of security," he now thought. "Are they not?"[316]

On February 8, Ōnishi departed Zhenjiang for repatriation. His emotions upon leaving China were complicated.[317] On the one hand, he declared, "from now on this is a China for Chinese people only. A peaceful Zhenjiang for only you, without any troubles. Please live your lives as you please, in good health. From my heart, I truly rejoice at a China of unadulterated Chinese people, at a Zhenjiang for Zhenjiang people only. Thank you for your trouble all this time. Thank you very much."[318] On the other hand, however, he could not suppress some darker feelings: "Along the track, there are old men, old women, children, etc. with a foul appearance. They come to sell us bread and the like. Who would buy things from dirty types like this—don't Chinese people realize this? Their clothing, their gaze, their conduct—when I recall they're a member of the victorious Allies, I'm overcome by an unspeakable sense of chagrin."[319]

That said, when he thought of how the Chinese and Japanese armies treated their respective POWs, he recognized that at least the Chinese army did not kill its prisoners or send them off to remote places for forced labor. Contemplating what it would have been like to be dealt with as a POW by his own army, he wrote, "If I just think about it, I somehow feel I've laid a finger on the most frightening thing in the world. Seeing it this way, I'm truly grateful for the way the Chinese army treats us. We can never thank them enough."[320] On March 5, Ōnishi landed at Sasebo. He returned to his home in Hyōgo Prefecture three days later and was soon reinstated at the Ikuno Prefectural Girl's High School.

FROM UMBRELLA SHOP SALESMAN TO PACIFICATION OFFICER IN THE NORTHERN CHINA EXPEDITIONARY FORCES

THE RECORDS OF A PACIFICATION OFFICER

Murakami Masanori, born the oldest son of an umbrella vendor in the town of Tsuma in Miyazaki Prefecture in 1915, became a pacification officer[321] for the Northern China Expeditionary Army in 1939 and was sent to Shanxi Province. In the autumn of 1941, he was employed by the secretariat of the "New People's Association" (*Xin min hui*) [322] in Changzi Prefecture and transferred there along with his family.[323]

After his graduation from Tsuma Middle School, Murakami had become head of the town's youth association (*seinendan*) and assisted in his family's umbrella-vending business. In 1938 he was selected as a member of the Great Japanese Union of Youth Associations Sympathy Group for Those in Military Service (*Dai Nippon rengō seinendan gun'yaku hōshi imondan*) and was sent to central China. With a history of pulmonary tuberculosis, Murakami did not think he was worthy to serve in the military, so he volunteered to be a pacification officer. When he was accepted, he wrote that he was so pleased he jumped for joy.[324]

Pacification officer training, in which it was proclaimed that "the confusion of the Chinese people, who are ignorant or mistaken in their thinking, must be crushed," sparked Murakami's enthusiasm to "rescue the people from the ravages of war and build a peaceful new China."[325] He led a security unit that took part in reconnaissance and punitive missions against the Chinese Communist Eighth Route Army in every part of Shanxi Province, beginning with Xiaoyi Prefecture. He bustled about with initiatives to win over the people such as an organization combining the New People's Association with "peace preservation" associations (*chi'an ijikai*), the establishment of Japanese-language schools, and the purchase of food. Murakami was aware that these activities aroused the antipathy of the Eighth Route Army, and he heard that there were rewards of five thousand *yuan* for the head of a pacification officer and one thousand *yuan* for his armband.[326]

Yet, believing in the construction of a "New Order in East Asia," after going back to his hometown to marry in March 1941, he returned to duty with his new wife in tow, seeking to integrate with the local population. His first son was born in March 1942, his second in May 1945.[327]

BETWEEN THE ARMY AND THE POPULATION

In the summer of 1941, Murakami had his first encounter with the suffering experienced by the Chinese people under Japanese occupation. The Japanese army vacated Xiaoyi Prefecture in response to maneuvers by the Nationalist Shanxi Army commanded by Yan Xishan. Chinese in the region who had been cooperating with the Japanese—prefectural officials, members of the New People's Association and cooperatives, police and security officers—feared execution as traitors and sought shared passage. Several of Murakami's Chinese employees tried to cling to a military truck. The soldiers kicked them off, beating them with their guns and boots; Murakami could do nothing but break down and cry out to them, "Please forgive me! Please forgive me!"[328]

In the autumn of 1942, he took up duties with the New People's Association of Zezhou. That year there was a great drought, and the harvest was sharply reduced. By the following year obtaining food had become a military imperative, and Murakami was faced with another painful dilemma, caught between orders from the Japanese secret service to purchase food and Chinese people groaning from hunger.[329] In the homes of the big landowners and men of influence—those who collaborated with the Japanese—there was enough food.[330] But for ordinary people the situation was dire.

Outside the walled city of Zezhou the drought led to a wave of refugees flowing in from Henan, with people dying every day of starvation.[331] Inside the walls, dozens were dying daily as well, and residents were reduced to grinding tree leaves, bark, and millet hulls for dumplings. Murakami and his fellow pacification officers set up a refugee aid center with their own funds, but a dangerously large throng pushed its way in and they quickly closed the center down again.[332] Purchasing in the sectors where the Eighth Route Army was active was carried out by military force. Going out to make purchases, Murakami witnessed Japanese soldiers killing captured POWs and the *kenpeitai* torturing and murdering civilians.[333] On a day he received "umbrellas from all" (万人傘) as gifts from the prefectural governor and others collaborating with the Japanese, Murakami wrote, "When I thought of how much the people were suffering from our food purchasing operations, I could not keep a chill from my heart."[334]

Around the autumn of 1943, Murakami became an advisor to the Qi Prefecture cooperative, in which role he continued to witness the toll of the Japanese purchasing operations. While residents appealed for relief from the army's unbearably heavy quotas, the chief of the secret service urged, "Even if you burn down their houses, even if you kill people, it's no problem. Squeeze them as much as they can be squeezed!"[335] A coercive purchase squad was assembled from among members of the secret service, who terrorized uncooperative farmers by cutting off their ears.[336]

Disgusted by such behavior, Murakami was proud of carrying out a survey of the true state of productivity, which led to a reduction of 30 to 50 percent in the quantity of goods demanded for delivery.[337] He also wrote of being thanked for proposing the capture of doves raised by major landowners to resolve simultaneously the demands of the army—troubled by a shortage of meat—and farmers worried about threats to their poultry.[338] But food purchasing activities remained his primary duty, and no matter how he conducted himself, there was no change in the fact that those operations were the source of widespread suffering. Amid ongoing drought, purchasing operations were to continue until Japan's defeat.

ALL LIKE BUBBLES ON WATER

Murakami learned of the surrender on August 15 from a radio broadcast of the emperor's speech. He had gone to Taiyuan to confirm the validity of a report of the surrender from an employee in the Qi Prefecture cooperative. "Dreaming the dream of constructing a new China for more than seven years, wandering at the edge of death many times as the agonies piled up one upon the other, all of this, too, had reverted to bubbles on the water"—these were his thoughts, he wrote, as his tears would not stop flowing.[339]

But Murakami's war was not yet over. Upon his return to Qi Prefecture, he found the advancing Shanxi Army and the smaller Japanese army garrison unit in a standoff, and he played a role in mediating between the two forces. An agreement was reached that allowed for a peaceful entry into the castle by the Shanxi Army, which awarded Murakami the title of Honorary Secretary of the Qi Prefectural Government.[340] At the end of 1945, ostensibly for the planning of Japan's reconstruction, Murakami and other former members of the cooperative began to purchase food and supplies for the Japanese army that was now under the command of the Shanxi Army, joining up with the Shanxi Province supply company. But this did not work out, and Murakami realized that his time in China was up; in March 1946 he returned to his hometown with his wife and children.[341]

After returning home, Murakami began manufacturing Japanese umbrella spindles (*rokuro*),[342] and he later ran a successful sewage disposal business.

FROM BREEDING STOCK CENTER EMPLOYEE TO 232ND REGIMENT INFANTRYMAN

THE RECORD OF A SOLDIER IN THE DANGYANG GUARDS

Born in 1914 in the village of Kyōwa Village in Yamaguchi Prefecture, Agari Masa'omi was called up in June 1943 and assigned to the 39th Division, Hamada Infantry 232nd Regiment, 10th Company, which was in Dangyang in the Chinese province of Hubei.[343]

After graduating from higher elementary school, Agari had been employed at the Yamaguchi Prefecture Breeding Stock Center. From arrival at the front through May 1945, he was on garrison duty, mainly in Hubei's Dangyang Prefecture. He also participated in the Changde Campaign in 1943.

Agari appears to have been a kind soldier with a caring heart. In 1944, while on sentry duty, he started a conversation with some elementary school children. After they gave him enough apricot blossoms to bury himself in, he wrote, "These children I will never see again—it was absurdly moving."[344] When he saw a farmer's wife tending to a rice paddy in an agricultural village in the vicinity of Shuangliansi, he was driven by "an urge to try joining her weeding together in the paddies," and without thinking about it he called to her, "Thanks for a job well done!" He later wrote, "The figures of women at work in the great paddies stretching off into the clear sky are something beautiful."[345]

Scouting out a "comfort station" in the town of Shuangliansi, he talked with the Chinese "comfort women" by candlelight while eating beans in the company of a soldier working in intelligence. Touched by the "refreshing" humanity of the "comfort women," Agari from then on "came to think that I should not insult these women or put them to shame."[346]

Yet according to what he wrote, his company requisitioned horses and donkeys and such foodstuffs as rice, pigs, beans, sausages, salt, pears, and peaches on a daily basis. He and his fellow soldiers also regularly commandeered both adults and children. In the spring of 1944, for example, his company "surrounded a village along the way from three sides" and commandeered women and children to carry firewood for battalion use "with no thought as to whether they were old, young, men, or women, seizing every last one of them."[347] He had no pangs of conscience about these sorts of activities. When he questioned a youth arrested on suspicion of being a spy in 1944, Agari assumed that the young man would avoid execution. This did not mean he would be released, however; rather, Agari sought to "use him for the time being to chop firewood or for odd jobs"—there is no indication that he felt any doubt about the justice of this.[348]

Reflecting on his service, Agari wrote, "I never saw or heard of anything such as massacres or rapes without cause."[349] But this was evidently untrue. Around the same time, when out on reconnaissance, he witnessed the shooting to death of a "good guy" (*ryōmin*) by an intelligence officer who failed to confirm guilt beforehand.[350] And during the same period, he captured a man in his thirties who was crossing a river in the middle of the night; the man was executed by the company after being tortured several times. Regarding the torture and execution, he wrote, "When I heard of the circumstances, I fell into a completely dismal mood. I also regretted his capture. In the end I even wished for his speedy death. . . . On the battlefield, maybe you can settle things [only] through killing."[351]

FOR THE SAKE OF "PEACE IN THE EAST"

Agari's acquiescence to such deeds may be attributed to his belief that his side was fighting for the sake of "peace in the East" and consequently for the sake of the Chinese. Having overheard the complaints of women who'd been requisitioned to carry firewood, he wrote:

> These people of the occupied territories, every time there's a battle we're sweating buckets and spilling our blood for the sake of their peace too. . . . Despite the fact that this is a peaceful march [of firewood porters], when I think of this it gets my ire up a bit.[352]
>
> . . . And now that we've gotten into this war with the world as our enemy, we're spilling our blood in China. The blood and sweat we've spilled are wiping clean the Chinese continent that's has been wounded and sullied [by the aggression of the Allied Powers]. When you put it that way you can't say our battle behavior is entirely without sense. . . . When it's a battlefield, the inhabitants suffer damage, and the destruction of the cultural heritage goes on and on. Yet we believe in peace in the East, and precisely for this reason we pay no regard to life-threatening danger.[353]

All the suffering of the Chinese people and the damage to their property was thus rationalized as inevitable. In May 1945, Agari departed Dangyang for Manchuria. Following the surrender, he was interned by the Soviet Union. Even after he returned to Japan in 1950, there was no change in his conviction about why the war had been fought.

FEATURES OF THE EXPERIENCES OF CHINA AND DEFEAT

Through the three individual cases examined above, certain features of soldiers' experience of the China front as well as of the defeat emerge quite clearly. As Ōnishi's diary shows, the war they served in was nothing other than one of naked aggression. Yet believing that the "holy war" was for the sake of the establishment of the "Greater East Asian Co-Prosperity Sphere" or for "self-defense," these men did not come to that realization during the period when they were called on to fight. The earnest intentions of the soldiers were completely incorporated into the prosecution of the war. These three examples reveal how much the good intentions of people who believed in the "holy war" were exploited on behalf of a war of aggression. At the China front, unlike in the Philippines or Burma, the Japanese army surrendered before it had been completely defeated. As illustrated in the example of Agari, many soldiers thus managed to avoid a confrontation with their beliefs, and so these persisted without alteration into the postwar years.

Yet the case of Ōnishi shows that it is also true that China's generous, broad-minded approach to dealing with Japanese people after the war gave soldiers an opportunity to reflect on their behavior. Looking back upon his bitter experience in Liu, where requisitions were conducted even in a community meant to be pacified, he wrote, "We too left our homes behind and were called up for a great war undertaken by the nation, and before we knew it our groundless fears went beyond the limits of self-defense and ended up bringing immeasurable harm to the people. In my heart I am deeply ashamed of this behavior, which cannot now be redeemed."[354]

The case of Murakami, who interacted closely with the Chinese people in the occupied territories, was all the more profound. After the defeat and his return home, the deaths of his wife and of his former subordinate Duan Bu-yun, and the news of the desertion of Wang Qing-feng to the Eighth Route Army (he had made vows of brotherhood to both men), Murakami was compelled to reexamine his China experience. He wrote,

> When we returned to Japan, we sweat blood day and night, and in the end it was [only] when my wife Sawa died that the wailing cries and the indescribable misery of Chinese people whose relatives had been killed or had died from starvation keenly shook my soul for the first time as something real. Those employees whom I trusted the most—those of the Xiaoyi Prefecture New People's Association and cooperative—they were clinging to the truck shouting "Help us!" and the soldiers beat them and kicked them off with great brutality. Unable to do anything to help them, we escaped encirclement by the Shanxi Army. . . . The sentimental, virtuous Prefectural Chief Cao, and the young men of Qi Prefecture too—most likely they've all been killed as traitors already. . . . My sworn brother Wang Qingfeng left his beloved wife and children behind and is probably still on the run. Feeling this and pondering that, I continued to be tormented by nightmares day and night. I couldn't bear it and wanted quickly to forget everything of those times. Just hearing Chinese, I hated it so much I wanted to block my ears. . . . This was clearly an extreme mental rejection. As this situation continued, before I knew it I'd completely forgotten my Chinese.[355]

He reflected deeply on the fact that the Japanese had in fact brought trouble and inflicted cruel treatment upon even those Chinese who had cooperated with them and with him personally. Murakami's reflections focused on Chinese people under Japanese army occupation, and there is no way to claim that his moral torment embraced what had occurred in the whole of the occupied territories, but along with the reflections of Ōnishi, they have a certain preciousness, which has implications for the formation of postwar society.

4
DEMOCRACY FROM
THE BATTLEFIELD

FASCISM DEVELOPS CRACKS

CRACKS IN SECRET

The people's strong support of imperial fascism was closely related to the information they received on the Asia-Pacific War situation. From the outbreak of war against the United States and Britain in December 1941 through the end of 1942, it was believed that Japan's overwhelming victories were continuing. The problem of rice shortages aside, the Ministry of Home Affairs had absolute confidence, reporting that "the people's hearts are cheerful and open. It is a situation in which no unrest or agitation of any kind is discernible."[1]

From early 1943 through late 1944—a period that began with reports of the battle death of Combined Fleet Commander-in-Chief Yamamoto Isoroku and the complete annihilation of the Attu Island Garrison[2] and ended with the commencement of sustained American bombing of the Japanese mainland—the Japanese military conducted a strategic retreat that transformed into a desperate resistance. But support for imperial fascism and fighting morale followed a trajectory different from that of the war situation, and that support only slowly broke down.

Surveying the outlook with regard to home-front security in January 1943, the Ministry of Home Affairs was forced to acknowledge that because military gains could no longer be expected and Japanese military losses would probably be considerable, "war-weariness" would gradually rise within Japan, and there was a fear that "the masses will slowly be led toward a mood of desperation."[3] The following January, the ministry issued the results of a survey of letters sent to China by people from Tokyo and the surrounding areas. According to the survey, while "most upper-class people are using their influence to pass the days without any shortages," among the lower classes—pushed into buying bonds and allotting a fixed portion of their incomes to postal saving accounts— representative correspondents spoke of "getting worn out"; one wrote, "In Japan too, I see before me a time when the so-called situational opportunists (*jikyoku binjōsha*) and privileged classes engorge themselves while the middle classes are ruined. If we continue like this it will certainly come."[4] Discontent over food and material shortages, formerly suppressed by the expectation of victory, reemerged and was increasingly directed against the military authorities, bureaucrats, and privileged classes—the leaders of imperial fascism.

Based on information gained through crackdowns on rumors in April 1944, the Ministry of Home Affairs highlighted a rise not only in criticism of the military and bureaucracy but also rumors such as "[a certain] island garrison has suffered complete annihilation." The ministry found, more generally, a growth in expressions of "bad, war-weary content,"[5] exemplified by the following: "If we lose this war important people might get killed, but they wouldn't kill us—peasants, workers, poor people. If we don't work there's nothing to eat, so whether we win or lose the war it doesn't make much difference."[6]

AFTER THE FALL OF SAIPAN

When Saipan Island fell in July 1944, popular anxiety grew. According to the Metropolitan Police Headquarters Intelligence Section, "at the level of the ordinary masses, they're feeling an extraordinary shock, and morale does not much improve; with the exception of a certain optimistic portion that sees the losses as something inevitable—as a tactic to entice the enemy—the majority appear to be unable to suppress a measure of anxiety and fear regarding the outlook for the war situation."[7]

In September, concerned at factory workers' "sluggish" will to produce, employees of the Special Secret Service Police Headquarters and all police departments were mobilized to survey their acquaintances, relatives, and work connections on the subject of "Why it's not possible to bring full capacities into play."[8] The following conclusions were reached: Topping the list of factors at 75 percent were "those for whom food shortages are the cause." Second most common, at 63 percent, were "those who see their real income as small." Other factors cited included "material and employee shortages" and that "those directing the workplace lack the enthusiasm and kindness befitting a company boss or executive." It was observed that many people had no choice but to miss work so they could make purchases. A worker was quoted as saying, "Better one rice ball than innumerable sermons."[9] The Metropolitan Police Headquarters First Economy Division offered the following list of five primary factors "obstructing increased production" in agricultural villages: (1) a shortage of agricultural labor and a steep rise in agricultural village wages caused by high illicit wages of between fifteen and fifty yen per day in munitions factories;[10] (2) shortages of fertilizer, materials, and farm tools and equipment (fertilizer was 60 percent short of requirements); (3) shortages of seeds and shoots and abuses of undifferentiated planting allocations; (4) the persistence of monthly delivery quotas that ignored produce growing requirements; and (5) unduly low delivery prices (while fertilizer, raw materials, and wages had to be paid for at black market rates, delivery prices were officially regulated, resulting in a profit gap). Except for factor 4, each point spoke to the failure of the war economy in agricultural villages.[11] As an example of the consequent spread of war-weariness, the fifty-six-year-old Hayami Kamematsu, who worked as a tool grinder and was head of the neighborhood association (*tonarigumi*) in Tokyo's Hongō Ward, was reported for saying the following to an acquaintance: "It would be better is we lose this war. If we're under American rule, goods will be plentiful. This war happened because Japan occupied Manchuria; it's not that America is bad. At the time of the Great [Kantō] Earthquake [in 1923], [America] gave us blankets and things. I myself got a blanket."[12]

CRACKS COME TO THE SURFACE

It was with the beginning of the bombing of the Japanese mainland by American planes based on the Mariana Islands from November 1944 onward—and above all when indiscriminate firebombing of cities across the length of Japan began in February 1945—that this trend came markedly to the surface.

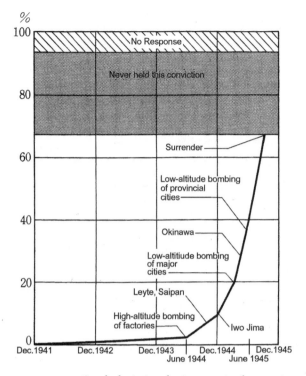

FIGURE 4.1   Graph depicting the increase in the conviction that Japan could not win the war.

While the U.S. Strategic Bombing Survey overemphasized the effectiveness of strategic bombing, its postwar investigations revealed that the indiscriminate bombing of 1945 contributed greatly to the collapse of the Japanese people's will to fight.[13]

With regard to graph 4.2, when the Strategic Bombing Survey investigated when and how the Japanese people reached the conviction that "Japan cannot achieve certain victory," respondents gave the following answers (more than one response was permitted, bringing the total over 100 percent):

❶ "Because of the aerial bombardment": 47 percent

❷ "I never believed that we could not win": 26 percent

❸ "Because of military losses and reversals in battle strength": 21 percent

❹ "Because I was aware of shortages of military materials": 5 percent

❺ "Because of shortages of consumer goods": 3 percent

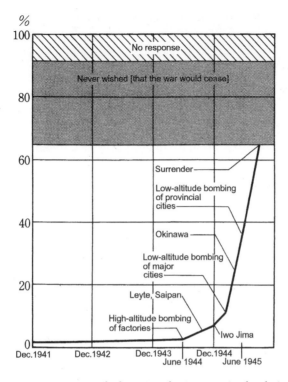

FIGURE 4.2 Graph depicting the increase in the desire that the war would end.

❻ "Because I always believed we would lose, and opposed the war from the beginning": 1 percent

❼ For "various [other] motives" and "no response": 13 percent[14]

While it can be said that shortages of war materiel and consumer goods produced war-weariness (amounting to 25 percent of the reasons respondents said they'd "wished that the war would cease"), this did not in itself suddenly give rise to the conviction that victory could not be achieved. Until their own city, residence, shop, or factory burned down before their eyes, it appears people did not become convinced that a Japanese victory was unlikely. Among those who said Japan could not achieve certain victory "because of the aerial bombardment," only 10 percent cited atomic bombs. Of those who answered "because of military losses and reversals in battle strength," the falls of Saipan Island, Leyte Island, and Iwo Jima were of overwhelming influence. Those who cited the defeat of Germany and the entry of the Soviet Union into the war numbered less than 1 percent of the total.

On the other hand, the fact that 26 percent of the respondents continued to believe that Japan could not lose until they heard the emperor's broadcast on August 15 reveals the tenacity of the people's fighting spirit. Furthermore, even the statement "I reached the conviction that we could not attain certain victory" (see graph 4.2) does not indicate a complete collapse of the will to fight. Most people remained ready to continue fighting until the end, and there were certainly no concrete steps toward the type of resistance that arose in Italy, which aimed to overthrow fascism and end the war.[15]

In April 1945, officials in the Department of Peace Preservation at the Ministry of Home Affairs assumed that among a certain portion of Japanese, "at careless moments—because of issues ranging from unease at the progress of the war to hardships in daily life deriving from food shortages and runaway goods prices on the black market—there are more than a few who let statements slip ranging from war-weary to pacifist." Because these sorts of statements were "deeply rooted in popular life" they tended to circulate, and the officials offered this dour analysis: "In tandem with the rapid changes in the war situation, including the enemy's recent invasions of the Philippines, Iwo Jima, and Okinawa and the intensification of the aerial bombardment of the mainland, the general popular sentiment is . . . becoming remarkably pessimistic, and the sense of losing the war is truly deepening."[16]

In July, the Home Ministry produced an even more pessimistic analysis based upon surveys conducted through June, when the aerial bombing of middle-sized cities was carried out.[17] Popular sentiment in areas that had suffered bombardment was gradually changing from relief or an "excited" hostility immediately after the attack—"We'll get them back!"—to "a sense of fear of aerial bombardment." Hearing reports of similar cities being bombed one after another, those in small- and medium-sized cities thus far spared were "generally assailed by an extreme sense of fear." As this fear "thickened," it spread throughout the nation, with the exception of agricultural and mountain villages.[18]

The ministry's analysis reached other significant conclusions: (1) not only was the general will to fight disappearing, but the people were coming to "think only of self-preservation," and the "phenomenon of a divergence between the war and daily life [was] growing serious"; (2) the "middle stratum," including urban white-collar workers and managers of small munitions workshops, who

FIGURE 4.3 A U.S. Air Force leaflet warning of the bombing of small- and mid-sized cities. Cities listed, counterclockwise from left: Otaru, Akita, Hachinohe, Fukushima, Urawa, Takayama, Iwakuni, Tottori, Imabari, Miyakonojō, Yawata, Saga.
Source: Hiroku: Bōryaku senden bira, ed. Suzuki Akira and Yamamoto Akira (Tokyo: Kōdansha, 1977), 96.

once benefitted from the war, were swiftly being reduced to "people living a lower-class life," and the "sturdy core stratum" who supported the war had virtually disappeared; (3) large numbers of people across the country were living in temporary shelters, including as many as 227,000 in Tokyo, and as many as eight million people burned out of their homes in the four great industrial zones had relocated to the provinces; and (4) phenomena revealing a collapse in the people's fighting spirit had spread nationwide. These included sharp rises in the expression of war-weary and "pacifist" sentiment (e.g., "Whether we win or lose this war, our lives could not be brought any lower than this. I don't care whether we win or lose"), the surfacing of a groundswell of antipathy vis-à-vis the military, "[social] class-type notions of antagonism between high and low," and general despair.[19] Confronted with the severely negative side of war, the people were finally beginning to separate from the imperial fascist state.

With the popular desperation thus spreading, when Imperial Headquarters announced the fall of Okinawa on June 25, there was no "exceptional reaction, contradictory to prediction," but only the "utmost" deepening of a "pessimistic defeatism" that foresaw the Japanese mainland turning into a battlefield and a "defeat from gradual pauperization" caused by the cutting off of relations with the outside world.[20]

FROM "MATTERS OF STATE AND SOCIETY" TO SELF-DEFENSE

From July to the beginning of August, war-weariness and the trend toward self-defense and "self-preservation" unfettered by the state grew extremely acute. As the statements of war leaders on the radio and in newspapers were repeatedly proved wrong, it was reported that in Tokyo "people abuse the military in the depths of their hearts" and that "a sense of mistrust toward officials" was growing conspicuous.[21] Whereas these sorts of things had hitherto been "spoken of in secret," and people had gone to lengths such as "being abusive to the military authorities in letters of complaint," reported the Metropolitan Police Department, they had now lost even the energy to bother. "Hope and willpower" had "gradually lost steam, and a resigned apathy that languishes around self-protection of one's immediate vicinity rather than matters of state and society" had grown "universal."[22]

Labor disputes in munitions factories, which had been rising since 1942, began to decline beginning from the second half of 1944. Yet according to a Special Secret Police report, this was partly because workers had been "driven into a situation of apathetic absent-mindedness" by the worsening of the war situation and the hardships of daily life.[23]

In the great mobilization to prepare for the decisive battle on the mainland, Japan was flooded with a massive army of 2.4 million people. Even in agricultural villages—in which the army had placed the most trust—"discontent over army high-handedness, particularly in connection with foodstuffs and transport," was becoming prevalent.[24]

The imperial fascist state was now just one step from self-collapse. But with the end of the war imminent, the last step to overcome was an extremely difficult one.

THE COLLAPSE OF A TENANT FARMER'S WILL TO INCREASE PRODUCTION

Abe Ta'ichi, a tenant farmer in the village of Ōizumi in Yamagata Prefecture, whose experiences through 1942 are profiled in chapters 1 and 2, was deeply unhappy about the state-imposed obligation to deliver rice. On February 28, 1944, just after he completed delivery of 95.7 percent of his total rice harvest, he resigned as chief of the Branch Economy Corps of the Imperial Rule Assistance Association and as a member of the village committee.[25] Soon after, his uncle went to the front.[26] Seeing him off as far as Tsuruoka Station keenly "brought the thought home" that "every last man [including myself] will have to be sent to the front" (March 3). On March 9, Abe's heart darkened as he heard stories of the deteriorating war situation and "talk of Korean independence and so forth" in a pharmacy in Tsuruoka.

A rice blight was spreading around the same time, and at a point when he was "feeling fed up," Abe heard news of the annihilation of the Japanese forces on Saipan and the fall of the Tōjō cabinet.[27] In his diary entry for July 19 he wrote, "I have an acute feeling of oppression, and my heart is gloomy." On August 13, at what he called "a moment of decision for the nation," Abe wrote that he too was prepared to be called up. In the meantime he continued his activities as an officer in the Imperial Assistance Adult Men's Association.

On October 19, just three days after being cheered by the announcement of a "great military achievement" in the Battle of the Taiwan Straits,[28] he received a telegram from his younger brother Yasukichi, then in Tianjin, China, who said he would be sending his wife back to Japan for the time being—the occupied areas too had become dangerous.

In January 1945, Abe couldn't even obtain a diary, and with no alternative he decided to write in his unused "student diary" from 1941. By now he'd lost his enthusiasm for agricultural management or increasing production and had little energy for writing in his diary either. That year's delivery quota for rice produced in 1944 was also exceedingly high,[29] and fertilizer was in very short supply. Seeking an alternative source of food, on January 18, Abe purchased a hunting rifle with money he got from selling a cow and became consumed with hunting pheasants, ducks, and rabbits. He was now just waiting to be mustered up for the decisive battle of the mainland.

THE AGITATION OF A DRAFTED WORKER AT NAKAJIMA AVIATION AND THE PSYCHOLOGY OF DEFENSE

Mori Isao, a lacquerer in Furukawa Township in Miyagi Prefecture,[30] was a drafted worker at Nakajima Aviation's Ojima factory. Given a shortage of duralumin—an aluminum alloy used in building airplanes—production at the coating factory had fallen precipitously. His workplace still maintained an exemplary attendance record—not a single employee had been recorded absent—but according to Mori, employees there each worked an average of just one hour per day (May 26, 1944).[31]

When the Tōjō cabinet resigned in July 1944, Mori wrote that the people around him "seem[ed] in fact to be feeling a sense of relief." He did not know whether it was a "holy war" that Japan was fighting, but in any case, he thought, "we must absolutely not lose this war" (July 24).[32] In a newspaper the following February, he read of the "Proposal for Dealing with Occupied Japan" issued by the Institute of Pacific Relations (IPR) and its discussion in Hot Springs, Arkansas (the article was published in the *Mainichi* and *Asahi* newspapers on February 19); the proposal covered such topics as the punishment of the Japanese military clique, the *zaibatsu*, and those responsible for the war; the thorough revision of the Japanese Constitution; the reeducation of the Japanese people; and the divestiture of acquired territory. Mori wrote, "Just thinking that this will happen to us if we lose the war, it's a war we cannot [afford to] lose."[33] This was just at the time that the aerial bombardments began.

When Ōta was first bombed on February 10, Mori felt no particular surge of anger toward the enemy. In fact, he and his fellow factory employees were glad they could miss work thanks to the air-raid warning. After another raid on February 16, Mori saw about twenty American planes flying leisurely away after dropping their bombs, and it occurred to him that he "couldn't agree with" the tactics of Japan's military.[34] He wrote that he was fed up with the unpleasantness of draftee life, the inefficiency of factory operations, and the absurdity of defense exercises in which employees trained with bamboo spears.[35]

Yet Mori did not entirely lose his fighting spirit. On May 5, a labor mobilization instructor named Kuroda foresaw the hard fight on Okinawa following the crushing defeat at Iwo Jima and argued that surrender—which he compared to a mercy killing in medical terms—was "the ultimate path to Japan's salvation," better than a hundred million honorable deaths. Hearing this, Mori wrote, "I do not believe in the humanitarianism of the American and English armies. . . . I'm thinking that Kuroda *sensei* is most likely a pacifist."[36] On June 23, when he was secretly shown an American leaflet guaranteeing humanitarian treatment from the Allied forces if Japan gave up its "pointless war," he was agitated—"conscious of myself having a kind of positive response, I shuddered at the thought."[37] Although he thought the American army's promise might be credible, he resisted accepting it on the basis that it would mean falling for an enemy scheme. Nor could he recognize the Soviet Union's declaration of war as a sign of Japan's inevitable defeat. Before the last step stood a great psychological wall. News of the defeat consequently took Mori completely by surprise: "It's true I was hoping that the war would end as soon as possible, but I was not hoping for defeat" (August 15).[38]

A TAKASHIMA STATION SWITCHMAN'S EXPERIENCE OF AERIAL BOMBARDMENT AND EXALTATION OF FIGHTING SPIRIT

Konagaya Saburō, a switchman at Takashima Station in Yokohama,[39] greeted New Year's Day, 1945, with a desire "to stir up a divine wind, blazing the trail for 440,000 [employees] of the National Railways. To be the young leader of a suicide squad."[40]

The Tokyo-Yokohama area was repeatedly bombed beginning in February, but Konagaya did not experience bombing up close until April 4. That day, bombs fell on Higashitakashima Station on the Tōyoko line; Konagaya, who participated in the rescue operation, saw blood-spattered corpses with their innards sticking out and feet shorn off. He wrote, "Enemy planes, I despise the lot of you, damn you! Come try me, I'll rip you to pieces!"[41]

Takashima Station was also struck in the great bombing raid of May 29, 1945, which involved 517 B29s and one hundred P-51s. Konagaya watched helplessly as the station bookstore, toilets, and congregation area were engulfed in flames. He ran from place to place thinking, "I wonder if I'll die now. . . . If I could, I'd throw my body at an enemy warship [in a kamikaze attack] and live eternally in the cause of right." After the bombing ended, Konagaya further stoked his will to battle, writing, "This is war. From here on out. Being able to fight down to one's naked body. . . . We'll surely defeat this foe" (May 30).[42] The next day, the call-up notice he'd been longing for arrived. He wrote, "If this is not heavenly guidance then what is it? . . . This cruel enemy who has wounded the station, the railway, and the workmates that I hold dear—now I shall take up arms and smash him relentlessly to smithereens!"[43]

THE AMBIVALENT FEELINGS OF A SUPERVISOR-TEACHER

If we take Konagaya as the model of a fiery youth, the following case is representative of a prudent man in the prime of life. Inoue Isamu, a biology teacher at Amagasaki City Higher Girl's School, led and directed students for labor duty mobilization while living out of his biology classroom, having left his wife and children behind in Akao.[44] The students were mobilized to ten workplaces, including Japan Internal Combustion, Riken Industries, Sumitomo Propeller, and the Amagasaki post office.

Born in 1903, Inoue had obtained a teaching certificate and entered the profession after graduating from Kōbe First Middle School. He expressed his support for the imperial system in ordinary ways, never failing to pay homage to the school shrine containing the emperor's portrait,[45] even when he went to the bathroom at night. Where the war was concerned, Inoue was convinced that a Japanese victory was inevitable. Like Mori Isao, he read the IPR's "Proposal for Dealing with Occupied Japan" in the newspaper on February 20, 1945, and described its recommendations for the complete occupation of Japan, changes in the "national polity" (*kokutai*),[46] and punishment of those responsible for the war as "true arrogance and insolence."[47] After drinking with teacher friends and students' parents on March 4, he recorded some of the statements made around the table: "It would have been good if we'd made peace at the time of the fall of Singapore" and "At least once it'd be nice to bomb the U.S. mainland."[48]

Once Inoue directly experienced aerial bombardment, his faith in victory quickly collapsed. On the night of March 13, 1945, he was caught in an American firebombing attack for the first time. That night Osaka was burned to the ground, and on March 17, Kōbe too was reduced to ashes.[49] After days of air-raid warnings, Inoue finally began to have doubts, writing, "Our fleet that's been so intensively trained—what in the world are they doing?" (March 31).[50] When he heard about the German surrender on May 11, he wrote, "Prospects for the future appear truly discouraging."[51]

Aerial bombardment resumed in June, resulting in the deaths of several of Inoue's students, the incineration of his family home in Kōbe, and the destruction of the homes of many of his colleagues and students. Student absences rose sharply. Of Japan Internal Combustion's 148 students, eighty attended on June 11 and just thirty-six on June 22.[52] "Like this Japan can never win," he said in the staff room on June 15. "Even if we draw the enemy into a decisive battle on the mainland and counterattack once, there'll be no end to it." When someone responded, "Do you think they'll give us the chance to counterattack? They'll land [only] after they've completely burned [Japan] into a field of ashes," Inoue was compelled to agree.[53] On June 30, an army officer delivered a lecture in the school's auditorium. Inoue listened as the officer explained how to use bamboo spears and said that if each person killed one enemy, Japan would eventually win because it had more people. Inoue thought this strange, but "no one said anything."[54] By this time, his fighting spirit had completely deteriorated.

One after another Inoue fielded requests for the evacuation of students from parents and guardians who'd been bombed out, which he had to reject because of the prefecture's policy of preserving labor power. The only thing evacuated was the emperor's photograph (*goshin'ei*). At last the factories were evacuated, however, and on July 27, led by Inoue, the group of students working at Japan Internal Combustion were evacuated to Hirotani Township in Hyōgo Prefecture.[55]

Four days later, at Hamasaka Station on his way home, Inoue heard drunken voices shouting, "Why don't we bomb the American mainland just once? They do nothing but swagger around." In his diary, he wrote of thinking to himself, "he talks big." His entry continued, "Right after that attack on Pearl Harbor, I wonder why they didn't let the aircraft carriers continue on and send in suicide squads? If we'd done that, we probably could have broken their fighting spirit."[56]

On August 5, Nishinomiya and Amagasaki were bombed once again.[57] Two fellow teachers were burned out of their homes. Reading Tōyama Mitsuru's[58] statement that "the aerial bombardment is a chastisement" cited in a newspaper article, the teachers were all indignant: "What nonsense he blurts out."[59] Yet Inoue half-believed an announcement saying that those in bomb shelters would be safe from the new type of weapon like the one dropped on Hiroshima, and that outside, you'd be protected from its heat rays if you wore a white shirt with long sleeves and white gloves—on August 14, he washed his shirt with this in mind.[60]

Then, the next day, he heard the radio broadcast of the defeat in the school staff room. "Mortified to no end," he worried for the future, but on the other hand he thought, "I'm lucky to have made it to today alive." He had long felt ashamed about being classified 4-F (unfit for service) because of his weak physical condition, but "from today," he wrote, "I've been liberated from my mental anguish."[61] He went to the Amagasaki post office on August 16, where everyone was greeting one another with comments like "If they were going to surrender, it would have been better to do it a month earlier!" "I feel the same way," he thought.[62]

Thus, in Inoue's case too, we can conclude that despite the progressive deterioration of his fighting spirit, it did not collapse entirely until he heard the emperor's surrender decree.

OVERCOMING THE COLLAPSE OF THE STATE

AUGUST 15, 1945

The Japanese people's reaction to the defeat has been understood up to now as a general stupefaction and despondence, accompanied by an indescribable, mysterious sense of liberation. Yet we must stress the fact that depending on each person's viewpoint, location, and situation, there was a considerable amount of variation—as is only natural. Drawing a distinction between those on the Japanese mainland and those overseas, this is concretely examined below.

JAPAN'S AUGUST 15

As we have already seen, on the Japanese mainland—with the exception of Okinawa, which experienced an intense land battle—even though the popular fighting spirit was just a step away from complete collapse, the reaction of the majority of the people who heard the emperor's August 15 surrender declaration was "either sadness, wretchedness, surprise, or disillusionment."[63] An investigation conducted by the U.S. Strategic Bombing Survey Research Unit between November and December 1945 posed the question, "How did you feel when you heard Japan had lost the war?" The answers were as follows:

❶ "Regret, grief, disappointment": 30 percent
❷ "Surprise, shock, confusion": 23 percent
❸ "A sense of relief or happiness the war was over and the suffering was also over": 22 percent
❹ "Fear or worry about treatment under occupation": 13 percent
❺ "Disillusionment, anguish, a sense of emptiness. I'd sacrificed everything for victory, and it had all been in vain": 13 percent
❻ "Shame, followed by a sense of relief—regret, but with acceptance. It was predicted, but it feels like a stain on the history of the nation": 10 percent
❼ "I predicted it and was resigned to it": 4 percent

❽ "I was concerned for the emperor. I felt embarrassed for the emperor. I apologized to the emperor": 4 percent

❾ No response or other responses: 6 percent[64]

Thus, while most of those surveyed met the defeat with chagrin, shock, and concern for the future, there were also many who felt a "sense of relief or happiness" that the war and the suffering it had caused were over. It is further worth noting that only a very small minority of people "apologized to the emperor" upon Japan's defeat.

THE SHOCK AND DESPONDENCE OF DEFEAT

To understand these experiences of defeat in greater detail, let us examine the records from Hino Township in Shiga Prefecture.[65]

The prevalent reaction was despondency: many residents, whose time-honored view of the world had collapsed, spent their days listlessly. Yamamoto Mitsuo, an eighteen-year-old student at Shiga Normal School who had been mobilized to work at the Sumitomo Metal Katada Factory, had foreseen the defeat, so his shock was not as great as others'. Yet he wrote of the thoughts "entangled in my mind": "Japan has lost after all. Bless me the war is over, I made it without dying. What will happen with the Japan to come?" He described himself as being listless for some time.[66]

In his memoirs, Tanaka Kōjirō, a thirty-five-year-old clerk at the Minami Hizusa village office at the time of the surrender, wrote, "Before long, beginning with the father of an only child killed in battle who went insane, suicides and mentally deranged people appeared one after another within the village as well. With the thick web of the war suddenly snapped, we passed days of emptiness within our hearts that at times resembled those of the insane."

Takagi Shige'ichi, thirty-six, a graduate of Tokyo Foreign Language University and a teacher at Misono National Elementary School, had assumed he would be told by the emperor to "prepare for the final battle of the mainland," so his "true feeling" when he heard of the surrender "was that my hopes had been betrayed." Takagi had encouraged many of his students to volunteer for the army, the navy, and the Manchuria/Mongolia Colonization Youth Volunteer Corps.[67] Recalling students saying "goodbye teacher" as they departed and his own declarations of "well done" at ceremonial village burials of students who'd died in battle, he wrote, "It felt inexcusable to the spirits of the war dead who'd taken my words as genuine, and my tears would not stop flowing."[68]

Among the many who had enthusiastically supported the war, there were also those who cursed the emperor—although they were in the minority. Ikeda Umeji, aged thirty-nine, was a model agent of imperial fascism; employed as an instructor at a Youth Training Center[69] from 1927 to 1937, he subsequently became branch chairman of the army reservist's association while also serving as manager of the Imperial Assistance Adult Men's Association,[70] a member of his village assembly, and a civil defense unit assistant chief in charge of the blackout unit. His civic duties left him no time to assist his wife in the management of their 3.43-acre farm. When he heard the emperor announce the surrender, he was "absolutely dumbfounded, losing all hope for living into the future," and he soon developed a neurosis that lasted for around two years. When he was purged from public office in 1947 by Edict Number One,[71] an indignant Ikeda directed his bitterness toward the emperor: "That I, who'd continued to devote faithful efforts during the war for the sake of the emperor . . . would be purged from public office when the end of the war came—is this the way of a sovereign with his subjects?"[72]

In light of the pillaging and acts of violence carried out by the Japanese military in every part of Asia they invaded, many anticipated the American occupation with fear. Yoshimura Seitarō, a forty-year-old town ward headman, spent days despondent because of a rumor that "women will be raped in a clean sweep, men are useless and so will be slaughtered." He wrote, "It's frustrating. I gave it my all, and it's that frustrating."[73]

THE LIBERATION OF DEFEAT

Then there were those who truly felt relief, even if it was accompanied by uneasiness and confusion. For Kogame Shizuko, a twenty-six-year-old housewife pregnant with her first child, the announcement of the defeat came as such a shock that she could not stand up. She thought, "Why didn't they fight to the end?" But as time passed, her feelings changed. "Bless me," she wrote, "now there won't be any air raids. I can sleep soundly."[74] Okazaki Denzaemon, aged forty-three and headman of Kitahitsusa, had "a strong feeling half-resembling resignation" that the inevitable had come to pass. After years of focusing entirely on contributing to the war effort, "gloomy days continued" as he pondered how he should now administer the village. Yet on the other hand, "there arose the lightness of a heart relieved, finally liberated from an indescribable feeling of heavy pressure."[75]

Takada Tokujirō, a thirty-seven-year-old teacher at Yōkaichi Elementary School who was leading students in land-reclamation construction work on the Noto River, was also "filled with unease." Having fought for three years in central China beginning in 1938, he "knew a little something about the fear of the battlefield," and after his youngest brother had died in battle in Burma in 1944, he'd passed every day in fear of being called up once again. Thus when he heard of the defeat, he "had a feeling of relief that my life was now entirely my own."[76]

There were also those who wondered with frustration why Japan had not surrendered sooner if it was going to lose anyway. For the thirty-eight-year-old farmer Okazaki Shigetarō, it took several days after the surrender announcement for the fact of defeat to hit home. When it did, he wrote of thinking, "Why didn't we surrender earlier?"[77] Hori Toranosuke, a forty-three-year-old employee at the Hikone branch of the Japan Kangyō Bank, experienced a combination of relief, woe, and concern for the future. He thought, "If this decision had been taken a year ago, or at least six months ago, it would have ended without us getting a baptism of atomic bombs, and without us losing tens of thousands of people. The military leadership that didn't know the word 'retreat'—I'm so angry at them I'm beside myself."[78] If such people had known that the majority of the 3.1 million Japanese who lost their lives in the war had fallen in its final year, and most of those in the final six months, their indignation would likely have been even stronger.

NATIONAL CONSCIOUSNESS THAT BLOCKED
MOVEMENT TOWARD REFORM

As we can see, even within a single township, the manner in which people reacted to the defeat varied considerably. Yet there is one consistent point: until the occupation army began to issue directives at the beginning of October, the people did not move to action on their own. With the occupation's policies not yet made plain and the special secret service police (*tokkō*) still functioning, there must surely have been a sense of caution about doing anything careless. People certainly had their hands full just looking after themselves as well, dealing with food shortages that had grown very serious in the final months of the war.

Yet beyond this, the Japanese people had still clearly not grasped the opportunity to free themselves from the constrictive power of the imperial state.

Many had grown deeply disillusioned with the imperial fascist order, and a hazy desire for change was beginning to arise, but there was still no clear vision as to how the state should be changed. Just after the defeat, the old political forces[79] began to act, but bound to the Meiji Constitution[80] and imperial fascist ideology, their outlook was divorced from the sentiments of the people, who had experienced the war in all its severity. On the Japanese mainland, it was thus necessary that the first blow to the power of the imperial state should come from the "outside."

"AUGUST 15" OVERSEAS

At the time of the surrender, there were approximately 7.06 million Japanese overseas: roughly 3.51 million soldiers and 3.55 million civilians.[81] Their reactions to the defeat were even more diverse than those of their countrymen on the mainland.

Unlike on the mainland, news of the defeat was not immediately transmitted everywhere abroad, so after August 15 considerable numbers of Japanese—unaware of the surrender—continued to risk death fighting with local people, retreating, wandering through jungles, and the like.[82] As a consequence, in considering the experience of Japanese overseas, we must examine the period between the end of the war and the moment when people actually comprehended the fact of the defeat.

"WE MUST NOT LOSE"

Examining only those whose modes of reaction to the defeat differed greatly from those on the mainland, the first type we can identify are those who maintained the belief that Japan was not losing. Twenty-five-year-old Yamada Tomiichi, a private superior class in the Independent Infantry 487th Battalion in Hunan Province, felt strongly that although the fighting was hard, "We haven't lost"— his unit still had enough weaponry and ammunition to keep fighting. On the day he learned of the defeat, "with desperation also lending a hand," he shot off the ammunition he had at hand in one go.[83] Iwaki Nobuyuki, who departed from Osaka Bay in March 1940, had fought in central China with the Wakayama Infantry 218th Regiment Infantry Gun Company. He too did not have a true sense of the defeat while he was overseas. It was only after landing in Sasebo in February 1946 and observing from the train window the scorched earth of Japan that "what I'd been convinced of on the continent—'we haven't lost'—completely vanished."[84]

According to a survey of Japanese civilians and military personnel in Beijing conducted by an officer in the U.S. Army Intelligence Department in December 1945, 47 percent agreed with the proposition that "Japan could have fought on for longer" (43 percent disagreed), and 87 percent rejected the proposition "China could probably have won the war even without American assistance" (8 percent agreed). An overwhelming majority thus felt that Japan had not lost to China.[85] In places such as China, Java, and Sumatra, where Japan had not suffered total military defeat at the time of the surrender, many Japanese remained unaware of the situation in other areas and on the mainland and so did not have a true sense of the defeat.

FEELINGS OF INSULT AND FRUITLESSNESS IN DEFEAT

A second type were those who personally witnessed the people of Asia welcoming Japan's defeat and took this as an insult, along with those seized by a deep sense of futility that the years of fighting and hardship had been for nothing. In China's Zhoushan Archipelago, children who had always been admiring of the seventeen-year-old navy communications officer Yamamura Tatsuo turned against him after August 15. Having once called him "Toiyashiisan" (Teacher of the East), they now said "Toiyapin, Bechiyarisha" [sic] (no-good soldier of the East). As a result, he wrote, "I was made intimately familiar with the melancholy of defeat, gnashing my teeth countless times."[86]

In Korea, Wagatsuma Masatoshi worked as a special secret service officer responsible for external affairs at the Awudi Police Department. After the surrender, pursued by Soviet troops and Korean security units, he made his escape over the 38th Parallel. Reflecting on his flight atop the roofs of railway cars and his witnessing of Japanese imprisoned in factory boarding houses formerly meant for Koreans, he keenly felt "the misery of defeat . . . and the misery of people in a colony without weapons, without national prestige."[87] With the defeat, he wrote, the Koreans had changed into "fierce tigers" where the Japanese were concerned, to which he was resigned as "a natural payback." He described himself as so miserable that his tears overflowed.[88]

When the army sanitation corporal Hashida Kiichirō, aged thirty-five, heard of the surrender in the jungle of Namatanai on the island of New Ireland in the Solomons, he secretly cheered that his wish to return home alive might be granted. Yet as he recalled the hardships of the many battles in which he'd fought in two tours of duty over more than five years—in central China, Mukden, Hainan Island, Thailand, Malaya, Singapore, Rabaul, and Namatanai—the faces of comrades killed in battle appeared before him, and he "had no choice but to be very angry at the worthlessness of it all."[89]

JOY IN THE COLLAPSE OF THE STATE

By contrast, some of those who'd experienced fierce combat, starvation, and other extreme hardships were openly joyful that the war had come to an end. At the edge of the Shittan River in Burma, twenty-six-year-old Kuno Jiken, a soldier in the 53rd Reconnaissance Regiment, observed the bodies of countless Japanese soldiers being borne along by the current. Just before the surrender, in a state of physical and mental exhaustion, he'd been reduced to sitting and waiting to die. But when he heard the order to cease hostilities around August 17, "happiness was reborn on everyone's faces, and my breast was filled with a relieved feeling of 'this is good.' "[90] Sumeragi Mutsuo, an engineer with the Philippine Expeditionary Army and graduate of the agriculture department of Kyōto University, was in Luzon's Asin Valley, starving, when he learned of the ceasefire on August 17. He recalled the scene:

> A navy unit above our hut, near the top of the mountain, was shouting *"banzai"* three times loudly. Anyone and everyone hailed the ending of the war. "We're going back to Japan!"—in the mountains, the potato fields, the Asin Valley, these were our happy words. . . . The faces of the high-ranking career officers in the army command, who were in the position of feeling responsible for the defeat, were also bright.[91]

At the base of Luzon's Mt. Pulog, Taniki Shunji, a recruit attached to the battalion headquarters of the Ifu Corps,[92] heard of the defeat from the regimental headquarters on August 26. When he communicated this to his command, he witnessed a warrant officer exclaiming, "Japan has lost, *banzai!*"[93] He also heard a story that soldiers in the Independent Motorized 321st Company had shouted " '*Banzai! Banzai!*' after learning that the war was over"—and were almost fired upon by a machine gun company as a result.[94]

On equatorial Halmahera Island, Ikeda Yoichi,[95] a peasant soldier who was on the verge of dying from starvation, described the sense of liberation he experienced in defeat: "You know I was glad. Everyone was glad. It's funny. There was a man who got too happy and went nutty. He got it into his head that he'd already returned home, and was walking around greeting everyone with 'Honey, I'm home!'"[96]

A substantial proportion of the soldiers who had directly experienced the worst of the war thus welcomed the cessation of hostilities. Whether or not one had personally endured extreme hardship had deep implications for whether one's old worldview collapsed, and whether it was replaced by absolute pacifism.

A POSTWAR SPIRIT IN THE MAKING— AND CONSCIOUSNESS THAT REMAINED INTACT

POSTWAR SPIRIT BORN OF THE ASHES

In November and December 1945, the Morale Division of the U.S. Strategic Bombing Survey reported on the attitude of Japanese civilians toward building a new nation (former soldiers were not surveyed). In response to the question of "how Japan should change," the most frequently expressed opinions were:

❶ "Change Japan into a peaceful nation and abolish control by the militarists and militaristic thinking": 22 percent

❷ "That sort of thing is too difficult for me—I don't know": 22 percent

❸ "Make Japan more democratic": 20 percent

❹ "Reduce the power of landlords and monopoly capitalists and do away with the gap between the classes": 7 percent[97]

Even after the occupation forces issued reform directives, many people lacked a vision of what should be done, but most demanded peace and democracy, based on their "great disillusionment with militarism." The report states that the Japanese people's deep discontent "was not clearly transforming into demands for concrete reform" but that "preparations for reform" and "broad expectations" existed, and these "were filled with potential," supported by an "extremely unsettled" social atmosphere. Only 5 percent of those surveyed said that "Japan should return to how it was before the war"—meaning a return to the limited, emperor-centered democracy of the 1920s, essentially what was desired by many among the old political establishment.[98]

Concerning the emperor, 62 percent of those surveyed said, "I hope for his [continued] reign." If we also interpret "No response" (12 percent), "I can't make any decision about that" (10 percent), "I am feel embarrassed for the emperor" (7 percent), and "I cannot talk about such a reverent subject" (2 percent) as expressions of continuing devotion to the emperor, then a total of only 7 percent expressed attitudes critical of him: "What happens to the emperor has nothing to do with me" (4 percent) and "He should be made to resign" (3 percent). According to the report, many respondents "stopped talking [or] hesitated" when asked about the emperor and gave an opinion only after being "prompted numerous times."[99] In sum, the survey suggests that the people's strong desire for reform did not encompass the abolition of the imperial system or the emperor's abdication. What can be inferred from the survey, conducted before the emperor's "declaration of humanity" (*ningen-sengen*) on New Year's Day, 1946,[100] is that the people were strongly demanding peace and democracy on the basis of retaining the emperor and the imperial system.

A POSTWAR SPIRIT BORN OF THE BATTLEFIELD

Turning to the viewpoints of Japanese overseas, an investigation by officers of the U.S. Army Information Division conducted in Beijing in December 1945 provides some insight.[101] Notably, the sense of racial superiority over Europeans and Americans had broken down, and as a result most of those surveyed had come to believe that the Japanese system of governance should be reformed and Western-style democracy adopted.

Concerning the proposition that "the Japanese race is superior to all other races," 49 percent disagreed, 41 percent agreed, and 10 percent gave no response. Sixty percent agreed that "democracy is the only form of political organization for Japan"; only 29 percent disagreed. There was an overwhelmingly favorable response to the suggestion that "the *zaibatsu* should be broken up": 71 percent of respondents were in favor and just 19 percent opposed.[102]

In overwhelming numbers, people thus supported a rebuilding of Japan accompanied by reform. Moreover, 66 percent agreed that "Japan's future will be just as bright (*akarui*) as if it had not lost the war" (27 percent disagreed). Fully 80 percent agreed that "if it is for the sake of rebuilding Japan, I will happily endure the same hardships I endured during the war"; just 10 percent disagreed. Overall, the Japanese surveyed had such an optimistic outlook that the U.S. forces were taken by surprise.[103]

"IMPERIAL" CONSCIOUSNESS THAT DID NOT COLLAPSE

Yet according to the same investigation, a sense of superiority toward non-Japanese Asians and an "imperial" consciousness continued to persist alongside traditional views of the emperor and the nation. Ninety-two percent of respondents agreed that "the Japanese emperor is a divine being"; only 4 percent disagreed. The split was 83 percent to 9 percent in favor of the statement "More than for my own happiness, I must work for the sake of the Japanese nation." By 86 percent to 9 percent, respondents concurred that "the Japanese are superior to people of the other nations of the Far East."

Other results confirmed the persistence of old viewpoints: "Korea will need at least 20 years before it is prepared enough for independence"—77 percent agreed, 14 percent disagreed; "Japan should retain Taiwan"—63 percent agreed, 26 percent disagreed; "The Chinese in Manchuria do not have the ability to run the industrial organizations Japan built"—69 percent agreed, 20 percent disagreed; "In order to maintain its present standard of living, Japan requires Chinese economic resources"—81 percent agreed, 7 percent disagreed (to the proposition that Japan's survival necessitated retention of its economic privileges in China, 72 percent agreed, 17 percent disagreed); "The natives of the southern regions prefer the Japanese to the European rulers"—50 percent agreed, 23 percent disagreed. Most of those surveyed believed that Taiwanese "hope to become a part of Japan" (63 percent in favor, 12 percent against); did not believe that "Manchurians resent the Japanese" (69 percent against, 15 percent in favor); felt that if the Chinese had understood Japan's "true intentions," Japan could have won the war (61 percent in favor, 30 percent against), because Japan had "only sought to assist" the Chinese in ruling China (64 percent in favor, 27 percent against); and believed that "the natives of the southern regions think extremely favorably of the Japanese" (63 percent in favor, 13 percent against).[104]

It appears that a solid majority of around 60 percent of respondents to this Beijing survey thus continued to maintain an "imperial" consciousness regarding Asia and did not feel responsibility for the war.[105] On the other hand, we should not overlook that among roughly 20 percent of those surveyed, "imperial" consciousness toward Asia had collapsed.

FORGOTTEN MEMORIES OF OPPRESSION
AND DISCRIMINATION

As postwar Japan moved toward democracy and economic prosperity, the Okinawans, Ainu, Uilta, and Chamorro peoples and the Koreans, Taiwanese, and others who had been mobilized for war were virtually forgotten.

Japan's doctrine of the renunciation of war and permanent peace was based on the Japanese people's dreadful experience. For the United States on the other hand, it was "a matter of, 'it's alright if the Japanese mainland is unarmed so long as Okinawa can be obtained as a nuclear base,' "[106] a doctrine built upon the sacrifice of the people of Okinawa Prefecture—a sacrifice that was completely ignored by "mainland" Japanese.

It was the same with regard to minority peoples. For a quarter-century or more after the war, there were virtually no efforts to compensate the minorities within the "Japanese Empire" who were oppressed and discriminated against under Japanese rule, just as there was virtually no self-inspection of these issues by the Japanese people. It was only in the 1970s that these matters began to be dealt with publicly.[107]

At the end of 1974, Suniyon (Japanese name Nakamura Teruo), a volunteer soldier of the Ami people, shocked Japan by returning alive after thirty years in the jungle.[108] After he participated in the Kitami People's History Course in 1975, Dahinieni Gendanu, who we encountered in chapter 2, overcame his fear of discrimination and prejudice, stopped hiding the fact that he was a Uilta, and—with support from Tanaka Ryō and other conscientious Japanese—began to assert his identity;[109] his memoir, *Gendānu*, was published in 1978. Katō Kunihiko's *At the Edge of Universal Brotherhood* (*Isshi dōjin no hate*),[110] which told the stories of Taiwanese civilian military employees, came out a year later. A start was made at dealing with the complaints of Taiwanese mobilized for Japan, but it was only in the 1980s that the National Diet began to deliberate on state compensation for Taiwanese conscripted as soldiers for the Japanese Empire.

Hashimoto Susumu's *North-South Monument* (*Nanboku no tō*), which chronicled an Ainu soldier's mobilization and combat experiences as well as an Ainu woman's journey of discovering her identity, was published in 1981. Utsumi Aiko's *Record of the Korean Class "B" and "C" War Criminals* (*Chōsenjin BC kyū senpan no kiroku*),[111] published in 1982, revealed the truth about Koreans who took the blame for war crimes because they served as guards at POW camps in Southeast Asia. Ishigami Masao's *Japanese, Do Not Forget!* (*Nihonjin yo wasurunakare*), which came out the following year, described how the people of the Japanese Trust Territories and Micronesia were conscripted as civilian military employees.

REFLECTING ON WAR RESPONSIBILITY

As hidden facts of the war came to light one after another following the defeat, Inoue Isamu, the teacher at Amagasaki Prefectural Higher Girl's School whose experiences in the final months of the war were discussed above, became embarrassed at his own ignorance. Seeing photos of victims of the atomic bombs in the newspaper on August 22, 1945, he "shivered even now at [his] own stupidity" in having once looked up at American planes and blurted out, "Go ahead and drop your new weapon!"[112] On August 28 there was a retirement ceremony for the now defunct Riken Industries; Inoue joined in singing the "Patriotic March" (*Aikoku kōshinkyoku*),[113] paid homage to the Japanese flag, and cried.[114] Reading an article about the surrender-signing ceremony on board the battleship *Missouri* on September 3, he felt ashamed for having once applauded at a lecture in which Admiral Takahashi Sankichi proposed that if submarines were stationed around the Japanese isles no enemy ships would get through and for having been excited by Ikezaki Tadataka's "Essay on Pacific Strategy" (*Taiheiyō senryaku ron*)[115]—after reading it, Inoue had triumphantly spread out a map in the staff room and persuaded his colleagues that "Japan's strategic position is impregnable!"[116]

When the arrest of suspected war criminals began, Inoue came to ponder the question of responsibility for the conflict. Learning of the Japanese army's brutality toward civilians and American POWs in the Philippines, he wrote on September 16, "This is a complete surprise, and as a Japanese something inexcusable."[117] The next day, he read a newspaper editorial, "The Crimes of the Tōjō Military Clique." He found this odd and felt that the newspapers should apologize—if there had been so much evidence, why had the newspapers failed to denounce the "criminals" in the lead-up to the war?[118]

Before the defeat, Inoue was in such difficult straits that he had been forced to catch frogs to eat. When he returned to Akō after a long absence on September 28, his children's faces were swollen from malnutrition. His wife complained of the extreme distress of the difficulty of making ends meet. The drawers in the house were almost empty, their belongings bartered for food. In reaction, Inoue wrote, "War—this is the thing we must not do. Provocateurs and agitators—those are the ones to be hated" (September 29).[119]

On November 25, Inoue attended a rally marking the establishment of the Japanese Socialist Party's Amagasaki branch and heard a speech by Sakamoto Masaru. He thought it a shame that Kawakami Jōtarō failed to appear but found himself "enjoying expecting a lot from [Kawakami]'s upcoming activities."[120]

CONSCIOUSNESS THAT DID NOT COLLAPSE, AND REFLECTION SUSPENDED

Even as Inoue's old worldview thus progressively broke down after the defeat— and even as he reflected upon his own responsibility for having participated in the war—his mental transformation was not complete. From a September 4 newspaper, Inoue learned that the Allied powers viewed the first Sino-Japanese War (1894–1895) and Russo-Japanese War (1904–1905) as the result of Japanese aggression and were demanding the return of Taiwan, the Pescadore Islands, and southern Sakhalin, along with the abandonment of the former mandated territory of Micronesia—"this," Inoue thought, "is cruelty in the extreme."[121] He based his view on the fact that these territories had formerly been recognized as part of the Japanese Empire by the United States and much of Europe; he evidently gave no thought to the inhabitants of those territories who had been suffering under Japanese rule.

On September 28, Inoue heard that Miki Kiyoshi,[122] who hailed from the same prefecture, had died in Toyatama Prison, but he does not appear to have been troubled that a political prisoner had remained behind bars after the defeat and died there.[123] After Prince Higashikuni's cabinet resigned en masse on October 6 after refusing to make changes in the existing imperial fascist order, including its repressive Peace Preservation Law, Inoue wrote, "I am extremely grateful to them for grappling with the great confusion of the time just after the defeat."[124] On October 12, reflecting on the release of Tokuda Kyūichi and other Communist Party leaders from prison, Inoue wrote, "I find it truly embarrassing" to have "preached the eternal glory of the *kokutai* to young people." At the same time, observing the many people who were coming forward proclaiming themselves to have been "noncooperators" with the wartime regime, he wrote, "I don't think I'd like it if they were to start accusing us [of collaborating with it]."[125] His reflections on the cruel behavior of the Japanese army in the

Philippines were likewise quickly cut off in favor of thoughts about the indiscriminate slaughter caused by the atom bombs: "It seems you can say that might makes right," he concluded.[126] For Inoue and people like him, the pursuit of war responsibility, the abandonment of the colonies and, to some degree, postwar reforms were things forced "from the outside."

What did not change after the defeat was general opinion regarding the emperor and the imperial system. At Inoue's school on October 25, staffers and people from the surrounding area formed a line along the fence around the school grounds to hail the Imperial Portrait (the emperor's photograph), which had been evacuated to Sasayama. On September 30, a ceremony was held at which the Imperial Rescript on Education was read out.[127] On November 3, a ceremony was held on the occasion of the birthday of Emperor Meiji, which Inoue attended in a morning coat.[128] When the newspapers began to address the question of the imperial system, Inoue wrote, "I'd be in favor of its maintenance" (November 6). Where the emperor himself was concerned, Inoue worried that he would be made to resign and charged with responsibility for the war. "The other day," he wrote, "Minister Without Portfolio Matsumoto said there will be no resignation, but I'm [still] uneasy that there might be something further."[129]

THE ESTABLISHMENT OF AN "EARNEST PRAYER AGAINST WAR" AND SUPPORT FOR THE "HUMAN EMPEROR"

Mori Isao, who had gone from lacquerer to drafted laborer, had been "praying for the victory of the motherland, whatever the doctrine of war." When he learned of the defeat, he could not grasp it and became psychologically unmoored.[130] As the truth about the war gradually became clear, he came to suspect that the Japanese people had been "completely deceived," but he could not bring himself unequivocally to accept this position like "someone jumping on the bandwagon of the day."[131]

With a retirement allowance from his factory, Mori bought up Japanese lacquer on the black market and started anew as a lacquerware maker. In the general election of April 1946, he was unable to decide for whom to vote; with "a feeling as if I was rolling the dice," he submitted a ballot with the names of two conservatives. He felt unable to trust only the Communist Party, whose national loyalties seemed to lie with Russia.[132]

Though he could not say that "the emperor is without a scrap of war responsibility," Mori wrote that he did "not feel this represents a basis for opposing
the imperial system," and he saw no choice but to withhold judgment on the
system's future (November 19, 1946).[133] On July 6, 1947, he went to greet the
imperial tour[134] and felt a "common people's sort of closeness" to the emperor,
who looked "little different from the white-collar workers around him." Without thinking about it, he wept and shouted, *"Banzai."* He was amused to spot
an acquaintance who was a member of the Communist Party also shouting
"banzai" three times.[135] He thus came to support the newly humble, "common
man's" emperor and imperial system "of around 1946 or '47," which issued the
"humanity declaration." He wrote that it would be problematic for the emperor
to go back to wearing a military uniform and straddling a white horse.[136]

Mori was irritated by the Tokyo Trials—the International Military Tribunal
for the Far East—and what he saw as their "victor's justice."[137] "Condemn the
offence but pity the offender," he wrote. Still, he believed that the "hatred of
war" should not be forgotten (November 12, 1948).[138] When he saw a news-
reel about the Korean War on August 23, 1950, he felt he could "not ignore
the problems of my neighbor" and that he "hated war from the bottom of my
heart." He also opposed the establishment of the Police Reserve Corps and Japan's rearmament.[139]

After the San Francisco Peace Treaty came into effect in 1952, Mori maintained his "earnest prayer against war"—even as he experienced a sense of nos-
talgia whenever he heard the "Battleship March," which played in the pachinko
parlors. In 1955, he helped seek signatures for a campaign to ban atomic
weapons.[140]

THE UNITED STATES: FROM "EXPEL THE BARBARIANS" TO PEACE AND DEMOCRACY

Konagaya Saburō, the switch operator at Yokohama Takashima Station who
was called up and served in Kumamoto Prefecture, returned to his home on
August 26, 1945, and to work at Takashima Station on August 31.[141]

After the defeat, Konagaya wrote of feeling "the weak-spiritedness that is
the birthright of the Japanese" and "the pallor of moral sensibility." He was
"infuriated" that his countrymen had forgotten "the consciousness of being
Japanese" and were blindly obedient to the United States and Soviet Union

(December 19). As "a wordless revenge on the Americans," he would not seek to rise in the world but would "only set my sights on becoming a train dispatcher or thereabouts, at the most."[142]

Konagaya's old worldview had thus not collapsed. He admitted that "if it's for the sake of the emperor, even now I would give my life. . . . I'm a member of the 'Expel the Barbarians' (*sonnō jōi*)[143] Party" (February 22, 1946). Yet his position led him to raise pointed questions about the occupying forces, questions that did not occur to many:

> Behind the justice, humanity, and everlasting peace that they advocate, what about the warlike national policy they hide in their clutches? We witness it. The shells and bombs they transport one after another by special train every day from Yokohama Bay to Haijima—what do they mean? What do you call this if not a warlike national policy? . . . Until the day I can believe theirs is a country of truth as they advertise, I will harbor antipathy to them.[144]

There was also the fact that the majority of the transport work Konagaya and his coworkers were doing involved U.S. materiel, revealing the role of the force of arms in the Allied domination of East Asia. Nonetheless, Konagaya had come to support the antifascist ideals of "justice, humanity, and everlasting peace" espoused by the Allies. Indeed, his criticism of the occupying army combined the sentiment of "expel the barbarians" with an antifascist perspective.

Even as he lamented "the deterioration of morality," Konagaya was active in union politics and voted in national elections. A youth division of the Takashima Station union local was established, and in the elections for its officials, he "made just a bit of an effort" to support one of the candidates for division chief (March 17, 1946).[145] In the April general parliamentary election—which used a preferential voting system—Konagaya put Kōno Ichirō at the top of his ballot, followed by Hirose Hiroshi and then Murobose Kōshin.[146] On September 2, Konagaya himself was elected to the governing committee of the Takashima union local. Leading up to a planned September 15 general strike to protest layoffs of National Railroad employees because of severe inflation, Konagaya wrote, "We union committee members have an increasingly great and heavy duty." Just before the strike was to take place, the state acceded to the union's demands.[147] In 1947 inflation grew still worse, and he felt as if "the crisis in making ends meet . . . has reached its limit." He supported the plan for a February 1 strike and headed to Yokohama Station "with a firm determination to hold the fort where the general strike is concerned, carrying several days' worth of food." When he learned that the strike had been suspended, he was "a bit disappointed" (February 1).[148]

Konagaya greeted the promulgation of the National Constitution on May 3, 1947, as "a shining first step toward democracy for our nation, Japan." Yet around the same time he also got married, and, feeling uneasy about food shortages and the difficulty in making ends meet, he wrote that "although we should be happy about the inauguration of the democratic constitution and grandly celebrating it, I can't stand having the feeling this is someone else's affair."[149]

A "HOLY WAR" VIEW AND CONCEPT OF PEACE COEXISTENT

In contrast to the growing popular aspiration for peace and democracy (as well as economic prosperity), many former agents of imperial fascism continued to hold strongly to their old worldviews. On August 15, Takahashi Minejirō, the Fujine Village branch chairman of the Imperial Reservists Association in Iwate Prefecture introduced in chapter 2, wrote in his diary, "The end of the war is decreed. I want to cry but cannot."[150] On September 6, he attended the ceremony at which the Reservists Association branch was dissolved; he kept the association flag, disobeying an order to burn it.

Of the students he encouraged and sent off to war, more than a hundred did not return. As he regarded the grieving parents, wives, and children left behind, he felt the need to atone. He worked from 1947 as an officiating priest for secret Buddhist prayer meetings, from 1948 as a district welfare officer, and from 1950 as a youth guardian, looking after the children of households on relief, mentally handicapped children, juvenile vagrants, and the like. In his book *A Hometown History of Fujine* (*Fujine kyōdoshi*), he wrote of his perspective on penitence: "To those who died in battle and their bereaved families, I have done something unforgivable. My heart grows darker and darker. I am cursed, hated. At this point there is nothing I can do. All I can do is apologize, visit the spirits of the war dead and apologize to them, soothe them, hold services for them, and look after their bereaved families for them."[151]

It was the same outlook that motivated Takahashi to bring homemade sake to Sugamo Prison to comfort former Army Minister Araki Sadao and the nine other Class A war criminals who received life sentences in the Tokyo war crimes trials. After the peace treaty went into effect in 1952, Takahashi sculpted a "Goddess of Peace" (*heiwa kannon*) with soil from all over Asia that soldiers had sent to him—one spoonful each—from the front. It was displayed in a "Goddess of Peace Hall" along with a framed text that read "Eternal Accomplishment" (*ihō banko*), with the signatures of the ten Class A war criminals.[152] Thus Takahashi's Goddess of Peace was premised on the old "holy war" perspective.

A CONTINUED "HOLY WAR" STANDPOINT AND
RECEPTIVITY TO DEMOCRACY

When she heard the broadcast of the surrender announcement, Itō Matsuo, the head of the Great Japan Ladies' Association in the Iwate Prefecture village of Oyama, was so shocked that she could not stand up.[153] After the defeat, she witnessed farmers hesitant to make compulsory rice deliveries and thought to herself, "Japan's farmers and others no longer have any pride or objective. Their conscientiousness and concept of duty are also collapsing." Regarding the agricultural reforms carried out soon afterward, she felt that small landlords were treated unfairly and found this "incomprehensible."[154]

For Itō, who had retained faith in such wartime slogans as "loyalty and patriotism" (*jinchū hōkoku*) and "the hundred million [Japanese] meeting honorable deaths" (*ichioku gyokusai*), the situation after the war, including the political reforms, was "a reality I truly had trouble comprehending."[155] She wrote of falling frequently into despondence and absentmindedness. In her memoir she declared, "Thanks to the new constitution, the fortress of feudalism came down; thanks to the agricultural reforms, the wall of social obligation and human feeling too was demolished; and under the name of democracy, it was a day for all to delight in freedom. And then it went from freedom to free license."[156]

Though she once tentatively stated that her cooperation in the war effort, including her work in the Great Japan Ladies' Association, was "perhaps a bad deed," Itō largely continued to affirm her support for the war: "I do not regret it. It was rather pure-heartedness itself, and I can even see it as something precious, these hearts united together for the sake of all, for the sake of the nation alone."[157] In this sense her thoughts did not extend beyond the boundaries of the nation, and her "holy war" perspective remained intact.

Yet even Itō might have been expected to welcome postwar democracy insofar as it incorporated the aim of elevating housewives' status. In September

1947, the Oyama Village Ladies' Association was established as a democratic body according to Allied standards[158] and launched a movement to reform daily life for the better. Working out of the association's headquarters in the village hall, Itō was charged with "the abolition of feudalism and banishing of superstition" and "home improvement" respectively. For the sake of "raising the status of farmer's wives and promoting their happiness," she campaigned for work-saving kitchen and other residential improvements.[159] To fund this campaign, she founded a "modern mutual finance association" (*bunka mujinkō*) and "modern savings" (*bunka chokin*).[160] On her recommendation, a farmer installed plumbing, a sink, and a kitchen counter in his and his wife's home; when she heard that he'd declared that "Everyone made fun of me, saying, 'What's your aim in performing such an act of piety for your wife?'" Itō wrote that she felt deeply that such "acts of piety" would be a source of happiness to the family.[161]

Thus, although Itō's support for the "holy war" did not collapse, her efforts to raise women's status made her an effective proponent of democracy. Those efforts, she wrote, were accompanied by an anguish that she compared to the sort associated with "removing and throwing away old clothing."[162]

THE CONTINUITY OF "IMPERIAL JAPAN" CONSCIOUSNESS AND THE "HOLY WAR" PERSPECTIVE

Among Japanese repatriated from overseas, Watanabe Chūzaburō—a soldier in the Kwantung army who did forced labor as a Soviet POW for roughly three years—is an example of those whose worldview was almost entirely unaltered by Japan's defeat.

Born in 1921 in Otowa Township, Aiichi Prefecture, Watanabe withdrew from Toyohashi City Commercial School and in 1938 moved to the city of Dairen in the Japanese puppet state of Manchukuo. In 1944 he was conscripted into the Manchuria Independent Motorized 70th Battalion. Stationed in Korea when Japan surrendered, he was disarmed on the outskirts of Pyongyang and interned in camps in Slovyansk and Ijun in the Ukraine, where he did heavy forced labor.[163] In Slovyansk, where he did factory construction and agricultural work, carried raw materials, bricks, coal, concrete and steel frames, and extracted oil, some of his fellow POWs died, and Watanabe came down with acute pneumonia and once fell through the ice of a frozen river.[164]

This dangerous forced labor contravened international law, and the treatment of POWs in the camps was also very harsh. The discipline of the Soviet soldiers and the Soviet standard of living both seemed extremely inferior to those Watanabe had known in Japan. Watanabe was thus unable to believe in Soviet-style socialism or what the Soviets called "democratization."[165]

Earlier, before he was disarmed on August 26, 1945, Watanabe had sought to take his own life—he was stopped by his squad chief.[166] He had decided to kill himself because he believed that if he returned to Japan he would live the rest of his life disgraced for "returning as a prisoner."[167] While interned in the USSR, he kept faith in "Imperial Japan" and the "Shinsōkan (*Kanro no hōu*)" doctrine: "We are the children of god."[168] Upon his return to Maizuru on November 2, 1948, he recited a poem revealing that his worldview had not changed:

We are now in Imperial Japan
I see it in a dream
My eyes blur—even mountains are invisible

THE CONTINUITY OF THE "HOLY WAR" PERSPECTIVE

The aforementioned cases of Agari Masa'omi, a garrison soldier in Dangyang in China, and Nitō Seikichi, a soldier in a heavy artillery unit stationed in Sumatra, are similar. After the war, Agari was interned in the Soviet Union for five years. Like Watanabe, he continued to believe in Japan's "holy war," defiantly maintaining that "in general, the cruelty, inhumanity, and obscenity of the battlefield have been conveyed contrary to the facts and perverted in an exaggerated way."[169]

As for Nitō, he did yield on the point that Japan "did damage in World War II," and he significantly believed that Japan should "make compensation for the crimes committed against Southeast Asia."[170] Yet he continued to maintain that if Japan were to carry out "development of agriculture and forestry" in Southeast Asia's undeveloped areas and establish a "co-prosperity sphere" as compensation, it would no longer be dependent on the United States for food, and then "our" service at the Southeast Asian front would not have been in vain.[171] In pursuit of this vision, he organized an agricultural and forest development project in Java and invested in it several million yen of his earnings from his transport business.[172]

THE ESTABLISHMENT OF A STANDPOINT OF ABSOLUTE PEACE AND OPPOSITION TO WAR

In contrast, among the Japanese who had experienced severe fighting, dealt closely with the people of Asia, or both, there were many who adopted a pacifist stance. We have already seen the examples of Ida Masakichi, staff member of the Sumatra military government; Sakimoto Takashi, who participated in the Imphal Campaign; and Fujioka Akiyoshi, who endured combat and starvation on Jolo Island—the so-called Island of Honorable Death (*gyokusai*). The case of Ni'imi Aya, who suffered starvation in the mountains of Luzon and lost her child, is similar. After the war, she became the owner of a retreat at a bamboo flute (*shakuhachi*) training center in Kumamoto Prefecture. Remembering her beloved husband and child, she would chant, "Everyone hold up your hands, and from up where the sun is, let's drive war out [of the world]."[173]

THE COEXISTENCE OF AN ANTIWAR STANCE AND A "HOLY WAR" PERSPECTIVE

What of those who served in the army during the Sino-Japanese War? Yamamoto Takeshi, who fought in central China for approximately two years beginning in 1937 and was introduced in chapter 1, was called up again in December 1944 and sent to Hachijō Island. When he learned of the surrender, he was simply dumbfounded. He wrote in his diary,

> Taiwan, Manchuria, Korea, acquired with the blood of our ancestors, working themselves to the bone building them up, are all returned to the hands of our enemies, and what's more even so much as southern Sakhalin is taken from us by the Soviet Union, like a lawless looter at the scene of a fire. And the most recent problem is that the Chinese continent too—where tens of thousands of my comrades in arms lie dead—must be handed over to Chiang Kai-shek. Disarmament everywhere on land, sea, and air. They're trying to make a reality as sad as one could imagine.[174]

Despite that expression of deep bitterness over the consequences of the defeat, when he returned safely to his home town on November 13, Yamamoto reflected on the preciousness of peace, observing, "Instead of the boisterous, carnival atmosphere like the time of my triumphant return home from the China Incident, this sense of euphoria of sitting around the *kotatsu* with just the family and being deeply happy together—that's wonderful."[175] Yamamoto's experience of the defeat thus became ambivalent. On September 9, 1981, in a document addressed to a former officer of the old 36th Infantry Regiment, he summarized his "postwar thoughts" under the following headings:

> Gratitude for a peaceful Japan, for the peace of our prospering nation
>
> Indebtedness toward the emperor
>
> Patriotism and a sense of mistrust etc. toward today's young people
>
> [Seeking] an early realization of visits to Yasukuni Shrine by government officials, beginning with the emperor[176]

In a letter to a former officer dated January 16, 1984, he wrote that he was "extremely proud" of "our supreme spirit and behavior of giving everything for the Empire, devoting our lives without a thought for ourselves," a story he said should be told to subsequent generations.[177]

Although Yamamoto maintained many of his old views concerning the emperor, the world, and the war, his perspective was affected by his combat experience, during which he saw many comrades in arms killed or crippled. Reflecting on this and on the fact that he had been driven into a war that led to the murders of a host of ordinary Chinese, including women and children, he wrote in the same letter, "We should not repeat the calamity of war that we've been through." And he had a habit of telling his children, "Just don't go to war again."[178]

A CHARGE OF WAR'S CRUELTY AND A PLEA FOR THE PRESERVATION OF PEACE

Marui Miyo, the younger sister of Imai Ryūichi, introduced in chapter 1, who died in battle in Shanghai, says that in his letters to her, her older brother "wrote of his hopes for the future as he readied himself for death" and that the cruelty of his "being already gone from this world a month and a half later" meant "many years passed with it being hard to read his diary and his many letters."[179] After the defeat, Marui strongly affirmed the cruelty of war and the greatness of peace. She found herself thinking about the grief of those like her brother "who continued, from their entry into the army, to entertain doubts about a life devoted exclusively to training for killing people; who, on the battlefield, had no way to resist and could only kill or be killed"; and who had never had the chance to enjoy the prosperity and freedom of the postwar period. In 1981, she published her older brother's diary with the aim of transmitting the feelings of those who were sacrificed for the war and, more generally, the experience of war's horrors, which was fading with the years.[180]

LIBERATION FROM THE FETTERS OF THE STATE

When the Japanese state and its military collapsed, those who had endured the war's most extreme hardships felt an unexpected and powerful sense of liberation. Among those who reported this sort of experience were Katō Mifumi, a staff member of the War Preparation Office of the Burma Defense Army; Miura Tokuhei, who fought in the intense battle of Myitkyina; Yano Masami, a soldier of the Tank Division Engineers Unit; and Fujioka Akiyoshi, who surrendered after fighting on Jolo.

For those who had this sort of experience, the building of a new Japan, based upon ideals of peace and democracy, was not something they saw as imposed "from outside" but rather the natural consequence of realizations they had come to themselves. Regarding the Japanese Constitution's appeal for the abandonment of war, for example, Fujioka, who returned to Japan in January 1947, writes, "This was extremely natural. At least this, I thought, we had to have."[181]

SELF-EXAMINATION OF THE
EXPERIENCES OF WAR AND ASIA

Many people found it extremely difficult to look back upon their experience of the war in Asia and examine their own responsibility for it. Yet it is inaccurate to say that the Japanese people have not done so at all. In one form or another, a considerable number of people have sought to take their own measure.

As we have already seen, after gaining permission from his comrades in arms, Miura Tokuhei recorded the slaughter of civilians in a Burmese village, and Yano Masami was compelled to acknowledge his participation in "murder, arson, robbery, rape—we've committed every sort of crime" on Luzon.[182] After the conflict was over, Ni'imi Aya came to recognize that "in this war, we imposed trouble upon the land, trees, and rocks of the Philippines, upon the people of the Philippines"; not content to pass all the blame for the war on to others, she published an account of her experiences in the Philippines as "my own small atonement. . . . I myself also bear responsibility."[183]

Reexamining his experiences during his service in the Sumatra military government, Ida Masakichi could find no positive aspect to the war.[184] Ishii Masaharu went even further. He acquired Indonesian citizenship, became a part of the local society, and ultimately recognized that the Japanese army—including himself—had unequivocally committed "aggression" (*shinryaku*).[185]

After the war, Kimura Genzaemon, who fought in northern China and was introduced in chapter 1, came to see that "the truth in which the nation believed it lived . . . was nothing more than a case of sheer buffoonery, a hallucination." Aiming to make this clear in service of his wish for "eternal peace and friendship between Japan and China," he published his war diary, which included descriptions of brutal behavior toward Chinese.[186] As a result of reexamining his own behavior, Murakami Masanori, who worked in a pacification unit in northern China, was consumed by intense self-loathing. Driven by a belief that war should not be pursued again and by the idea that "from the heart, I must apologize to the people of China," who had "been the victims of an aggressor," he published his own account. Ōnishi Katsumi's[187] diary similarly revealed the true nature of the war of aggression. Following its publication, Ōnishi's Fourth Mortar Battalion Veteran's Association (*Haku'yon kai*) published a unit history in which the former soldiers expressed a desire to "declare our heartfelt feeling of repentance toward the Chinese people, to whose lives and property we caused direct and indirect damage." The introduction and the afterword stated that the book used "personal diaries that their providers might even now hesitate to make public" but whose "publication we forced" with the "silent permission" of the parties involved because they "represented the facts of the soldier's lives."[188]

At the close of Japan's eight-year total war, which inflicted immeasurable damage upon the people of Asia and yielded 3.1 million Japanese dead, the Japanese people bore witness to the apotheosis of a drive to modernize that had begun during the Meiji period, modeled on Europe and America. From the overseas battlefields and the ashes of the homeland, people arrived at the concepts of everlasting peace and the abandonment of the capacity to wage war—ideas almost entirely alien to the nations of Europe, the United States, and the developing countries of Asia, Africa, and Latin America. These basic concepts led in turn to the development of the Three Non-nuclear Principles[189] and bans on the exportation of weapons and deployment of troops abroad, along with a nonaggressive defense policy and a ceiling on defense expenditures of 1 percent of GNP—which, although they presuppose a certain war capacity, represent checks against its transformation into a means of foreign conquest.

From reflection on the defeat, furthermore, the Japanese people sought to adopt a Western-style democratic system and pursue the sort of economic prosperity enjoyed by Americans. They carried out a new experiment in the twentieth century: economic development under a lightly armed, peaceful state. Because this experiment was rooted in popular experience, it was able to penetrate to the furthest reaches of society.

Yet it seems that the significance of the very experiences that gave rise to these phenomena— experiences of the battlefield and bombed-out ruins—are gradually fading from view. This has come about in part because of the passage of time since the end of war, but there is also—behind the established antiwar, pro-peace outlook—the continued existence of the "holy war" perspective, defects and suspension of reflection regarding cooperation in the war and war responsibility, and the persistence of an "imperial" attitude toward Asia—all characteristic of many Japanese people, which can be seen to have a profound relationship with the contemporary state of affairs.

During the postwar period, furthermore, the Japanese people were largely unable to achieve a meaningful reconciliation with the peoples of surrounding countries, to compensate those who were oppressed and mobilized for war, or to secure the rights of minority peoples within Japan itself. These failures too are not unrelated to Japanese views of war responsibility and the persistence of "imperial" attitudes.

Still, the fact that more than a few people have sincerely reflected on their experiences and examined their own beliefs and actions is a sign that the Japanese people are taking the first steps toward a resolution of these problems. Is it not therefore urgent that we now assemble and examine the precious insights that the Japanese people arrived at in the abyss of war and the postwar period's many examples of reflection and self-examination?

POSTSCRIPT

Eleven years have passed since I became interested in the problems of Japanese fascism and war, after previously focusing my studies on the history of Japan's social movements. During that time, my view of these problems shifted substantially. At a point when I was thinking of putting together research under the rubric of Japanese fascism theory, I received an invitation from the Contemporary History Research Association (*Gendai rekishigaku kenkyūkai*). As I took part in the association's lively debates, and as I observed the reactions of students to my university lectures, I came to feel strongly that I should cast my view down to the ground level and explore the problem of ordinary people's reactions to, and attitudes concerning, fascism and war.

In reference to Japan's recent history, scholars were extremely cautious about grappling with the issue of popular consciousness. In truth, I too hesitated in stepping into this territory, and I moved in this direction only a little bit at a time. I eventually realized that a huge variety of records of war experience (most of them diaries, accounts written immediately after the defeat, or memoirs composed after retirement) were being published publically and privately, especially since the beginning of the 1970s. These sorts of records had not received much consideration as objects of historical study.[1] As I moved ahead with the writing of this book, which is based on the examination of precisely these sorts of records—in particular the records of ordinary people, excluding officers—there came news of the speeches by the West German president Richard von Weizsäcker and former chancellor Helmut Schmidt marking the fortieth anniversary of Germany's defeat in World War II. While I did not agree with everything the two men had to say, I was nevertheless moved by the following passages:

> May 8 is the day of remembrance. Remembering means recalling an occurrence honestly and without distortion so that it becomes a part of our very beings. . . . In particular we commemorate the six million Jews who were murdered in German concentration camps. We commemorate all nations who suffered in the war, especially the countless citizens of the Soviet Union and Poland who lost their lives. . . . We commemorate the Sinti and Romany Gypsies, the homosexuals and the mentally ill who were killed, as well as the people who were put to death for their religious or political beliefs. We commemorate the hostages who were executed. We recall the victims of the resistance movements in all the countries occupied by us.
>
> (*R. Weizsäcker, "He Who Closes His Eyes to the Past Is Blind to the Present"*)[2]

> Japan does not have close relations with any country comparable to those among the members of the European Union, or the European countries with the U.S. and Canada. . . . Germans have keenly felt the need to solemnly analyze their recent history, and the future. They have conducted a deep personal inspection, and as a result they have reached a precise acknowledgment of their personal injustices. In the neighboring countries that suffered under Hitler's control too, this has gradually been understood. Yet in Southeast Asia, we hear no accounts whatsoever that Japan has conducted such a self-inspection, or that today's peaceful Japan is deeply trusted and accepted for that reason.
>
> (*Schmidt, "Friendless Japan"*)[3]

Here the good sides of postwar West Germany's social structure—in particular, the recognition of the rights of ethnic and other minorities, the acknowledgment of war responsibility on a national level, and the establishment of friendly relations with neighboring countries based upon self-examination—are contrasted with the Japanese state's failure as a whole to engage in a deep "self-inspection." With regard to the state, the observation is unfortunately nothing other than accurate.

I took Weizsäcker's and Schmidt's declarations as encouragements to the Japanese people and pushed forward with my research, which I had tended to leave off. In the process, I realized that through the various personal records of the war experience, as well as the investigations and research being conducted by journalists and scholars, more than a few people were carrying out the sort of self-examination that Schmidt was talking about. This reaffirmed to me the great importance of the building of a peaceful Japan based upon the Japanese people's various experiences of the war. This book, then, brings together the records of many of those experiences.[4]

I received the support of many people in putting it together. Ishigami Masao, Ida Masakichi, Katō Mifumi, Sakimoto Takashi, Ni'imi Aya, Nitō Seikichi, Fujioka Akiyoshi, Marui Miyo, Miura Tokuhei, and Yano Masami were of great assistance, donating various records of their war experiences, answering inquiries in interviews and letters, and making other sources available to me. Kuboi Ritsuo lent me Ōnishi Katsumi's *Ichiheishi no yasen nikki*, and Saitō Yoshimichi allowed me the use of various letters to Saitō Takao as illustrations. The National Diet Library assisted me during my examination of various records of war experience. Tazaki Nobuyoshi provided the "Abe Tarō nikki." I received a large amount of material from Awaya Kentarō and Yoshida Yutaka, and Hora Tomio provided assistance with sources. I have many fond memories of visiting government offices, archives, and libraries together with Yoshida and Ikō Toshiya as they edited the eleven-volume *Shiryō Nihon gendaishi*, which is referenced often in this book. Fujiwara Akira did me the favor of reading the portion concerning "war memoirs" (*senki*). I received guidance regarding the *kana* transcription of Korean names from Kajimura Hideki and the *kana* transcription of Chinese and Taiwanese names from Ishijima Noriyuki. My thanks from the bottom of my heart.

Interaction with the members of the Contemporary Japanese History Research Association (*Nihon gendaishi kenkyūkai*) for more than ten years—along with the members of the Contemporary History Research Association for more than six years—has provided me with fresh inspiration. Furthermore, this book would not have appeared without the warm support of Watanabe Isao of Tokyo University Press. Here I would like to express my deep gratitude.

YOSHIMI YOSHIAKI
MAY 1987

NOTES

TRANSLATOR'S INTRODUCTION: THE PEOPLE IN THE WAR

1. This translation project was made possible by generous grants from the Netherlands Institute for War Documentation (NIOD) and the Isaac Alfred Ailion Foundation. I would like to thank Yoshimi Yoshiaki for his indispensable and generous cooperation, collaboration, and patience at every stage of its preparation. My acknowledgments also to Rikki Kersten for her assistance in securing project funding, to Alan Tansman and the other (anonymous) reviewer for Columbia University Press for their enthusiasm and constructive advice on improving the manuscript, to Dan Geist for his generous assistance in refining its writing and editing, and to Carol Gluck, Anne Routon, and the staffs of Columbia University Press and the Weatherhead East Asian Institute for their support in seeing it through to publication.

2. *War Without Mercy: Race and Power in the Pacific War* is the title of an award-winning 1987 study of Japanese and American mutual images by John Dower (New York: Pantheon) that documents the ubiquitous racism characteristic to perceptions of the conflict on both sides and the escalating brutality that it helped engender.

3. Qualities frequently mentioned in this context have included blind obedience to authority, racism, xenophobia, provincialism, conformism, anti-individualism, readiness for self-sacrifice, and a tendency to violence.

4. John Fairbank, Edwin O. Reischauer, and Albert Craig, *East Asia: Tradition and Transformation*, rev. ed. (Boston: Houghton Mifflin, 1989), 724–725.

5. The contemporary staying power of such conceptualizations is reflected, for example, in both the title and the contents of Nicholas Tarling's *A Sudden Rampage: The Japanese Occupation of Southeast Asia, 1941–1945* (Honolulu: University of Hawaii Press, 2001). It

should be noted that in a recent trend that receives further attention below, an increasing body of scholarship has taken issue with such conventional views, characterizing inter-war Japanese fascism and imperialism as essentially modern responses to the tensions and contradictions of modern mass society and capitalist industrial development and accompanying multiple (economic, political, social, cultural, and imperial) crises of the global international system experienced in Europe and the United States in the same period. In English, see, for example, Andrew Gordon, *Labor and Imperial Democracy in Prewar Japan* (Berkeley: University of California Press, 1992); Louise Young, *Japan's Total Empire* (Berkeley: University of California Press, 1998); Harry Harootunian, *Overcome by Modernity: History, Culture, and Community in Interwar Japan* (Princeton, N.J.: Princeton University Press, 2000); and Alan Tansman, *The Aesthetics of Japanese Fascism* (Berkeley: University of California Press, 2009).

6. "Japan in this period is better labeled militarist than fascist," continue the authors of the above textbook. "The basic state apparatus was not new or revolutionary, but merely the old 'establishment,' now dominated by the military elite, overlaid by controls, and swept up in a spiritual nationalism." Other leading Japan scholars classifying wartime Japan as other than fascist have included George Wilson, James Crowley, Mark Peattie, Richard Smethurst, Gordon Berger, Ben-Ami Shillony, Richard Mitchell, Peter Duus, and Daniel Okimoto. In a more recent comparative study, Robert Paxton, a leading historian of the fascist period in Europe, agrees: "The Japanese empire of the period 1932–45 is better understood as an expansionist military dictatorship with a high degree of state-sponsored mobilization," he wrote, "than as a fascist regime." Robert Paxton, *The Anatomy of Fascism* (New York: Knopf, 2004), 200.

7. The term was first coined by Maruyama Masao, whose analysis is discussed in further detail below.

8. Maruyama Masao, "Theory and Psychology of Ultra-Nationalism," in *Thought and Behavior in Modern Japanese Politics*, trans. and ed. Ivan Morris (New York: Oxford University Press, 1963); originally published in *Sekai* (May 1946): 21.

9. Carol Gluck, "The Idea of Shōwa," *Daedelus* 119 (Summer 1990): 12–13.

10. In its powerful combination of historical narrative and personal testimony, *Grassroots Fascism* can be seen as foreshadowing a more recent international trend represented by such works as Alessandro Portelli, *The Order Has Been Carried Out*, on Italy in World War II (New York: Palgrave Macmillan, 2003); Jean Yves Le Naour, *The Living Unknown Soldier: A Story of Grief and the Great War*, on French veterans of World War I (New York: Holt, 2005); and Drew Gilpin Faust's *The Republic of Suffering* on American experiences of the Civil War (New York: Knopf, 2008).

11. See, for example, the introduction and essays in Frederick Cooper and Anne Laura Stoler, eds., *Tensions of Empire* (Berkeley: University of California Press, 1997).

12. See Mark Mazower, *Hitler's Empire: How the Nazis Ruled Europe* (New York: Penguin, 2008).

13. A similar point has been made regarding the evolution of Japanese Marxist historiography in the early and mid-twentieth century, a part of global history still little known out-

side of Japan. As Germaine Hoston observed in 1986, "over the last several decades, Western Marxists like Maurice Dobb and Paul Sweezy have been engaged in a controversy on the character of the development of capitalism in Western Europe. In confronting the issue of whether an external force, world trade (Sweezy), or some factor inherent in the feudal system (Dobb) was the principal factor that precipitated England's evolution of industrial capitalism, these scholars have addressed important gaps remaining in Marx's original theory. The participants in the debate on Japanese capitalism undertook this endeavor twenty years before Western Marxists did, and in their study of a non-Western case, spoke to the question of the relationship between the universal and the particular that is fundamental to any conception of political development, whether Marxist or non-Marxist." Germaine Hoston, *Marxism and the Crisis of Development in Prewar Japan* (Princeton, N.J.: Princeton University Press, 1986), 99.

14. First published in book form in 1995 and subsequently appearing in English as *Comfort Women: Sexual Slavery and the Japanese Military During World War Two*, trans. Suzanne O'Brien (New York: Columbia University Press, 2000).

15. The remaining portion of this translator's introduction presents an in-depth discussion of *Grassroots Fascism*'s formative and contemporary contexts as well as an assessment of the challenges, strengths, and weaknesses of Yoshimi's distinctive approach. Both cite and draw substantially on interviews with the author. Readers with less time or interest for issues of the book's progeny and its location in the domestic and global scholarly landscape may wish to skip directly ahead to the start of the translation.

16. Although the social status of schoolteachers was relatively high in prewar and early postwar Japan, their salaries were notoriously low. This situation was represented in the prewar expression "pauper in Western clothes" (*yōfuku saimin*)—referring to those possessing modern cultural sophistication but disadvantaged materially—for which schoolteachers served as a standard example. As in Europe in the same period, frustrated ambitions among underprivileged low-ranking state officials of this sort may well have represented potent fuel for "grassroots" support of fascism. On Europe, see, for example, Michael Mann, *Fascists* (Cambridge: Cambridge University Press, 2004).

17. When the war started, Yoshimi's father was just too old to be drafted; when it ended, Yoshimi's oldest brother was just too young. Personal interview with Yoshimi Yoshiaki at his office at Chūō University, Tokyo, January 17, 2007.

18. Ibid.

19. Ibid.

20. In accordance with the pacifist precepts of its postwar constitution, Japan did not send troops to Vietnam, but it remained in a military alliance with the United States throughout the conflict, offering passive support in the form of continued U.S. military access to Japanese sea, air, and land space. For more on the Japanese experience of the Vietnam War, see Thomas R. Havens, *Fire Across the Sea: The Vietnam War and Japan, 1965–1975* (Princeton, N.J.: Princeton University Press, 1987).

21. Personal interview with Yoshimi, Tokyo, January 17, 2007.

22. Personal interview with Yoshimi, Tokyo, January 19, 2007.

23. Personal interview with Yoshimi, Tokyo, January 17, 2007.

24. This was the historian Kamei Katsuichirō's assessment of *Shōwashi* (authored by Imai Sei'ichi, Fujiwara Akira, Tōyama Shigeru, et al. [Tokyo: Iwanami shoten, 1955]) in the March 1956 issue of *Bungei shunju*, as cited in Tōyama Shigeru, *Sengo no rekishigaku to rekishi ishiki* (Tokyo: Iwanami Shoten, 1968), 227.

25. Personal interview with Yoshimi, Tokyo, January 17, 2007.

26. Ibid.

27. Under the prewar education system from 1907 onward, students attended the so-called ordinary elementary school for a period of six years, followed by the so-called higher elementary school for another two years. Attendance usually began at age six.

28. Personal interview with Yoshimi, Tokyo, January 17, 2007.

29. Ibid.

30. Ibid.

31. See, for example, *Nihon fashizumu no keisei*, ed. Eguchi Kei'ichi, a volume in the series *Taikei Nihon gendaishi* (Tokyo: Nihon hyōronsha, 1978).

32. See Peter Duus and Daniel I. Okamoto, "Fascism and the History of Prewar Japan: The Failure of a Concept," *Journal of Asian Studies* 39, no. 1 (November 1979): 65–76; Ben-Ami Shillony, *Politics and Culture in Wartime Japan* (Oxford: Clarendon, 1981); and Itō Takashi, "Shōwa seijishi kenkyū no ichi shikaku," *Shisō* (June 1976): 215–228.

33. Ōishi Kaichirō, "Kindaishi josetsu," in *Iwanami kōza nihonrekishi kindai 1* (Tokyo: Iwanami shoten, 1975), 6.

34. Furuya Tetsuo, "Nihon fashizumu ron," in *Iwanami kōza nihon rekishi* (Tokyo: Iwanami shoten, 1976), 20:84–86.

35. Ibid.

36. Personal interview with Yoshimi, Tokyo, January 19, 2007.

37. Ibid.

38. Ibid.

39. As evidence for this "failure," scholars typically cite the successes of bureaucratic and big-business interests in blocking full implementation of military-backed attempts to establish one-party rule in the form of the Imperial Rule Assistance Association under the leadership of Konoe Fumimaro (1940) and state economic control under the "Economic New Order" (1941). Frequently cited is the scholar E. H. Norman's 1940 observation that "experienced bureaucracy has gradually snuffed out all signs of genuine democratic activity, but on the other hand it has blocked the victory of outright fascist forces." In the same year, observing the resistance of Japanese big business to Nazi-style attempts at nationalization in the same, Norman wrote, "it seems as if Japanese business circles have profited from the experience of Germany, where complete Nazi control over state and foreign policy has eventually become a Juggernaut menacing some of the very interests and men who helped it to power." E. H. Norman, cited in John W. Dower, "E. H. Norman, Japan, and the Uses of History," in *Origins of the Modern Japanese State: Selected Writings of E. H. Norman*, ed. John W. Dower (New York: Pantheon, 1975), 73; the second quote is from Norman, *Japan's Emergence as a Modern State*, in ibid., 114. On the other hand, Norman's contemporary John Gunther, a sharp-witted journalist for the *International Herald Tri-*

bune and author of the late-1930s international bestsellers *Inside Europe* and *Inside Asia*, observed the following in 1939: "A movement to abolish the parliamentary facade and to inaugurate a single Fascist-totalitarian party replacing the old parties began several years ago . . . its leadership was to go to Prince Konoye [Konoe], who later became prime minister. . . . But the plan collapsed. Konoye became shy of the idea, and other leaders were coy. Apparently they feared that Japan was not ready for such a formally totalitarian step. Then came national preoccupation with the China war, *which made it in a way unnecessary.*" John Gunther, *Inside Asia* (New York: Harper and Brothers, 1939), 65, emphasis added.

40. Yoshimi, *Kusa no ne no fashizumu*, 78.
41. See, for example, Ethan Mark, "Asia's Transwar Lineage: Nationalism, Marxism, and 'Greater Asia' in an Indonesian Inflection," *Journal of Asian Studies* 65, no. 3 (Autumn 2006): 461–493.
42. Ibid.
43. Yoshimi, *Kusa no ne no fashizumu*, 13.
44. Personal interview with Yoshimi, Tokyo, January 19, 2007.
45. Yoshimi, *Kusa no ne no fashizumu*, 23–24.
46. E. P. Thompson, *The Making of the Working Class* (London: Gollancz, 1963), 12. An outstanding example of such scholarship in the American context is Howard Zinn, *A People's History of the United States: 1492–Present* (New York: Harper Collins, 1980).
47. Carol Gluck, "The People in History: Recent Trends in Japanese Historiography," *Journal of Asian Studies* 38, no. 1 (November 1978): 25–50.
48. More progressive than both the previously known constitution drafts drawn up by leaders of the Popular Rights Movement and the Western sources it drew upon for inspiration, the constitution was authored by the wandering son of a well-to-do farm family who had enthusiastically spread the gospel of popular rights among the people.
49. Irokawa Daikichi, *Meiji no bunka* (Tokyo: Iwanami shoten, 1970).
50. See, for example, Neil Waters, *Japan's Local Pragmatists: The Transition from Bakumatsu to Meiji in the Kawasaki Region* (Cambridge, Mass.: Harvard University Press, 1983), 3–30.
51. See, for example, Gluck, "The People in History."
52. "City residents, for whom opportunities were relatively numerous, were beneficiaries of war," writes Yoshimi. "In contrast, in each war since the first Sino-Japanese conflict [1894–1895], the people of farming, mountain, and fishing villages had born great sacrifices, contradictions, and difficulties." *Kusa no ne no fashizumu*, 10.
53. Personal interview with Yoshimi, Tokyo, January 23, 2007.
54. Ibid.
55. In a critical 1979 reexamination of the concept "Japanese fascism," American scholars Peter Duus and Daniel I. Okamoto indeed highlighted what they saw as a need for research on the war period inspired by work "of the sort that Irokawa Daikichi has done on the 1870s and 1880s and Kano Masanao has done on the 1910s and 1920s" in order to similarly "enrich our sense of those periods and correct oversimplified aggregate portrayals." Duus and Okamoto, "Fascism and the History of Prewar Japan."

56. Personal interview with Yoshimi, Tokyo, January 19, 2007.

57. *Grassroots Fascism* was eventually to appear as the eighth in the twelve-volume series alongside works treating topics such as Indian nationalism, Islam and the Russian Revolution, social revolution in the Hungarian countryside, imperialist consciousness in England, African perspectives in the age of "the carving up of the continent," German imperialism and Poles in the Ruhr region, Asian socialism, identity and modernity in Mexico, and testimonies of Palestinian refugees.

58. Personal interview with Yoshimi, Tokyo, January 17, 2007.

59. Yoshimi, *Kusa no ne no fashizumu*, 301.

60. Personal correspondence with Yoshimi Yoshiaki, January 3, 2011.

61. Yoshimi, *Kusa no ne no fashizumu*, 301.

62. See John Dower, *Embracing Defeat* (New York: Norton, 2000), 22.

63. For a consideration of this phenomenon in the Indonesian context, see Ethan Mark, "Suharto's New Order Remembers Japan's New Order: Oral Accounts from Indonesia," in *Representing the Japanese Occupation of Indonesia*, ed. Remco Raben (Zwolle: Waanders, 1999), 72–84.

64. Personal interview with Nakajima Masachika, Saitama, August 8, 1995.

65. Personal interview with Yoshimi, January 17, 2007.

66. See, for example, the narrative based on the diary entries of Fujioka Akiyoshi, authored in a POW camp after the surrender, where Fujioka retroactively ascribes to himself an awareness of his status as merely "one of the tools of imperialism" in a mid-1944 diary entry. In his summary and analysis at the conclusion of the account, Yoshimi reproduces and confirms Fujioka's version of events: "If we first examine things from the standpoint of his Philippine experience, Fujioka was already well enough aware of the nature of the Japanese army as victimizer, conscious from the beginning that he was 'one of the tools of imperialism.'" While it is impossible to determine the truth of this characterization, it is also impossible to rule out potential modification in light of postwar reality. Yoshimi, *Kusa no ne no fashizumu*, 215, 219.

67. Personal interview with Yoshimi, January 17, 2007.

68. In subaltern history in the Indian case, see, for example, Dipesh Chakrabarty, "Subaltern Studies and Postcolonial Historiography," *Nepantla: Views from South* 1, no. 1 (2000): 9–32.

69. Ibid.

70. Their numbers include Edward Said, Frederick Cooper, Anne Laura Stoler, Peter van der Veer, Nicholas Dirks, and Dipesh Chakrabarty.

71. A hint as to the often complex relationship between the Japanese occupiers and the Indonesian nationalist elite, for example, appears at the conclusion of the Indonesia section of chapter 3. Here Yoshimi notes that during the occupation the Japanese civilian and former Sumatra resident Ida Masakichi interacted heavily with a number of "pro-Japanese" Indonesians who later came to hold high positions in independent Indonesia (one an officer trainee who later became postwar commander of the South Sumatra Defense Army, another a military government police department chief who later became governor-general of Sumatra, the third a military government employee who later became governor of Palembang State).

72. Personal interview with Yoshimi, Tokyo, January 19, 2007.

73. On the Japanese war experience see, for example, Haruko Taya Cook and Theodore F. Cook, *Japan at War: An Oral History* (New York: New Press, 1992); Hildi Kang, ed., *Under the Black Umbrella: Voices from Colonial Korea* (Ithaca, N.Y.: Cornell University Press, 2001); Samuel Yamashita, ed., *Leaves from an Autumn of Emergencies: Selections from the Wartime Diaries of Ordinary Japanese* (Honolulu: University of Hawaii Press, 2005); Frank Gibney, ed., *Sensō: The Japanese Remember the Pacific War: Letters to the Editor of the* Asahi Shinbun (Armonk, N.Y.: M. E. Sharpe, 2006); and Emiko Ohnuki Tierney, *Kamikaze Diaries: Reflections of Japanese Student Soldiers* (Chicago: University of Chicago Press, 2006). On the American side, see, for example, Paul Fussel, *Wartime: Understanding and Behavior in the Second World War* (New York: Oxford University Press, 1989); Samuel Hynes, *The Soldier's Tale: Bearing Witness to a Modern War* (London: Penguin, 1998); and Paul Fussel, *The Boys' Crusade: The American Infantry in Northwestern Europe, 1944–1945* (New York: Modern Library, 2003).

74. See Andrew Gordon, *Labor and Imperial Democracy in Prewar Japan* (Berkeley: University of California Press, 1991); Louise Young, *Japan's Total Empire: Manchuria and the Culture of Wartime Imperialism* (Berkeley: University of California Press, 1998); and Harry Harootunian, *Overcome by Modernity: History, Culture, and Community in Interwar Japan* (Princeton, N.J.: Princeton University Press, 2000).

75. *Ajia/taiheiyō sensō shiriizu Nihon kindaishi* (Tokyo: Iwanami shoten, 2006–2008), vols. 1–8.

76. See, for example, Leslie Pincus, *Authenticating Culture in Imperial Japan* (Berkeley: University of California Press, 1996); Harootunian, *Overcome by Modernity*; Tansman, *Aesthetics of Japanese Fascism*; Kenneth James Ruoff, *Imperial Japan at Its Zenith: The Wartime Celebration of the Empire's 2600th Anniversary* (Ithaca, N.Y.: Cornell University Press, 2010); and the essays in Alan Tansman, ed., *The Culture of Japanese Fascism* (London: Duke University Press, 2009). In Japanese, see also Akazawa Shirō and Kitagawa Kenzō, ed., *Bunka to fashizumu: senjiki nihon ni okeru bunka to kōbō* (Tokyo: Nihon keizai hyōronsha, 1993).

77. See, for example, Oguma Eiji, *Nihonjin no kyōkai: Okinawa, Ainu, Taiwan, Choōsen, shokuminchi kara fukki undo made* (Tokyo: Shinyosha, 1998); and Tessa Morris-Suzuki, *Reinventing Japan: Time, Space, Nation* (Armonk, N.Y.: M. E. Sharpe, 1998).

78. See, for example, Prasenjit Duara, *Sovereignty and Authenticity: Manchukuo and the East Asian Modern* (Lanham, Md.: Rowman and Littlefield, 2003); Leo Ching, *Becoming Japanese: Colonial Taiwan and the Politics of Identity Formation* (Berkeley: University of California Press, 2001); Hyun Ok Park, *Two Dreams in One Bed: Empire, Social Life, and the Origins of the North Korean Revolution in Manchuria* (London: Duke University Press, 2005); Jun Uchida, *Brokers of Empire: Japanese Settler Colonialism in Korea, 1876–1945* (Cambridge, Mass.: Harvard University Press, 2011); and Takashi Fujitani, *Race for Empire: Japanese as Americans and Koreans as Japanese in World War Two* (Berkeley: University of California Press, 2011).

79. Yoshiaki, *Comfort Women*; and Yoshimi Yoshiaki, *Doku gasu sen to Nihon gun* [Poison gas warfare and the Japanese army] (Tokyo: Iwanami shoten, 2004). Yoshimi's most recent

work, *Yakeato kara no demokurashii: kusa no ne no senryōki taiken* [Democracy from the ashes: The grassroots occupation experience] (Tokyo: Iwanami shoten, 2014), is a two-volume exploration of popular experiences of the U.S. occupation period that can be seen as a postwar sequel to the present volume.

80. For a brief and accessible overview of the history of Japan's war in Asia and the Pacific, a good place to start is Andrew Gordon's *A Modern History of Japan: From Tokugawa Times to the Present*, 3rd ed. (New York: Oxford University Press, 2013), chaps. 10–12. Consciously written as part introspective personal history and part general history, Ienaga Saburō's *The Pacific War*, first published in 1968 and in English translation in 1979 (New York: Pantheon), remains a classic introduction to the Asia-Pacific War.

❶ FROM DEMOCRACY TO FASCISM

1. In the Manchurian Incident, the Japanese Kwantung Army, responsible for guarding the South Manchurian Railway, used a bombing incident near the city of Shenyang (then Mukden) as a pretext to occupy southern Manchuria. Facing international criticism, the Japanese government was initially indecisive in response to this autonomous army action, but sharing a perception of Manchuria's colonization as a solution to Japan's domestic and international woes in the midst of the Great Depression, the Japanese military, mass media, business community, and public displayed great enthusiasm for it. This helped embolden the Kwantung Army to occupy all of Manchuria and install a puppet regime there in 1932, a move that led to the eventual Japanese withdrawal from the League of Nations the following year. On this event and its profound social ramifications in Japan in English, see Louise Young, *Japan's Total Empire: Manchuria and the Culture of Wartime Imperialism* (Berkeley: University of California Press, 1998); and Sandra Wilson, *The Manchurian Crisis and Japanese Society, 1931–1933* (London: Routledge, 2002). (EM)

2. Tatsuo Takayoshi, *Taishō demokurashii* (Tokyo: Iwanami shoten, 1974), 7.

3. The Taishō period refers to the reign period of the Taishō emperor, which lasted from 1912 to 1926. The term "Taishō democracy" refers to the increasing influence and popularity of parliamentary democracy, democratic movements, and democratic ideals that characterized the period and the years on either side of it. However, democracy in prewar Japan was limited by a number of factors, including the continued political and legal centrality and unassailability of the emperor and his advisors, the political power of nonelected bodies such as the House of Peers, the military's influence and independence from parliamentary control, and suppressive measures such as the infamous 1925 Peace Preservation Law. The degree to which one can describe the prewar Japanese order as "democratic" remains therefore debated and controversial. For a discussion of "Taishō democracy" in English, see Andrew Gordon, *Labor and Imperial Democracy in Prewar Japan* (Berkeley: University of California Press, 1991). (EM)

4. The "emperor system" is a general, critical term of reference to the prewar Japanese social and political order constructed with the emperor as its centerpiece. Favored by scholars to the left of the political spectrum since the early postwar period, its usage reflects a conceptualization of prewar Japan as an authoritarian and oppressive social and political sys-

tem distinguished by the emperor's unique role as both political and religious leader and legitimator. At the same time, its scholarly usage in compounds such as "emperor-system democracy" and "emperor-system liberalism" reflects an acknowledgment that the *coexistence* of support for the imperial institution on the one hand and progressive conceptualizations of society and politics on the other, however contradictory and troubling, was not only possible but indeed characteristic of Japanese prewar and wartime ideology. Andrew Gordon uses the term "imperial democracy" in a similar vein. See Gordon, *Labor and Imperial Democracy*. Following Gordon, the Japanese terms "emperor-system democracy" and "emperor-system fascism" are henceforth translated here as "imperial democracy" and "imperial fascism." (EM)

5. Amemiya Shōichi refers to this sort of liberationism as "emperor-system authoritarian democracy-ism" (*tennōsei ken'i shugiteki minshūshugi*, abbreviated as *ken'i shugiteki minshūshugi* or "authoritarian democracy-ism"). He links it to the people who gathered around Prime Minister Konoe Fumimaro and implemented national reorganization at the time of the New Order Movement [at the beginning of the 1940s—EM], along with their supporters: businessmen and industrialists in small- and medium-sized enterprises and owner-cultivators, cultivator-landlords, and cultivator-peasants in provincial cities and rural villages. Amemiya traces its evolution from "imperialism externally, social renovation internally" (from World War I onward) to "Asian Monroe Doctrine–ism externally, national socialism internally" (at the stage of the Sino-Japanese War). Amemiya Shōichi, "Taisei yokusankai keisei katei ni okeru shoseiji chōryū," *Ibaraki daigaku kyōyōbu kiyō* 15 (1983): 31–32. Yet he treats this "authoritarian democracy-ism" as a special characteristic of a social grouping one rank higher than the people, the "class of prominent men in residence" who carried out "self-renovation." Regarding Asian Monroe Doctrine–ism, this was a Japanese foreign policy idea that gained strength from the end of World War I, which maintained that Western power must be expelled from Asia and that Asians should manage Asia's affairs, but that only Japan was fit to be the leader of this mission—a doctrine of rejection and exclusivity regarding the West and of domination and discrimination toward Asia. Eguchi Kei'ichi, "1930-nendai ron," in *Taikei/Nihon gendaishi*, ed. Eguchi Kei'ichi, 1:17–18. Eguchi identifies this as one of the representative lines of Japanese imperialism.

6. The "February 26 Incident" refers to a failed coup d'état attempt led by a group of twenty-two young army officers and approximately 1,400 soldiers in Tokyo between February 26 and 29, 1936. Calling for national renovation in the emperor's name, the rebel units enjoyed the backing of several high-ranking army officers of the so-called Imperial Way Faction (*kōdōha*), known as ideological proponents of domestic spiritual and social reorganization. The rebels assassinated a number of big-business leaders and several prominent politicians, including Finance Minister Takahashi Korekiyo, and occupied the Army Ministry, the General Staff Office, the Imperial Diet, and the Prime Minister's Residence, but they failed to gain the emperor's backing. The army command at first declared martial law, but in light of strong protest against the coup attempt from the navy, the business community, and the emperor himself, it subsequently moved to suppress the rebels. In contrast to the treatment of military and right-wing perpetrators of several previous ter-

rorist acts earlier in the decade, the February 26 coup leaders and their direct supporters were punished harshly. Nineteen of the young officers, along with their accused political mentor Kita Ikki, were summarily executed, and four generals who had backed them were purged from duty. The crackdown resulted in a resolution of a longstanding rivalry within the army command between the Imperial Way Faction and the Control Faction (*Tōseiha*) in decisive favor of the latter. Represented by such figures as Tōjō Hideki, those associated with the Control Faction were generally more conservative than the Imperial Way Faction regarding domestic social renovation, but they proved no less adventurous with regard to waging war, imperialist expansion, increasing military prerogatives, and the pursuit of radical domestic policies to these ends. For further information in English, see, for example, Ben-Ami Shillony, *Revolt in Japan: The Young Officers and the February 26, 1936, Incident* (Princeton, N.J.: Princeton University Press, 1973). (EM)

7. *Yuasa Kurahei kankei monjo*, Yamaguchi Prefectural Archives.

8. Saitō Takao (1870–1949) was a member of the Minseitō Party and known for his outspoken parliamentary criticism of the military in the late 1930s, criticism that eventually saw him purged from the Diet in 1940. While he attacked the military for arrogance and flawed policies, Saitō was himself a proponent of Japanese imperialist expansion in China, and his antimilitary criticisms were largely those of means rather than ends. For more on Saitō in English, see Earl H. Kinmonth, "The Mouse That Roared: Saito Takao, Conservative Critic of Japan's 'Holy War' in China," *Journal of Japanese Studies* 25, no. 2 (Summer 1999): 331–360. (EM)

9. *Shiryō Nihon gendaishi*, ed. Awaya Kentarō and Otabe Yūji (Tokyo: Ōtsuki shoten, 1984), 9:398.

10. Ibid., 9:409–410.

11. Ibid., 9:436.

12. Ibid., 9:418.

13. After the resignation of the Hirota Kōki cabinet in late January 1937, the emperor called upon the former army minister and general Ugaki to form a new cabinet. Ugaki's nomination faced unexpectedly strong opposition from within the army, however, centered around Colonel Ishiwara Kanji of the General Staff Office, a former proponent of the Manchurian Incident of 1931. Army critics cited suspicion of Ugaki's involvement in an abortive coup d'état in 1931 as well as deep links with the political parties and big business, which, they argued, made him unfit to pursue necessary political reforms. In response, the army chose not to recommend any active-duty officer as army minister—an old requirement under the Meiji Constitution that had been abandoned in the 1910s but recently readopted by the Hirota cabinet—thus thwarting Ugaki's attempt to form a cabinet. On February 2, 1937, General Hayashi Senjurō became prime minister with army backing. The requirement that ministers of army and navy be active-duty officers was thus shown to provide the military an effective veto power over cabinet formation, and in subsequent years this threat was used to leverage increasing army influence in the political arena. In English, see, for example, Gordon Mark Berger, *Parties Out of Power in Japan, 1931–1941* (Princeton, N.J.: Princeton University Press, 1977). (EM)

14. *Shiryō Nihon gendaishi*, 9:447.

15. Ibid., 9:450.
16. Ibid., 9:467.
17. In cooperation with agencies such as the Central Agriculture and Forestry Council.
18. From Minamikata Village, Miyagi Prefecture. This and the following citations are from "Tendencies of Thinking during the [China] Incident in Farming, Mountain, and Fishing Villages." Naikaku jōhōbu, ed., "Jihenka ni okeru nōsangyoson no shisō dōkō," repr. in *Shiryō Nihon gendaishi*, ed. Yoshimi Yoshiaki, Ikō Toshiya, and Yoshida Yutaka (Tokyo: Ōtsuki shoten, 1984), 11:319. This was a classified manuscript printed under the name of the Cabinet Information Bureau, comprising a survey of attitudes toward the Sino-Japanese War in thirty-eight towns and villages throughout the country conducted by the Cabinet Planning Board's Industry Section between November 1937 and January 1938. Most of the data was collected in November 1937. It appears that those in charge in the Planning Board were associates of Wada Hiro'o. [Wada Hiro'o (1903–1967) was one of several figures on the Cabinet Planning Board suspected of communist sympathies and arrested for violation of the Peace Preservation Law in 1941 (the so-called Planning Board Incident). He was finally acquitted in 1945. After the war Wada served as minister of agriculture, economic advisor, and socialist party MP and had a hand in occupation-era land reform and economic recovery policymaking. (EM)] The survey method involved assembling a composite view of the tendencies of each municipality, and it is possible that the results were heavily biased according to the respective powers of observation and subjective interpretations of the pollsters in each locality (whose observations and interpretations in turn likely represented a summation of the views of well-informed people of local influence). But this in itself does not constitute grounds for dismissal; in reports from municipalities in which close observation was conducted, one may judge that they were near to reflecting the true situation.
19. *Shiryō Nihon gendaishi*, 11:320.
20. Ibid., 11:310.
21. Ibid., 11:319.
22. The quote is from Mikata Village, Hyōgo Prefecture, ibid., 11:311, 321–322.
23. From Okugawa Village, Fukushima Prefecture, ibid., 11:319.
24. From Meiji Village, Ibaraki Prefecture, ibid.
25. From Tomioka Village, Ishikawa Prefecture, ibid., 11:320.
26. From Takaichi Village, Nara Prefecture, ibid.
27. The First Shanghai Incident, which began in January 1932, was precipitated by a Japanese military scheme to suppress Chinese anti-Japanese protests and distract world attention in the wake of the Japanese invasion of Manchuria. The scheme involved the staging of an attack by Chinese upon a Japanese Buddhist monk in Shanghai, which was then used as a pretext to land a large military force to occupy the city. The Japanese troops faced unexpectedly stiff and sustained resistance from the Chinese 19th Army, who enjoyed widespread popular support. In the face of Chinese protests to the League of Nations, complaints from the European and American imperial powers also resident in Shanghai, and fears of further stoking popular anti-Japanese unrest, the Japanese were compelled to conclude a ceasefire agreement in May of the same year. The Second Shanghai Incident

occurred in August 1937 within the context of Japanese moves to expand the local conflict that began at Marco Polo Bridge the previous month into all-out war. (EM)

28. Naikaku jōhōbu, ed., *Jihenka ni*, 321.

29. Ibid., 315.

30. The Movement for Total National Spiritual Mobilization was advocated nationwide by the First Konoe cabinet as the Sino-Japanese War flared into a full-scale conflict. From 1938 its participant organizations included the Imperial Military Reservists' Association, the National Shinto Priests' Association (全国神職会), the National Mayor's Association, and the Japanese Council of Labor Unions. (EM)

31. From Minamisabaishi Village, Niigata Prefecture. Naikaku jōhōbu, ed., *Jihenka ni*, 327.

32. From Shufu Village, Ehime Prefecture, ibid., 324.

33. From Kawashima Town, Kagawa Prefecture, ibid., 322.

34. Ibid., 323.

35. An observer for the Cabinet Planning Bureau.

36. "Chūgoku Shikoku chihō jikyoku jōkyō shisatsu hōkoku," in Naikaku jōhōbu, ed., *Jihenka ni*, 411.

37. Ibid., 320.

38. Midono Village, Aichi Prefecture, ibid., 320.

39. Shiratori chō senbotsusha no tegami, ed., *"Shiratorichō senbotsusha no tegami" henshū i'inkai* (Gifu: Shiratorichō kyōiku i'inkai, 1976), 11.

40. *Nōmin heishi no koe ga kikoeru—7000 tsū no gunji yūbin kara*, ed. Iwate-Waga no pen (Tokyo: Nihon hōsō shuppan kyōkai, 1984), 211.

41. Ibid., 228.

42. Nomonhan is a small village on the Chinese side of the Mongolia-Manchurian border. The "Nomonhan Incident" refers to a large-scale but clandestine series of border clashes between the Japanese Kwantung army and Mongolian and allied Soviet Russian forces in the summer of 1939. By September, infantry units of the Kwantung Army had suffered severe losses at the hands of Soviet armored divisions, with some 17,000 casualties out of a fighting force of 56,000. For more on Nomonhan in English, see Alvin D. Cox, *Nomonhan: Japan Against Russia, 1939* (Redwood City, Calif.: Stanford University Press, 1990). (EM)

43. Okamura Toshihiko, *Hodabi* (Tokyo: Bunkensha, 1961), 285.

44. Regarding their "feelings, frankly stated," when sent to the front, a summer 1985 *Asahi* newspaper poll of 289 members of the Veteran's Association of the former Aizuwakamatsu 65th Infantry Regiment resident in Tokyo yielded the following results: "I felt it could not be helped," 60%; "I was happy to depart for the battlefield," 29%; "I hated it beyond all words," 3%; "other," 8%. *Asahi Shimbun* (August 15, 1985). Those who responded totaled 222, or 77 percent of those polled. The respondents included twenty-five officers, the remainder comprising one hundred noncommissioned officers, ninety-six enlisted men, and one unidentified. But even taking into account the efflorescence of memory given the passage of forty years since the war's end, the figure of only 3 percent in the category "I hated it beyond all words" is remarkable.

45. Iwate ken nōson bunka kondankai, *Senbotsu nōmin heishi no tegami* (Tokyo: Iwanami shoten, 1961), 226–229.

46. Yamamoto Takeshi, *Ichiheishi no jūgun kiroku* (Fukui: Yasuda shoten, 1985), 192.

47. *Senbotsu nōmin heishi no tegami*, 74.

48. Ibid.

49. Asahi shimbun Yamagata shikyoku, *Kikigaki: aru kenpei no kiroku* (Tokyo: Asahi shimbunsha, 1985), 26, 152.

50. Chairman of the Jinan Council of Commerce and Industry.

51. Kimura Genzaemon, *Nitchū senso shussei nikki* (Akita: Mumyōsha shuppan, 1982), 185, entry for February 23, 1939.

52. *Hodabi*, 268.

53. Ibid., 299.

54. Murata Washirō, *Nitchū senso nikki* (Tokyo, Hōwa shuppan, 1983), 5:112.

55. The Japanese measurement was three *chō* (3 x 2.45 acres = 7.353 acres), two *tan* (2 x 0.245 acres = 0.490 acres), and six *se* (6 x 0.0245 acres = 0.147 acres).

56. Tazaki Nobuyoshi, "Kosaku nōka no keieishiteki bunseki—1931–03—1936–02," no. 1, *Shakaigaku kenkyū* (Hitotsubashi daigaku) 21 (1982): 314.

57. Ibid., 322.

58. Hereafter "Abe Ta'ichi nikki," dated from January 1, 1931, through January 31, 1945, unpublished document in the possession of Abe Ta'ichi.

59. Tenant struggles for rent reductions in rural Japan arose from the late 1910s through the 1920s, peaking in radicalism during the early stages of the Great Depression but slowing in the 1930s amid a mix of government suppression and intervention. In English, see, for example, *Farmers and Village Life in Twentieth-Century Japan*, ed. Ann Waswo and Nishida Yoshiaki (London: RoutledgeCurzon, 2003). (EM)

60. Founded in 1922, the Japanese Communist Party was broken up and forced underground as a result of wide-scale police suppression that began in 1928 under the draconian Peace Preservation Law (*Chi'an iji hō*) of 1925, which was revised that year to target not only members of the communist party but also their alleged sympathizers in trade unions, the academy, the literary world, etc. The law banned organizations aiming to "alter Japan's *kokutai*" (national polity) and their supporters, imposing a maximum penalty of death. On *kokutai*, see note 258 of chapter 2. (EM)

61. Abe Ta'ichi nikki," entry for January 31, 1937.

62. A song popularized in the context of the Village Revitalization Movement of the 1930s. For more in English on this movement and associated attempts to renegotiate and redefine relations of state and rural society in the wake of the Great Depression, see Kerry Smith, *A Time of Crisis: Japan, The Great Depression, and Rural Revitalization* (Cambridge: Harvard University Press, 2001). (EM)

63. Until the postwar constitution instituted equal inheritance rights regardless of age and gender, primogeniture (right of inheritance by the firstborn son) was Japanese social norm and the law of the land. This meant gross discrepancies in status and prospects among sons (let alone daughters) and can be seen to account in large part, for example,

for correspondingly great differences in family reactions to the conscription of different sons, as vividly illustrated in the case of Abe Ta'ichi. (EM)

64. First established in 1901, the *Aikoku fujinkai* was a private women's organization with a mostly elite membership, which was mainly concerned with supporting and collecting funds for gravely injured soldiers and families of the war dead. By the time of the Russo-Japanese War (1904–1905), its membership had spread throughout the country and numbered close to half a million. After the Manchurian Incident, the *Aikoku fujinkai* competed with the army-sponsored Great Japan National Defense Women's Association (*Dai Nippon kokubō fujinkai*), launching movements for "patriotic savings" and the like. In February 1942 it was fused into the Great Japan Ladies' Association (*Dai Nippon fujinkai*) sponsored by the Imperial Rule Assistance Association. On the Imperial Rule Assistance Association, see note 13 of chapter 2. (EM)

65. Abe Ta'ichi nikki, entry for July 14, 1937.

66. *Mugi to heitai* was the first of a bestselling trilogy of battlefront accounts written by Hino (1907–1960) in 1938 and 1939 after being drafted and serving at the China front. The remaining titles were *Tsuchi to heitai* [Mud and soldiers] and *Hana to heitai* [Flowers and soldiers]. Popular for its vividly "realistic," gritty depiction of the lives of Japanese soldiers in the field, the *heitai* trilogy proved exceptionally effective modern propaganda. Avoiding reference to atrocities or pronouncements on the war's meaning, the books portrayed Japan's soldiers as tough and sometimes crude but ultimately sincere and admirable. A graduate of the elite, private Waseda University, Hino was one of many former 1920s student radicals who had undergone a change of political stance (literally, *tenkō*, "change in direction") toward a patriotic, proimperialist position after arrest and release from prison in the early 1930s. His first novel, *Funshōtan* [Tales of human excrement], won the prestigious Akutagawa Prize for literature in 1937. The most in-depth treatment of Hino's work and its postwar legacy in English is David M. Rosenfeld, *Unhappy Soldier: Hino Ashihei and Japanese World War II Literature* (Lanham, Md.: Lexington, 2002). (EM)

67. The North China Transport Company was a government-controlled corporation (*kokusakugaisha*) under the South Manchurian Railway Company Group, established in 1938 to operate railways and bus lines in north-central China. Headquartered in Beijing, it employed roughly 110,000 staff, of whom approximately 70 percent were Chinese. It became defunct with Japan's defeat in 1945. Chae-sŏng Im, "Nitchū sensōka no kahoku kōtsū no seiritsu to senji yusō no tenkai," *Rekishi to keizai* 193 (October 2006). (EM)

68. Also undergoing the examination were men who had requested deferments that had now expired, ranging in age between twenty and twenty-eight. What follows draws upon the "General Outlook of the Survey of Thinking of Men of Conscription Age, 1940" (*Shōwa 15-nendo sōtei shisō chōsa gaikyō*), produced by the Office of Social Education of the Ministry of Education (*Mombushō shakai kyōikukyoku*) (Tokyo: Mombushō, 1941). These were fifteen-minute interviews conducted in 1940 by officials of the conscript education survey, staff of young men's schools or elementary schools and the like, either on the day before or the day of the conscription examination, with the target group totaling 28,711. The ten subjects of the opinion survey included "attitude toward life," "attitude

toward Serving Asia's Development Day," "opinions on the China Incident," and "hopes for current politics," with the format consisting of the circling of the statement that appeared closest to one's own thinking from among four to eight predetermined choices. It was anonymous, but one did enter one's current address, date of birth, most recent educational history, occupation, and relationship to the head of household. Additionally considering that this was a survey conducted at the moment of the conscription examination, those who might have entertained serious doubts about the war were not likely to have revealed their thoughts. In this regard in particular, it can be assumed that there was a considerable bias, but bearing in mind that the great majority already supported the war beforehand, we can assume that the true situation was reflected with considerable accuracy at least so far as the breakdown according to categories and educational history.

69. *Shōwa 15-nendo sōtei shisō chōsa gaikyō*, 79.

70. Ibid., 47.

71. Government-run Teacher Training Schools (*shihan gakkō*) first appeared in 1872 and were formalized in 1886. Entry was open to qualified graduates of higher elementary schools (*kōtō shōgakkō*). A second higher type, with entry from secondary school (*chūtō gakkō*), was established in 1907. All were abolished under the postwar occupation reforms. In a 1934 text, the Marxist critic and philosopher Tōsaka Jun observed that the teacher training colleges favored "moral training" over "intellectual training" and were the focus of intensive Education Ministry efforts to spread imperial ideology and eliminate "dangerous thought." Tōsaka Jun, *Gendai Nihon no shisō tairitsu* (1934), collected works vol. 5. (EM)

72. Established in 1935, the *Seinen gakkō* were practical schools for working youth that combined the existing Supplementary Trade Schools (*Jitsugyō hoshū gakkō*, established in 1893) with Youth Training Centers (*Seinen kunrensho*, established in 1926), whose staff and curricula was indeed often already shared. Students entered after completing elementary school. Attendance for males was made mandatory from 1939, with an increasing focus on military education. (EM)

73. Mombushō shakai kyōikukyoku, ed. *Shōwa 15-nendo sōtei shisō chōsa gaikyō*, 82.

74. Ibid., 49. The move toward a wartime control economy was heralded by the implementation of the National Mobilization Law in May 1938, which granted the state virtually dictatorial powers over "human and material resources." The consequence was a great mobilization, concentration, and diversion of industry, labor, and resources away from consumer-related production into that stipulated necessary for military-strategic purposes, with a corresponding decline in the consumer economy. Big business collaborated closely with the state and in so doing also successfully resisted state attempts at full nationalization. On the wartime control economy in English, see, for example, Chalmers Johnson, *MITI and the Japanese Miracle: The Growth of Industrial Policy, 1925–1975* (Palo Alto, Calif.: Stanford University Press, 1982); and *Japan's War Economy*, ed. Erich Pauer (London: Routledge, 1999). (EM)

75. Mombushō shakai kyōikukyoku, ed. *Shōwa 15-nendo sōtei shisō chōsa gaikyō*, 48.

76. Ibid., 28.

77. On the term "emperor system" as used by Japanese scholars, see note 4, above.

78. Ibid.
79. The Eastern Army command, located in Tokyo, was established in August 1940, when the Japanese home army was divided into the Eastern, Central, and Western Armies.
80. "Shōwa 15-nen zenpan shisō jōsei," *Shiryō Nihon gendaishi*, 11:280.
81. On Saitō's speech, see note 8, above.
82. On December 22, 1938, observing the escape of Wang Jing-wei and other members of the nationalist government's "surrender faction" from the nationalist capital Chungking, then Prime Minister Konoe Fumimaro issued the so-called Konoe Three Principles (the Third Konoe Declaration) as a basic policy for the adjustment of Sino-Japanese relations, with this faction as partner. From this point onward, these were taken as Japan's official war aims, and the prosecution of the war too was meant to adhere to these "principles." The Three Principles were stated as "neighborly friendship" conditional upon the cessation of resistance to Japan and the recognition of "Manchukuo"; "mutual defense," meaning the recognition of the right of the Japanese army to station troops in China; and "economic cooperation," whose conditions were the recognition of Japanese freedom of residence and business operation and the furnishing of facilities for the development and exploitation of resources in the regions of northern China and "Inner Mongolia." The advance toward "the construction of a New East Asian Order" in cooperation with the Chinese surrender faction was proclaimed based upon these principles, in conjunction with the "expectation of a thorough military mopping-up of the anti-Japanese Nationalist Government." In addition, a text was attached stating that if China were to acknowledge these fundamental principles, Japan would make no issue of territory or reparations, Chinese "sovereignty" would be "respected," "extraterritoriality" would be "abolished," and serious attention would be paid to the issue of "the return of settlements." It goes without saying that the essence of the Konoe Declaration lay in the first part, with the added text at the end nothing more than a façade.
83. Kawami Tei'ichi, ed., *Saitō Takao seiji ronshū* (Saitō Takao sensei kenshōkai, 1961), 30–32.
84. This and the following citations are from "Saitō Takao ate shokanrui" (1940–), reprinted in *Shiryō: Nihon gendaishi*, 11:209.
85. Ibid., 11:188.
86. Ibid., 11:207.
87. Ibid., 11:216. Each self-censored word was marked by a single circle corresponding to one unit of text (*Kanji*) deleted by Satō in fear of the censor. The words intended seem clear however: The first was probably "blood," the second and third clearly 弱 and 強, forming together the expression 弱肉強食 (*jakuniku kyōshoku*, "the strong eat the meat of the weak"), which translates as "the survival of the fittest," "the right of the strongest," or "the law of the jungle." (EM)
88. Ibid., 11:210.
89. A port city on the southern tip of Hokkaidō, Japan's northernmost island.
90. Ibid., 11:208.
91. Ibid., 11:194–195.
92. On the Third Konoe Declaration, see note 82 above. Wang Jingwei (1883–1944) was a prominent member of the Chinese Nationalist Party who broke ranks with Chiang Kai-

shek and entered into collaboration with Japan in December 1938, heading a puppet nationalist regime in Nanjing. He failed to draw significant popular political support. For more in English, see, for example, John Hunter Boyle, China and Japan at War, 1937–1945: The Politics of Collaboration (Cambridge, Mass.: Harvard University Press, 1972). (EM)

93. *Shiryō: Nihon gendaishi*, 11:194–195.

94. Ibid., 11:210.

95. "The settlements" refers to areas in Chinese port cities inhabited by and under the administration of one or more of the imperial powers as a result of imposed treaties. At the time of the outbreak of the Sino-Japanese War there were twenty-seven such settlements. The regaining of sovereignty over these areas was a top priority for Chinese nationalists. (EM)

96. Ibid., 11:197.

97. Ibid., 11:191.

98. Ibid., 11:205. Komori hailed from Osaka City's Higashi Ward.

99. Ibid., 11:211.

100. Ibid., 11:187, 189.

101. "Geppō," 13, supplement of *Shiryō Nihon gendaishi*, vol. 11.

102. What follows draws upon Imai Ryūichi, *Tōkakan no jinchū nikki* (Ichinomiya, Aichi: privately published, 1981), 7, supplemented in part by a correspondence addressed to the author from Imai's younger sister, Marui Miyo. Composed during breaks in the fighting, this diary represents a high-quality record that vividly describes the thirteen-day period between August 20 and September 1, 1937. On the true situation of the war between the battle of Shanghai and the capture of Nanjing, Yoshida Yutaka, *Tennō no guntai to Nankin jiken—mō hitotsu no nitchū sensō* (Tokyo: Aoki shoten, 1985); and Honda Katsuichi, *Nankin e no michi* (Tokyo: Asahi shimbunsha, 1987) offer detailed and realistic analyses.

103. Co-opting older traditions of village youth groups that were in decline during the Meiji period, the Youth Associations were established under the auspices of the interior and education ministries in the years after the Russo-Japanese War in 1904–1905, reaching a nationwide administration during the Taishō period. From the 1920s onward, military influence over the associations gradually increased. Under military direction, the Imperial Japanese League of Youth Associations was founded by the Education and Interior ministries in 1924. It was later merged into the Imperial Japanese Youth and Boy Scout's Association in 1941. In English, see, for example, Kenneth B. Pyle, "The Technology of Japanese Nationalism: The Local Improvement Movement, 1900–1918," *Journal of Asian Studies* 33, no. 1 (1973): 51–65; and Richard J. Smethurst, *A Social Basis for Prewar Japanese Militarism: The Army and the Rural Community* (Berkeley: University of California Press, 1974). (EM)

104. Correspondence from Imai's younger sister, Ms. Marui Miyo, to the author dated September 21, 1986. *Chūō kōron* and *Kaizō* were both general-interest, mass-circulation literary journals aimed at the better-educated classes, the latter with a pronounced association with the political left but both equally popular during the interwar period. A publication with the title *The Works of Three Northern Europeans* appeared in Japan as the twenty-seventh and last volume in a world literature series from the publisher Shinchōsha first published in 1928. (EM)

105. Irie Takako (1911–1995) was a popular film actress beginning in the late 1920s. She became a major star following her appearance in Mizoguchi's Kenji's 1933 film *Taki no shiraito* [The water magician], appearing often and remaining extremely popular throughout the war period. (EM)

106. I am taking the liberty here of assuming that while Imai wrote *pinta*, he in fact meant *binta*, meaning a "slap." Slaps to the head and other parts of the body were commonplace in the training of Japanese troops in this period and seen as a legitimate and effective form of disciplining. In English, see, for example, Edward Drea, *In the Service of the Emperor: Essays on the Imperial Japanese Army* (Lincoln: University of Nebraska Press, 1998); and Yuki Tanaka, *Hidden Horrors: Japanese War Crimes in World War II* (Boulder, Colo.: Westview, 1996). (EM)

107. Imai, *Tōkakan no jinchū nikki*, 12–13, 15–16.

108. Ibid., 25.

109. Ibid., 30.

110. Ibid., 39–40. Here and in subsequent citations below from this source, the breaks marked by periods are in the original.

111. Ibid., 47–48. Letter of August 31, 1937.

112. Ibid., 51–53. Letter of September 1, 1937.

113. Ibid., 48–50. Letters of August 31 and September 1, 1937.

114. The following draws upon Yamamoto Takeshi, *Ichiheishi no jūgun kiroku*, supplemented in part by Yamamoto Takeshi, *Waga jinsei kaikoroku* (Fukui: Yasuda shoten, 1984). The former is a memoir assembled in daily sequence after the war based upon a detailed diary from the battlefront and represents a source whose high value is comparable to that of a diary.

115. Yamamoto, *Waga jinsei kaikoroku*, 37. On the mass arrests of communists and suspected communist sympathizers that began in 1928, see note 60, above. "Proletarian literature" refers to a socialist literary movement broadly popular from the mid-1920s until the early 1930s. From the late 1920s, its publications and authors faced increasing suppression under the Peace Preservation Law. (EM)

116. The army reservists' organizations were nationally unified and placed under central military administration from 1910 onward. They played an important role in enabling and expanding army influence and monitoring over the population. From the 1920s onward the military increasingly employed the reservists' organizations to propagate social and spiritual movements for militarization and war preparedness. For more on the reservists' associations and their social and political significance in prewar Japan in English, see Smethurst, *A Social Basis for Prewar Japanese Militarism*. (EM)

117. Yamamoto, *Waga jinsei kaikoroku*, 61.

118. Ibid., 52. In the Sino-Japanese War, Japan made no declaration of war and made no attempt to adhere to international agreements such as the Treaty Regarding the Rules and Conventions of Land War (1907) or the Geneva Convention Regarding the Treatment of Prisoners (1929), failing even to establish prison camp facilities. For this reason, whether directed explicitly or inexplicitly, there were extremely numerous cases in which there was a policy of killing Chinese army soldiers who had lost the will to fight or had surren-

dered. Given that there were no prisoner-of-war camps, there were a great many cases in which soldiers on the front, puzzled as to what to do with soldiers who had surrendered, executed them in obedience to orders from above. Disobedience was not allowed. Thus it must be said it was the Japanese war command at the highest level, which chose such a policy, that created the cause of the killing of Chinese prisoners and army soldiers who had lost the will to fight—and that the greatest responsibility must also lie there. The second responsibility lies with local Japanese commanders at every level who issued such orders and directives. Regarding Japanese on the home front, although it can be said that they had been dispossessed of clues to the war's true causes and that their lack of sovereignty was a constraint, it would seem undeniable that, in raising their voices in support of what they believed to be a "holy war" and sending troops to the front, they bear a secondary responsibility. There were not a few cases in which soldiers on the front lines, unfamiliar with international law and acting out of passions of enmity or out of genuine intent, killed Chinese army soldiers who had lost the will to fight or had surrendered. But even if we leave out cases of killing out of genuine intent, when considering the issue of responsibility it is absolutely necessary to take the following background into account. The Prisoner Information Office, whose duty it was to gather information and assemble records regarding prisoners, was established only after the opening of hostilities with the United States, on December 27, 1941, and the "Rules Regarding the Treatment of Prisoners"—aimed primarily at Europeans and Americans—appeared only in March 1942. After the war, furthermore, the problem of the state ignoring international law and the resultant ignorance of soldiers regarding international law returned to haunt the soldiers themselves in the form of war crimes trials. Moreover, this precipitated the following sort of situation: As a result of the inhuman behavior of the Soviet Union, more than seventy thousand Japanese POWs imprisoned in Siberia lost their lives, and more than forty thousand suffered injuries and illness. But had these POWs known of the Geneva Convention Regarding the Treatment of Prisoners, they could have asserted their rights as prisoners and should thus have been able to protect themselves. (I owe this point to Ubukata Naokichi.) The following words of Saitō Rokurō, the plaintiff in the case demanding compensation for forced laborers in Siberia, are truly poignant: "What caused the death of nearly 20 percent [of the POWs] after the fighting was, from the first, the inhumane behavior of the Soviet Union. But we must not forget that one reason that the victims were so numerous was that—myself included—we knew absolutely nothing of the [Geneva] Convention on [the treatment of] POWs." Saitō Rokurō, "Kesshin ni saishite," *Zen'yokukyō kōhō* 82 (1987): 3.

119. Yamamoto, *Waga jinsei kaikoroku*, 67.
120. *Tokumuhei* (特務兵), equivalent to a soldier charged with the transport of military supplies, formerly referred to as a *Shichō yusotsu* (輜重輸卒).
121. Ibid., 82–84.
122. The word "men" here is modified with the adjective *setaikusai* (世帯くさい), literally "stinking of the domestic," whose intended meaning in this context is unclear. (EM)
123. Ibid., 85, 87. In this way, accounts of requisitioning appear again and again. These, moreover, coincide with statements of returning soldiers that appeared in the memorandum

from the undersecretary of the army, "Matters Pertaining to the Guidance and Control of Speech of Units and Soldiers Returning from the Area of the China Incident." Namely, such as: "If you got caught requisitioning cows or pigs in the area of the supply base you'd get a good scolding, but since you can't fight if you don't eat, once we were on the front lines we killed them as we found them one after another"; "the most pleasurable thing during the fighting was looting, and on the front lines, even the superior officers pretended not to see it, so there were men who looted to their heart's content"; and "if you examine each soldier who participated in the war one by one, you'll find they're all nothing but criminal [perpetrators] of massacres, robbery, and rape." *Geppō*, 13–14. Yamamoto's record contains no references to rape, but a statement does appear in which he expresses indignation after learning of its reality afterward. Again, this is all strongly reminiscent of Fuji Masaharu's war novel, based upon his own experiences, an excerpt from which follows. His experiences began in 1944: "Whether you call it requisitioning or whether you call it emergency purchasing, in the end it was getting something for nothing, no more than robbery by another name. Goods were requisitioned, people were forced to carry requisitioned materials as coolies without notice; women who seemed worthy of raping had their private parts requisitioned first, and then if there was too much requisitioned stuff they were made to carry it. Requisitioned were items like rice, pigs, chickens, and seasonings, but there were also men who collected paper money and precious metals thinking they might come in handy at some point. Vegetables were taken with the audaciousness of plucking grass, and if we happened to take a rest by the side of a kumquat mountain, shortly thereafter, branches overflowing with kumquats would be marching along—it was funny, in the middle of the mountains of the continent, hardly where I would have expected it, among other things it brought Macbeth to my mind." Fuji Masaharu, *Daba Yokomitsugō* (Rokkō shuppan, 1980), 63–64; cited in Hikosaka Tei, *Hito wa dono yō ni shite hei to naru no ka* (Tokyo: Keshi shobō, 1984), 1:12. In its operations, the Japanese army hardly implemented the supply of clothing or supplementary food, and since even the supply of the staple food rice was exceedingly insufficient under wartime conditions, soldiers were forced into a situation in which they had no choice but to make requisitions. The brunt of the responsibility thus lies with the Japan Army High Command, which produced this situation. This is hardly to say, however, that soldiers in the front lines who made requisitions bear no responsibility. Cases of requisition for personal gain or out of genuine intent or desire are particularly problematic. Among these, rape could by nature not be justified under any possible definition. Takasaki Ryūji, "Chūgoku sensen de no gōkan ga oyoboshita shisōteki eikyō," *Shisō no kagaku* 61 (1985), 27. It must no doubt be said that this sort of requisitioning—or more frankly put, looting—was ubiquitous within the Japanese army in China (and in Southeast Asia) through to the war's end in 1945.

124. Yamamoto, *Ichiheishi no jugun kiroku*, 97.

125. Since soldiers' diaries and memoirs make no distinction between official soldiers of the Chinese army, militiamen, and village self-defense forces, I include all three of these among "Chinese army soldiers."

126. Ibid., 98.

127. Ibid., 103. It would appear that the behavior of the Kyōto Sixteenth Division had been mistakenly conveyed as that of the Sixth Division.

128. The battle of Xuzhou, which took place between mid-April and May of 1938, comprised an attempt by the Japanese North China Area and Central China Expeditionary Armies to encircle a large Nationalist force of six hundred thousand men and secure control of the main rail line between Beijing and Nanjing to the south. Following on the unexpected Japanese defeat at Tai'erzhuang in early April, the fierce battle resulted in an eventual Japanese victory, with the Chinese suffering approximately one hundred thousand casualties to the Japanese thirty thousand. But Japanese forces were unsuccessful in trapping and eliminating the larger Chinese armies, which withdrew westward and subsequently opened the dikes of the Yellow River to slow the Japanese pursuit toward Wuhan. (EM)

129. Ibid., 139.

130. Ibid., 140.

131. Ibid., 141.

132. Ibid., 142.

133. Ibid., 149.

134. Ibid., 151.

135. Ibid., 140.

136. It appears rather in the afterword by Inaki Nobuo.

137. Ibid., 307. This is taken from the afterword by Inaki Nobuo.

138. Ibid., 35.

139. Ibid., 119. Diary entry dated March 22, 1938.

140. Ibid., 120. Diary entry dated March 25, 1938.

141. The extended Japanese campaign against Wuhan, China's second-largest city at the time and its inland traffic center along the Yangtze River, took place between June and October 1938 and involved more than one million nationalist Chinese and approximately 350,000 Japanese troops. Although ultimately a Japanese victory, the Japanese army failed to annihilate the Chinese army as intended. Casualties were high on both sides, but the much larger Chinese armies remained intact, and Japanese forces ended the campaign significantly weakened. In its wake the war moved to a stalemate, and Japan was to mount no further major campaign in China until 1944. For more on the campaign in English, see Stephen R. MacKinnon, *Wuhan, 1938: War, Refugees, and the Making of Modern China* (Berkeley: University of California Press, 2008). (EM)

142. Yamamoto, *Ichiheishi no jugun kiroku*, 154. Diary entry dated July 27, 1938.

143. Ibid., 178.

144. Ibid., 223.

145. Ibid., 207, 222.

146. Ibid., 223. The *Yokusan sōnendan*, founded in January 1942 with army support, took the Nazi storm troopers as its model and has been described as the most militant of Japan's wartime semiofficial organizations. It enlisted men over twenty-one and conducted activities to urge the people to maximum patriotic service in production, fundraising, and supporting the military. During the Imperial Rule Assistance Association election campaign of April 1942, the corps staged rallies and parades in support of state-approved

candidates and intimidated unapproved candidates and their supporters. See Ben-Ami Shillony, *Politics and Culture in Wartime Japan* (Oxford: Oxford University Press, 1981). (EM)

147. *Nōmin heishi no koe ga kikoeru*, 71–75. Diary entry from November 1937.

148. In Japanese usage, "Nanjing rice" refers to rice imported from China and/or Southeast Asia, seen as being of inferior quality to Japanese rice. (EM)

149. Ibid., 79, 81. Diary entry for November 1937.

150. Ibid., 57. Entry for May 11, 1938.

151. During the extended, failed Japanese expedition to suppress Soviet Russia after the Russian Revolution, 1918–1923 (EM).

152. Ibid., 98–99. Entry for November 20, 1937.

153. Ibid. Entry from Langfang, 1937.

154. Ibid., 99. Entry for November 20, 1937. It goes without saying that these sorts of feelings and behavior toward Chinese people were not limited to low-ranking soldiery alone. An elite graduate of Tokyo University's law department with a job at Nippon Steel Company who departed for the northern China front in March 1938 and subsequently commanded subordinates as an officer in northern and southern China wrote the following sorts of things in his diary: "We seek warmth by turning household belongings and implements into firewood. It is a sad thing. Oh natives of China, where will you go?" (March 11, 1940). "When I got to the field, it got truly savage, I didn't think twice about killing *nii* [derogatory term for Chinese]. . . . Yesterday too, the soldiers asked if it was all right to fire a warning shot, and when I allowed it, the second shot unfortunately hit a *nii*, and he began to wail very loudly. I felt sorry for him, but I had them fire another round and kill him" (April 30, 1940). I heard a commanding officer who'd captured a guy who's some sort of enemy spy say he'd have the new recruits stab him, but [on February 11] I snatched him [instead], and, for the first time in my life, I cut the head off a *nii* with a Japanese sword. I cut his shoulders and the upper part of his neck. I did kill him with the first blow of the sword, but I didn't make a very clean job of it" (February 17, 1941). Thus not only was there little difference between the elite and the people, but rather elite incitement and leadership was a significant aspect in the rise of these sorts of perceptions and behavior. *Chi no sazamegoto*, ed. Kyūsei Shizuoka kōtō gakkō senbotsusha ikōshū henshū i'inkai (Shizuoka: Kyūsei Shizuoka kōtō gakkō senbotsusha irei jikkō iinkai, 1966), 38, 43, 53.

155. This may be a reference to Japanese New Year's according to the old Chinese calendar. (EM)

156. *Senbotsu nōmin heishi no tegami*, 65.

157. Ibid., 75–76. Letter of September 1, 1938.

158. Ibid., 71. Letter from autumn 1938.

159. The following account draws upon Kimura Genzaemon's detailed diary from the front, *Nitchū sensō shussei nikki*. Under the prewar education system, students attended the so-called Ordinary Elementary School for a period of four years, followed by the so-called Higher Elementary School for another two to four more years. The school type at which Kimura taught contained both schools side by side. Attendance usually began from age six. (EM)

160. Takai Yū'ichi, "Kaisetsu," in Kimura, *Nitchū sensō shussei nikki*, 282–285.

161. Ibid., 19.

162. Ibid., 30.

163. Ibid., 53. Entry of January 5, 1938.

164. Ibid., 68.

165. *Nihon Hyōron* was a monthly current affairs magazine that appeared from 1926 to 1956. (EM)

166. Kawai Eijirō (1891–1944) was a renowned liberal economist and thinker who famously opposed both Marxism and fascism. In 1938, the same year the above publication appeared, his works were banned. He was forced into retirement the following year. (EM)

167. Kimura, *Nitchū sensō shussei nikki*, 89–90.

168. Ibid., 207, 233.

169. Ibid., 141. Entry of September 11, 1938.

170. Ibid., 145. Entry of September 21, 1938.

171. Ibid., 213. Entry of May 28, 1939.

172. Ibid., 115. Entry of July 14, 1938.

173. Ibid., 247, entry for September 5, 1939.

174. The "East Asian Cooperative Body" was a theory first proposed by the political philosopher Miki Kiyoshi, head of the Cultural Problems Research Group of the Shōwa Research Association, an academic policy think-tank assembled under Prime Minister Konoe Fumimaro in 1937. In the association's *Principles of Thought for a New Japan* (1939), Miki noted that the creation of regional economic blocs and spheres of political and cultural influence was the basic trend of the times and argued that it was Japan's "world-historical mission" to enable "the East" to determine its own destiny, creating a "cooperative body" (*kyōdōtai*) in East Asia with a "new East Asian culture" based upon "cooperativism" (*kyōdōshugi*). Cooperativism was defined as an alternative to both liberalism and socialism in which the state's economic structure would be unified and "classes will cease being classes and become [incorporated into] an occupational order within a higher whole," thus eliminating the evils of capitalism and class struggle. Japan's imperial policy within this framework was to be one of "liberating" China from Western imperialism, eschewing the narrow "racialism" of old, and establishing a relationship of "mutual respect" between the two nations in which Chinese national aspirations were to be acknowledged. As the price of entry into this brotherly New East Asian Order, the Chinese for their part would be expected to transcend "simple nationalism." See, for example, Miles Fletcher, *Intellectuals and Fascism in Prewar Japan* (Chapel Hill: University of North Carolina Press, 1982). (EM)

175. On the genesis of Konoe's "New East Asian Order" slogan, which first appeared in 1938, see note 82, above.

176. Ibid., 266.

177. Ibid.

178. What follows is drawn from Murata Washirō's detailed seven-volume diary from the front *Nitchū sensō nikki* [China war diary] (Tokyo: Hōwa Shuppan, 1984–1986).

179. Meiji University is a large private university in the Chiyoda district of Tokyo. First founded as a law school in 1881, it became a university in 1920. (EM)

180. Murata, *Nitchū sensō nikki*, 1:133–134.

181. Ibid., 1:165.

182. Ibid., 1:171.

183. Ibid., 1:173.

184. Enma (Sanskrit: *Yama*) is the fifth of the seven judges of the Buddhist realm of the dead, usually regarded as the ruler of Hell. (EM)

185. Ibid., 2:34–35.

186. Ibid., 2:12. Entry of February 15, 1938.

187. Ibid., 2:31. From "Ankitsu (Huzhou) chiku zanteki tōbatsuki," same month.

188. Ibid., 2:126. Entry of June 6, 1938.

189. Ibid., 2:127, 180, 187. "Greater Asianism" refers to a contradictory but profoundly popular Japanese wartime ideology that linked a Japanese "world-historical" mission of "Asian liberation" to the reinvigoration of the Japanese empire, thus combining anti-imperialist and anti-Western rhetoric with faith in Japan's natural role as Asia's "leader" and imperial hegemon. Its spokesmen argued that Japan's "holy war" in Asia was nothing like Western imperialism because Japan, and Japan's relationship to Asia, was different. As domestic Japan cleansed itself of the modern social ills and tensions associated with Western culture and institutions, so the aim of its battle in Asia was to liberate its Asian brethren from the scourges of Western imperialism and capitalism through an "Asian" social and cultural renovation, in the process reuniting and developing an Asia whose peoples and lands had long been divided. Japan—as the only industrialized Asian country that had escaped colonization and thus retained its ancient Asian culture while at the same time succeeding in technological modernization—was billed as the sole country qualified for this mission, the "older brother" that would lead the way. (EM)

190. Ibid., 2:190. Entry of July 27, 1938.

191. Ibid., 2:205.

192. Ibid., 3:38.

193. Ibid., 3:87.

194. Ibid., 4:116. Published in 1716, the *kangsxi zidian* was the representative Chinese dictionary of the Qing dynasty, which established the standard 214 radicals and contained some 47,000 characters. (EM)

195. Ibid., 4:151.

196. Ibid., 4:220.

197. Ibid., 4:231.

198. Ibid., 5:38.

199. Ibid., 5:70.

200. Ibid., 5:132. On Hino Ashihei (1907–1960) and his blockbuster wartime trilogy of novels based on his experiences at the China front, see note 66, above. (EM)

201. Ibid., 5:142, 191.

202. Ibid., 6:91.

203. Ibid., 2:126. Diary entry of June 6, 1938.

204. Ibid., 6:34. Diary entry of September 2, 1939.

205. Ibid., 6:82. Diary entry of September 17, 1939.

206. Ibid., 6:101, 126.
207. Ibid., 7:17–18. Diary entry of January 6, 1940.
208. Ibid., 6:120. Diary entry of October 7, 1939.
209. Ibid., 7:56. Diary entry of January 24, 1940.
210. Ibid., 7:172. Diary entry of April 2, 1940.
211. Ibid., 7:183. Diary entry of April 10, 1940.
212. Ibid., 7:198.
213. The number of soldiers discharged and repatriated were as follows: 1938: 60,000; 1939: 120,000; 1940: 120,000. *Senji kokumin dōin shi*, vol. 2: *Heiryoku dōin*, ed. Kokumin keizai kenkyūkai/kinzoku kōgyō chōsakai (1946).

❷ GRASSROOTS FASCISM

1. *Gendaishi shiryō*, ed. Nakamura Takafusa and Hara Akira (Misuzu shobō, 1970), 43:739–740, 753.
2. "Yamaguchi chihō saibansho kenji kyoku kannnai ni okeru saikin no keizai jōsei," *Shisō geppō* (July 1940): 163.
3. Harada Kumao, *Saionji kō to seikyoku* (Iwanami shoten, 1952), 8:228.
4. Ibid., 8:324.
5. Kunugi Toshihiro, "Makino Nobuaki ate Yoshida Shigeru shokan ni tsuite," *Shien* 41, no. 1 (1981): 86–87.
6. Both reports appeared in *Shisō geppō* (July 1940): 137–138, 142–143.
7. Ibid., 130.
8. Ibid., 143–145.
9. Ibid., 145.
10. Ibid., 150.
11. Inspired by Nazi German models, the government-sponsored Industrial Patriotic Movement sought to maximize war production and minimize friction between labor and management by replacing "horizontal" trade unions representing workers across industries with "vertical" company unions combining labor and management in single enterprises. Launched as the Industrial Patriotic League in July 1938 at the behest of the public-private social policy organ the Labor-Capital Cooperation Association (*kyōchōkai*), it met with a lukewarm response from workers and employees, upon which the state assumed direct oversight and initiated the national-level Industrial Patriotic Association in November 1940. The movement, which was maintained until the end of the war, mandated national standards for productivity, working hours, holidays, wages, welfare facilities, and medical treatment. See, for example, Andrew Gordon, "The Invention of Japanese-Style Labor Management," in *Mirror of Modernity: Invented Traditions of Modern Japan* (Berkeley: University of California Press, 1998). (EM)
12. *Shisō geppō* (July 1940): 113.
13. In 1940, as part of the New Order Movement under the second cabinet of Prime Minister Konoe Fumimaro, momentum arose among military, government, and popular circles for the dissolution of existing political parties and their replacement with a single mass

party. This resulted in the formation of the Imperial Rule Assistance Association (*Taisei yokusankai*) in October 1940, in which all members of the Diet were enrolled. Although Konoe and his associates had envisioned the IRAA as a genuine mass party of national unity and real political strength comparable to the European fascist parties, in practice it was placed under the direction of local officials and as such it actually functioned as little more than an apolitical auxiliary channel of bureaucratic administration. (EM)

14. *Shisō geppō* (July 1940): 149.
15. Ibid.
16. Ibid.
17. The original Japanese term literally translates as "emperor-system fascism." On the significance of this term in Japanese scholarship see note 4 of chapter 1. On the Imperial Rule Assistance Association, see note 13, above. First proposed by reformist bureaucrats in the second Konoe administration's Cabinet Planning Board in July 1940, the New Economic Order originally represented a sweeping plan to place privately owned industries under direct state control. It encountered heavy opposition from private industrial interests, who offered a counterproposal to the Diet involving close state-business consultation and coordination rather than direct state takeover. The latter become the basis for the New Economic Order as finally enacted. (EM)
18. "Rokudai toshi niokeru beikokutūchōsei jisshi nitomonau tianjō yōchūi gendō nikansuru chōsa," *Shisō geppō* 83 (May 1941): 1.
19. Ibid., 8.
20. Ibid., 6.
21. Ibid., 6.
22. On the National Mobilization Law, see note 74 of chapter 1. Under the provisions of this law, the National Conscription Ordinance, issued in July 1939, empowered the Minister of Health and Welfare to conscript labor forcibly as needed in war-related industries. Under it, through 1945, some 1,600,000 workers were eventually mobilized. (EM)
23. "Saikin niokeru rōdōsha no shisō dōkō," *Shisō geppō* 87 (September 1941): 2.
24. Ibid., 3.
25. "Kokumin chōyōrei niyoru hichōyōsha sonota no ippan dōkō," *Shisō geppō* 88 (October 1941): 2.
26. *Shisō geppō* 87 (September 1941): 31.
27. "Kyōto fuka niokeru tōseikeizai nikansuru tōsho no dōkō," *Shisō geppō* 85 (July 1941): 44.
28. "Shokuryō husoku nitomonau syōhisya no dōkō nikansuru chōsa," *Shisō geppō* 92 (March 1942): 1–2.
29. Ibid., 2.
30. Ibid., 30.
31. The Rice Riots of August and September 1918 occurred as a spontaneous response to substantial inflation in commodity prices in the wake of strong economic growth during World War I. The latter was a result of heightened global demand for Japanese goods and services during that period. An estimated 700,000 people in approximately five hundred mainly urban locations nationwide took direct part in the riots, which met with large-scale police and military intervention. The scale, intensity, and unpredictability of the

riots engendered nervousness among Japan's elites, precipitating the fall of the Terauchi cabinet and its replacement by Japan's first true party cabinet led by Prime Minister Hara Kei. In English, see, for example, Gordon, *Labor and Imperial Democracy*. (EM)

32. Itō Sei, *Taiheiyō sensō nikki* (Tokyo: Shinchōsha, 1983), 1:12. Entry of December 9, 1941. Itō (伊藤整, 1905–1969) achieved prominence in the 1930s as an author and critic of literature by and for young women and as a translator and interpreter of such modern Western classics as *Lady Chatterley's Lover* and *Ulysses*. (EM)

33. Ibid., 1:59. Entry of February 15, 1942.

34. Kikuchi Keiichi, *Nanasentsū no gunji yūbin* (Tokyo: Hakuju-sha, 1983), 216.

35. The *Seinen kunrensho* were military training centers for laboring youth established in Japanese villages and towns nationwide by government edict in 1926, linked to local elementary and trade schools. In many cases they did not employ specialized instructors but rather local schoolteachers or army reservists under the direction of local elementary or trade school principals, and the curriculum often overlapped with that of those schools. From 1935 they were combined with these schools into the "Youth Schools" (*Seinen gakkō*). In English, see, for example, Smethurst, *A Social Basis for Japanese Militarism*. (EM)

36. Takahashi had served as a medic in the Russo-Japanese War.

37. This is taken in the main from Kikuchi, *Nanasentsū no gunji yūbin*, 173–174.

38. An affectionate abbreviation of Takahashi Minejirō.

39. Kikuchi, *Nanasentsū no gunji yūbin*, 20.

40. Ibid., 164.

41. Uchida Yasuke, *Kōgun shōhei imonjō tsuzuri* (Minamichita-chō, Aichi Prefecture: Kōgun shōhei imonjō tsuzuri kankōkai, 1979), 1:11.

42. Ibid., 1:19.

43. Ibid., 1:49–50.

44. Ibid., 1:60.

45. Ibid., 1:60, 76.

46. In what is known as the "First Konoe Declaration," issued on January 16, 1938, Prime Minister Konoe Fumimaro declared that the Japanese government would no longer negotiate with Chiang Kai-shek and announced a desire for the establishment of a new Chinese administration without him. Konoe thus effectively broke contact with the Chinese nationalist government and closed off any possibility for a peaceful settlement of hostilities. (EM)

47. Uchida, *Kōgun shōhei imonjō tsuzuri*, 1:76. Dismissive and racist representation of participants in the Chinese resistance against Japan as "bandits" and "thieves," in combination with adjectives such as "treacherous" and "cowardly," were a staple of Japanese media and propaganda in the 1930s and 1940s, reinforcing Japanese convictions of the legitimacy of their continued domination and their faith in ultimate victory. See, for example, Young, *Japan's Total Empire*. (EM)

48. Uchida, *Kōgun shōhei imonjō tsuzuri*, 2:428.

49. Uchida, *Kōgun shōhei imonjō tsuzuri*, 4:9.

50. Ibid., 4:72.

51. In the twenty-first Diet elections, held on April 30, 1942, voters were presented with a slate of government-approved candidates meant to take the place of the party politicians whose parties had earlier been dissolved to make way for the Imperial Rule Assistance Association (*Taisei yokusankai*). The slate of candidates approved by the Home Ministry, police, and military received government support and funding. While nonapproved candidates (mainly former party politicians) were also on the ballot, government obstacles prevented them from running an active campaign. Nevertheless, 14 percent of the representatives chosen and approximately 35 percent of the votes cast went to unapproved candidates. Through neighborhood organizations and the like, the population was heavily mobilized to go to the polls, and the resultant turnout was an extremely high 82 percent. See for example Berger, *Parties out of Power*; and Shillony, *Politics and Culture*. (EM)

52. Nakano was elected as the top candidate. Uchida, *Kōgun shōhei imonjō tsuzuri*, 4:140.

53. Ibid., 4:381.

54. Ibid., 4:379.

55. On the *fujinkai*, see note 64 of chapter 1.

56. Itō Matsuo, *Ishikoro no harukana michi* [A faraway gravel road] (Tokyo: Kōdan-sha, 1970), 13, 68, 92.

57. Ibid., 158–159. It is well known that the celebrated activist Ichikawa Fusae, who devoted her life to the women's liberation movement, including the movement for woman's suffrage, reacted as follows upon witnessing the fast-paced spread of the National Defense Women's Association (*Kokubō fujinkai*) system down to her home village during the Sino-Japanese War. "For ordinary farming village wives, who had never before had anything such as free time, just being released from the home for half a day to listen to a lecture was women's liberation. In this sense, driven by circumstances, the fact that the Women's Patriotic Association spread like wildfire from one village to another may be something we can be happy about." See also Ichikawa Fusae, *Ichikawa Fusae jiden, senzen hen* (Tokyo: Shinjuku shobō, 1974); and Awaya Kentarō, "Fashoka to minshū ishiki" in *Taikei/Nihon gendaishi*, vol. 1., ed. Eguchi Kei'ichi (Tokyo: Nihon hyōronsha, 1978). It can be argued that in some places Itō's devotion to the Ladies' Patriotic Association as detailed above shares something with the sentiments of Ichikawa.

58. Itō, *Ishikoro no harukana michi*, 160–161.

59. Ibid., 161.

60. Ibid., 162–163.

61. Ibid., 163.

62. Ibid., 165.

63. See the first part of chapter 1.

64. The following is from "Abe Ta'ichi nikki," dated from January 1, 1931, through January 31, 1945, unpublished document in the possession of Abe Ta'ichi.

65. Abbreviation of *sangyō kumiai*.

66. The village is no longer known by this name.

67. On the Imperial Rule Assistance Association, see note 13, above.

68. The "Special Maneuvers of the Kwantung Army" was the purposely deceptive heading given to a massive mobilization of Japanese military forces in July 1941 in preparation

for an invasion of the Soviet Union that never finally transpired. The largest military mobilization in the history of the Japanese army up to that time, it was initiated in light of Germany's surprise invasion against the Soviet Union in June 1941, whose early victories encouraged opportunism among the army staff despite the recent signing of a nonaggression pact between Japan and the Soviet Union. As a result the size of the Kwantung Army swelled to 700,000 men. Approximately 140,000 horses were also drafted into service. In August, with Russian resistance against the Germans stiffening and a lower-than-expected number of Soviet troops moved from the Far East to reinforce those on the Western front, the Japanese high command decided to forego any invasion plans for that year, ultimately choosing a move southward instead. (EM)

69. On the *Yokusan sōnendan*, see note 145 of chapter 1.
70. On the *Yokusan senkyo*, see note 51 of chapter 2.
71. Tazaki, "Senjika kosakunōka no jinushi kosaku kankei," 327.
72. "Mori Shintarō nikki," in *Yokohama no kūshū to sensai,* ed. Yokohama no kūshū wo kirokusuru kai (Yokohama: Yokohama no kūshū wo kirokusuru kai, 1975), 2:71.
73. Ibid., 2:22.
74. Ibid., 2:83.
75. An announcement from Imperial Headquarters.
76. Ibid., 2:71.
77. Ibid., 2:72.
78. At Japan Steel Pipe there were three ranks: company employee, junior company employee, and worker.
79. An island in the Solomon archipelago.
80. Two U.S. battleships and three cruisers were reported sunk, but U.S. losses were exaggerated.
81. A special-issue postal lottery ticket whose proceeds went toward the war effort.
82. Ibid., 2:73–74.
83. Ibid., 2:77.
84. Ibid., 2:80.
85. During the New Year's holiday, the longest and most sacred of Japan's holiday celebrations, workers traditionally stay home several days into January. (EM)
86. Ibid., 2:83.
87. Ibid., 2:84, 90.
88. Mori Isao, *Shōwa ni ikiru* (Tokyo: Heibon-sha, 1957), 22.
89. Ibid., 22–23.
90. Ibid., 23–24.
91. Ibid., 26–27. The term *hakkō ichiu*, literally meaning "eight directions, one roof/house" and interpreted variously to read "all the world under one roof" or "all the world as one family," was an abbreviation of a statement that appeared in the ancient *Nihon shoki*, attributed to the legendary emperor Jimmu. *Hakkō ichiu* became a slogan of Japanese policy from its employment in the Konoe cabinet's statement of the "Basis of National Policy" in July 1940, which described Japan's mission as "encouraging the achievement of world peace based upon the great spirit of national founding that unites the eight di-

rections under one house." Interpreters almost always equated the "roof" (*u*, alternate reading *ie*) in *hakkō ichiu* with "house" (*ie*), a Japanese term whose meaning encompasses both that of a physical "house" and the people who inhabit it, a family. *Hakkō ichiu* can thus be read to represent at once both a geopolitical mission of empire building and a moral mission of achieving brotherhood among those of an imagined single (Asian) family. (EM)

92. Ibid., 47. Diary entry for July 13, 1942.

93. Ibid., 30. Diary entry for December 13, 1942.

94. Ibid., 88.

95. Ibid., 85.

96. Ibid., 86. Diary entry for November 18, 1943.

97. Ibid., 99.

98. "Konagaya Saburō nikki," in *Yokohama no kūshū to sensai*, ed. Yokohama no kūshū wo kirokusuru kai (Yokohama: Yokohama no kūshū wo kirokusuru kai, 1975), 2:40.

99. For example, the novelist Itō Sei wrote, "Amid sudden excitement, I felt a strangely quiet sense of relief bubbling up, a sense of okay, this will do, now it will be alright, it's been decided." His fellow novelist Dazai Osamu, who was later to achieve great celebrity for his ironic, dark postwar fiction, also recalled feeling that "Japan too, from this morning on, is a different Japan." Yamada Fūtarō, ed., *Dōjitsu dōkoku* (Rippū shobō, 1979), 41, 65). The words of the writer Shiga Naoya, broadcast on NHK radio on February 17, 1942, just after the Japanese army had occupied Singapore, are famous: "This is a good lesson for the insolent, godforsaken America and England. It is also truly delightful in bringing hope to our young people. Our feelings are bright and uncommonly relaxed." See *Shiga Naoya zenshū* (Iwanami shoten, 1974), 7:251; and Sakuramoto Tomio, *Daihon'ei happyō Singapōru wa kanraku seri* (Aoki shoten, 1986), 151–161.

100. "Konagaya Saburō nikki," 2:41–42.

101. Ibid., 2:42.

102. The Tokyo Railroad Bureau Patriotic Service Association (*hōkōkai*) Takashima Station Youth Corps.

103. Ibid., 2:44, 47.

104. Ibid., 2:48.

105. Ibid., 2:53.

106. Ibid., 2:54.

107. The fall of Saipan to U.S. forces in July 1944 was a strategic disaster that starkly heralded Japan's defeat, as possession of the island put U.S. B-29 bombers within range of the Japanese mainland for the first time. (EM)

108. Ibid., 2:55.

109. The following is based on Zaichūkaminkoku (Beijing) Nihon teikoku taishikan keimubu (Imperial Japanese Embassy [Beijing]), *Shōwa 15-nen hokushi ryōjikan keisatsushochō kaigiroku* [Records of the meetings of northern China embassy police departments of 1940], U.S. Library of Congress ed., Microfilm of the Foreign Ministry of Japan Documents, R. WT50.

110. "Japanese" here includes Koreans and Taiwanese.

111. Koreans following in the wake of the Japanese army were victims, their sources of livelihood and native villages stolen by the Japanese. Nevertheless, according to the words of the Japanese consular police chief of Qingdao, "many of our Korean brethren are actively advancing to the front along with the Imperial Army, and their achievements laboring in the sincerity of sacrificial service are such that I cannot begin to enumerate." In this sense, we can say that they cooperated with the Japanese army, and in seeking to turn a profit from this, they were also victimizers where the people of China were concerned. Yet a considerable number of these sorts of Koreans had no choice but to become illicit traders. Behind this fact lay the following sorts of circumstances: "In terms of their character, their cultivation, and the like, Koreans in China nowadays have made great advances compared to several years ago; among young men there are not a few with education beyond a secondary level. [Given the choice,] would young people with such refinement and backbone really seek to engage in illegitimate business? That they long for employment as public officials, in banks or in businesses—there is no need to waste words on this. Yet [Japanese] society's attitude toward fulfilling these demands is, at present, heartless." Though they might stream into northern China, because of discrimination in hiring, Koreans still had no choice but to engage in illicit business to make ends meet. And though they were in control of the occupied areas, Japanese left the dirty work to Koreans (and Taiwanese).

112. The *fabi* (lit. "legal tender") currency was introduced by the Chinese nationalist government in 1935 and remained in circulation until 1948. The rival *lianyin* banknotes were first issued by the Japanese-sponsored United Preparatory Bank of China (中国聯合準備銀行) upon its founding in March 1938. (EM)

113. *Kaigai Hōjin no gendō yori mitaru kokumin kyōiku shiryō (an)* [Sources for the education of countrymen, observed from the words and actions of overseas Japanese], draft manuscript, ed. Takasaki Ryūji, Jugonen sensō gokuhi siryoshū 1 (Ryūkei shosha, 1976), 6–8.

114. Ibid., 10–14.

115. Ibid., 19.

116. Ibid., 24–26.

117. Ibid., 32–33.

118. Ibid., 34–35.

119. Ibid., 37–38.

120. Ibid., 40.

121. Ibid., 40–41.

122. The Concordia Society was the only government-sponsored political and publicity organization in the Japanese puppet state of Manchukuo. Launched in July 1932 with the Manchukuo government and the Kwantung Army as its president and director respectively, it functioned primarily as a state propaganda organ, purveying slogans such as "The Five Races in Harmony" (*Gozoku kyōwa*) and "A Realm of Peace and Prosperity" (*Ōdō rakudō*). In 1936 its form was changed into that of a nationwide mass movement, and as such it subsequently served as a model for mass social organizations in Japan's other

colonies as well as the Imperial Rule Assistance Association. After 1941 the *kyōwakai* and its activities was incorporated into the Manchukuo government. See, for example, Young, *Japan's Total Empire*. (EM)

123. Ibid., 44–45.

124. Ibid., 80–81.

125. Ibid., 15, 84, 86, 88.

126. Ibid., 102.

127. Ibid., 100.

128. Ibid., 81, 99.

129. From here on, following Soejima Shōichi, in his "Nitchū sensō to Ajia taiheiyō sensō," *Rekishi Kagaku* 102 (1981): 22–23, I have chosen to refer to Japan's war from December 8, 1941, to the defeat in 1945 as the Asia-Pacific War (*Ajia taiheiyō sensō*). Also see Eguchi Kei'ichi, *Jugonen sensō shōshi* (Aoki Shoten, 1986), 6. Hitherto the term "Pacific War" (*Taiheiyō sensō*) has been used, but this term has the problem of overemphasizing the image of the war between Japan and the United States at the expense of the war in China and Asia. The use of the term "Greater East Asia War" (*Dai tōa sensō*), on the other hand, includes the possibility of a biased appraisal of the war as a "holy war" to establish a "Greater East Asian Co-Prosperity Sphere" (*Daitōa kyōei ken*) and a "New Order in Greater East Asia" (*Daitōa shin chitsujo*); its usage is inappropriate, unless done so in irony or to indicate the fact that the war was so referred to at the time.

130. Shiratori chō senbotsusha no tegami, ed., *"Shiratorichō senbotsusha no tegami" henshū i'inkai* (Gifu: Shiratorichō kyōiku i'inkai, 1976), 107.

131. Ibid., 103–104.

132. Tsubokura Junji, *Hitō kōryaku senki—yobi Tsubokura jōtōhei jinchū nikki* (Yayoi-chō, Kyōto: private publication, 1983), 27–28.

133. Ibid., preface, 2.

134. Ibid., 1–3.

135. It seems likely Tsubokura's family were tenant farmers.

136. Ibid., 4. After landing before the enemy at Ramon Harbor, Tsubokura entered Manila. He then participated and was wounded in the assault on Mariveles. Many lost their lives in these battles, and on January 2, 1943, Tsubokura wrote that if the deciding battle had been fought in Manila, several thousand Japanese would not have lost their lives. Compared to burying this many officers and men, "reducing Manila to ashes would have been a very small price to pay" (122).

137. The following draws upon *Ware aka aka to ikitari—higashimikawa chihō senbotsusha no ikō kara*, ed. Ishikawa Yukio and Hyōdō Masao (Tokyo: Tokuma shoten, 1969).

138. Ibid., 134. Letter dated August 11, 1945.

139. Ibid.

140. The specialized term "sublate" (in Japanese 止揚, *shiyō*) is associated with Hegelian philosophy. It is defined as to negate or eliminate but preserve as a partial element in a synthesis within the Hegelian dialectic. (EM)

141. Ibid., 136.

142. Literally "Victory Cry," apparently referring to some sort of candy. (EM)

143. Yamagata hōsō hōdōbu ed., *Yamagata/senbotsu heishi no tegami* (Yamagata: Yamagata hōsō, 1981), 120. Letter of April 8, 1944.

144. Created in 1890, the order of the Golden Kite was awarded to members of the Japanese military and military affiliates for bravery, leadership, or command in battle. During the course of the Sino-Japanese and Asia-Pacific Wars, more than 800,000 of them were conferred, the vast majority of the lowest sixth and seventh grades. (EM)

145. Ibid., 168. Letter of October 24, 1944.

146. Ibid., 135. Letter of May 1944.

147. Abe was a postal employee from Sakata City, born in 1909.

148. Ibid., 97–98. Letter of April 11, 1942.

149. Alternately referred to in English as the Lantern Festival or the Festival of the Dead, the Obon is an annual three-day Japanese Buddhist festival to honor the spirits of one's deceased ancestors. It is celebrated in the summer at different times in different parts of Japan, with the August celebration the most common. (EM)

150. A reference to the day Abe would return to Japan.

151. Ibid., 104.

152. Shiratori chō senbotsusha no tegami, ed., *"Shiratorichō senbotsusha no tegami" henshū i'inkai*, 118.

153. Hamano Kenzaburō, *Senjō—Ruson haisen nikki* (Tokyo: Seitōsha, 1979), 122.

154. The Japanese colonial doctrines and policies of *dōka* ("assimilation," dating from the beginning of the twentieth century) and *kōminka* ("imperialization" or "imperial subject making," dating from the mid-1930s) both involved the imposition of Japanese culture, or "Japanization," upon the colonized in ways that nevertheless preserved essential status distinctions between colonial subjects and Japanese citizens. Reflecting the intensified "total" mobilization mentality and policies of the war era, *kōminka* was more radical than its *dōka* predecessor, amounting to "the forced draft regimentation of all aspects of colonial life." See Mark R. Peattie, *The Japanese Colonial Empire, 1895–1945* (Princeton, N.J.: Princeton University Press, 1984), 41. For more on *dōka* and *kōminka* theories and policies in English, see E. Patricia Tsurumi, *Japanese Colonial Education in Taiwan, 1895–1945* (Cambridge, Mass.: Harvard University Press, 1977); and Leo T. S. Ching, *Becoming Japanese: Colonial Taiwan and the Politics of Identity Formation* (Berkeley: University of California Press, 2001). (EM)

155. On this the committee received advice from Hayashi Hirofumi.

156. Ryūkyū shimpō shakaibu, ed., *Shōwa no Okinawa* (Naha: Niraisha, 1986), 238–239.

157. Higa Syunchō, *Higa Syunchō zenshū* (Naha: Okinawa Taimusu-sha, 1971), 3:238–243.

158. Before the Meiji period, the Ryūkyū Islands (the string of islands between Kyūshū and Taiwan that includes Okinawa as its largest island) was a tributary state of China but also conducted extensive trade with the Satsuma domain, which in turn claimed political supervision over the Ryūkyūs; formal Japanese sovereignty over the archipelago was asserted with the creation of Okinawa Prefecture—against Chinese and local objections—in 1879. (EM)

159. Ryūkyū shimpō shakaibu, ed., *Shōwa no Okinawa*, 237.

160. *Ōsaka asahi shimbun*, Kagoshima Prefecture ed. (February 8, 1939).

161. Ryūkyū shimpō shakaibu, ed., *Shōwa no Okinawa*, 240.

162. Ibid., 207–208.

163. Nahashi kikakubu shishi henshūshitsu, ed., *Nahashishi*, shiryōhen, vol. 2, no. 3 (Naha: Naha shiyakusho, 1970), 355.

164. In the midst of total war—and as an integral part of its mobilization—the year 1940 was deemed and widely celebrated as marking the 2,600th anniversary of the founding of the enthronement of Emperor Jimmu in 660 BC. On the celebrations and their significance, see Ruoff, *Imperial Japan at Its Zenith*.

165. Ibid., 356.

166. Ibid., 368–369.

167. Ibid., 444.

168. Ibid., 367.

169. A reference to Okinawa's culture and dialect.

170. Ibid., 357.

171. Nahashi kikakubu shishi henshūshitsu, ed., *Nahashishi*, shiryōhen, vol. 3, no. 8 (Naha: Nahashi kikakubu shishi henshūshitsu, 1981), 499.

172. Ibid., 451–454.

173. Ibid., 455.

174. From Nakagusuku Village on Okinawa's main island.

175. Ryūkyū seifu, ed., *Okinawa kenshi*, vol. 9, *Okinawa sen kiroku* 1 (Naha: Ryūkyū seifu, 1971), 345–346.

176. Ibid., 349.

177. From Nishihara Village on Okinawa's main island, aged forty at the time of the battle of Okinawa.

178. Literally the "Stone" and "Bravery" Units, respectively the 62nd and 9th Divisions.

179. Ibid., 647–648.

180. Ibid.

181. Ibid., 654.

182. Aged twenty at the time of the battle of Okinawa.

183. Ibid., 251–260.

184. Ibid., 261, 263.

185. Ibid., 265, 260. Ellipses in the original.

186. Ibid., 246–247.

187. Ibid., 250–251. Okinawa's inhabitants suffered extremely numerous mass killings, coerced group suicides, and the like at the Japanese army's hands. Yet Ishihara Masae points out the following as one of the inherent issues: namely, incidents of mass killings of the population in Okinawa happened as a result of Japanese army officers and men scheming to protect themselves or stay alive, but not only this; in many cases, the village community was involved, and where participation in mass murder of the population was concerned, "it can generally be said that this was a result directed by the village war leadership stratum in order to provide to the soldiers of the imperial army proof of their identity as imperial subjects." See Ishihara Masae, "Okinawa sen to sonraku kyōdōtai," *Okinawa*

kokusai daigaku bungakubu kiyō, shakai kagaku hen 4, no. 1 (1976): 63. See also Ishihara, *Gyakusatsu no shima——kōgun to shinmin no matsuro* (Tokyo: Banseisha, 1978). If this was in fact so, it must be said that policies of assimilation (*dōka*) and the making of imperial subjects (*kōminka*) carried an exceedingly profound significance.

188. Ryūkyū seifu, ed., *Okinawa kenshi*, 252–253.

189. The term for "natives," *dojin*, has a derogatory connotation in Japanese similar to that of its English counterpart. Takakura Shin'ichirō, *Shinpan ainu seisakushi* (Tokyo: San'ichi shobō, 1972), 392; and Matsumoto Shigemi, Akima Tatsuo, and Tate Tadayoshi, *Kotan ni ikiru* (Tokyo: Gendaishi shuppankai, 1977), 210.

190. "Ainu kankei shimbun kiji," comp. Kōno Tsunekichi, in *Ainu shiryōshū* 2, vol. 7 (Sapporo: Hokkaidō shuppan kikaku sentā, 1984), 12–13.

191. Enforced in Hakodate, Fukuyama, and Esashi in 1877, with the enforcement area subsequently expanding, covering all of Hokkaidō by 1898.

192. Hokkaidōchō, *Hokkaidō kyūdojin* (Hokkaidōchō, 1911); repr.: *Ainu shiryōshū* (Sapporo: Hokkaidō shuppan kikaku sentā, 1980), 1:67–68.

193. Ezo or Emishi were indigenous peoples who lived in the Kantō and Tōhoku regions of Japan's main island of Honshū as well as on Hokkaidō from ancient times through the middle ages.

194. A mythological figure appearing in the ancient Japanese "Record of Ancient Matters," a collection of myths regarding the origin of the four Japanese home islands authored in the eighth century. (EM)

195. Sarashina Genzō, *Ainu to Nihonjin—denshō ni yoru kōshōshi* (Tokyo: Nihon hōsō shuppan kyōkai, 1970), 20–27.

196. A discriminatory term for Koreans. Hashimoto Susumu, *Nanboku no tō—Ainu heishi to Okinawa sen no monogatari* (Tokyo: Sōdo bunka, 1981), 47.

197. Ibid., 84.

198. Ibid., 83.

199. Ibid., 87.

200. Ibid., 89.

201. Ibid., 84.

202. Ibid., 94–98.

203. Ibid., 124.

204. Teshi Toyoji (as told to Yamada Sadao), "Okinawa ken de tatakatta," in *Zoku kataritsugu sensō taiken*, ed. Nihon jidō bungakusha kyōkai/Nihon kodomo wo mamoru kai (Tokyo: Sōdo bunka, 1983), 2:53.

205. Because the Conscription Law did not grant drafting privileges to the secret service (*tokumu kikan*) and since the Uilta (the Ainu of Sakhalin referred to the Uilta as the "Orok"), the Nivkh (in the Manchurian appellation, "Gilyak"), the Kirin, and the Sanda Yakut peoples had no family register, they should not have originally fallen under the Conscription Law. Beginning in 1942, however, each year the secret service distributed thirty "call-up notices" and mobilized people every winter and summer, using minorities for anti-Soviet intelligence. After the war, Gendanu applied for a military pension, but the Japanese government rejected this, saying that the only way to see it was that he had not been drafted

as a soldier but as a *gunzoku* (civilian in military employ), and *gunzoku* required an eighteen-year draft period in order to qualify for a pension, whereas in Gendanu's case he had completed fewer than thirteen years.

206. The following draws upon Tanaka Ryō/Dahinieni Gendanu, *Gendanu: Aru hoppō shosūminzoku no dorama* (Tokyo: Gendaishi shuppankai, 1978), in some places supplemented with *Karafuto nenkan*, 1939 ed., ed. and pub. Karfuto Shisuka jihōsha (repr. Tokyo: Kokusho kankōkai, 1980), along with issues of *Kanpō*.

207. From 1905 to 1945, the southern half of Sakhalin Island, off the coast of southern Siberia, was part of the Japanese empire. The 1855 Treaty of Shimoda had granted both Japan and Russia joint rights of occupation of the island without specifying a border between them. Japan was granted official sovereignty rights below the fiftieth parallel through the Portsmouth Treaty at the end of the Russo-Japanese War in 1905, after which the area came under the administration of the Karafuto Agency (*Karafutochō*). In the period through World War II Japan gained increasing privileges in the northern portion of the island as well, establishing oil and mining companies there. The Soviet Union occupied the entire island at the end of World War II, and Japan renounced all claims to Sakhalin in 1952. (EM)

208. July 1909, Sakhalin Edict no. 17 of the same year.

209. September 1921, Sakhalin Edict no. 35 of the same year.

210. April 1924, Edict no. 88.

211. Ainu repatriated from Hokkaidō had family registers, and other, indigenous Sakhalin Ainu acquired family registers under Imperial Edict no. 373, enforced on January 1, 1933 (Matters of Reform Within the Sakhalin Enforcement Law Special Edict).

212. Tanaka Ryō/Dahinieni Gendanu, *Gendanu: Aru hoppō shosūminzoku no dorama*, 30. Katakana is one of the two syllabaries used in written Japanese, along with hiragana. In modern Japanese katakana is used most often for transcription of foreign words as well as for onomatopoeia; hiragana is used for transcription of words of native origin and inflections of words expressed in Chinese characters or kanji. In the period through 1945 katakana interspersed with kanji was also used as the standard written language in official documents. (EM)

213. Ibid., 34–35.

214. Ibid., 43.

215. Ibid., 44.

216. Ibid., 16, 63–64.

217. The trainers were both commissioned and noncommissioned officers. Established in 1940, the Nakano School was an intelligence school named after the neighborhood in Tokyo where it was located in the former Army Signal Corps Center. Most of its graduates were assigned to "special duty agencies" (*tokumu kikan*) and charged with special operations, making contact with local populations and conducting intelligence and counterintelligence operations in the occupied areas. (EM)

218. First issued in 1882 and written in simple language, the Imperial Instructions for Soldiers (*gunjin chokuyu*) formed the basis for the spiritual training of the prewar army and navy. Its preamble emphasized the role of the emperor as the supreme commander of the

armed forces, and a lengthy five-article text enjoined the emperor's soldiers to be loyal, courteous, brave, faithful, and frugal. (EM)

219. The Code of Battle (*senjinkun*) was a code of military conduct issued in January 1941 by General Tojo Hideki to shore up the fighting spirit and behavior of soldiers in the face of the ongoing war in China. It demanded that soldiers "realize the principles of the national polity" (*kokutai no hongi*) and listed a number of concrete rules to be followed, including the injunction "do not suffer the shame of being captured alive," a principle under which many soldiers were compelled to sacrifice their lives. On *kokutai* and *kokutai no hongi*, see note 258, below. (EM)

220. "Takasago zoku" (高砂族) was the Japanese appellation for Taiwan's aboriginal peoples during the period of Japanese colonial rule. The postindependence term is Gaoshanzu (高山族, pronounced "kōzanzoku" in Japanese). (EM)

221. The terms "discharged" and "called up" appear between quotation marks to highlight the unofficial, extralegal nature of such orders, since the secret service did not have lawful drafting privileges. (EM)

222. Families of soldiers who died in battle received financial compensation, and the spirits of the deceased enjoyed the honor of enshrinement at the Yasukuni national cemetery. In the case of death from illness there was only rarely compensation and no enshrinement at Yasukuni. (EM)

223. Ibid., 109, 115. After the war, the former member of the Shiska secret service who distributed the "call-up notices," Nanbu Yoshimasa (pen name Hagiri Masayoshi), along with Ogasawara Sadako, a member of the House of Councilors who was cooperating toward Gendanu's receipt of a military pension, made the following statements respectively regarding the mission of secret service operatives who were mobilized: "While in charge of the [twelve outstanding men] who had finished the second training, I dispatched mobile units to what was in fact the tundra region along the Poronai River in order to expose Soviet spies. Until the outbreak of war [with the Soviet Union on August 8, 1945], these mobile units traversed the border region, arresting Soviet spies dozens of times." Hagiri Tadayoshi, "Horobiyuku orokko zoku—senjichū nihongun ni kyōryku shita hitobito," *Shi to shinjitsu* 331 (1977): 44. "Led by his superior, a Nakano School graduate, he received a reprimand and then, in the broad tundra region of the northern fiftieth parallel, he faithfully—truly faithfully—carried out his mission. On the orders of his superior, he was sometimes made to do such extreme things as killing people and kidnapping people of his own ethnicity on the Soviet-held side." Ogasawara Sadako's interpellation in the Diet, *Sangi'in naikaku i'inkai kaigiroku* 4 (May 13, 1976): 13.

224. Tanaka Ryō/Dahinieni Gendanu, *Gendanu: Aru hoppō shosūminzoku no dorama*, 125.

225. Their survival was remarkable considering that their mission took them directly into the face of rapidly advancing Soviet forces. (EM)

226. Ibid., 127.

227. Ibid., 130. Soviet advances soon made this decision irrelevant. (EM)

228. Ibid., 135.

229. Ibid., 146–147, 170–171.

230. Ohōtsuku minshūshi kōza, ed., *Minshūshi undō—sono rekishi to riron* (Tokyo: Gendaishi shuppankai, 1978), 84–85, 88.

231. Ishigami Masao, *Nihonjin yo wasuru nakare—nanyō no tami to kōkoku kyōiku* (Tokyo: Ōtsuki shoten, 1983), 125–126, in part supplemented by correspondence from Ishigami to the author.

232. Ibid., 27.

233. Ibid., 34. For more on Japanese colonial society and policy in Micronesia in English, see Mark R. Peattie, *Nan'yō: The Rise and Fall of Japanese Micronesia, 1885–1945* (Honolulu: University of Hawaii Press, 1988). (EM)

234. Ibid., 87.

235. *Daihōrin* 1 (October 1934): 265.

236. Ishigami, *Nihonjin yo wasuru nakare*, 106, 125–126.

237. Ibid., 128.

238. Ibid., 140–147.

239. Ibid., 158–159.

240. Ibid., 184, 189.

241. Ibid., 166–167. It was said that inhabitants arrested along with him were killed.

242. The Japanese transliteration of the brother's name is "Baddomeru"; the original name could not be traced. (EM)

243. Ibid., 194–200.

244. Miyata Setsuko, *Chōsen minshū to "kōminka" seisaku* (Tokyo: Miraisha, 1985), 42–43.

245. The Navy promulgation was in July 1943.

246. Korean family registers could not be moved to Japan, thus making permanent the distinction between Japanese and Koreans and effectively denying Koreans the possibility of moving permanently to the Japanese mainland. (EM)

247. As part of Japan's wartime "imperialization" policies, Koreans were compelled to recite the Imperial Subject's Pledge not only in schools but at every sort of public gathering, at the start of the day in workplaces, before film showings in movie theaters, etc. The pledge included statements such as "I am a subject of the Japanese empire," "we unite our hearts in loyalty to the emperor," and "with endurance and discipline we shall become countrymen great and strong." (EM)

248. Miyata, *Chōsen minshū to "kōminka" seisaku*, 68–69. The drought of 1939, which particularly afflicted the Nakdong River basin, was the worst since the beginning of modern measurement. Six major districts of the southern area were unable to transplant rice, and the average yield was reduced by 37 percent. (EM)

249. The following relies on Chōsengun shireibu, "Rikugun tokubetsu shiganhei jōkyō chōsa," *Rikushi mitsu dai nikki* 73 (October 1939), in the possession of the Bōeichō bōei kenkyūsho Military History Library (*senshi toshokan*).

250. Waku Masashi, "Aoge! Ko Ri Jinshaku (I Inseok) jōtōhei no shukun," *Chōsen* 299 (Seoul, April 1940): 65.

251. "Oh my!"

252. Chōsengun shireibu, "Rikugun tokubetsu." In the protocol, I insoku's name is suppressed—appearing as "a certain unit" and "a certain volunteer soldier"—and the "evalu-

ation" of this death in battle is also low. It therefore cannot be imagined that the circumstances of this death in battle were fabricated or whitewashed in the protocol.

253. Miyata, *Chōsen minshū to "kōminka" seisaku*, 75.

254. On the *kōminka* movement, see note 154 of this chapter.

255. Kyōiku sōkanbu, "Chōsen shusshin hei no kyōiku sankō shiryō," *Chōsen kenkyū* 88 (August 1969): 59.

256. Karashima Takeshi, "Chōsen gakutohei no saigo," *Bungeishunjū* 42, no. 10 (1964): 268–269.

257. Miyata, *Chōsen minshū to "kōminka" seisaku*, 176–177.

258. Literally reading "national body," *kokutai* is a highly politically charged term referring to Japan's supposedly unique "national character," centered around its so-called unique, "unbroken" imperial institution and culture of harmony, selflessness, and sacrifice. First coined by patriotic scholars of the Mito domain in the late Tokugawa era, *kokutai* assumed a central place in the nationalist orthodoxy of the Meiji state and received particularly heavy emphasis in the nationalist and imperialist propaganda of the 1930s and 1940s. For an elaborate and influential example of official, state-sponsored propaganda regarding the meaning and significance of *kokutai*, see *Kokutai no hongi*, co-authored by the philosopher Watsuji Tetsurō and published by the Ministry of Education in 1937, appearing in translation under the same title by Robert K. Hall (Cambridge, Mass.: Harvard University Press, 1949). (EM)

259. Kyōiku sōkanbu, "Chōsen shusshin hei no kyōiku sankō shiryō," 59, 61.

260. At the end of 1941, it was announced that a mandatory education regulation would be enacted in 1946.

261. Shihōshō keijikyoku, "Chōsen ni taisuru chōheisei shikō no kakugi kettei kōhyō ni kansuru hankyō chōsa," *Shisō geppō* 95 (June 1942): 7–8.

262. Ibid., 8,10.

263. A city in southwestern Korea and historical center of learning, culture, and politics, Kwangju lent its name to a student's independence movement that spread throughout Korea in 1929. (EM)

264. Ibid., 21.

265. Utsumi Aiko, "Chōsenjin senpan," *Chōsen kenkyū* 121 (1972): 32.

266. Takeda Shigetarō, "Waga natsukashiki heiei seikatsu," *Shinhyōron* 198 (1970).

267. Beatings and slappings for the slightest of offences were commonplace in the Japanese military in the interwar years, part of a disciplinary intensification initiated in the wake of the Russo-Japanese War and World War I aimed at shoring up battlefield obedience and hardiness as the military increased dramatically in size. See, for example, Tanaka, *Horrors in the East*. Former Navy Recruit Masayo Enomoto, interviewed in the late 1990s for the associated BBC television documentary *Horror in the East*, recalled a boot camp routine called "self-punishment": "Once the instructor gets tired of beating you up, they have recruits face each other, and slap each other. . . . Gradually I felt that I'd missed out on something if by nighttime I hadn't been beaten up at least once." Recruits of a lower social status such as Koreans and Taiwanese were all the more subject to such routine violence. Interviewed in the same documentary, the former Taiwanese recruit Toyoshige

Karashima recalled, "sometimes you'd be hit with fists and sometimes you'd be hit with bamboo sticks. Sometimes in the evening we couldn't eat our food because our faces were so swollen." (EM)

268. Takeda, "Waga natsukashiki."

269. Tamura Sadakichi, *Sen to shingeki—Chūgoku tairiku ni jūgun shita ichiheishi no kiroku* (Shizuoka: private publication, 1976), 5, 61.

270. I'io Kenshi, *Kaimondake* (Tokyo: Shūeisha, 1985), 130.

271. Ibid., 172–173, 250.

272. Ibid., 249.

273. Gwak Gui-xun, "Chōsenjin kanbu kōhosei no shuki," in *Chōsen/Hiroshima/han nihonjin*, ed. Pak Sunam (Tokyo: Sanseidō, 1973; new ed., 1983), 160.

274. Ibid., 161–163.

275. Ibid., 164.

276. Nickname for the badge worn by staff cadets.

277. Ibid., 166.

278. Ibid., 168.

279. Oh Rim-jun, *Kiroku naki shūjin—aru Chōsenjin senchūha no seishin shi* (Tokyo: San-ichi shobō, 1969), 178, 185, 195, 208.

280. Ibid., 213.

281. Ibid., 89.

282. Ibid., 171.

283. Ibid., 134–135, 171.

284. Oh Rim-jun, "Dai Nippon teikoku shiganhei to shite," *Ushio* 144 (1971): 226.

285. Ibid., 227–228.

286. All elementary schools for young Taiwanese.

287. Taiwangun shireibu, "Hokushi jihen wo tōshite mitaru hontōjin no kōminka no teido," dated September 1937, U.S. Library of Congress, microfilm reproductions of selected archives of Japanese Army, Navy, and other government Agencies, 1868–1945, T. 874, R. 111. The introductory passage of this top-secret report described those hoping for a Chinese victory as being in the majority.

288. Zhong Zheyuan (1885–1940) was a Chinese general during the Chinese civil war and the Sino-Japanese War. Allied with Chiang Kai-shek, he commanded the nationalist 29th Army stationed in southern Shanxi Province, from where his troops resisted Japanese encroachments in the area of the Great Wall in 1932. The 29th Army was involved in heavy fighting in the Marco Polo Bridge incident that opened the Sino-Japanese War in 1937 and suffered heavy casualties in the war's early months. For more detail on Zhong and his complex relationship with the nationalists and the Japanese in the period leading up the Sino-Japanese War in English, see Marjorie Dryburgh, *North China and Japanese Expansion 1933–1937: Regional Power and the National Interest* (Richmond: Curzon, 2000). (EM)

289. Taiwangun shireibu, "Hokushi jihen wo tōshite mitaru hontōjin no kōminka no teido."

290. The following is from Taiwangun shireibu, *Shina jihen to hontōjin no dōkō*, nos. 1 (dated October 1, 1937, Library of Congress, microfilm reproductions of selected archives of Jap-

anese Army, Navy, and other government Agencies, 1868–1945, T. 879, R. 111), 5 (dated February 1, 1938, T. 888, R. 111), and 8 (dated May 1, 1938, T. 893, R. 111).

291. Ibid., no. 1.

292. Ibid., no. 5.

293. Ibid., no. 8.

294. Tai Kuo-hui (戴國輝), "Sengo nittai kankei wo ikiru," *Sekai* 480 (1985): 167.

295. "Banjin" (蕃人) was a derogatory Japanese appellation for Taiwanese aborigines during the colonial period. (EM)

296. Katō Kunihiko, *Isshi dōjin no hate——Taiwanjin moto gunzoku no kyōgū* (Tokyo: Keisō shobō, 1979), 133.

297. Named after the mountainous district in which it took place, the Wushe Rebellion (referred to in Japanese as the "Musha Incident") was the last of several armed rebellions by the Gaoshan peoples against Japanese colonial oppression and discrimination, in particular against policies of police control that ignored Taiwanese customs and ways of life. Representing at once an ethnic movement, a social movement, and an agrarian movement, the uprising was brutally suppressed by combined Japanese military and police forces. In its aftermath, apart from a small increase in the colonial government's welfare budget, there was little change in the status quo. (EM)

298. Katō, *Isshi dōjin*, 134.

299. Ibid., 137.

300. Until he was discovered on Morotai Island in 1974, Suniyon of the Ami people—mobilized and enlisted in 1943 and sent to the Philippines as one of roughly five hundred men who comprised the first installment of the "Takasago People Army Special Volunteer Soldiers"—spent thirty years hiding in the jungle. It is said that when he was found alive he used the name "Nakamura Teruo" but that when he returned to Taiwan the name "Lee Kuan Hui" was awaiting him. Tai Kuo-hui, *Taiwan to Taiwanjin* (Tokyo: Kenbun shuppan, 1979), 188–189.

301. Lin Chin Min, *Shirazaru Taiwan—Taiwan dokuritsu undoka no sakebi* (Tokyo: Sanseidō, 1970), 86.

302. Ibid., 85–86.

303. Ibid., 86.

304. Ibid., 87.

305. Ibid., 131.

306. Isomura Seitoku (Kō Sheng De), *Ware ni kaeru sokoku naku—aru Taiwanjin gunzoku no kiroku* (Tokyo: Jiji shimpōsha, 1981), 9–10.

307. Kō's father was likely able to return to occupied Java as part of a prisoner exchange, as was the case with many other captured Japanese residents of the Netherlands East Indies. Even if unable to meet his father, Kō saw this as a way to get closer to where he was. (EM)

308. Ibid., 11.

309. Ibid., 31.

310. Ibid., 49.

311. Ibid., 63.

312. Ibid., 99, 148–149.

313. Ibid., 209.
314. Ibid., 219–220.
315. Ibid., 230.

❸ THE ASIAN WAR

1. Nitō Seikichi, *Yokosuka jūhō butai tōnan Ajia jūgunki* (Tokyo: private publication, 1979), 7. This text was written with the idea of leaving behind a war record of a "soldier and non-commissioned officer engaged in real blood-stained battles" (5).
2. Nitō, *Meiji hinoeuma umare no shinnen*, vol. 1 (of 3) (Tokyo: private publication, 1980), 94–95.
3. Nitō, *Yokosuka jūhō butai tōnan Ajia jūgunki*, 9, 25.
4. A materials supply route from Hong Kong to the nationalist government in Chungking.
5. Ibid., 18–19, 37.
6. Ibid., 40.
7. Ibid., 59.
8. Ibid., 67–68.
9. Japanese, apparently a kind of knife.
10. Ibid., 83, 86.
11. Ibid., 97.
12. Ibid., 87, 90.
13. Ibid., 97.
14. Ibid., 114, 117.
15. Ida Masakichi, *Watashi no 'Sumatora' tokō monogatari* (Kumagaya: private publication, 1983), 305; supplemented in part by conversations between Ida and the author.
16. Ida Masakichi, *Haruka naru hoshi wo mitsumete* (Kumagaya: private publication, 1982), 233–236.
17. Ida, *Watashi no 'Sumatora' tokō monogatari*, 74–75.
18. Ibid., 82–83.
19. The Pasemah (or Besemah) people, currently numbering approximately half a million, live mainly in what is now the province of South Sumatra, Indonesia, with a minority in Bengkulu Province. At the center of their territory is the volcanic peak of Mount Dempo. The town of Pagar Alam is its historical political center. Their principal economic activity is agriculture, based on the three crops rice, rubber, and coffee. Most Pasemah are Sufi Muslims. (EM)
20. Ibid., 84–85, 88–89.
21. Ibid., 283–284.
22. Ibid., 289.
23. Ibid., 129. After the war, Noh became a commander of the Sumatra Defense Army.
24. Ibid., 289–290.
25. Ibid., 291–295.
26. Ibid., 328.

27. Ida, *Yume no nampō gunsei jidai wo ikite* (Kumagaya: private publication, 1984), 23.

28. Ibid., 27–28.

29. Ibid., 35, 53, 75, 89.

30. This development reflected a more general consolidation and "normalization" of military rule and administrative structures in the conquered areas of Southeast Asia in late 1942, roughly half a year after Japan's successful military campaigns there had ended, in which civilian officials assumed increasing duties while large numbers of military men were transferred to active fronts to the east and west. All such policies and structures were required to adhere to the "Guidelines on the Administration of Occupied Areas" issued by the General Headquarters–Government Liaison Conference in November 1941, which described Japan's primary goals in Southeast Asia as the "rapid acquisition of important defense resources" and the "securing of self-sustenance of operating military forces in the field." In this aim, it ordered that "existing government structures be used to the utmost and former government organizations and folk customs be respected." Within this framework, each occupying force (for example, the 25th Army that occupied Sumatra and Malaya, the 16th Army in Java, and naval detachments in Indonesia's outer islands to the north and east) made its own administrative arrangements according to perceived local needs and circumstances and with limited mutual communication or coordination, subject to approval from the Southeast Asia command at Singapore and the high command in Tokyo. The result was a fragmented ruling structure, often with substantial political and administrative variation as well as political divisions between the different areas. See Ethan Mark, *Appealing to Asia: Nation, Culture, and the Problem of Imperial Modernity in Japanese-Occupied Java, 1942–1945* (Ph.D. thesis, Columbia University, 2003), AAT 3088380; Ōkuma kinen shakai kagaku kenkyūjo, *Japanese Military Administration in Indonesia*, U.S. Department of Commerce, Office of Technical Services, Joint Publications Research Service (Washington: U.S. Department of Commerce, 1963), translation of *Indoneshia ni okeru Nihon gunsei no kenkyū* (Tokyo: Kinokuniya shoten, 1959); and Yoji Akashi, "Bureaucracy and the Japanese Military Administration, with Specific Reference to Malaya," in *Japan in Asia, 1942–1945*, ed. William Henry Newell (Singapore: Singapore University Press, 1981). (EM)

31. Ida, *Yume no nampō gunsei jidai wo ikite*, 178–179.

32. Ibid., 230.

33. Ibid., 215–219.

34. Ibid., 258–259.

35. Ibid., 281.

36. Ibid., 277, 279–280. In response to the author's questions on April 22, 1987, regarding this incident, Ida states the following: "The result of the trial was that more than a dozen men received a death sentence, and I heard afterward they were shot to death in front of holes they'd dug at an airfield. At the time I, who entertained the conceit of knowing the feelings of the local people better than anyone, felt a great compassion, and I thought the Japanese army self-centered. Thinking about it now, I feel they were martyrs to the Indonesian independence movement."

37. Ibid., 142–144.

38. State councils (*shū sangi'in*) were established by the Japanese military administrations in Sumatra and Java under the propaganda heading of allowing native political partici-pation; in Java a Central Council (*Chūō sangi'in*) was also eventually established in late 1943. But like the colonial Dutch-sponsored local and central councils (*volksraad*) of the prewar period, members were appointed by the colonial ruler, and their function was strictly advisory. Discussion topics and issues were furthermore limited to those deter-mined by the Japanese. (EM)

39. Ibid., 237–239.

40. The training and deployment of *heiho* as assistants to Japanese army units began in the spring of 1943. Indonesians who signed up—including many from the working class, des-perate for employment—often faced extreme exploitation and discrimination and later starvation and death as conditions at the front worsened. The establishment and training of the more elite, exclusively Indonesian military units (the *Peta* or "Defenders of the Homeland" units in Java, followed by the *giyūgun* in Sumatra and Malaya) followed in late 1943, partly prompted by the requests of Indonesian nationalists eager to take advantage of Japanese military knowhow for nation-building and national-defense purposes. The timing of the formation of the *giyūgun* reflected a deteriorating war situation and a resul-tant change of heart among a largely conservative Japanese command heretofore hesitant to "arm the natives." In English, see Joyce Lebra, *Japanese-Trained Armies in Southeast Asia: Independence and Volunteer Forces in World War II* (Hong Kong: Heinemann, 1977). (EM)

41. Ida, *Yume no nampō gunsei jidai wo ikite*, 295, 332–333.

42. With the status of an active-duty soldier.

43. Ibid., 343–344, 358.

44. Ibid., 359, 363, 369.

45. Ibid., 377–378.

46. Ibid., 380.

47. Along with Java, the historically prosperous, cosmopolitan, and devoutly Muslim Mi-nangkabau region of West Sumatra was a hotbed of Indonesian nationalism from the movement's inception in the early 1920s, contributing a substantial share of nationalist leadership that included the movement's cofounder and subsequent first vice president of independent Indonesia, Mohammad Hatta. (EM)

48. Ibid., 386–387. The British were under Allied orders to reoccupy Indonesia and "maintain order" until the Dutch colonial rulers returned; this included countering resistance from the Indonesian nationalist movement. With Allied soldiers as yet few in number, Japa-nese units were often temporarily called upon to assist and were allowed to keep their weapons in this aim. Such policies placed the often ambivalent Japanese in an extremely awkward position, and while some complied, others took no action or made their weap-ons available to Indonesians. This was the case in Surabaya, East Java, where nationalist resistance to British attempts to occupy the city on behalf of the Dutch in November 1945 flared into a full-blown three-week military confrontation that marked the start of the Indonesian Independence War. See Gotō Ken'ichi, "Caught in the Middle: Japanese

Attitudes Toward Indonesian Independence in 1945," *Journal of Southeast Asian Studies* 27 (March 1996): 37–48. (EM)

49. Ida, *Yume no nampō gunsei jidai wo ikite*, 388, 391, 397.

50. Ibid., 404.

51. Nickname for a World War II–era slow cargo ship. (EM)

52. Ibid., 405–406.

53. Interview with Ida Masakichi, April 22, 1987.

54. Ishii Masaharu, *Minami kara—Indoneshia zanryū moto Nihonhei no kaisō* (Tokyo: Nishida shoten, 1984), 67.

55. Ishii's father was subsequently head of an agricultural experiment station at Moshiriya in the suburbs of Kushiro, Hokkaido.

56. Japan ruled Saipan after seizing it from German control during World War I, and its colonial hegemony was extended by League of Nations mandate in 1922. Following European and American examples, agricultural experimental stations were established in Japan and in its colonies under both public and private auspices to explore means of increasing agricultural productivity through the use and development of new seed varieties, tools, and planting and harvesting techniques. (EM)

57. Established in 1872, the Imperial Guards were a select army division officially charged with the prestigious duty of protecting the imperial house. (EM)

58. Ibid., 21, 28–29.

59. Ibid., 32, 39, 44, 67.

60. Ibid., 84.

61. Ibid., 85–86.

62. Ibid., 87–91.

63. Ibid., 93.

64. Ibid., 94.

65. Ibid., 96–97.

66. Japanese transliteration of an Indonesian place name that could not be traced. (EM)

67. Ibid., 99–100.

68. The Arabic title *hadji* (in contemporary Indonesian spelling, *haji*) refers to one who has made the pilgrimage to Mecca. Previous to the accessibility of relatively inexpensive air travel, participation in such a pilgrimage from Southeast Asia was an extremely expensive and thus exclusive undertaking, according—and associated with—high social status. (EM)

69. Ibid., 102–115.

70. Ibid., 116–120.

71. Lit. "Special Information Squad."

72. Modeled on those in Japan proper with the same name, youth training centers were variously established in Java and elsewhere in occupied Indonesia to offer spiritual and military training to select young adult Indonesian men, serving as a forerunner to the volunteer armies established later in the occupation and coming to encourage the dream of an independent Indonesia, although not always with such goals in mind from the start. In Java the first such center was initiated as an ad hoc program by several young civilian

students attached to the Java Propaganda Squad shortly after the Dutch surrender; this was followed by a more rigorous and systematic but still "unofficial" military training under the auspices of army intelligence and directed by Lt. Yanagawa Munenari, a Nakano School graduate. As the former Indies resident and intelligence operative Togashi Takeomi himself later admitted, when the latter center first opened under Java Special Intelligence Unit (*Beppan*) auspices in January 1943, "it was by no means for the purpose of forming anything like the *giyūgun*. The aim was to set up an Indonesian edition of the *Nakano Gakkō* . . . to train young Indonesians, stubborn, mentally tough youth, for use as assistants in general duties. . . . To educate people for use as spies." Togashi Takeomi, *Intabyū kiroku, Tokuteikenkyū 'bunka masatsu,'* series A: *Nihon to Ajia*, interviewer: Shiraishi Takashi (November 13, 1978), 16. For more in English on Japanese paramilitary training of Indonesians, see Joyce Lebra, *Japanese-Trained Armies*; and Mark, *Appealing to Asia*. (EM)

73. Ishii, *Minami kara—Indoneshia zanryū moto Nihonhei no kaisō*, 236.

74. Ibid., 120.

75. Ibid., 126, 128, 132.

76. Ibid., 134–135, 152.

77. The Netherlands launched large-scale military campaigns in Indonesia on two separate occasions in 1947 and 1948, attempting to restore hegemony over its former colonial possession and facing determined resistance from the nationalist movement, whose leaders Sukarno and Mohammad Hatta had declared independence two days after the Japanese surrender to the Allies on August 17, 1945. Under pressure from the United States and others, the Netherlands finally conceded its colonial claims in the Den Haag Treaty of November 1949, which established Indonesia as a sovereign nation-state. (EM)

78. Ibid., 138, 141,143–147.

79. Ibid., 203, 211.

80. Tanaka Toshio was a sergeant on a *kenpeitai* team in Semarang in Java (who subsequently changed his name to Mohammad Hasan). The reason he participated in the independence war was that he had escaped from Cipinang Prison, where he was being held on suspicion of war crimes. Tochikubo Hiroo, *Nikkei Indoneshiajin* (Tokyo: Simul shuppankai, 1979). In the case of Imperial Guards Division Transport Corps sergeant Hayakawa Kiyoshi in Sumatra, too, it was because he was kidnapped by the Batakaro people, and his cooperation in the independence movement was requested by the village headman. Hayakawa Kiyoshi, *Bōkyaku no seishun—Indonesia dokuritsu senki* (Tokyo: Kyōiku shuppan sentā, 1980).

81. Nitō, *Yokosuka jūhō butai tōnan Ajia jūgunki*, 121.

82. Ida, *Yume no nanpō gunsei jidai wo ikite*, 409.

83. Ishii, *Minami kara*, 202.

84. Ibid., 246.

85. Katō Mifumi, *Biruma no nagareboshi* (Okazaki: private publication, 1979), 1–2.

86. Correspondence from Katō to the author, September 2, 1986.

87. Katō, *Biruma no nagareboshi*, 1.

88. Correspondence from Katō to the author, September 2, 1986.

89. Katō, *Biruma no nagareboshi*, 2.

90. Ibid., 9.

91. Ibid., 12, 15, 19.

92. Ibid., 22–23.

93. Ibid., 24–26.

94. Ibid., 29.

95. Ibid., 54.

96. Ibid., 50–51.

97. Ibid., 60.

98. Ibid., 63–64.

99. Ibid., 89.

100. Ibid., 104–109.

101. Ibid., 110–111.

102. Ibid., 124, 132.

103. Ibid., 141.

104. Ibid., 146.

105. Ibid., 146–147.

106. Ibid., 152.

107. Ibid., 158–159.

108. Ibid., 161.

109. Ibid.

110. Ibid., 193, 212.

111. Ibid., 221.

112. Ibid., 221, 223–224, 226, 232.

113. Ibid., 233–234.

114. Correspondence from Katō to the author, September 2, 1986.

115. Katō, *Biruma no nagareboshi*, 101.

116. Ibid., 177–178.

117. Ibid., 233.

118. Miura Tokuhei, *Ichi kashikan no Biruma senki—Mītokīna kanraku zengo* (Fukuoka: Ashi shobō, 1981), 1–2. *Ichi kashikan no Biruma senki* was written based on memos (*Butai kōdō nisshi*, lit. a "Unit Action Diary") that Miura always carried with him and brought back. It is an excellent and bold record, seeking to reveal and not conceal even things that the army normally considered "dishonorable," for the sake of passing on the true sense of the war to subsequent generations. Moreover, this record is valuable in that it was passed around and read among his war comrades, with Miura choosing to make it public as the outcome of mutual debates.

119. Of Western clothing.

120. Ibid., 1.

121. Ibid., 12.

122. Correspondence from Miura to the author, March 3, 1987. The slogan "Greater East Asian Co-Prosperity Sphere" (*Dai tōa kyōeiken*) was first used by Japan's Foreign Minister Matsuoka Yōsuke in August 1940. (EM)

123. Miura, *Ichi kashikan no Biruma senki*, 26.

124. Ibid., 41–43, 48.

125. In 1943 Major-General Orde Wingate (1903–1944) formed and trained a "long-range penetration force" to operate behind Japanese lines after the Allied retreat from Burma. Eventually known as the Chindits—a corrupted version of the name of a mythical Burmese lion—they were supplied by air and fought for some six weeks before withdrawing. Wingate trained and commanded a second, larger force that was landed by air in early 1944. (EM)

126. Ibid., 95.

127. Ibid., 129.

128. Ibid., 105.

129. Ibid., 146.

130. *Sasaegi*, lit. trees of support. (EM)

131. Ibid., 210–211.

132. Ibid., 210, 214. All were popular hit songs of the 1930s. The first and second were made famous by Fujiyama Ichirō in 1931 and 1932 respectively, the last was the title of a poem written by Takehisa Yumeji in 1910 and made into a popular song in 1918 that saw renewed popularity in 1938 as a film's title song. (EM)

133. Ibid., 230.

134. Ibid., 237, 239.

135. Ibid., 240.

136. In response to the author's questions on this, Miura responds as follows: When he first saw prisoners executed in China, he was unable to eat for two days. Before long, however, it had become nothing at all. During the peaceful times of the Burma occupation, he says, everyone's spirit was calm, and they didn't think of killing anyone, but once they got to the front and the fierce fighting began, their spirits became something entirely different from those of peacetime. Interview with Miura, April 25, 1987.

137. This order was transmitted between the night of July 31 and the morning of August 1. Miura, *Ichi kashikan no Biruma senki*, 243–244.

138. Ibid., 248.

139. Ibid., 265.

140. The ill-fated Imphal Campaign was launched in the spring of 1944. Japanese 15th Army forces, accompanied by a regiment of the Indian National Army under the command of the nationalist leader Subhas Chandra Bose, aimed to surround and capture the British stronghold of Imphal, a plain near the Burma-India border, and from there to proceed deeper into India. By July, lacking supplies and exhausted by fighting, disease, and monsoon rains, the Japanese and Indian armies were compelled to retreat, having suffered heavy casualties. (EM)

141. Ibid., 98.

142. Ibid., 268–269.

143. Correspondence from Miura to the author, March 3, 1987.

144. Miura, *Ichi kashikan no Biruma senki*, 269.

145. Sakimoto Takashi, *Biruma no tatakai—retsu heidan ichi tsūshinheishi no shuki* (Izumi, Kagoshima Prefecture: Izumi bunka no kai, 1982), 1.

146. Ibid., 2.

147. Ibid., 28.

148. Correspondence from Sakimoto to the author, February 28, 1987.

149. Sakimoto, *Biruma no tatakai*, 41.

150. Ibid., 42.

151. Ibid., 51–53.

152. Although a Japanese victory, the battle of Sangshak resulted in heavy losses on both sides, and the resultant one-week delay in the Japanese advance allowed British and Indian reinforcements to occupy the strategically vital Kohima ridge. (EM)

153. Ibid., 76.

154. Ibid., 89.

155. Ibid., 95.

156. The abandonment of the Miyazaki Detachment was based on the orders of the 15th Army headquarters, and it is said that the division commander opposed this measure to begin with.

157. Ibid., 99.

158. Ibid., 103.

159. Ibid., 113.

160. Ibid., 115–116.

161. Ibid., 119. Identifying commanders by name, another Allied propaganda leaflet highlighted the Japanese leadership's "strategic blunders" in the Imphal Campaign. See Suzuki Akira and Yamamoto Akira, eds., *Hiroku: bōryaku senden bira* (Tokyo: Kōdansha, 1977), 49.

162. Sakimoto, *Biruma no tatakai*, 121.

163. Ibid., 127–128.

164. Ibid., 135.

165. Ibid., 121.

166. Ibid., 204.

167. Lit. "people as sovereign–ism."

168. Ibid., 226–227.

169. Ibid., 245.

170. Ibid., 258–259.

171. Ibid., 260.

172. Ibid., 264. Sakimoto joined the Japan Socialist Party around 1960 and left it in 1980.

173. Yano Masami, *Rusontō haizan jikki* (Tokyo: Sanju shobō, 1986), 15. This is a brave record, written immediately after repatriation, that does not conceal things inconvenient to its author, based upon memos composed in the form of daily diary entries and written on toilet paper during Yano's time as a prisoner. In response to a question from the author regarding the book's dating of his period of wandering in the mountains, furthermore, Yano replies, "I believe it is 95 percent accurate." Correspondence from Yano to the author, June 8, 1987.

174. Yano's small physique—he stood just 165 centimeters tall and weighed only fifty-two kilograms—was an additional factor in his desire to leave the army as quickly as possible. It made it difficult for him to carry out assigned tasks, caused him to suffer excessively from the harsh Manchurian climate, and made him a target for abuse.
175. Yano, *Rusontō haizan jikki*, 8–10.
176. Ibid., 11.
177. Ibid., 16.
178. Ibid., 37, 57.
179. Ibid., 69.
180. The popular love song "Longing for Your Shadow," written by Chiyako Satō and made famous in 1932 by the singer Ichirō Fujiyama, which Yano's friend Hirose was noted for playing. (EM)
181. Ibid., 74–75. Entry of November 3, 1944.
182. Ibid., 88.
183. On this occasion, Yano says he used the stolen fabric to make a loincloth.
184. Ibid., 79–80.
185. Ibid., 111.
186. Ibid., 114–115.
187. Ibid., 120.
188. Ibid., 124. After American forces landed, the Japanese army's view of Filipinos grew ugly. Hamano Kenzaburō, a contracted employee of the Department of Information of the Philippine Expeditionary Army and head of a battlefield propaganda attack unit, for example, wrote the following in his diary on February 15, 1945. Hamano was a member of the intelligentsia, a graduate of Waseda University's English Department: "At the front, they say they're killing each and every Filipino as they find them. The Filipinos are people of the enemy side. From the point of view of carrying out military operations too, this is unavoidable. Seeing these children [who make fun of the Japanese army], we can't help succumbing to a ferocious feeling of 'shoot them to death!' No lying, this is my feeling at present. I say it again. Burn the Philippines flat! Shoot the anti-Japanese Filipinos to death! The renaissance of the Philippines will begin after that." Hamano, *Senjō*. From June 1945 on, Maeda Takejirō, a warrant officer of the 103rd Division Rapid-Fire Gun Unit, was compelled to make a hunger march in the mountains of Luzon; according to his detailed battlefront diary, this was also a requisition march. Maeda Takejirō, *Hitō kiga kōgun nikki* (Fukuoka: Tōtekisha, 1985). The seizure of items such as cows, horses, pigs, chickens, rice, potatoes, sugarcane, and vegetables appears repeatedly in this diary, most looted from the inhabitants. This caused conflicts with the local people defending themselves, and when Japanese soldiers got killed, there were reprisals. For example, Maeda's diary records the following sequence of events at a location two kilometers north of Sinaben: "We put all our energy into finding goods. My group discovers unhulled rice . . . there are no further battle results. After hiding in the mountain recesses for a while, it seems like the natives are moving elsewhere" (July 21). "Myself and the seven men under me split up in the dense jungle in the hills behind us, spend five hours chasing the

footprints of the inhabitants in hiding, and then—discovering smoke from a cooking fire in the valley—we make a surprise attack, netting a number of items in addition to Type 38 guns. The inhabitants were moreover just at the point of making a meal, so we all had a feast" (July 28). "Myself and all the men under me, along with a member of the work unit, make a clean sweep of the whole river and valley of Sinaben, launch a surprise attack on the Igorot tribe, and seize foodstuffs etc. along with blankets. We also capture nine women and children, but the mistresses were all ill. They too have no food and are quite weak, running from place to place in the mountains. How wretched" (July 30).

189. Yano, *Rusontō haizan jikki*, 126.

190. Ibid., 153.

191. Ibid., 164.

192. Ibid., 172.

193. Ibid., 175, 180.

194. Ibid., 183.

195. Ibid., 185.

196. Ibid., 187.

197. Ibid., 186.

198. Ibid., 188–189.

199. Ibid., 198–200.

200. Ibid., 202–203.

201. Ibid., 220. Entry for August 17, 1945.

202. Ibid., 226.

203. Ibid., 251.

204. Ibid., 263.

205. Ibid., 271.

206. Ibid., 275–276.

207. Ni'imi Aya, *Watashi no Firipin monogatari* (Kumamoto: private publication, 1976), 4. Ni'imi Aya and Okada Keiko, *Ruson ni kieta hoshi* (Tokyo: Mainichi shimbunsha, 1980), 109. Ni'imi wrote this record after her return in 1946, during a period of peddling soap and picking up fallen coal along the railroad tracks while recovering from malnutrition. The first of the above sources is this record, and the second is a partially revised version of the same; the citations are based upon the first (a private publication), which well conveys the intensity of the text.

208. Ni'imi, *Watashi no Firipin monogatari*, 4–5.

209. Ibid., 9.

210. Ibid.

211. The Japanese granting of nominal independence to the Philippines—as earlier with Burma in August 1943—was prompted partly by the worsening war situation and local discontent, partly by a need to be seen to match or exceed prewar promises of future independence by the former colonial ruler, and partly by ongoing, increasing concerns over local loyalties against this background. Japanese de facto control over political, economic, military, and foreign policy remained in any case little changed. (EM)

212. A Japanese knitted-goods enterprise that had advanced into the Philippines in 1918.

213. The return of the dollar signified a declining faith in the legitimacy and longevity of the Japanese currency and the Japanese order it represented. (EM)

214. Ibid., 19.

215. Ibid., 22–23. The term *jōdo* means "heaven" or "paradise." It is also the name of the most widely practiced school of Buddhism in Japan, the *jōdoshū*. (EM)

216. Ibid., 25.

217. Ibid., 43.

218. Ibid.

219. Ibid., 50–52.

220. Ibid., 54–58.

221. Ibid., 63.

222. Ibid., 75.

223. Ibid., 77–78.

224. Ibid., 83, 96–97.

225. Ibid., 104–105.

226. Ibid., 111.

227. Ibid., 131.

228. Ibid., 109.

229. Fujioka Akiyoshi, *Haisen no ki—gyokusai chi Horo tō no kiroku* (Tokyo: Sōrinsha, 1979), 23. *Haisen no ki* is a record written after the war in an American POW camp; from Fujioka's second call-up to his arrival at Jolo Island and from his surrender to American forces onward, the entries are written in daily diary form.

230. Fujioka Akiyoshi, *Uijin no ki* (private word-processor publication, 1986), 1–3. Interview with Fujioka, April 13, 1987.

231. Published in 1947 and based on the author's own experiences, Noma's antiwar novel *Shinkū chitai* (*Zone of Emptiness*) profiled the brutality and dehumanization of life in the imperial army through a tracing of the interactions and experiences of soldiers of different social backgrounds in an Osaka barracks and their involvement with the military legal system in the desperate final year of the war. It is considered one of the finest war novels produced after World War II, intimately revealing the distinctive dynamics of the Japanese military, and it met with a great public response at the time of its publication. It was made into a movie in 1952. (EM)

232. Fujioka, *Uijin no ki*, 80.

233. Ibid., 17.

234. Ibid., 27. After arriving, Fujioka was told that his unit was not among those predicted to be lost at sea (33).

235. Ibid., 33. Entry of September 1, 1944.

236. Fujioka, who passed his youth, including his time at Ōsaka Commercial College (from which he graduated in 1938) imbibing "a liberal social atmosphere under the influence of Taishō democracy etc.," says that he, like many Commercial College graduates, viewed the Sino-Japanese War as an aggressive war from the beginning. Because he "was of a mind" that the nations of Europe and America were "countries that Japan should take

as models [and that] we should learn from them and follow their lead," the notion of the derogatory wartime term "brutish British and Americans" (*kichiku bei'ei*) and a romanticized view of the emperor were "out of the question." Yet the fact that there were completely different views of the war, Europe and America, and the emperor among those just a few years younger—even among graduates of the same college—was something he would realize fully during his time in the American POW camp. Interview with Fujioka, April 13, 1987.

237. A type of artillery piece designed for rough terrain which can be broken down and transported in pieces. (EM)

238. The Bōeichō senshishitsu (Defense Agency Military History Room), *Shō-gō rikugunsakusen (2)*, numbers the force of arms at the time of the American invasion at a small 3,425 men, with the Independent Combined 55th Brigade (the Suga Brigade) as its nucleus (645). Yet according to Ministry of Health and Welfare sources the number of those who died in battle on Jolo Island during the Asia-Pacific War was 6,030. Listed in Nishimoto Masami, *Tsuisō no Firipin* (Tokyo: Philippine Information Center, Senseki hōmondan jimukyoku and Yōseisha, 1975), 328.

239. Fujioka, *Haizan no ki*, 50.

240. Ibid., 51, 54.

241. Ibid., 59–66.

242. Ibid., 59.

243. Ibid., 83.

244. Ibid., 105–106.

245. Ibid., 106–112.

246. Ibid., 118.

247. According to *Shō-gō rikugunsakusen (2)*, the army corps commander, who was commander-in-chief, also died in battle between July 31 and August 2, 1945 (646).

248. Fujioka, *Haisen no ki*, 132.

249. Ibid., 133.

250. Ibid., 138.

251. Ibid., 155.

252. Ibid., 157.

253. The number of survivors cited in *Shō-gō rikugunsakusen (2)* is 135 (647).

254. On *hakkō ichi'u*, see note 91 of chapter 2.

255. Fujioka, *Haisen no ki*, 183. Entry of December 5, 1945.

256. In response to questions on this point from the author, Fujioka says, "Unlike in China and Luzon, contact with the Moro people was limited, and it was difficult to have a real sense that the Japanese army was encroaching upon their lives. Still, the Japanese did take the liberty of going there and making trouble for them, so in a general sense, I think you can't think of it as anything other than aggression against the Moro." Interview with Fujioka, April 13, 1987.

257. Fujioka, *Haisen no ki*, 170. Entry of October 7, 1945.

258. Ibid., 172. Entry of October 30, 1945.

259. Ibid., 174. Entry of November 2, 1945.

260. Ōnishi Katsumi, *Ichiheishi no yasen nikki* (Tokyo: Hakuyonkai, 1976), 1, 18. This is a detailed diary written on the battlefield. Ōnishi had someone returning to Japan send the portion of his diary through January 29, 1944, to his home by mail after he got back. The portion from January 30 through mid-May of that year did not reach his empty house. Fearing confiscation after the defeat, he burned the portion of his diary dated from then on. Immediately after his repatriation, he wrote down the portion for which there was no original diary (his period as a recruit and from January 30, 1944, onward), relying on his memos and his memory. The period described is that from January 14, 1941, to March 8, 1946; both the original diary, which covers the Zhejiang campaign, and the portion written just after repatriation, which covers the *Tairiku datsū* ("through the China continent") campaign, are substantial.

261. Ibid., 4. Entry for January 16, 1941.

262. Ibid., 22.

263. Ibid., 41, 64.

264. Ibid., 76.

265. Remembered in the United States as the "Doolittle Raid," after its commander Lt. Col. James Doolittle, this daring long-distance, one-way bombing run involving sixteen B-25 bombers launched from aircraft carriers deep within enemy waters did little physical damage but was widely publicized and provided a boost to American fighting morale during a period in which there was little other positive news from the Pacific front. (EM)

266. Ōnishi, *Ichi heishi no yasen nikki*, 114.

267. Ibid., 112.

268. Ibid., 114.

269. Ibid. In the Zhejiang campaign, the active use of poison gas by the Japanese army expanded. From June 3 onward in particular, 13th Army Headquarters "encouraged" the 15th, 22nd, 32nd, and 116th divisions under its command to use poison gas, and as a result, above all the 22nd division "used it to great effect." "Se-gō [Sekkan or Zhe-Gan] sakusen keika gaiyō," Bōeichō Bōeikenkyusho Library. According to Ōnishi's diary, we can see that his 116th division used it from the beginning of the campaign.

270. Ōnishi, *Ichi heishi no yasen nikki*, 115.

271. Ibid., 117–118.

272. Ibid., 118.

273. Ibid., 118, 121.

274. Myōken is a type of shrine particularly numerous in Ōnishi's home region of western Japan, at which the Buddhist saint of that name was worshipped. (EM)

275. Ibid., 123, 125.

276. Standard company procedure was to fire thirty projectiles and thirty red shells.

277. Ibid., 128.

278. Ibid., 129.

279. Ibid., 130.

280. Ibid., 131.

281. Ibid., 134–135. Entry of July 6, 1942.

282. Ibid., 137. Entry of July 30, 1942.

283. Ibid., 146.

284. Ibid., 118.

285. Ibid., 139.

286. Ibid., 151.

287. Ibid., 205. Entry of November 7, 1943.

288. Ibid., 205.

289. Ibid., 230–267.

290. Ibid., 252.

291. Ibid., 302.

292. Ibid., 372.

293. Ibid., 360.

294. Ibid., 308. Diary entry for September 9, 1944.

295. Ibid., 430.

296. Ibid., 443. Ōnishi says that the inhabitants trapped in the cave managed to escape via a secret exit.

297. Ibid., 439–440.

298. Ōnishi also heard that it was in the aim of doing battle with the Soviet Union.

299. A term referring to villages targeted for Japanese propaganda and seen as pro-Japanese. (EM)

300. Ōnishi expresses this notion of ingratitude with the old idiom *shiri kurae kan'on* (尻くらえ観音), which refers to how people appeal to the Buddhist god of mercy *kan'on* in hard times but soon forget their debt when their luck is better. (EM)

301. Ibid., 476.

302. Ibid., 551. Entry of June 23, 1945.

303. Fearing that Japanese military scrip would soon become worthless, the population sought to exchange military scrip for items that would retain value, including silver coins. On August 8, Ōnishi would sell shirt fabric and futon lining. Ibid., 643.

304. Ibid., 554.

305. A propaganda phrase referring to the expulsion of the Western enemy from Asia. (EM)

306. Ibid., 570.

307. Ibid.

308. Ibid., 598.

309. Ibid., 651.

310. Ibid., 663.

311. An allusion to the famous opening words of the essay the *Hōjōki* ("Record of a Ten-Foot Hut"), written by the medieval Buddhist monk and poet Kamo no Chōmei (1155–1216), which ruminates on the fleetingness of life, comparing people's lives and dwellings to bubbles in a flowing river. (EM)

312. Ibid., 667.

313. Earlier name of the "Through the Continent Campaign" derived from the Japanese reading of the first characters of the two Chinese cities Xiangjiang and Guilin. (EM)

314. Ibid., 772.

315. Ibid., 799.

316. Ibid., 806.

317. Ibid., 816.

318. Ibid.

319. Ibid.

320. Ibid., 817.

321. Northern China Expeditionary Army "pacification officers" (*senbukan*) were assigned to carry out "pacification" (*senbu*) of the Chinese people that the army alone could not do sufficiently and were attached to the secret service (*tokumu kikan*) as civilians in military employ (*gunzoku*). There were two types of units: "army-accompanying pacification" (*jūgun senbu*) units charged with propaganda aimed at the enemy, information gathering, and convincing war-displaced refugees to return home (*kirai kankoku*, lit. "advising to return"); and "fixed pacification" (*teichaku senbu*) units charged with wide-ranging duties including political activities, "peace-preservation" activities, railroad protection operations, economy and industry reconstruction work, and educational and cultural activities. As of March 1940 there were 1,626 Japanese and 1,299 Chinese pacification unit members. Once the war had subsided a bit, the need for pacification units declined, and in February 1940, the army integrated the pacification units and the *Xin min hui* (on the *Xin min hui*, see note 322, below) together. Only in Shanxi Province were pacification units still deemed necessary, and their integration was delayed. See Aoe Shunjirō, *Dai Nippongun senbukan—aru seishun no kiroku* (Tokyo: Fuyō shobō, 1970), 191–192, 327.

322. The *Xin min hui* was established in 1937 as a propaganda and cultural organization to promote Japan's agenda in China through the secret service (*tokumu kikan*) under General Kita Sei'ichi of the North China Area Army. Leadership came mostly from Japanese in the employ of the Kwantung Army–sponsored Concordia Society (*Kyōwakai*) in Manchukuo or connected with the East Asia Common Culture Academy (*Tō'a dōun shoin*) in Shanghai. Its most active Chinese member was its central executive office head Miao Pin. For more on the *Xin min hui* in English, see Akira Iriye, "Toward a New Cultural Order: The Hsin-Min Hui," in *The Chinese and the Japanese: Essays in Political and Cultural Interactions*, ed. Akira Iriye (Princeton, N.J.: Princeton University Press, 1980). (EM)

323. Murakami Masanori, *Kōdo no zanshō—aru senbukan no kiroku* (Miyazaki: Kōmyakusha, 1983), 27, 77. It is said this account is based upon a 1,200-page manuscript written shortly after Murakami's return to Japan.

324. Ibid., 20, 22.

325. Ibid., 23.

326. Ibid., 30.

327. Ibid., 59.

328. Ibid., 66–68.

329. Ibid., 103, 116–118.

330. Ibid., 127. Murakami was impressed by this as a sign of the "sturdiness" of the Chinese, but in fact it was probably the result of plundering from the people.

331. Ibid., 121–122.

332. Ibid., 125.

333. Ibid., 142–143, 154.

334. Ibid., 138–139.

335. Ibid., 169.

336. Ibid., 176.

337. Ibid., 181–185.

338. Ibid., 188.

339. Ibid., 251–253.

340. Ibid., 269–272.

341. Ibid., 295–300.

342. The spindle at the top of an umbrella shaft.

343. Agari Masa'omi, *Yume no Kohoku—hei no tsuioku* (Shūhō-chō, Yamaguchi Prefecture: private publication, 1982), 11, 230.

344. Ibid., 164.

345. Ibid., 188.

346. Ibid., 115–116.

347. Ibid., 81.

348. Ibid., 143.

349. Ibid., 230.

350. Ibid., 117.

351. Ibid., 183–184.

352. Ibid., 83.

353. Ōnishi, *Ichiheishi no yasen nikki*, 141.

354. Murakami Masanori, *Kōdo no zanshō*.

355. Ibid., 336–337.

❹ DEMOCRACY FROM THE BATTLEFIELD

1. Naimushō, "Zōgen higo torishimari no jōkyō" (December 12, 1941), in *Kindai shomin seikatsushi*, ed. Minami Hiroshi and Satō Kenji (Tokyo: San'ichi shobō, 1985), 4:432.

2. Japanese forces occupied the Aleutian Islands of Attu and Kiska in June 1942 in the aim of gaining control over Pacific shipping routes and preventing an American counterattack across the North Pacific. After a long campaign under extreme conditions, the Japanese force at Attu was almost completely wiped out at the end of May 1943, and remaining Japanese forces at Kiska Island were evacuated without a fight at the end of July. (EM)

3. Naimushō keihokyoku, "Chi'an taisaku yōkō" (January 13, 1943), U.S. Library of Congress, *Microfilm of Oriental Japan*, MJ 144 R. 3.

4. Naimushō keihokyoku gaijika, "Tsūshin ken'etsu yori mitaru saikin no shokuryō jijō to kokumin shisō no dōkō" (January 19, 1944), U.S. Library of Congress, *Microfilm of Oriental Japan*, MJ 144 R. 8.

5. Naimushō keihokyoku hoanka, "Shisō junpō" no. 2 (April 20, 1944), Minami et al., *Kindai shomin seikatsushi*, vol. 4, *Ryūgen* (Tokyo: San'ichi shobō, 1985), 407.

6. Ibid., 407.

7. Keishichō jōhōka, "Saikin ni okeru shojōsei" no. 7 (August 29, 1944), Library of Congress, *Microfilm Reproductions of Selected Archives of the Japanese Army, Navy, and Other Government Agencies, 1868–1945*, T. 1528 R. 225.

8. Keishichō jōhō i'inkai, "Jōhō tekiroku" no. 1 (September 10, 1944), in ibid.

9. Ibid.

10. It goes without saying that military and labor drafts were surely the more essential reason for such shortages.

11. Ibid.

12. Ibid.

13. United States Strategic Bombing Survey Report no. 14, "The Effects of Strategic Bombing on Japanese Morale," Tōkyō kūsyū wo kiroku suru kai, *Tōkyō daikūsyū sensaishi* (Tokyo: Tōkyō kūsyū wo kiroku suru kai, 1973), 5:402–403; as well as Awaya Kentarō, "Kokumin sōdōin to teikō," *Iwanami kōza nihon rekishi* (Tokyo: Iwanami shoten, 1977), 21:163–165.

14. Tōkyō kūshū wo kiroku suru kai, *Tōkyō daikūsyū sensaishi*, 5:404.

15. Ibid., 5:405.

16. Naimushō keihokyoku hoanka, "Saikin ni okeru minshin no dōkō" (April 1945), in *Tōkyō daikūsyū sensaishi*, 5:350.

17. Naimushō keihokyoku hōanka, "Kūshū gekika ni tomonau minshin no dōkō" (July 1945), in ibid.

18. Ibid., 5:364.

19. Ibid., 5:364–365.

20. Naimushō keihokyoku hoanka, "Okinawatō shikkan ni tomonau minshin no dōkō" (July 10, 1945), in ibid., 5:365–367.

21. Keishichō, "Keishichō yori mitaru shakai jōsei ippan" (July 1945), U.S. Library of Congress, *Microfilm Reproductions*, T. 1528 R 225.

22. Ibid.

23. *Tokkō geppō*, manuscript of August 1945 issue, in *Tōkyō daikūsyū sensaishi*, 5:373.

24. Fujiwara Akira, "Taiheiyō sensō," *Iwanami kōza Nihon rekishi* (Iwamami shoten, 1963), 21:185.

25. Tazaki, "Senjika kosakunō no jinushi-kosaku kankei," 51.

26. The following is from "Abe Ta'ichi nikki," dated from January 1, 1931, through January 31, 1945, unpublished document in the possession of Abe Ta'ichi.

27. The Tōjō cabinet fell in mid-July 1944 in the wake of the fall of Saipan and was replaced by a cabinet led by the army general Koiso Kuniaki. (EM)

28. At the time, Japan's Imperial Headquarters announced that Japanese airplanes had sunk no fewer than twenty aircraft carriers and five battleships of the U.S. task force. This was a dramatic error, as Imperial Headquarters had publicized a mistaken report from an airplane occupant without checking it first. No U.S. ships were sunk.

29. According to Tazaki Nobuyoshi's calculations, the figure amounted to 84.1 percent of the total harvest. Tazaki, "Senjika kosakunō no jinushi-kosaku kankei," 51.

30. Introduced in chapter 2.

31. Mori Isao, *Shōwa ni ikiru* (Tokyo: Heibon-sha, 1957), 118.

32. Ibid., 121–122.

33. Ibid., 135.

34. Ibid., 149.

35. Because of an acute nationwide shortage of firearms, millions of Japanese in this period trained for a final showdown against advancing U.S. military forces with sharpened bamboo spears. (EM)

36. Ibid., 161–162.

37. Ibid., 160.

38. Ibid., 185.

39. Introduced in chapter 2.

40. "Konagaya Saburō nikki," in *Yokohama no kūshū to sensai*, ed. Yokohama no kūshū wo kirokusuru kai (Yokohama: Yokohama no kūshū wo kirokusuru kai, 1975), 2:271.

41. Ibid., 2:274.

42. Ibid., 2:277–278.

43. Ibid., 2:278.

44. Inoue Isamu, *Nikki shōwa nijūnen* (Kobe: Nojigiku bunko, 1974), 4.

45. A reference to the so-called *hōanden*, constructed and compulsorily worshipped in schools throughout Japan in the decades through 1945. (EM)

46. On the concept of *kokutai*, see note 258 of chapter 2. (EM)

47. Inoue, *Nikki shōwa nijūnen*, 27.

48. Ibid., 31.

49. Ibid., 35–36.

50. Ibid., 40.

51. Ibid., 53.

52. Ibid., 66, 72.

53. Ibid., 68.

54. Ibid., 77.

55. Ibid., 92–93.

56. Ibid., 95.

57. Ibid., 98.

58. Tōyama Mitsuru (1855–1944) was an influential right-wing militant and imperialist agitator active behind the scenes in Japanese politics from the early Meiji period through World War II. (EM)

59. Ibid., 103. Entry of August 11.

60. Ibid., 104.

61. Ibid., 105.

62. Ibid., 106.

63. Amerika senryaku bakugeki chōsadan sen'ibu (United States Strategic Bombing Survey Morale Division), "Haisen chokugo no kokumin ishiki" ("National Consciousness Just After the Defeat"), in *Shiryō nihon gendaishi*, trans. Miyazaki Akira, ed. Awaya Kentarō (Tokyo: Ōtsuki shoten, 1980), 2:122.

64. Ibid. Because there were also people who indicated more than one response, the total comes out to 125 percent.

65. Amalgamated in 1955, this township comprises six villages including North and South Hizusa Villages. The following draws upon *Shūsen no hi: sono hi watashi wa*, ed. Shūsen no hi kiroku kankōkai (Hinochō, Shiga Prefecture: Shūsen no hi kiroku kankōkai, 1978).

66. Ibid., 104. Regarding reactions to the defeat in agricultural villages that had been spared bombing, the Home Ministry states, "People in the village districts had long believed in victory in the Greater East Asia War and devoted themselves to increasing agricultural output, deliveries, and labor service, and because of this, where the weighty broadcast of August 15 is concerned—hearing the unexpected imperial announcement of the end of the war in a situation where many had expected an order to be given for the [nation of] one hundred million to make a unified mass attack—it is observed that their discouragement and shock were extremely great and that they were therefore aimless for a time, and it is acknowledged that their desire to increase production and deliveries declined sharply." Naimushō keihokyoku hoanka, "Sensō shūketsu ni kansuru byōgi kettei zengo ni okeru chian jōkyō" (August 26, 1945), in Awaya, ed., *Shiryō Nihon gendaishi*, 2:34.

67. Founded in 1937 and sponsored by the Colonial Ministry, the Manchuria/Mongolia Colonization Youth Volunteer Corps assembled young men between the ages of fourteen and twenty-one as soldiers and settlers on the Manchurian frontier. In all they accounted for more than a third of the total number of Japanese settlers emigrating to Manchuria between 1937 and 1945. Schoolteachers played an essential role in recruitment in the localities, particularly as fewer people volunteered from 1940 onward. See Louise Young, *Japan's Total Empire*. (EM)

68. Shūsen no hi kiroku kankōkai, *Shūsen no hi: sono hi watashi wa*, 118–119.

69. On the Youth Training Centers (*Seinen kunrensho*), see note 35 of chapter 2.

70. On the Imperial Assistance Adult Men's Association (*Yokusan sōnendan*), see note 145 of chapter 1.

71. A reference to the so-called Potsdam Edict Number One of January 1947. Section Six of the 1945 Potsdam Declaration issued by the Allied Powers declared, "There must be eliminated for all time the authority and influence of those who have deceived and misled the people of Japan into embarking on world conquest." A "categorical" purge of individuals seen as having aided and abetted militarism and ultranationalism began with a SCAP order of January 4, 1946, applying to "all positions in the central Japanese and prefectural governments and all of their agencies and local branches, bureaus, and offices." Precisely one year later, Imperial Ordinances numbers 1 and 4 along with a Home Ministry Ordinance extended the objects of the purge to include local government officials. See John Dower, *Embracing Defeat: Japan in the Wake of World War II* (London: Allen Lane, 1999); and Kurt Steiner, *Local Government in Japan* (Stanford, Calif.: Stanford University Press, 1965). (EM)

72. Shūsen no hi kiroku kankōkai, *Shūsen no hi: sono hi watashi wa*, 135–136. After the San Francisco Peace Treaty went into effect, Ikeda received the explanation that he had been purged from public office in order to keep him from being arrested, and he once again had a change of heart, once more coming to believe in the "great heart" of the emperor (137).

73. Ibid., 17.

74. Ibid., 83.

75. Ibid., 51.

76. Ibid., 12.

77. Ibid., 108.

78. Ibid., 78.

79. A reference in particular to the postsurrender reemergence of the old party politicians who had come to occupy the center of the prewar political order before being sidelined by the wartime military-bureaucratic leadership. (EM)

80. Promulgated in 1889 and in effect until 1947, the Meiji Constitution formed the basis of an extremely conservative prewar political and legal order with the emperor at its apex, with little allowance for democratic representation or control over the state apparatus and the military and limited civil protections. Over the course of the early twentieth century, popular struggles for expanded democratic rights and parliamentary rule (the so-called Taishō democracy movement) met with some success, but the absolute prerogatives of the emperor and the independence of the military from civilian control remained unassailable, and the party politicians themselves remained largely those of a conservative bent reflective of their elite social class and status. For more in English, see, for example, Andrew Gordon, *Labor and Imperial Democracy in Prewar Japan* (Berkeley: University of California Press, 1992); and R. P. G. Steven, "Hybrid Constitutionalism in Prewar Japan," *Journal of Japanese Studies* 3, no. 1 (Winter 1977): 99–133. (EM)

81. The figure for soldiers is taken from a table included in Hara Akira, "Senji tōsei keizai no kaishi," in *Iwanami kōza nihon rekishi* (Tokyo: Iwanami shoten, 1976), 20:240; and that for civilians from Research Officer Tate, *Shikoku kyōdō sengen jutaku ni tomonau jinkō seisaku jō no shomondai* (unfinished manuscript), U.S. Library of Congress, *Microfilm of Oriental Japan*, MJ 144, R. 3.

82. It was the same for people in Okinawa who refused to surrender and wandered in the mountains.

83. Shūsen no hi kiroku kankōkai, *Shūsen no hi: sono hi watashi wa*, 284–285.

84. Nanshōkai, ed., *Chūshi no sanga tōkeredo*, no. 1 (Shirahama City, Wakayama Prefecture: Nanshōkai, 1980), 20–21.

85. Department of State, Office of Research and Intelligence, "Survey of Political Opinions of Japanese in Pei-P'ing" (April 30,1946), in *OSS/State Department Intelligence and Research Report, II, Postwar Japan, Korea and Southeast Asia, A Microfilm Project of University Publication of America, Inc., 1977*, reel II-28.

86. Shūsen no hi kiroku kankōkai, *Shūsen no hi: sono hi watashi wa*, 250.

87. Wagatsuma Masatoshi, *Kita Chōsen no omoide* (Yonezawa-shi: private publication, 1979), 68.

88. Ibid., 8–9, 82, 145.

89. Shūsen no hi kiroku kankōkai, *Shūsen no hi: sono hi watashi wa*, 328.

90. Ibid., 337–338.

91. Sumeragi Mutsuo, *Ruson sen to Firipinjin—Ruson de Nihongun wa nani wo mitaka* (Tokyo: Rakuyū shobō, 1981), 310.

92. A recruit unit assembled from all regiments from the Tōhoku region in the north of Japan's main island of Honshū. Taniki was assigned to the 72nd infantry Regiment Second Battalion.

93. Taniki Shunji, *Lusontō sentō kiroku* (Isawa-chō, Iwate Prefecture: private publication, 1983), 25. Upon hearing this, Taniki at first reacted with bitterness, however.

94. Ibid.

95. A graduate of higher elementary school and a lance corporal at the time of the defeat.

96. *Nōmin heishi no koe ga kikoeru—7000 tsū no gunji yūbin kara*, ed. Iwate-Waga no pen (Tokyo: Nihon hōsō shuppan kyōkai, 1984), 178.

97. United States Strategic Bombing Survey, Morale Division, "Haisen chokugo no kokumin ishiki" ("National Consciousness Just After the Defeat"), in Awaya, ed., *Shiryō Nihon gendaishi*, 2:127.

98. Ibid., 2:127–128.

99. Ibid., 2:129.

100. The "Imperial Rescript to Promote the National Destiny" of January 1, 1946, in which the emperor renounced the (prewar) notion of his own divinity, thus ending the pretense of divine descent that had formed the basis of prewar emperor worship. (EM).

101. The following draws upon Department of State, Office of Research and Intelligence, "Survey of Political Opinions of Japanese in Pei-P'ing." This investigation involved the distribution of a questionnaire to Japanese civilians and soldiers containing 150 items, with an aggregate taken of those agreeing, disagreeing, and providing no response (in places the totals exceeded 100 percent). The selection of participants was carried out by the local Japanese army and Japanese residents' association. Respondents comprised 301 civilians and eighty-four military men, with the majority of civilians employed in connection with the North China Development Company, and approximate levels of education relatively high: (old-system) high school graduates and above comprising 43 percent; (old-system) middle school graduates, 40 percent; and graduates of higher elementary and elementary schools, 17 percent. Among the military men too, 66.7 percent were officers, with field officers numbering twenty-six, company officers thirty, and noncommissioned officers twenty-eight. More than a "grassroots" people's consciousness, this therefore represents a "middle-class" consciousness of Japanese of considerably higher status than average, but we are left to depend on this, as no other reliable investigation exists.

102. Ibid., 379.

103. Ibid., 382–383.

104. Ibid., 375–377, 380.

105. Regarding the question "how do you feel about the fact that Japan fought a war with China?", according to a survey conducted by the Japanese Public Opinion Research Association (*Nihon yoron chōsakai*) in 1972, 46.6 percent said "there was no choice," and 8.4 percent said "in the interests of self-defense, it was only natural"—together totaling 55.0 percent—against which only 26.4 percent said "I believe we did something wrong." Yoshida Yutaka, "Jūgonen sensōshi kenkyū to sensō sekinin mondai," *Hitotsubashi ronsō* 97, no. 2 (1987): 37. According to a poll of members of the veteran's association of the

former Aizuwakamatsu 65th Infantry Regiment resident in Tokyo published in the August 15, 1985, edition of the newspaper *Asahi,* when asked "what do you now think of the war that Japan carried out?", 59 percent responded "it was an unavoidable war" (with 2 percent calling it "a correct war"), and 32 percent said "it was an aggressive war." Broadly speaking, both tendencies were roughly the same as those in the U.S. Army poll above. On the other hand, when this author conducted the same poll as that in the *Asahi* newspaper among first-year students just entering the Faculty of Commerce at Chūō University in the spring of 1986 (first portion 176 students, second portion 173 students), 75.1 percent said "it was an aggressive war," 16.3 percent said "it was an unavoidable war," and 1.7 percent said "it was a correct war." Those that had not even learned of the Nanjing Massacre in high school, however, numbered 44.1 percent.

106. Arai Shin'ichi, *Genbaku tōka e no michi* (Tokyo: University of Tokyo Press, 1985), 270.

107. Ienaga Saburō's *The Pacific War* (*Taiheiyō sensō*) (Tokyo: Iwanami shoten) appeared in 1968. A second edition was published in 1986.

108. On the Indonesian island of Morotai. (EM)

109. Ohōtsuku minshūshi kōza, ed., *Minshūshi undō—sono rekishi to riron* (Tokyo: Gendaishi shuppankai, 1978), 85–86.

110. Katō Kunihiko, *Isshi dōjin no hate——Taiwanjin moto gunzoku no kyōgū* (Tokyo: Keisō shobō, 1979). "Isshi dōjin," an expression coined by the ancient Chinese poet Han Yu, was a Japanese colonial propaganda slogan meant to refer to Japan's so-called impartial treatment of and affection for all imperial subjects. (EM)

111. Utsumi Aiko, *Record of the Korean Class "B" and "C" War Criminals* (*Chōsenjin BC kyū senpan no kiroku*) (Tokyo: Keisō shobō, 1982).

112. Inoue Isamu, *Nikki: shōwa nijūnen,* 109.

113. This was the name of a stirring popular patriotic song whose lyrics were chosen from among tens of thousands entered in a national competition sponsored by the Cabinet Information Bureau in 1937 to boost war mobilization. The winning musical entry was composed by the navy band conductor Setoguchi Tōkichi. The nationalistic lyrics included references to the imperialist slogan *hakkō ichi'u* and to the "everlasting prosperity of the imperial land." (EM)

114. Ibid., 112.

115. Authored in 1932 (Tokyo: Senshinsha), this popular text by Ikezaki (1891–1949), who was earlier known as a literary critic, predicted a fateful coming military showdown between Japan and the United States. (EM)

116. Inoue Isamu, *Nikki: shōwa nijūnen,* 114–115.

117. Ibid., 122.

118. Ibid., 123.

119. Ibid., 131–132.

120. Ibid., 154. Kawakami Jōtarō (1889–1965) was a Tokyo-born, Tokyo University–educated politician elected to the Diet from the socialist Japan Labor Farmer Party (*Nihon rōnōtō*) in the first universal election of 1928 and later as a representative of the Social Masses Party, which chose cooperation with the wartime state. He served as a manager in the wartime Imperial Rule Assistance Diet of 1940. Purged by SCAP, he subsequently be-

came one of the founders and leaders of the postwar Socialist Party, representing its right wing. (EM)

121. Ibid., 115.

122. Miki Kiyoshi (1897–1945) was a prominent philosopher and political theorist. A student of the philosopher Nishida Kitarō at Kyoto Imperial University who also studied with Martin Heidegger in Germany, his humanistic writings were particularly influential among the younger intelligentsia. He was associated with the political left but during the early stages of the Sino-Japanese war, as head of the Cultural Problems Research Group in Prime Minister Konoe Fumimaro's think-tank the Shōwa Research Association, he produced a theory of the "East Asian Cooperative Body" that legitimated Japan's imperial expansion. He was arrested as a suspected communist party member in 1944 and died in prison shortly after the Japanese surrender. See also note 173 of chapter 1. (EM)

123. Ibid., 131.

124. Ibid., 134.

125. Ibid., 136.

126. Ibid., 122.

127. The Imperial Rescript on Education, issued in 1890, is seen as one of the defining documents of the conservative prewar political order. In it the emperor declared the purpose of education as learning to serve society and state. It invoked the age-old Confucian values of filial piety and loyalty, with their primary objects defined as not only the family but also the nation, the throne, and the Constitution; its faithful observance was proclaimed as the duty of all subjects toward the "imperial ancestors." (EM)

128. Ibid., 145–147.

129. Ibid., 148–149.

130. Mori, *Shōwa ni ikiru*, 185–186.

131. Ibid., 192.

132. Ibid., 199–200.

133. Ibid., 211.

134. Following the official renunciation of his divinity at the beginning of 1946, and now dressed in civilian clothes, the emperor embarked on tours to almost every prefecture of Japan to confirm his new postwar status as a modern monarch appropriate to a democratic society. (EM)

135. Ibid., 214, 217.

136. Ibid., 217.

137. A reference to the highly publicized Allied trials of Japan's wartime leaders classified as suspected "Class A" war criminals, held from May 1946 to December 1948. (EM)

138. Ibid., 222.

139. Ibid., 227–228.

140. Ibid., 232–233. This was part of a movement against atomic weapons that assumed mass proportions following the exposure of the crew of a Japanese fishing boat to nuclear fallout from a U.S. hydrogen bomb test in the Bikini Atoll in March 1954. (EM)

141. "Konagaya Saburō nikki," 344.

142. Ibid., 345.

143. The slogan *sonnō jōi*, literally "revere the emperor, expel the barbarians," became a rallying cry of the samurai opponents of the Tokugawa regime at the time of Japan's forced opening to the West in the 1850s. (EM)

144. Ibid., 346. Entry of February 22.

145. Ibid., 348.

146. Kōno, a protégé of the future LDP founder and prime minister Hatoyama Ichirō, was a member of Hatoyama's Liberal Party; Hirose and Murose were independents. (EM)

147. Ibid., 352.

148. Ibid., 354. To the dismay of progressives and the relief of conservatives, the occupation authorities (SCAP) banned the general strike just before it was set to take place. For progressives, the move has since been viewed as signaling the beginning of a U.S. "reverse course" in its occupation political priorities, a shift from encouragement of democratization, unionization, and demilitarization to a Cold War preoccupation with suppressing the threat of communism and shoring up Japan's conservative state and capitalist establishment. (EM)

149. Ibid., 355.

150. Kikuchi Keiichi, *Nanasentsū no gunji yūbin* (Tokyo: Hakuju-sha, 1983), 166.

151. This is taken in the main from ibid., 174.

152. Ibid., 174–175.

153. Itō Matsuo, *Ishikoro no harukana michi* (Kōdan-sha, 1970), 179.

154. Ibid., 187, 190. Itō's husband was purged from public office.

155. Ibid., 191.

156. Ibid., 192.

157. Ibid., 161.

158. As defined in the Potsdam Declaration.

159. Ibid., 193–196.

160. Ibid., 199. *Bunka chokin* refers to a movement to encourage postal savings. Already associated in the prewar period with notions of (Western-style) modernity and progress, the word *bunka* (lit. "culture") quickly returned to fashion after the war as a predicate for all manner of social-reform initiatives. (EM)

161. Ibid., 203.

162. Ibid., 191, 217.

163. Watanabe Chūzaburō, *Watashi no hōryo nikki* (Anjō Aichi Prefecture, private publication, 1978), 5.

164. Ibid., 174.

165. Ibid., 180–187.

166. Ibid., 172.

167. Ibid., 18.

168. Ibid., 174. This is the doctrine of the Japanese religion Seichō no ie, founded by Masaharu Taniguchi, a former member of the Ōmotokyō in 1930. Concerned primarily with notions of healing, prior to 1945 Seichō no ie was also an ultranationalist movement proclaiming that Japan was the center of the universe and the emperor its master. After 1945 its beliefs were modified but they retain a strong element of emperor worship. Seichō no

ie ' s following in Japan is estimated at more than three million, and it also has numerous branches in the Americas as well as in Europe and Africa. (EM)

169. Agari Masa'omi, *Yume no Kohoku—hei no tsuioku* (Shūhō-chō, Yamaguchi Prefecture: private publication, 1982), 230.

170. This feeling that compensation should be made is an extremely precious thing.

171. Nitō Seikichi, *Yokosuka jūhō butai tōnan Ajia jūgunki* (Tokyo: private publication, 1979), 121. This desire to believe that one's participation in the war was not in vain is one shared by a great many people. In the introduction to a collection of memoirs, for example, an organization of veterans from a unit that was also in Sumatra recognizes that "we caused a large amount of trouble, even if this was unintended." It nevertheless states the following: "The developmental period of central Sumatra that we pursued together with the people of this nation, sharing in the hardships during our sentimental youth now long past—then a wilderness as if at the end of the earth, yet now the site of Southeast Asia's largest oil fields—we believe that our efforts bore fruit." Chūsuma kai, *Omoide no bunshū*, 2 vols. (Tokyo: Chūsuma kai bunshū kankō i'inkai, 1981), 1:2.

172. Nitō, *Yokosuka jūhō butai tōnan Ajia jūgunki*, 120–121.

173. Ni'imi Aya, *Watashi no Firipin monogatari* (Kumamoto: private publication, 1976), 149.

174. Yamamoto Takeshi, *Ichiheishi no jūgun kiroku* (Fukui: Yasuda shoten, 1985), 272. Entry of August 16, 1945.

175. Ibid., 286.

176. Ibid., 296.

177. Ibid., 301.

178. Ibid., 301, 305. "Believing" their father's words "were right," Yamamoto Fujio and his four siblings were emboldened to publish their father's records.

179. Correspondence from Marui Miyo to the author, October 3, 1986.

180. Ibid. In the case of Murata Washirō, who fought in southern China, he too tenaciously worked to have his diary published, thinking that he would "like to have many people know the true nature of this cruel war in order to protect the peace of the present." *Yomiuri shinbun* (August 17, 1986). For Ōnishi Katsumi as well, among the motivations for publishing his diary was the thought that "a 'human' should not kill another 'human.' The act of war should on all accounts, definitely and certainly be eradicated for all eternity." Ōnishi, *Ichiheishi no yasen nikki* (Tokyo: Hakuyonkai, 1976) 1043. The publishing of reliable records itself, furthermore—including that of the five brothers and sisters of the Yamamoto family— bears an extremely positive significance, representing a self-examination of the experiences of war and Asia by Japanese themselves.

181. Fujioka, in correspondence addressed to the author, September 19, 1986.

182. Yano Masami, *Rusontō haizan jikki* (Tokyo: Sanju shobō, 1986), 271.

183. Ni'imi, *Watashi no Fuiripin monogatari*, 2.

184. Ida, *Yume no nampō gunsei jidai wo ikite* (Kumagaya: private publication, 1984), 409.

185. Ishii Masaharu, *Minami kara—Indoneshia zanryū moto Nihonhei no kaisō* (Tokyo: Nishida shoten, 1984), 246.

186. Kimura Genzaemon, *Nitchū sensō shussei nikki* (Akita: Mumyōsha shuppan, 1982), 153.

187. Introduced in chapter 3.

188. "Jo" and "Atogaki": in *Hakugeki dai yon daitai shi,* ed. Haku yon kai daitai shi hensan i'in kai (Tokyo: Haku yon kai honbu jimukyoku, 1985), 1, 1076. See Nagao Ryūichi's review of the above documents, "Jijitsu wo kiroku to shite nokosu ('Hakugeki dai yon daiyondaitaishi,' 'Yasen no omoide' shohyō)," *Shūkan dokushojin* (September 22, 1986). Without this sort of earnest self-inspection, it is also true that there can be no peace and friendship across borders. Again, groping toward "frank, sincere human intercourse" (Okabe Makio, "Nihon gun no zangyaku kōi wo megutte," *Sekai* 479 [1985]: 124), including technological assistance in agriculture and industry, etc., and the sending of books and organs, etc., carried out upon the basis of this sort of reflection—that is, precisely a groping toward human-to-human intercourse among peoples—carries a constructive significance.

189. The Three Non-nuclear Principles state that "Japan shall neither possess nor manufacture nuclear weapons, nor shall it permit their introduction into Japanese territory." They were outlined by Prime Minister Eisaku Satō in a speech to the Diet in 1967 during negotiations over the return of Okinawa from the United States. The Diet formally adopted the principles in 1971. (EM)

POSTSCRIPT

1. Ienaga Saburō's *The Pacific War,* 2nd ed. (*Taiheiyō sensō,* Tokyo: Iwanami shoten, 1986) draws upon numerous sorts of records of war experience.

2. *Asahi Journal* (December 27, 1985): 24–25. The English translation of this excerpt is from http://www.mediaculture-online.de/fileadmin/bibliothek/weizsaecker_speech_may85/weizsaecker_speech_may85.htm. (EM)

3. *Sekai* 494 (1986): 118–119. Originally in "Im Erfolg isoliert," *Die Zeit* (July 11, 1986).

4. Because of the limitations of my abilities, I was unable to analyze in this book issues of the war and the *hisabetsu burakumin* (one of Japan's main minority groups that has historically experienced profound discrimination dating back to its categorization as an "untouchable" caste during the Tokugawa era) as well as those of the war and the physically handicapped and was able to deal only partially with issues of the war and women.

INDEX

(*see* Indonesia; Java; Sumatra); Iwo Jima, fall of, 222f, 223, 223f, 224; Japanese casualties, 174–75, 179, 180–81, 186, 196–98, 255, 313(n253); Japanese military governments in Southeast Asia, 156–58, 303(n30), 304(n38); Japan's defeat welcomed by Asian peoples, 237–38; Japan's early success, 20; Japan's goals, 20, 60, 80, 83, 251, 284(n188), 303(n30); Leyte Island, fall of, 222f, 223, 223f; Okinawa, battle of, 124–27, 128–29, 224, 228, 321(n82); pacifism as postwar response to, 159, 177–78, 183, 252–54; Pearl Harbor attack, 95–96, 103, 115, 231; preparations for battle on mainland Japan, 226, 229, 231, 319(n35); public support for, during war, 91, 95–96, 99–102, 104–10, 219–32; Saipan's fall, 109–10, 220, 222f, 223, 223f, 290(n107); Singapore's fall and occupation, 95–96, 103, 107, 108, 152–53; soldiers' initial support for, 114–19; soldiers' postwar views on, 165–66, 177–78, 183, 188–89, 251, 313(n256), 326(n171); Solomon Islands battles, 105; start of, 9; Taiwanese soldiers in, 146–49; Taiwan Straits, battle of, 227, 318(n28); terms for, 292(n129); Yamamoto's plane shot down, 106. *See also* Allied forces; army (Japanese); British forces; Japan's surrender; military (Japanese); prisoners of war (Allied or Chinese); prisoners of war (Japanese); Second World War; soldiers (Japanese); *and specific countries, locations, and individuals*
assimilation and imperialization: of ethnic minorities, 127–28, 130, 132; of Koreans, 135–36, 138–40, 298(n247); in Okinawa Prefecture, 121–24; as policy, 293(n154), 294–95(n187); of Taiwanese, 144, 147
atom bombs: atomic weapons ban, 246, 324(n140); horror of, 1–2, 5, 243, 244–45; misinformation about, 231

Attu Island, 219, 317(n2)
Aung San, 168, 178
"authoritarian democracy-ism," 269(n5)
Awi (Matsuoka Tsuneo), 146

bamboo spears, 195, 228, 231, 319(n35)
Beijing, resident Japanese in, 110
"Beijing and Tientsin" (Kawai), 79
Biak Island, 148
British forces: British POWs, 176, 308(n136); in Burma, 174–77, 179–82, 308(n125), 309(n152); and the Indonesian nationalist movement, 159, 304(n48); treatment of Japanese POWs, 175, 177–78, 182–83
Burma, 166–83; Burma Defense Army, 168, 169; independence, 169, 173, 179; Japanese campaign in, 166–68, 173–83, 238, 308(nn136–37, 140), 309(nn152, 156, 161); Japanese occupation of, 168–74, 308(n136); map, 167f

Cabinet Planning Board, 16, 44, 271(n18). *See also* New Economic Order
cannibalism, 188
capitalism, in pre-war Japan, 3–4
Chamorro people, 132–33
chemical warfare, 71, 200, 202–3, 206, 314(n269)
Chiang Kai-shek, 59, 62, 99, 276–77(n92), 287(n46)
children: discrimination by, 128; Filipino children, 310(n188); Japanese child's death in the Philippines, 190–93; killed by Japanese soldiers, 126 (*see also* civilians, torture and killing of); malnutrition in, 243; taken by Japanese soldiers, 204, 215. *See also* education
China (nationalist/PRC), 201–6; anti-Japanese feeling in, 6; Japanese interventionism in, 9; Japanese POWs in, 211; Marco Polo Bridge incident, 9; Taiwanese feelings about, 143–44, 145; Zhejian-Jiangxi